BEETHOVEN

A documentary study

compiled and edited by

H. C. ROBBINS LANDON

THE MACMILLAN COMPANY

PICTURE EDITOR: ELSE RADANT

CHIEF PHOTOGRAPHER: PIERO MALVISI

DESIGNER: GEORGE ADAMS F.S.I.A. TYPOGRAPHY AND JACKET

PUBLISHED BY ARRANGEMENT WITH UNIVERSAL EDITION A.G., ZÜRICH

© UNIVERSAL EDITION A.G., ZÜRICH 1970

Printed in Switzerland and bound in Holland

The Macmillan Company
866 Third Ave., New York, N.Y. 10022

Collier–Macmillan Canada, Ltd.,
Toronto, Ontario

Translated from the German by Richard Wadleigh and Eugene Hartzell

Library of Congress Catalog Number: 77–101293

First American Edition 1970

Contents

83984

Foreword

Experts the world over have subjected Beethoven's life and works to the most minute scrutiny, and a vast literature exists about this genius whose name is, for many people, synonymous with music itself. Even in the field of iconography, there are excellent studies by Stephan Ley (*Beethovens Leben in Bildern*, Berlin 1925) and, more recently by Robert Bory (*Ludwig van Beethoven, his life and work in pictures*, London and New York 1960). One might therefore presume that no pictures or documents remain unknown.

In connection with an extensive research project which the author, together with a small group (Christine Swenoha, Else Radant and Fritz Schmidt), undertook for the new Beethoven biography by George Marek (New York 1969), it was – rather astonishingly – discovered that there was, indeed, an enormous amount of authentic iconographical material, particularly about Beethoven's friends, patrons, etc., most of which was not only unpublished but completely unknown to the scholarly and musical world. This has encouraged us to prepare the present book, which appears in the year when the musical world celebrates the two-hundredth anniversary of Beethoven's birth.

It has been our great fortune to uncover many hitherto unknown portraits of those close to Beethoven, for example, miniatures or portraits in oils of Countess Josephine Deym and her husband, Countess Clary, Count Waldstein, Princess Hermenegild Esterházy, Archduke Rudolph, Prince and Princess Odescalchi, Prince and Princess Liechtenstein, Princess Marie Christine Lichnowsky, and others. We were also able to discover the miniature of Baroness Ertmann which had disappeared from sight years ago.

Of Beethoven himself, it was not expected that we could discover any new portraits. The great Beethoven scholar, Theodor von Frimmel, published several brilliant iconographical reports on Beethoven, beginning in 1887 and concluding with *Beethoven im zeitgenössischen Bildnis* (Vienna 1923) and the *Beethoven-Handbuch* (Leipzig 1926). But even here, we were fortunate enough to track down, at considerable effort, the Isidor Neugass painting (known as the 'Brunsvik' portrait), the first colour reproduction of which graces these pages. We would like to record our special thanks not only to the owner, Madame Françoise de Cossette, but also to M. Antonio de Almeida, who laboured energetically on our behalf to have the picture photographed.

We have banned from the book almost all non-contemporary portraits of Beethoven: an exception is the rather mysterious series of sketches by Lyser, the origin of which has never been satisfactorily explained. Wherever possible, we have tried to find a contemporary portrait of Beethoven's friends and acquaintances, and contemporary engravings or paintings of the places he knew and visited. Mostly we were able to do this; occasionally, there was no contemporary likeness available and we were forced to accept a non-contemporary one.

As far as the reproductions of Beethoven's music are concerned, it will be noted that we have published for the first time various autographs and authentic parts, for example, a page from the *cantus firmus* work Beethoven did in 1793 with Albrechtsberger's corrections; similarly we have tried to reproduce little-known or newly discovered material for the symphonies. We trust that readers will be interested to learn that the Scherzo-Trio of the Fifth Symphony was originally about twice as long as in its final state: we have been able to discover fragments of the 1808 performance material which clearly show the uncut version. We have also reproduced a page of the 1814 performance material of the Seventh Symphony with an angry comment by Beethoven to the copyist, and a page of the first performance material of the Eighth and Ninth Symphonies, both with interesting holograph changes. It was felt that the Beethoven expert would thus find considerable material to interest him, while the amateur does not need to know these musicological details to enjoy looking at a page from which Beethoven's musicians played his music for the very first time.

It was decided to combine the late Otto Erich Deutsch's documentary system with this iconography, so that the pictures and the contemporary documents complement one another. In compiling the documents, we gratefully used the standard Thayer and Schindler biographies, and Friedrich Kerst's *Die Erinnerungen an Beethoven* (Stuttgart 1913), as well as Stephan Ley's *Beethoven, Sein Leben in Selbstzeugnissen, Briefen und Berichten* (Berlin 1939); but wherever possible, we have returned to the original texts which were often – especially in the case of Kerst – inaccurately transcribed. We should add, however, that it was not our intention to produce a strictly scholarly text with a vast amount of explanatory footnotes; this procedure would, it was felt, defeat the book's purpose and would, moreover, have increased its size by at least one-third. Some of the documents, as will be seen, are new to Beethoven scholarship. Our intent, in the choice of both documents and pictures, was to bring Beethoven's world closer to us, to show him and his surroundings in contemporary word and picture.

The picture editor and general editor would like to thank our friend, Piero Malvisi, whose handsome photographs form the bulk of our illustrations. Signor Malvisi's sense of humour, his duty to the job and his professional efficiency all made this book possible. We would also like to register a special vote of thanks to our many Czech colleagues who, in the Spring of 1968, helped us in innumerable ways to locate and photograph many of the most interesting portraits and engravings reproduced in the book. We also owe the Beethovenhaus in Bonn, and Dr Schmidt in particular, many thanks for all their assistance. In Vienna, we would like to single out the Gesellschaft der Musikfreunde (its Director Professor Rudolph Gamsjäger and its librarian Frau Dr Mitringer), who generously placed their priceless archives at our disposal; the Historisches Museum der Stadt Wien, who are the custodians of much Beethoveniana; the Österreichische Nationalbibliothek; and the Stadtbibliothek (Dr Fritz Raček).

The Freies Deutsches Hochstift Frankfurter Goethemuseum (Frau Almut Sack) was particularly helpful. Clothilde Countess Clam-Gallas was of enormous assistance in finding portraits of the Austro-Hungarian nobility. The Galerie Liechtenstein (Vaduz-Vienna, Dr Wilhelm) placed its beautiful collection at our disposal. Edward Croft-Murray, Esq., of the British Museum, was charming and helpful, as always.

There follows a list of the persons and institutions from whom we received information and material; we wish to thank them all for much courtesy and kindness.

Austria

Eisenstadt: Haydnmuseum

Linz: Oberösterreichisches Landesmuseum
Stadtmuseum

Salzburg: Professor Wolfgang von Karajan
Mozarteum

Vienna: Archiv der Stadt Wien
Burgtheater, Portraitsammlung, Bundes-
theaterverwaltung
Clothilde Countess Clam-Gallas
Josef Count Deym
Gesellschaft der Musikfreunde
Gilhofer and Ranschburg, Buch- und
Kunstantiquariat K. G. Gilhofer
Historisches Museum der Stadt Wien
Kunsthistorisches Museum, Münzkabinett
Frau Traudl Lessing
Galerie Liechtenstein, Sammlungen des
Regierenden Fürsten von Liechtenstein,
Vaduz-Wien
Herr Ingo Nebehay, 'Wiener Antiquariat'
Österreichische Nationalbibliothek;
Musiksammlung; Theatersammlung; Bild-
archiv
Palais Kinsky, Palace Administration
Andreas Count Razumovsky
Konsul Otto Reichert
Stadtbibliothek
Sturm family (Frau Hella Sturm)
Herr Kurt Stümpfl
Professor Hans Swarowsky

Czechoslovakia

Chlumec: Castle administration

Chomutov: Museum

Duchcov: Museum

Hluboká: Castle administration

Hradec u Opavy: Beethoven Society

Kroměříž: Museum (the Archbishop's residence)

Prague: Národní Museum
Národní Museum, Hudební oddélení.

Teplice: Museum

England

London: Mrs Eva Alberman
British Museum, Department of Prints
and Drawings Royal College of Music

France

Paris: Bibliothèque Nationale, Departement de la
Musique
Mme Françoise de Cossette
M. André Meyer

Germany

Berlin: Deutsche Staatsbibliothek, Musikabteilung
Staatsbibliothek, Preußischer Kulturbesitz,
Musikabteilung

Bonn: Beethovenhaus
Kreisarchiv
Stadtarchiv
Städtische Sammlungen

Brühl: Castle administration

Frankfurt am Main: Freies Deutsches Hochstift,
Frankfurter Goethemuseum

Kiechlingsbergen (Breisgau):   Frau von Gleichenstein

Oberrotweil (Breisgau):   Herr Hans Joachim von
Gleichenstein

Stockach (Baden):   Herr Viktor von Gleichenstein

Winkel am Rhein (Rheingau):   Herr Achim von
Brentano

Italy

Buggiano Castello: H. C. Robbins Landon, Esq.

Rome: Principe Livio Odescalchi
Marchesa Maria Pallavicini

Switzerland

Schloß Arenenberg bei Ermatingen: Museum administration

Unites States of America

New York: Walter Hinrichsen, Esq.

Washington: Library of Congress, Music Division

H. C. R. L.
E. R.

Buggiano Castello,
July, 1969

The figures in the margins refer to illustration numbers

Introduction
to a Beethoven Iconography

We owe the first recorded portrait of Beethoven to his friends, the Breuning family: a silhouette, showing the young composer at about the age of sixteen. The silhouette was first published in the *Biographische Notizen* by F. A. Wegeler and F. Ries in 1838, and the original has since disappeared – not so great a tragedy as it might otherwise be, for a silhouette is easily reproduced. The artist was one Joseph Neesen, possibly an amateur; in any case, he was very obscure and is known only for his silhouettes of Beethoven and the Breuning family; perhaps he was a friend of theirs. *9*

If the first Beethoven portrait survives as something of a happy accident, the next one, chronologically, owes its existence to the composer's rapidly growing fame in Vienna at the turn of the century. It is an engraving published in 1800 by Giovanni *80* Cappi, formerly a business partner in the famous house of Artaria & Co. In a letter to Wegeler of 19 January 1801, Beethoven refers to the publisher as Artaria; either Artaria issued it first and later passed it on to Cappi when the latter founded his own business, or Beethoven still thought of Cappi as part of the Artaria establishment. The print is based on a design by Gandolph Ernst Stainhauser von Treuberg, and was engraved by Johann Neidl, who often worked for Artaria (he engraved, for instance, the portrait of Haydn based on the Zitterer painting). Neither Stainhauser nor Neidl is an artist of the first rank, but we can gain through the engraving our first impression of Beethoven as a famous young man in Vienna at the turn of the century: wavy dark hair; sideburns; a serious, rather full face; elegant clothing of the period. The engraving was presumably copied in Leipzig, without naming the artist; it was issued there by Beethoven's friend and brother-Mason Franz Anton Hoffmeister at his 'Bureau de Musique' in 1801. There is also a possibility that Beethoven sent Hoffmeister the original Stainhauser drawing and that the C.F. Riedl engraving thus represents a new *87* 'original source'. That Beethoven was an interesting subject to artists even at this relatively early date is clear from a passage in a letter to Christine Gerhardi, undated but evidently written in the 1790s, in which he refers to a portrait issued without his knowledge.*

The first really good Beethoven portrait is the beautiful miniature signed and dated 1803 by Christian Horneman, the Danish artist who worked in Berlin and then *103* came to Vienna about 1798 with a letter of recommendation to the famous portraitist, Johann Heinrich Füger. Many of Horneman's miniatures have been preserved, including portraits of King Friedrich Wilhelm III and Queen Luise of Prussia as well as Joseph

---

*Dear Chr[istine], [Vienna, 1797]
You said something yesterday about that likeness of me – I do wish that in this matter you would proceed rather circumspectly. For I fear that if we choose F. to return it, perhaps that wretched B. or that extremely stupid Joseph will interfere and, in that case, the affair may then become a trick to be played upon me; and that would be really deplorable. I should have to revenge myself again; and surely the whole populace don't deserve that. Try to get hold of the thing, if it is at all possible to do so. I assure you that after this experience I will appeal in the Press to all painters not to paint me again without my knowledge. I really did not think that this face of mine would ever cause me embarrassment. . . .
(Emily Anderson, *Letters of Beethoven*, London 1961, v. I, p. 29.)

Haydn (the latter reproduced by Karl Geiringer, 1932, in his *Joseph Haydn*). Beethoven gave the miniature to his friend Stephan von Breuning, and it remained in the Breuning family for more than a hundred years before passing to the famous Beethoven collector, Dr H. C. Bodmer, and from him to the Beethovenhaus in Bonn. Comparison *175* with the Klein mask (see below) shows that Horneman accurately represented Beethoven's facial features and proportions – even to the disfiguring pock-marks – except, perhaps, the nose. There is no doubt, however, that the Horneman miniature is the most important Beethoven portrait before the life-mask of 1812.

The dapper Beethoven of this period is not, incidentally, a figment of these artists' flattering imagination: we have corroborative evidence from no less a figure than the Austrian playwright Franz Grillparzer, who met the composer about 1804 or 1805 and later described him, 'contrary to his later habits', as being most elegantly dressed. *126* A life-size painting of about this period shows us a slightly idealized but none the less interesting portrait of the composer: the artist was Willibrord Joseph Mähler, a fellow countryman of Beethoven's from the Rhineland, who, although an amateur, gained considerable reputation as a portraitist of musicians. Mähler appears to have been a friend of Beethoven's, and we may therefore assume that the composer actually sat for the portrait; it remained in Beethoven's possession till his death. Some ten years ago, it was cleaned and expertly restored by the Historisches Museum of the City of Vienna, to which it now belongs. A careful comparison with the 1812 life-mask shows the general features to be for the most part accurate, though, as said above, idealized. An undated note from Beethoven to Mähler refers to this portrait: 'I beg you to return my portrait to me as soon as you have made sufficient use of it – if you need it longer I beg of you at least to make haste – I have promised the portrait to a stranger, a lady who saw it here, that she may hang it in her room during her stay of several weeks. Who can withstand such *charming importunities*, as a matter of course a portion of the lovely favours *which I shall thus garner* will also fall to *you*.'*

The great Beethoven scholar A. W. Thayer spoke with Mähler (who did not die till 1860) about this portrait**: 'To the question what picture is here referred to, Mr Mähler replied to the author [Thayer] in substance: "It was a portrait, which I painted soon after coming to Vienna, in which Beethoven is represented, at nearly full length, sitting; the left hand rests upon a lyre, the right is extended, as if, in a moment of musical enthusiasm, he was beating time; in the background is a temple of Apollo. Oh! If I could but know what became of the picture!"'

'"What!" was the author's answer, to the great satisfaction of the old gentleman, "the picture is hanging at this moment in the home of Madame van Beethoven, widow, in the Josephstadt, and I have a copy of it."'

Thayer's copy, which has been widely photographed, is now in the New York Public Library.

157 The next portrait to follow the Mähler painting is that of Isidor Neugass, who had just before [1805/6] painted the rather ugly, but by no means unrealistic, portrait of Haydn holding a sheet of the *Creation* in his hand (Eisenstadt Castle: reproduced in László Somfai, *Joseph Haydn, Sein Leben in zeitgenössischen Bildern*: Kassel-Basel-Paris-London 1966; p. 201). Two versions of the Neugass painting are known, neither of

---

Thayer's Life of Beethoven (ed. by Elliot Forbes), Princeton 1967, I, 337. See also Anderson I, 125.
**Ibid.

which has ever been reproduced before in colour (for black-and-white reproductions of both, see C. Bory's *Beethoven*, p. 119*). The one which is probably the original is signed and dated 'peinte par Neugass Wienne 1806'; it was commissioned by Prince Carl Lichnowsky, and hung for many years in Grätz Castle, Lichnowsky's country estate. It is still in the family's possession and is now in South America. The other, now in Paris, is the so-called 'Brunsvik portrait'; it was formerly in one of the Brunsviks' castles, either Korompa or Márton Vasár. Theodor von Frimmel, the great Beethoven scholar, was able to prove that Neugass himself executed the 'Brunsvik portrait', even though it is not signed or dated. In his *Beethoven-Handbuch* (Vol. I, p. 43) Frimmel quotes a letter from Therese von Brunsvik to her brother dated 1807: 'During the last few days I have seen a lot of Beethoven.... A certain Neigart has painted him and has the portrait in his studio.' Therese meant, of course, Neugass; in this same letter, she says that the portrait is to be sent to her sister Josephine. In later years, the Neugass 'Brunsvik' portrait was in Florence; it is now in private possession in Paris. Neugass is not a first-rate artist, and his Beethoven portraits are rather stylized, but they are useful, as any authentic iconographic documentation of Beethoven must be. Note, for example, the chain round the neck which obviously carried Beethoven's double lorgnette (Grillparzer noted that in 1804–05 Beethoven wore spectacles when reading); even at this relatively early period, he was not only hard of hearing, but also short-sighted. Note, also, the almost foppish elegance of Beethoven's clothing and general appearance.

Beethoven at the period of the *Fifth Symphony* is shown to us in an amusing pencil sketch by an artist who was very famous at the time, Ludwig Ferdinand Schnorr von Carolsfeld.** The drawing, done in a sketchbook of Beethoven's friends, the Malfatti family, is dated 'about 1808 or 1809' in a note written on the same page. Though hastily executed, the drawing is very faithful to Beethoven's features and lively – rather like a snapshot today.

Without any question, the most important documentary evidence of Beethoven's features is the life-mask made by the Austrian sculptor Franz Klein in 1812, as well as the bust prepared by Klein on the basis of that mask. Theodor von Frimmel was able to learn some hitherto unknown facts about the mask from descendants of the Streicher family, for it was evidently the piano manufacturer Andreas Streicher who commissioned Klein to make the mask. Klein's first attempt failed – Beethoven thought he would suffocate under the wet gypsum. The bust is therefore especially valuable because of its realistic portrayal of Beethoven's hair – something which was naturally missing from the facial mask. On the other hand, the mask preserves with complete accuracy the proportions of Beethoven's face, even to the ugly pock-marks and scars.

The spectacular success of Beethoven's *Battle at Vittoria* and the charity concerts of 1814 were no doubt responsible for a new engraving of the composer, since the engraved portrait issued in 1800 was by now out of date. Fortunately A. W. Thayer

*Robert Bory, *Ludwig van Beethoven, His Life and his Work in Pictures*, Zürich/London/New York 1960.

**Otto Erich Deutsch, in his article 'Beethovens Leben in Bildern' (*Österreichische Musikzeitschrift*, 16. Jahrgang, Heft 3, March 1961), suggests that not Ludwig but his father Johann Veit (Veit Hans) von Carolsfeld is the author of the sketch.

found Blasius Höfel, the engraver of the new print, still alive in 1860, and was able to learn from him the facts surrounding the new portrait. Artaria – still one of Beethoven's principal publishers – had engaged the fashionable French artist Louis Letronne to

188 make a drawing of Beethoven as the basis for a new engraving. Blasius Höfel, then a young man at the beginning of his career, found the drawing unsatisfactory and requested Beethoven to sit again for him; the composer agreed and Höfel refashioned the drawing. Contemporaries agreed that it was an excellent portrait: Aloys Fuchs, the great Viennese music collector, said to Thayer: 'Thus I learned to know him [Beethoven]', obviously a very literal translation of 'So habe ich ihn kennengelernt'. Nevertheless the engraving of 1814 is somewhat idealized: there are no pock-marks, for instance. What makes the engraving interesting is the undeniable impression of strength which seems to jump out from the face on the printed page. Recently, what purports to be the original Letronne drawing has come to light in Paris; it is not so bad as its reputation, but it does make Beethoven rather a French dandy. Beethoven himself sent a good many copies of the engraving to his friends. One, quoted by Frimmel (*Beethoven-Handbuch*, I, 219), was sent to Antonia von Brentano, and an autograph inscription on it reads: 'Hochachtungsvoll der Frau Von Brentano gebohren Edle Von Birkenstock von ihrem Sie verehrenden Freund Beethoven'. Höfel, who was some twenty-two years old in 1814, became very successful as a result of the Beethoven engraving. The Thieme-Becker *Allgemeines Künstler-Lexikon* (XVII, 1924) writes of it: 'Höfel's first engraving, which made him famous and brought him many commissions, was the excellent Beethoven portrait after Louis Letronne.'

Beethoven's fame at the time of the Congress of Vienna provided the occasion for
193 several other portraits. One is Mähler's second attempt to paint the composer. The portrait exists in at least three versions, of which the finest – recently cleaned by the Historisches Museum of the City of Vienna – is owned by Wolfgang von Karajan in Salzburg. Of the others, the Gesellschaft der Musikfreunde copy has a curiously lifeless appearance with rather cold eyes, while the third was made for Beethoven's friend Ignaz von Gleichenstein and sent to Germany; this 'German' version is still owned by the Gleichenstein family. The Gesellschaft der Musikfreunde version has been widely reproduced, the others less so. On the whole, the second Mähler portrait – which was first mentioned in a report dated August 1815 – is not entirely satisfactory. The proportions of the face are not exact if we compare them to the Klein mask of 1812, and the painter has certainly not caught the composer's 'inner life' on the canvas. Nevertheless it does not deserve the rather casual dismissal it receives from Frimmel (*Beethoven-Handbuch* I, 44).

183 The best thing about another portrait supposedly executed in 1815, that of Johann Christoph Heckel, is – as opposed to Mähler's – the expression. It shows the same stubborn, rebellious and square-jawed Beethoven that we know to be truthful from the
224 Klein mask and which has been rendered famous through the Waldmüller painting of 1823. The Heckel portrait, for which Beethoven sat at Streicher's piano rooms, was in private possession for many years and was last owned by the Lehman family, who gave it to the Library of Congress. Heckel's conception of the lower part of Beethoven's face is not entirely accurate.

Another Beethoven portrait from the period of the Vienna Congress is a pencil
200 sketch by Gustav Adolph Hippius, who was in Vienna during the years 1814 to 1816. In

12

some respects, the Hippius sketch may be profitably compared to the earlier pencil drawing of 1808: neither is great art nor even great portraiture, but each contains a certain snapshot-like atmosphere. The Hippius sketch remained unknown until its discovery in Russia and subsequent publication by Theodor von Frimmel.

147

The well-known German artist August Carl Friedrich von Kloeber painted Beethoven at Mödling in 1818. The circumstances are related below, in the documents. Unfortunately the big painting – of which a very detailed contemporary description survives*, and which also included Beethoven's nephew Carl, sleeping under a tree – has long disappeared. We have three preliminary sketches, of which we reproduce the one showing the composer's head. Although very famous, and often reproduced, the *201* Kloeber sketches are not very impressive. The hair is obviously well done, but the features are, once again, not entirely accurate and the expression is curiously lacking in feeling. Part of the difficulty which most artists found when drawing or painting Beethoven seems to have been due to the fact that the composer was impatient and would not sit still for long. Some of the Beethoven portraits were done under highly unfavourable circumstances, and sections later completed from memory. Conversely, some artists managed not to disturb Beethoven and did their work while he was composing or improvising at the piano (e.g. Blasius Höfel and, later, Schimon).

In the autumn of 1818, a young Austro-Hungarian artist, Ferdinand Schimon, a pupil of Lampi the younger, painted Beethoven's portrait. It has since become very *203* famous and is certainly one of the most interesting and persuasive of all the known oil portraits of the composer. Felix Anton Schindler, Beethoven's friend and biographer, considered it the most interesting, and relates in detail how the portrait came into existence. He writes:** 'From an artistic point of view Schimon's work is not a distinguished work of art, yet full of characteristic truth. In the rendering of that particular look, the majestic forehead, this dwelling-place of mighty, sublime ideas, of hues, in the drawing of the firmly shut mouth and the chin shaped like a shell, it is truer to nature than any other picture.' Schindler owned the portrait which, he later reports, 'has unfortunately darkened greatly'; it went to the Royal Prussian (later State) Library and is now in the Beethovenhaus in Bonn. The composer, incidentally, was satisfied with Schimon's work.

Equally famous, and as often reproduced as the Schimon portrait, is the famous picture made in 1819 by the Munich artist Joseph Carl Stieler; the portrait is signed *207* and dated 1819 but was not in fact completed until the next year. Contemporaries, including Schindler, thought it a good likeness, though the hands were completed from memory. Stieler was a clever diplomat and managed to persuade the composer to sit for him three times – something of a feat for anyone. The conversation books contain several entries in Stieler's hand, e.g. (December 1819 or January 1820): 'Setzen Sie sich doch gefälligst, als wenn Sie schreiben, um die Stellung zu probieren ... Wenn ich Ihnen winke, bitte in der Stellung zu bleiben, die Sie gerade haben.'*** Some further extracts are cited below, in the documents. Astute observers will notice

*Wiener Zeitschrift für Kunst, Literatur und Mode, 1818, p. 1134. Quoted in extenso in Frimmel's Beethoven-Handbuch, I, 280.

**Translation from Thayer's Life of Beethoven, op. cit., II, 742.

***'Please sit as if you were writing, so as to try out the position ... When I wave to you, please remain in the very position you are in.' W. Nohl's edition of the conversation books, I, 327, 336.

a considerable difference in the Beethoven of Schimon and that of Stieler. Schindler explains it by saying that 'the startling difference ... is the result of the long illness that had intervened'.* The best thing about the portrait is undoubtedly the 'thoughtful expression' (Frimmel). In 1826, Mathias Artaria published a lithograph of the Stieler portrait by the artist's nephew Friedrich Dürck. Later the famous artist Joseph Kriehuber made a lithograph based on the Stieler portrait. The original oil painting is owned by Walter Hinrichsen in New York City.

Joseph Daniel Böhm, a young artist and engraver, managed to persuade Beethoven to sit at least once – possibly twice. We find an entry in one of the conversation books of 1820: 'Der Böhm wünscht, dass Sie ihm noch eine Sitzung schenken möchten',** but we do not know if the answer was yes or no. Böhm made two sketches of Beethoven walking – the originals are now in the Beethovenhaus – and later he himself prepared silver plates of these sketches; copies of the silver plate versions, which are signed with Böhm's initials, are owned by André Meyer in Paris. Böhm also intended to strike a medal of Beethoven, and for this purpose prepared a wax medallion: a rather dim copy, made by Frimmel, was given to the Beethovenhaus, but the original has disappeared.

At this period it became fashionable to do sketches of the famous Beethoven on his walks. Quite a number of these interesting sketches have been preserved, some contemporary and some apparently posthumous. Martin Tejček is supposed to have observed Beethoven walking, and his sketch was used as the basis for a lithograph issued at Prague in 1841: it is useful primarily for its detailed view of Beethoven's clothing. Another drawing, the original of which has disappeared, is an amusing and realistic picture of Beethoven walking in the pouring rain, the collar of his greatcoat turned up against the wind: the original was a water-coloured pen-and-ink drawing by Johann Nepomuk Hoechle. Joseph Weidner, who supposedly made a portrait of the composer in oils, fashioned a characteristic sketch of Beethoven *a tergo*, brandishing a walking stick and lost to the world: it is one of the best of these sketches, which were undoubtedly made without Beethoven's knowledge. It is something of a mystery why the talented Danish artist Johann Peter Theodor Lyser made so many sketches of Beethoven, for according to Lyser experts it appears that the two men were never in the same place at the same time. It is thought that possibly Lyser had at his disposal a sketch or sketches by some other artist. Dr Gerhard von Breuning, the son of Beethoven's friend Stephan, with whom Frimmel discussed the Lyser drawings about 1880, thought the heads badly drawn, but the walking figure well observed.

Recently an interesting wax relief of Beethoven was discovered in Vienna, together with reliefs – apparently by the same hand – of other popular figures such as the Emperor Franz I, the Empress Caroline Augusta and Nicolò Paganini. This small but interesting collection belongs to the Historisches Museum of the City of Vienna, and in a recent publication Franz Glück, former Director of the Museum, was able to ascribe all these wax reliefs with confidence to the rather obscure artist Joseph

211, 213

210

215

209

208, 214,
226, 229

88

*Schindler: *Beethoven As I Knew Him*, edited by Donald. W. MacArdle, Chapel Hill and London 1966, p. 451. Throughout this present book we have gratefully used the MacArdle edition but have always done our own translations or, occasionally, used those in *Thayer's Life of Beethoven*.

**'Böhm wishes that you would sit for him once more'. See Frimmel, *Beethoven-Handbuch* I, 53.

Nikolaus Lang (1776–1835). Lang also made a medal to commemorate Beethoven's death in 1827.* Obviously the wax relief is the model for the medal, but, as Glück points out, the relief is much finer artistically and it was probably made during the composer's lifetime. Glück dates the relief 1815–1818 (*op. cit.* p. 209) and we have no reason to dispute this tentative dating.

It is interesting that young artists – like young people in general – were attracted to Beethoven. Another promising Austrian artist was the sculptor Anton Dietrich, for whom Beethoven sat in 1819–1820, when the artist was just turned twenty-one. Dietrich also took Klein's life-mask as the model for his bust, which was first shown in 1820. Dietrich made at least half-a-dozen copies, including life-size ones, some of them dated 1821 (one such variant is illustrated here); later he did a not very realistic *216* drawing. The Dietrich busts, judged *in toto*, are accurately proportioned but highly idealized and slightly cold. Franz Glück, in the interesting article mentioned above, also discusses the Dietrich busts at some length. Since Frimmel wrote about them the five Dietrich busts known at that time have all, except for the one owned by the Historisches Museum of the City of Vienna, disappeared from sight. From extant photographs, Glück was able to show that there seem to be two basic versions which Dietrich made: of the first, the museum owns a version of 1821; of the other, rather more formal bust *à l'antique*, no copy seems to exist at present. Glück considers, and we beg leave to concur, that the Museum version, with its strong jaw and the realistic portrayal of the hair, is the better of the two *Ur*-versions. Glück was also able to make an important discovery in the identification of the document quoted in connection with this bust.

In 1823, when Beethoven was particularly irritable, the great Austrian painter Ferdinand Georg Waldmüller was commissioned by Breitkopf & Härtel in Leipzig to do a portrait of the composer. The unfavourable circumstances in which this *224* portrait was painted are described below, in the documentary section. It led Schindler to a sweeping denunciation of the Waldmüller painting; after quoting the document in question, Schindler continues:

'In a word, the Waldmüller portrait is, if possible, further from the truth than any other. It is the likeness of a venerable pastor whose thoughts are occupied with elaborating a homily for the edification of his congregation. Even in its outlines, it has nothing in common with the head of Beethoven, the composer in whose mind there was evolving at that time the Ninth Symphony.'**

But Waldmüller was by far the greatest artist ever to paint Beethoven, and his work cannot be dismissed so lightly. Theodor von Frimmel, writing of the portrait, says:

'Nevertheless it is a highly valuable document which presents us a Beethoven as he "growls and scowls". Waldmüller's quite exceptional memory for shapes has given us, in any event, something more valuable than small talents with days of effort'.***

---

*Franz Glück *Prolegomena zu einer neuen Beethoven-Ikonographie*, Festschrift Otto Erich Deutsch zum 80. Geburtstag am 5. September 1963, hrsg. von Walter Gerstenberg, Jan LaRue und Wolfgang Rehm, Kassel, Basel, Paris, London, New York 1963. Photograph after p. 208.

**Schindler, *op. cit.*, 454.

***Beethoven-Handbuch* I, 46.

The original oil painting in the offices of Breitkopf & Härtel was destroyed during World War II, but a colour photograph exists. At least one authentic copy by Waldmüller has survived.

Beethoven, a few days after the first performance of the *Ninth Symphony*, is shown *241* to us in the realistic chalk drawing by Stephan Decker (May 1824), of which a lithograph was published in the *Wiener Allgemeine Musikalische Zeitung* on 5 June 1824 (wherein Decker's drawing is also mentioned as having been made 'a few days' after the famous concert). Beethoven looks grey and rather forbidding, but the master obviously approved of the lithograph because he occasionally presented one with a personal inscription. On 4 September 1825, when the composer was taking the cure at Baden, he dedicated a Decker lithograph to the publisher Moritz Adolf Schlesinger.* As far as can now be determined, Decker's is the last portrait of Beethoven before the composer lay on his deathbed.

The well-known portraitist Joseph Teltscher, a member of the Schubert circle, *245, 246* made three drawings of Beethoven on his deathbed (one, of the bed only without Beethoven, has been omitted from our illustrations) – profoundly moving documents of the dying man, his body beneath the bed-clothes swollen with dropsy. Theodor von Frimmel discovered these fascinating drawings in the famous collection of Dr August Heymann in Vienna, and published them for the first time in May 1909. There were later in the Stefan Zweig collection and are now owned by Zweig's heir, Mrs Eva Alberman.

Tragic in a curiously impersonal, objective way – quite unlike the pathetic and *250* terribly private sketches by Teltscher – is the sketch of Beethoven in death made on 28 March 1827 (the day after his death) by Joseph Danhauser – again, another young artist making a pilgrimage to the great composer. (Teltscher, too, was young: he was born in 1802, Danhauser in 1805.) Danhauser published a lithograph of the drawing. *253, 256* He also made the famous death-mask, which, it was hitherto believed, showed the composer horribly disfigured by the autopsy which had been made before Danhauser could begin his work. Beethoven's organs of hearing were removed for study, and to facilitate this the temporal bones had to be sawed out, thus causing the facial muscles to 'sag'. Franz Glück, in the article about Beethoven iconography quoted before, uncovered a document concerning the death-mask which seems to have escaped the notice of Beethoven scholars. It is a letter by Carl Danhauser, Joseph's brother, and it seems to suggest that the mask and drawing may both have been done before the autopsy, and in any case very early in the morning of 28 March 1827. This document is perhaps not precise evidence as to whether the autopsy had in fact been made or not: the subject is not specifically mentioned. On the other hand, other contemporaries are careful to state that Danhauser did not begin his work until the autopsy was finished. What is perhaps of vital importance to us is the condition of the death-mask itself. Glück is quite correct in pointing out that it is not nearly the second-rate document it has frequently been described to be, and that most writers – including to a certain extent Frimmel – have concentrated on the third- or fourth-hand copy in the Beethovenhaus in Bonn rather than on the superb cast from Franz Liszt's collection, now owned by the Historisches Museum of the City of Vienna, and here reproduced in two views. As Glück concludes: 'On the basis of the death-mask, we would know him, this great man, even if we did not know whom it represents.'

*Beethoven-Handbuch I, 47.

16

Documents and Plates

Anderson	Emily Anderson, *The Letters of Beethoven*, London 1961, 3 vols.
Breuning	Gerhard von Breuning, *Aus dem Schwarzspanierhaus*, Vienna 1874.
Czerny	Carl Czerny, *Über den richtigen Vortrag der sämtlichen Beethoven'schen Klavierwerke sowie das 2 und 3 Kapitel des IV Bandes der vollständigen theoretisch-praktischen Pianoforte-Schule Op. 500*. Edited and revised by Paul Badura-Skoda, Vienna 1963. (Wiener Urtext Ausgabe).
Du Montet	Baronne du Montet, *Souvenirs 1785 – 1866*, Paris 1914. (German version, *Die Erinnerungen der Baronin Du Montet*, translated by Ernst Klarwil, Zürich 1925).
FRBS	Theodor von Frimmel, *Beethoven Studien*, Leipzig 1905–06, 2 vols.
HJB II	Haydn Yearbook II, 1963/64. E. Olleson, *Haydn in the diaries of Count Zinzendorf*, Vienna 1964.
HJB III	Haydn Yearbook III, 1965. E. Olleson, *Georg August Griesinger's correspondence with Breitkopf und Härtel*, Vienna 1965.
HJB V	Haydn Yearbook V, 1968. Else Radant, *The diaries of Joseph Carl Rosenbaum*, Vienna 1968.
Hist. Tb.	*Historisches Taschenbuch. Mit besonderer Hinsicht auf die Oesterreichischen Staaten. Geschichte des 19. Jahrhunderts*, Vienna 1805–09. 3 vols.
KAL	Alfred Chr. Kalischer, *Beethoven's sämtliche Briefe*, Berlin 1909, vol. I.
KFR	Kalischer-Frimmel, vol. II of Kalischer's edition of Beethoven's letters, revised by Theodor von Frimmel, Berlin 1910.
Kerst	Friedrich Kerst, *Die Erinnerungen an Beethoven*, Stuttgart 1913, 2 vols.
	(N.B. Kerst is a compilation of material from original sources, some of which is derived from unpublished documents, letters, diaries, etc. These are given, as well as Kerst references.)
KHV	Georg Kinsky, *Das Werk Beethovens. Thematisch bibliographisches Verzeichnis seiner sämtlichen vollendeten Kompositionen*, completed and edited after the author's death by Hans Halm, Munich 1955.
Konv. N.	Walther Nohl, *Ludwig van Beethoven, Konversationshefte*, first half-volume, Munich 1924.
Konv. Sch.	Georg Schünemann, *Ludwig van Beethovens Konversationshefte*, vol. 2, Books XI – XXII, Berlin 1942.
Reichardt	Johann Friedrich Reichardt, *Vertraute Briefe, geschrieben auf einer Reise nach Wien, Ende 1808 und Anfang 1809*, edited by Gustav Gugitz, Munich 1915, 2 vols.
Schindler	Anton Schindler. *Ludwig van Beethoven*, fifth edition, newly edited by Fritz Volbach, Münster 1927.
Sonneck	O. G. Sonneck, *Beethoven Letters in America*, New York 1927.
TDR	Alexander Wheelock Thayer, *Ludwig van Beethovens Leben*, von Hermann Deiters neubearbeitet und von Hugo Riemann ergänzt, Leipzig 1901–11, 5 vols. (This biography was originally written in English, but the first edition appeared in a German version by Deiters.)
Thürheim	Countess Lulu Thürheim, *Mein Leben*, edited by René van Rhyn, Zürich 1923, 4 vols.
WRBN	Dr F. G. Wegeler and Ferdinand Ries, *Biographische Notizen über Beethoven*, Coblenz 1838.

Works of Beethoven are identified according to KHV (see above); WoO means *Werk ohne Opuszahl* (Work without Opus number).

The documents have been arranged in chronological order which, for obvious reasons, sometimes had to be disturbed. To go with Beethoven's portraits, we have attempted to present contemporary descriptions of his appearance, piano-playing, and descriptions of his character which, as far as possible, were arranged to coincide with the chronology of the portraits themselves.

Bonn was a pretty provincial town and the seat of the Archbishop and Elector of Cologne. Ludwig van Beethoven was born there, probably on 15 December 1770 (he was christened on 17 December but he always considered the 15th his birthday), the son of Johann van Beethoven and Maria Magdalena née Keverich. Johann was a tenor in the Court Kapelle, and Ludwig's grandfather, the Kapellmeister at Bonn, who also bore the name Ludwig or Louis, was still alive when the composer was born: he died in 1773 and Beethoven revered his memory throughout his life, keeping the portrait on his wall in Vienna. At the time Beethoven was born, the Elector and Archbishop of Cologne was Maximilian Friedrich, Count of Königsegg-Aulendorf, who was succeeded, in 1784, by Maximilian Franz, youngest brother of the Emperor Joseph II. Among Beethoven's earliest friends were the families of von Breuning and Wegeler. Members of both families later published their memoirs about Beethoven, which are of particular importance for the Bonn period in Beethoven's life.

Description of Bonn by Thomas Pennant: 1, 2

[English original]

July 2

The country is much the same as far as an isle with a convent called Neuwied. On each side of the Rhine the hills increase in height, terminate in conic shapes, and on the tops of three are ruined castles composed of lofty slender towers. From this place the left shore is quite flat, that on the right continues till near opposite Bonne.

Landed there about seven o'clock. The palace makes a fine figure from the water, having a most extensive front. The town is large, the streets narrow and ill built, the fortifications strong but seem to have been long in a pacific state – the ditches being fruitfull gardens and the ramparts covered with vines.

The Elector's palace is adjacent, a very large white pile, seemingly built at several times. The staircase is very handsome, cased with a mock marble and well stuccoed; the ceiling is exceedingly well painted, the subject Phoebus and several of his attendants that are made to float very lightly.

In the first wing I entered was but little furniture, most being sold on the death of the late extravagant Elector . . . .

The apartments on the right side of the palace are called le Buen Retiro and very finely furnished. The little closet called the rose cabinet is neat, wainscoted with wood painted in the Indian taste. The floor is prettily inlaid with Indian animals, an Elephant leaning against a Palm tree, crocodiles & ca.; the roof is thick, set with silver and copper color roses. The state bedchamber is exceedingly rich; the bed is so richly embroidered with gold as to seem quite massive; the rails, columns and arches that divide it from the rest of the room are carved wood, a most elegant light open work, gilt and painted with green . . . . In a small apartment walled with tyles is a very large marble cistern for a bath, – from this you enter into a number of little closets, a sort of maze, that surround a bed room. The view from the windows is fine, commanding the Rhine and hills; the gardens are filled with fine orange trees – their only beauty.

Thomas Pennant, *Tour on the Continent 1765*, London 1948, p. 145.
(Pennant made a journey across Europe in the course of which he visited Bonn.)

Every year, on Saint Magdalen's day, the name and birthday of Madame van Beethoven would be celebrated festively. The music stands would be brought out of the *Tucksaal* [correctly *Doxal*, a room in the church adjoining the organ: in the Bonn church it was located on the right above the choir; the chairs and music-stands were stored there]. The chairs would then be placed right and left in the rooms facing the street and a canopy set up in the room where the portrait of Grandfather Ludwig van Beethoven hung, and handsomely decorated with flowers, laurel branches and foliage. Early in the evening Madame van Beethoven would be requested to retire betimes, and by ten o'clock everyone would be assembled and ready in the most complete silence. The tuning up would now begin and Madame van Beethoven would be awakened. She would then dress and be led in and seated on a beautifully decorated chair under the canopy. At that very moment magnificent music would strike up, resounding throughout the whole neighbourhood so that everyone who was preparing to go to bed became gay and cheerful. When the music ended a meal would be served up and the company ate and drank until those who had become light-headed and wished to dance would take off their shoes and dance in their stockinged feet in order not to make a commotion in the house. In this fashion the celebration would come to an end.

When Ludwig van Beethoven had become a little older he went to the teacher Huppert [presumably Rupert] in the elementary school in the Neustrasse [Neugasse] which runs into the Rheinstrasse, at number 1091. Later he went to the Cathedral school. According to his father, he did not learn very much at school; that is why his father so early seated him at the clavier and kept him at it so severely. Cäcilia Fischer related that when his father led him to the clavier he had to stand on a small bench to play. Oberbürgermeister Windeck also saw this . . . . Ludwig van Beethoven also received daily instruction on the violin. Once he happened to be playing without notes when his father came in and said 'What is all that silly nonsense you are scraping away so badly? You know that I cannot stand it. Scrape from notes, otherwise all your scraping will not be of any use to you.' When Johann van Beethoven received an unexpected visitor and Ludwig happened to come into the room, he would generally walk around the clavier and press down the keys with his right hand. Then his father would say 'What are you splashing there again; go away or I'll box your ears.' His father finally paid attention to him when he heard him play the violin; he was again playing out of his head without notes. His father said 'Don't you ever stop doing that in spite of what I have told you.' The boy went on playing and said to his father, 'But isn't that beautiful?' His father replied, 'That is another matter. You are not ready to play things out of your head. Work hard at the clavier and on the violin. Play the notes correctly; that is more important. When you have become good enough, then you can and will have to work out of your head hard enough.' Ludwig van Beethoven later also received daily lessons on the viola.

TDR I, 132, 426. (Beethoven's parents lived in the Fischer family's house. Beethoven also grew up there. Later the son of the Fischer family wrote his reminiscences of Beethoven.)

The Fischer manuscript:

In the year 1776, Madame van Beethoven allowed herself to be persuaded by the Court musician Brandt to move to his house on the Neugasse (992), where she would have been closer to the Court, to the market and to the church. But this did not suit Johann van Beethoven; he was afraid that he would not be able to accommodate his belongings there. Moreover he thought that the outlook onto the wall of the Franciscan monastery was too gloomy. After the great fire of the palace in 1777, Beethoven feared for his home and went weeping to the Fischers. Since the apartment was vacant, the family moved there. Beethoven's children were happy and said, 'It is a good thing that we are here again; in the Rhine there is enough water to put out a fire.'

TDR I, 427.

Gerhard von Breuning writes about his father, Court Councillor von Breuning:

In my grandparents' house in Bonn there used to be what might be termed a daily guest, an elderly general who was an intimate friend of the family. This was Baron Ignaz de Cler, Governor of the city. Whether it was breakfast time or evening he was always a sort of oral gazette of recent events in the city and of novelties of every kind. Once, it was on 13 January 1777, he came into the room with a visibly perturbed expression, hunched-up even more than was usual with him, and sat down, deep in thought, crossing his hands on the handle of his walking stick. His appearance suggested some unusual occurrence; naturally there was no lack of requests, on the part of those present, for an explanation of the cause of his distress.

'A strange fact', he finally began to tell, 'was reported to me today. The sentry who was on guard from midnight to one o'clock in the Buenretiro Court had to be taken to the hospital. The relief found the poor man unconscious. In the guard-room, and again this morning to my adjutant, he reported the following; he had hardly taken up his station when he noticed that the sky, which until then had been dark, had begun to grow light. A patch of sky above the palace became increasingly bright until finally, from a break in the cloud a rain of fire poured down upon the palace, without, however, setting anything alight. This fire rain lasted a good ten minutes. Then the darkness closed in again about him and the rent in the cloud came together once more. But immediately the cloud divided again and against the blue background of the sky he saw distinctly a large and elegant coffin and around it he saw seven smaller and more poorly decorated coffins. Upon seeing this vision he was overcome with terror and fell into a faint.'

'That is my coffin,' said Joseph von Breuning (my Grandfather) in a most peculiar manner when the General had finished telling his tale. Those present were astounded at this remark, as unexpected as it was strange. And although everyone made a great effort to persuade themselves as well as my Grandfather, of the frivolity of such a remark, it was not possible to avoid a certain feeling of uneasiness and the company broke up in a less cheerful mood than was usual.

12

Two days later, on 15 January, a fearful fire broke out in the wing of the Elector's palace that faces the city. It contained not only many art treasurers but also archives and offices. As soon as this was reported to him, my Grandfather, a Court Councillor, who lived in the neighbouring Münsterplatz, hastened to the scene in order to rescue the most important papers in his chancery. Twice he was able to carry out, single-handed, piles of documents; a third time he got as far as the palace entrance with a similar load and had almost reached safety, when a burning beam fell on him and broke his spine. He died the following day, after several hours of agony. Born on 11 October 1740, he was only 36 years old. Seven workmen also perished in the fire.

Breuning 13 ff.

A description of Bonn:

[English original]
29 November 1780.
Bonn is a pretty town, neatly built, and its streets tolerably well paved, all in black lava. It is situated in a flat near the river. The Elector of Cologne's palace faces the south entry. It has not beauty of architecture and is all plain white, without pretensions.

We went to court and were invited to dine with the Elector (Königsegge). He is 73 years old, a little, pale, black man, very merry and affable. His table is none of the best. No dessert wines handed about, nor any foreign wines at all. He is easy and agreeable, having lived all his life in ladies' company, which he is said to have liked better than his breviary. The captains of his guard, and a few other people of the court, formed the company, amongst whom were his two great-nieces, Madame de Hatzfeld and Madame de Taxis. The palace is of immense size, the ballroom particularly large and low . . . . The Elector goes about to all the assemblies and plays at tric-trac. He asked me to be of his party but I was not acquainted with their way of playing. There is every evening an assembly or play at court. The Elector seems very strong and healthy and will, I think, hold the Archduke a good tug yet.

The Courts of Europe at the close of the last century, by the late Henry Swinburne, ed. by Charles White, 2 vols, London 1841, vol. I, p. 371 f.

The Fischer manuscript:

At Christmas time when the Elector, as Bishop, celebrated Mass in the Court chapel, from 11 to 12 midnight, the musicians and the Court Choir ladies in the Court *Tucksaale* had to give proof of their best strength and ability. All the Court nobility and servants attended in gala dress. The Electoral bodyguard lined each side in parade uniform, the entire regiment from the Koblenzer gate to the Palace chapel in full dress. After the first Gospel, half-way through the Mass and also after the last Gospel, they would fire three volleys followed by the cannon on the city ramparts.

At this season it was often very cold. After the celebration, when Beethoven and his family with other friends had arrived home, following an old custom, they broiled fresh sausages and drank hot wine, punch and coffee. In this way, Christmas Eve would be celebrated and come to an end.

When Herr Johann van Beethoven had to sing in the Court *Tucksaal* he would suck a fresh raw egg or eat two prunes, on the morning before. He recommended this as being good for the voice.

Court musicians in gala dress. [Ludwig van Beethoven's attire]: sea-green tail coat, short green knee-breeches with buckles, white or black silk hose, shoes with black bows, a white flowered silk waistcoat with flap pockets, the waistcoat bordered with pure gold cord, hair dressed in curls and pigtail, a cocked hat under his left arm and a sword, carried also on the left, with a silver sword belt.

TDR I, 432, 429, 434.

The Kurfürstlich – Bönnisches Intelligenzblatt *reports the arrival of Maximilian Franz as*   6, 10
Coadjutor in Bonn:

Gnädigst privilegiirtes

Kurfürstlich=Bonnisches

Intelligenz=Blatt

—————

XX. Stück

den 12ten August 1780.

————◆————

Bonn, den 12 August.

Der Wunsch unseres theuersten Landesfürstens (Segen Gottes über Ihn den Liebling seines Volkes!) ist erfüllt. Von der Vorsicht ausersehen, ein Band daurender Glückseligkeit zwischen Ahnen und Enkeln zu knüpfen, hat Er nun seinem treuen Volke in der Person des Durchl. Erzherzoges von Oestreich Maximilian Franz einen Coadjutor am Erzstifte geschenkt. Was der gerührte Unterthan, der immerhin mit einem kindlich liebenden Herzen an seinem Fürsten hieng, bey dieser Gelegenheit empfunden, lässt sich aus der Sprache des Herzens in eine wörtliche eben so wenig übertragen, als zuverlässig sich daraus der feyer-

liche Schluß ziehen läßt, daß herzlicher und kindlichtrauter ein Fürst von seinem Volke nicht geliebt werden könne, als Maximilian Friederich von dem Seinigen.

Am 7ten dieses Nachmittags gegen 1 Uhr erhielten Se. kurfürstl. Gnaden durch Hochführen Oberstjägermeister Freyherrn von Weichs die Nachricht von der zu Köln glücklich geschlossenen Coadjutorwahl. Gleich darauf verfügten Sich Höchstdieselben zur Franziskanerkirche, allwo unter Läutung aller Stadtklocken ein feyerliches musikalisches; Te Deum abgesungen wurde, während welchem von dem im Schloßgarten stehenden von Kleistischen Regimente eine dreymalige Salve gegeben, und mit einer dreymaligen Losbrennung des groben Geschützes von den Stadtwällen beantwortet wurde. Die übrigen Feyerlichkeiten dieses Tages, als: große Tafeln, Beleuchtung und freyer maskirter Ball waren einzig der Stadt Köln vorbehalten.

Der folgende Tag aber war der hiesigen Residenz zum Feste bestimmt, wozu sich eine fast unglaubliche Menge von Fremden eingefunden. Des Mittags ward bey Hofe öffentlich an zwoen Tafeln, deren eine zu 54 die andere zu 24 Gedecken besetzt war, gespeiset, Abends gegen halb neun Uhren ward die ganze Stadt beleuchtet. Das wetteifernde

Bestreben eines jeden frohen Unterthans, hier nach Maßgabe seiner Kräfte, ein Merkmal von Ehrfurcht und Liebe gegen seinen geliebten Landesfürsten abzulegen, zeigte sich im Ganzen so ausnehmend herrlich, daß, nach einhelliger Aussage der ältesten Einwohner dieser Stadt noch niemals Bonn in einer so prächtigen Beleuchtung erschienen ist. Das Rathhaus und die Häuser verschiedener Herrschaften, der Vorhof des akademischen Schulhauses verschiedene Klöster und die Judengasse haben sich bey dieser Gelegenheit besonders ausgezeichnet.

Se. kurfürstliche Gnaden, Höchstwelche nach geendigtem Appartement diese herrliche Beleuchtung mit einem Gefolge von einigen und zwanzig Wagen, in Augenschein zu nehmen geruhten, haben an den merkwürdigsten Plätzen mit dem Wagen eine Weile stille halten, und überall in den huldreichsten Ausdrücken und Minen Ihr gnädiges Wohlgefallen blicken laßen. Hierauf verfügten Sich Höchstdieselben zur Abendtafel, wo wieder höffentlich und zwar zu 82 Gedecken gespeiset wurde. Nach Endigung derselben ward ein maskirter Ball eröffnet, wozu jedem anständig gekleideten Unterthan sowohl als Fremden der Eingang offen stand, und der erst gegen 7 Uhren des Morgens geschlossen wurde.

Bonn, 12 August 1780

The desire of our most precious Prince (God's blessing on him, the beloved of his people) has been fulfilled. With the intention of linking together ancestors and descendants with a bond of unbroken happiness, he has now presented his faithful people with a Coadjutor of the Archbishopric in the person of His Serene Highness the Archduke of Austria, Maximilian Franz. The feelings of the grateful subject, who has always looked up to his Prince with a childlike loving heart, may on this occasion be expressed in heart-felt terms as little exaggerated as they are sincere, namely; that no Prince could be loved more devotedly and with childlike trust by his people than is Maximilian Friedrich loved by his.

On the 7th inst., at one o'clock noon, His Electoral Grace received from the Noble Colonel Master of the Chase Baron von Weichs, the news of the happy outcome of the election of the Coadjutor, held in Cologne. Immediately His Grace went to the Church of Saint Francis where, to the accompaniment of all the city bells, a solemn *Te Deum* was sung, while a detachment from the Kleist Regiment fired a three volley salute, answered by a triple salvo from the mighty cannon of the city ramparts. The remaining festivities for this day, such as great banquets, illuminations and a public masked ball were reserved for the city of Cologne.

On the following day, however, the Electoral Palace in our city was the appointed scene for the festivities attended by an unbelievable crowd of visitors. At midday, a dinner was held at court where there were two tables, one laid for 54 and the other for 24 guests. In the evening at half-past eight, the whole city was illuminated. The competitive effort of each and every happy subject, according to his ability, to demonstrate reverence and affection for his beloved ruler expressed itself with such exceptional grandeur that, according to the unanimous opinion of the oldest inhabitants, never have such gorgeous illuminations been seen hitherto in Bonn. The city hall, the houses of many of the gentry, the forecourt of the Academic School building, several monasteries and the ghetto excelled particularly on this occasion. His Electoral Grace, at the end of his Levée, condescended to view this superb illumination in person, taking an escort of some one-and-twenty carriages. He halted his carriage for a while in several of the most remarkable places and showed his gracious pleasure with the most laudatory expressions of admiration and approval. Thereupon His Grace went in to dinner at which once more a large company was assembled at a table with 82 places. This was followed by the opening of a masked ball, entry to which was open to all respectably dressed citizens, as well as visitors, and which did not end until about 7 o'clock in the morning.

Kreisarchiv Bonn, Sign. Ia, 6.

10   *Baron von Seida und Landensberg describes the Elector Maximilian Franz:*

From his large blue eyes shone the reflection of his noble soul. His countenance was open and engaging, although his friendliness could quickly turn to an austere seriousness. His nose was slightly hooked, his mouth well formed, the lips slightly pouting, his forehead was very high and only lightly covered with hair. Because of this feature, and his all too prominent jowls, the eurhythmics of his particularly well complexioned face were somewhat marred. His gait was quick and firm, his voice manly, resonant and clear. His speech was somewhat Austrian, while his personal habits as well as his dress were simple in the utmost degree. Avoiding all ostentation, which is so often a sign of vanity, he almost always wore either a simple grey frock-coat or else court dress.

TDR I, 160. (The Baron wrote an article in praise of the Elector in the *Zeitung für die Elegante Welt.*)

Henry Swinburne on Maximilian Franz:

[English original]
Maximilian is a good natured, neither here-nor-there kind of youth.

Swinburne, *op. cit.*, vol. I, p. 343.

Wolfgang Amadeus Mozart writes to his father on 17 November 1781, about Maximilian Franz:

When God grants an office, He also grants understanding. And this is truly the case with the Archduke. Before he became a priest he was much more witty and clever, talked less but more sensibly. You should see him now! Stupidity peeks out from his eyes, he talks and speaks without ceasing and everything in a falsetto. He has a swelling in his throat. In a word, it is as if the man had changed completely.

TDR I, 161.

Dr Franz Gerhard Wegeler about Bonn:

Altogether it was a wonderful and in many ways an exciting time in Bonn as long as it was under the rule of the personally brilliant Elector Max Franz, Maria Theresa's youngest and favourite son.

TDR I, 162. (Dr Wegeler was Beethoven's friend in youth and later married Eleonore von Breuning.)

The Fischer manuscript:

At the time of the Elector Clemens August, in the year 1724, there lived in the house [Rheingasse 934], the Court Kapellmeister and good singer Maria Joseph Balluinesius [Balduin?] Ludowikus van Beethoven, together with his wife. They had one child, a son, Johann van Beethoven, and lived as tenants on the second floor.

    The Court Kapellmeister's son Johann van Beethoven had already received instruction on the piano and in singing at an early age. Later he too was appointed to the post of Court Tenor singer.

7

Johann van Beethoven also early became an expert in wine-tasting and before long a hearty wine drinker as well; he was light-hearted and merry, being easily satisfied and not intemperate.

When Johann van Beethoven introduced his beloved in person to his father, it was his intention, upon which he insisted and from which he would not waver, that she should become his wife. His father did not consider her as suitable or worthy, although she was a pretty and slender person, with whom no one could find fault, of good law-abiding burgher stock. Moreover, she could prove by means of old references that she had served in good houses where she had received a good up-bringing and training.

But after the Court Kapellmeister had obtained information regarding her and had discovered that she had once been a chambermaid, he was very much opposed to the marriage and said to his son, 'I would never have believed or expected of you that you should sink so low.'

The son of the Court Kapellmeister, Johann van Beethoven, Court Tenor, was married in Bonn in the old parish chruch of Saint Remigius on 12 November 1767; to Anna Maria Magdalena Keferig, named Beethoven, born in the valley of Ehrenbreitstein. Madame van Beethoven later used to recall that as far as she was concerned she could have had a fine wedding, but that her father-in-law obstinately refused to attend. Because of this the ceremony was brief.

Johann van Beethoven was of medium height, with a long face, broad forehead, a round nose, broad shoulders and serious eyes. He had some scars on his face and wore a thin pigtail. His wife was rather tall, longish face, a nose somewhat bent, spare, earnest eyes. Madame van Beethoven was a clever woman; she could give converse and reply aptly, politely and modestly to high and low, and for this reason she was much liked and respected. She occupied herself with sewing and knitting. They led a righteous and peaceful married life, and paid their house-rent and baker's bills promptly, quarterly and on the day. She was a good domestic woman, she knew how to give and also how to take in manner that is becoming to all people of honest thoughts.

After the Beethovens had had three children, on fine summer days they would be taken out by the serving maids to the Rhine or to the Palace garden, where they played in the sand with other children. At the proper time they would have to find their own way home. When the weather was not favourable, the children played in the Fischers' courtyard with the Fischer and other children from the neighbourhood.

When Johann van Beethoven received visitors and wanted to get rid of the children because they disturbed him, the maid would take them to the lower floor, set them down on the bare floor and control their pranks. The children would then crawl to the entrance door on their hands and knees. As a result of a chill, Nicola [called Johann] suffered an abscess on his head; this resulted in a scar which is still visible.

Beethoven's children were not brought up with gentleness; they were often left in the charge of serving maids. Their father was very strict with them. When the children were with others of their age they could amuse themselves peacefully for a long time. Ludwig liked to be carried piggy-back, which made him laugh heartily.

Johann van Beethoven, the Court Tenor, carried out his duties punctiliously. He gave lessons on the piano and in singing to the sons and daughters of the local English, French and Imperial Envoys, to the gentlemen and daughters of the nobility and to distinguished burghers as well. He often had more to do than he was able, hence his household was well taken care of. The Envoys regarded him with much favour; they had instructed their major-domos that, should he be short of wine, he would send a message and the cellar servants were to bring him full measures of wine to his house. Beethoven, however, availed himself but sparingly of this privilege.

TDR I, 416 f., 420 f., 423 ff.

Beethoven soon displayed an enormous musical talent, and his father obviously wished to present him as a child prodigy much in the way that Leopold Mozart had capitalized on his son Wolfgang's talents. Johann van Beethoven introduced his son to the world at a concert in Bonn held on 26 March 1778. By this time, Beethoven had begun serious study not only on the organ and piano but also on the violin and viola; he was later to be listed among the viola-players of the Court orchestra. Among his various local teachers the most important, without any question, was Christian Gottlob Neefe (1748–98), who was the Court organist and theatre director at Bonn; from Neefe Beethoven learned Johann Sebastian Bach's *Well-Tempered Clavier*, which he used to play even during his early years in Vienna.

Notice.

On today's date, 26 March 1778, in the hall of the Musical Academy in the Sternengasse, the Court Tenor of the Elector of Cologne BEETHOVEN will have the honour of presenting two of his pupils, namely Mdelle Averdonc, Court Alto singer, and his young son of six years. The former will have the honour to oblige with several beautiful Arias, the latter with various piano Concerti and Trios. He flatters himself that they will give all the distinguished Ladies and Gentlemen complete satisfaction, all the more so since both have had the honour of performing to the greatest satisfaction of the whole Court.

The performance will begin at 5 o'clock

For those Ladies and Gentlemen who do not hold season tickets the price of admittance is one gulden. The tickets may be obtained at the above-mentioned hall of the Academy, also at Herr *Claren* on the Mühlenstein stream.

TDR I, 120. (Ludwig was in fact seven years old.)

Dr Franz Gerhard Wegeler on Christian Gottlob Neefe: 11

Neefe had little influence on the education of our Ludwig. The latter even complained about Neefe's too sharp criticism of his first attempts at composition.

TDR I, 138.

Beethoven writes to Christian Gottlob Neefe:

Thank you for the counsel you have so often given me in the progress of my God-given art. Should I ever become a great man, you will have contributed to it. . .

Spazier's *Berliner Musikzeitung*, 26 October 1793.

The Fischer manuscript:

When Johann van Beethoven visited the Fischer family of a Sunday evening, he talked about a number of things. Then he also said: 'My son Ludwig, he is now my only comfort in life. He is improving in his music to such an extent that he is admired by everyone. My Ludwig, my Ludwig, I foresee that in time he will be a great man in the world. Those of you who are gathered here and see it come about, remember these words of mine.'

Ludwig van Beethoven, when he was somewhat older, was often dirty and unkempt, so much so that Cäcilia [Fischer] said to him: 'How dirty you look. You really should be tidier.' To which he answered: 'What difference does it make. When I become a gentleman no one will notice.'

Once Ludwig van Beethoven was sitting at the window of his bedroom overlooking the courtyard. He held his head in both his hands and looked very pensive. Cäcilia Fischer, coming across the courtyard, called up to him: 'What are you looking at, Ludwig?' But she received no answer. Later she asked him: 'What does that mean? No answer is also an answer.' He said: 'Oh no, it's not that. Forgive me; I was so taken up with profound and beautiful thoughts that I could not bear to be disturbed.'

Looking back, one could not say that Ludwig ever cared for companionship or for society. In fact, it was only when he was pondering over music, or had to occupy himself alone that he would assume quite a different aspect, and would be conscious of the respect due to him. His happiest hours were those when he was free of all company, when his family had all gone out and he could be alone.

TDR I, 442, 427, 436, 434.

> Beethoven soon began to compose. Unlike Mozart, who was born with a mercurial temperament and a Mendelssohnian facility, Beethoven had to work extremely hard at his compositions, sketching and polishing his works over and over again until he considered them finished; this was a trait of Beethoven's entire career. Since he was a virtuoso on the relatively new piano (in German *Hammerklavier*, generally referred to as Fortepiano), it was natural that many of Beethoven's earliest compositions should be for the piano. His first published works were a set of variations, composed in 1782. His most important compositions of this earliest period, however, were undoubtedly the three piano Sonatas dedicated to the Elector Maximilian Friedrich, WoO 47.

C. F. Cramer's Magazin der Musik *writes about Beethoven, 2 March 1783:*

Ludwig van Beethoven, son of the above-mentioned Tenor, is an eleven-year-old boy and of very promising talent. He plays on the piano in a very finished manner and powerfully, reads at sight and, to put it briefly, he plays the greater part of the Well Tempered Clavier of Sebastian Bach which Herr Neefe gave him. Those who are familiar with this collection of Preludes and Fugues in every tonality (which one could practically term the *non plus ultra*) will know what this means. Herr Neefe, insofar as his other duties permitted, has given him instruction in thorough–bass. Now he is teaching him composition and in order to encourage him, has had engraved in Mannheim 9 Variations on a March. This young genius deserves a subsidy in order to enable him to travel. He will undoubtedly become a second Mozart, if he progresses as well as he has begun.

Magazin der Musik, year I, 394.

Beethoven's dedication on the first edition of the so-called 'Elector Sonatas':

> Three Sonatas for Clavier, dedicated to the Right Worthy Archbishop Elector of Cologne, Maximilian Friedrich, my gracious Sovereign, composed by Ludwig van Beethoven, aged 11 years. Speier, in the Edition of Councillor Bossler. [1783]

Most Exalted and August Lord!
Since my fourth year music has become the foremost of my childish occupations. At so early an age I met the beautiful Muse who led my spirit to pure harmonies: I won her and it has often seemed to me that she loves me in return. I have now reached my eleventh year and since then, in the hours of dedication, my Muse often whispers to me, 'Attempt it and write down the harmonies in your soul'. Eleven years, I thought, and what figure would I cut as an author? What would the men of the arts say? I was almost too shy. But my Muse demanded – I obeyed and wrote.

And now, may I, <u>Most Exalted and August Lord</u>, make so bold as to lay the first-born of my juvenile works on the steps of Thy throne? And dare I hope that <u>Thou</u> wilt grant them the enhancing approval of Thy gentle fatherly glance? Oh yes, for the sciences and the arts have ever found in <u>Thee</u> their wise protector, their generous patron under whose paternal care their talents thrive.

Filled with this encouraging confidence, I presume to approach <u>Thee</u> with these juvenile attempts. Accept them as a pure offering of a childish reverence and look down, <u>Most Exalted and August Lord</u>, upon them and their youthful author.

Ludwig van Beethoven.

TDR I, 147 f. (The family, and for a long time Ludwig himself, thought he was born in 1772.)

Respectful Pro-Memoria regarding the Electoral Court Musique:

[Bonn, 25 June 1784] . . .

8 Johann Beethoven has a definitely decaying voice; he has been long in service, is very poor, of respectable conduct and married.

13 . Christian Neefe, the organist, according to my unprejudiced judgment, could be relieved of this post since he is not particularly accomplished on the organ, is moreover, a foreigner of no particular merit and of the Calvinist religion.

14 . Ludwig Beethoven, a son of Beethoven sub no. 8, receives no stipend but, in the absence of Kapellmeister Luchesy, has taken over the organ. He has good ability, is still young and his conduct is quiet and upright . . .

TDR I, 175 ff.

Tenors.
Messrs. Johann van Beethoven . . .
Organists.
Christian Neefe.
Ludwig van Beethoven . . .
Viola players . . .
Ludwig van Beethoven . . .

Stadtarchiv Bonn.

14   *Anton Schindler writes about Hofrätin Helene von Breuning:*

Even in his later years he [Beethoven] called the members of this family his former guardian angels and liked to recall many of the reprimands of the lady of the house. 'She knew how to keep the parasites from the flowers,' he said. By this, he meant certain friends who had begun to endanger the natural development of his talent as well as the right balance of his artistic consciousness and, because of their adulation, might have aroused vanity in him. He was well-nigh to regarding himself as a renowned artist and consequently preferred to give ear to those who fostered this delusion, rather than to those who made him aware of the fact that he had as yet to learn everything which turns an apprentice into a master.

Schindler I, 17 f.

20   *Letter from Beethoven to Dr Franz Gerhard Wegeler:*

[Vienna, between 1794 and 1796]

Dearest and best friend!
In what horrible guise have you portrayed me to myself. I admit it and do not deserve your friendship. You are so noble, so well-meaning that, for the first time, I cannot place myself on your level, for I have fallen far beneath you. For many long weeks I have distressed my noblest and best friend. You believe that I have lost the goodness of my heart, but no, heaven be thanked, it was no intentional premeditated wickedness on my part that made me act as I did, but an unpardonable thoughtlessness that led me to see the thing in a false light. Oh, how ashamed I am for you and for myself – I hardly dare to beg once more for your friendship.

Oh Wegeler, my only consolation lies in the fact that you have known me almost from my childhood and yet, oh let me say it myself, I was always good and ever attempted to be honest and worthy in my actions. Otherwise, how would you have loved me? Could I possibly now, in so short a time, have changed so terribly, and so much to my disadvantage – impossible. Could those feelings for the great and the good have been completely extinguished within me all of a sudden? No, Wegeler, beloved and best friend, oh, try once more to throw yourself unreservedly into the arms of your B, encourage the good qualities which you always found in him. I assure you that the pure temple of sacred friendship which you will build upon them will stand firm and forever. No incident, no storm will be able to shake its foundations – firm – eternal – our friendship – forgiveness – oblivion – a new life for the dying, declining friendship. Oh Wegeler, do not cast away this hand of reconciliation; give me yours in mine – oh God – no more – I myself will come to you and throw myself into your arms and plead for the prodigal friend, and you will give yourself to your repentant, loving, never forgetting

Beethoven
once more.

I have at this very minute received your letter, as I have only just come home.

KFR 17 f. Anderson 15.

Dr Gerhard von Breuning describes the von Breuning family: *14, 17, 18*

The already widowed Hofrätin Helene v. Breuning, daughter of the Elector's personal physician Stefan Kerich, was only 26 years old. Of her children:

Christof was born on 13 May 1771 in Bonn.

Eleonora Brigitte on 23 April 1772 in the same place.

Stefan (my father), generally known as Steffen, also born in Bonn on 17 August 1774, while Lorenz, nicknamed 'Lenz', born half-a-year after the death of his father as a posthumous son, followed in the summer of 1777.

The widow, apart from longer or shorter periods spent with her father-in-law at Kerpen (a village between Cologne and Aachen), or with her sister-in-law, Margarete von Stockhausen in Beul an der Ahr (now Mineralbad Neuenahr), henceforth remained in the family house in Bonn until 1815. . .

A brother of my late lamented grandfather, Johann Lorenz von Breuning, Prebendary of Neuss (known throughout the family as 'Uncle von Neuss') immediately moved to Bonn to supervise the upbringing of the four orphaned children and – as the head of the family of his deceased brother – to look after the affairs of the family, until his death in Bonn in 1796, at the age of 58. . . .

The amiable and eager character of a poor student soon made him a daily comrade in the house. This was Franz Gerhard Wegeler, the son of an Alsatian burgher, who <div align="right">*20*</div> early felt a strong aspiration for learning which would enable him to break the fetters of his humble origins and to achieve that which he and his contemporaries later did achieve.

Already a naturalized member of the household in 1782, he made the acquaintance of the son of a musician in the Electoral Court Chapel who, although still a boy rather than a youth, was as ardently enraptured with the Muse of music as was the other with science and the arts, and already played excellently on the piano.

Eleonore and Lenz required a piano teacher, while Wegeler's young friend needed to give lessons in order to support himself and his parents. So the young Ludwig van Beethoven was introduced into the hospitable house of my grandmother. He quickly took a fancy to this lady and she soon became a second mother to him. In many ways she exercised a moderating influence on the occasionally hot-heated obstinacy of his character. But a lasting bond of friendship was established between the children and Beethoven.

Breuning 17 f.

Dr Franz Gerhard Wegeler describes Beethoven in the family circle of the von Breunings:

17, 18 In this family there reigned a youthful high spiritedness and an unaffected, cultured tone. Christoph von Breuning early tried his hand at writing short poems, as Stephan von Breuning was to do later, and not without success. The intimates of the house distinguished themselves in convivial entertainments in which the useful was combined with the pleasurable. It should also be noted that before the war [1790s] this was a fairly prosperous household, so it is quite easy to understand that it was here that Beethoven experienced the first happy discoveries of his youth. Beethoven was soon treated as a son of the house. Not only did he spend the greater part of the day there, but sometimes even the night. Here he felt himself free; here he could move about with ease; everything combined to make him cheerful and to develop his intellect. . . . It was in the midst of the von Breuning family that Ludwig received his first introduction to German literature, particularly poetry, as well as his first lessons in the social amenities.

WRBN 10, 9.

Beethoven soon began teaching, and one of his pupils was Maria Anna Wilhelmine, Freiin von Westerholt, who became an excellent pianist. Beethoven fell in love with her and this is probably the first of his many, and mostly tumultuous, love affairs. She later married a Freiherr Friedrich Clemens von Elverfeldt, also known as Beverförde-Werries.

Spazier's Berliner Musik Zeitung *reports on 19 October 1793:*

19 The fiery Madame von Elverfeldt [played] a difficult Sonata by Sardi with such speed and precision that one must admire her. [The father] himself played the bassoon and he had a sort of private band formed from his household staff, mostly of wind instruments.

TDR I, 263.

Dr Franz Gerhard Wegeler writes about Beethoven's love-life:

The truth is, as my brother-in-law Stephan von Breuning, as Ferdinand Ries, as Bernhard Romberg and I discovered, that Beethoven was never without a beloved, and generally infatuated with her in the highest degree. These love-affairs diminished as he grew older and left as little mark on him as they had awakened in the objects of his love. In Vienna, at least so long as I lived there, Beethoven was always involved in some love relationship and sometimes he made conquests which would have been if not impossible, exceedingly difficult for certain Adonises to achieve.

WBRN 42 f.

1. Bonn from the Rhine. Coloured engraving for camera obscura by Balthasar Friedrich Leizel, 1780. Stadtarchiv Bonn.

In Bonn, which then had about 10,000 inhabitants and was the residence of the electors and archbishops of Cologne, Ludwig van Beethoven was born and was christened on 17 December 1770. His exact date of birth is not known.

2. New fountain at the Markplatz, Bonn. Coloured engraving for camera obscura by Balthasar Friedrich Leizel, 1780. Stadtarchiv Bonn.

Beethoven's parents lived for some time near the Marktplatz. In the rear of the picture to the left is the Bonn Rathaus (town hall), built during the reign of Elector Clemens August. On the Marktplatz there was also the inn 'Der Zehrgarten', and the innkeeper was the mother of Babette Koch, an intimate friend of Eleonore von Breuning. The attractive Babette was also on friendly terms with the young Beethoven.

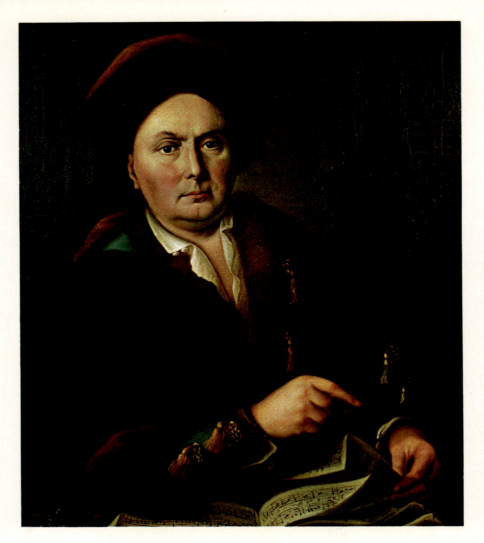

3. Ludwig van Beethoven (1712–1773). Portrait in oils by Leopold Radoux. Konsul Otto Reichert, Vienna.

Ludwig (Louis) van Beethoven, the grandfather of the famous composer and the first musician in the family, was born in Antwerp. He later moved to Bonn, where he became Hofkapellmeister of the Elector's Court. A contemporary report describes him as 'a big, handsome man with a longish face, a broad forehead, round nose, large, prominent eyes, fat red cheeks, and a very serious demeanour.' Beethoven, who held his grandfather in high regard, had this portrait sent from Bonn to Vienna in 1801; after his death the painting went to his nephew Carl and his wife.

4. The Electoral Palace (*Residenz*) in Bonn after the fire in 1777. Coloured engraving for camera obscura printed in reverse, engraved in 1780 by Balthasar Friedrich Leizel. Städtische Sammlungen, Bonn.

The Elector loved music, opera, theatre and ballet. Frequently the aristocratic members of his court put on theatrical performances during which the electoral musicians, later including the young Beethoven, assisted.

34

5. Maximilian Friedrich, Count of Königsegg-Aulendorf, Elector and Archbishop of Cologne (1708–1784). Anonymous portrait in oils. Städtische Sammlungen, Bonn.

Maximilian Friedrich was a good-natured, indolent man who, after the excesses of his predecessor, the Elector Clemens August of Bavaria, severely reduced court expenses. But he did engage Beethoven's grandfather, who had been a bass singer in the Electoral Chapel, as Kapellmeister.

6. Arrival of the Coadjutor Maximilian Franz, Archduke of Austria (1756–1801) in Bonn, 1780. Detail from a painting by Franz Jakob Roussaux. Stadtarchiv Bonn.

7. The house No. 934 in the Rheingasse, Bonn. Engraving by
Conrad Caspar Rordorf. Gesellschaft der Musikfreunde, Vienna.

In 1776, the Beethoven family moved into the
house of the baker Fischer. The baker's son
Gottfried later wrote a kind of diary which is of
considerable importance to our knowledge of
Beethoven's life and especially his youthful
years, described by Fischer in some detail.

> ## AVERTISSEMENT.
>
> Heut dato den 26ten Martii 1778. wird auf dem musikalischen Akademiesaal in der Sternengaß der Churköllnische Hoftenorist BEETHOVEN die Ehre haben zwey seiner Scholaren zu produciren; nämlich: Madlle. Averdonc Hofaltistin, und sein Söhngen von 6. Jahren. Erstere wird mit verschiedenen schönen Arien, letzterer mit verschiedenen Clavier-Concerten und Trios die Ehre haben aufzuwarten, wo er allen hohen Herrschaften ein völliges Vergnügen zu leisten sich schmeichlet, um je mehr da beyde zum größten Vergnügen des ganzen Hofes sich hören zu lassen die Gnade gehabt haben.
>
> Der Anfang ist Abends um 5. Uhr.
>
> Die nicht abbonnirte Herren und Damen zahlen einen Gulden.
>
> Die Billets sind auf ersagtem musikalischen Akademiesaal, auch bey Hrn. Claren auf der Bach im Mühlenstein zu haben.

8. The hand-bill of a concert given on 26 March 1778 during which Ludwig van Beethoven made his first public appearance. Original document destroyed; from a photograph at the Beethovenhaus Bonn.

Father Johann van Beethoven attempted to make a kind of *Wunderkind* out of his son, as once Leopold Mozart had done with Wolfgang.

9. Ludwig van Beethoven, *c.* 1786. Silhouette by Joseph Neesen; photograph Beethovenhaus Bonn.

The first known portrait of Beethoven. It served as frontispiece to F. G. Wegeler and F. Ries, *Biographische Notizen über Ludwig van Beethoven*, Coblenz 1838. The original has long disappeared.

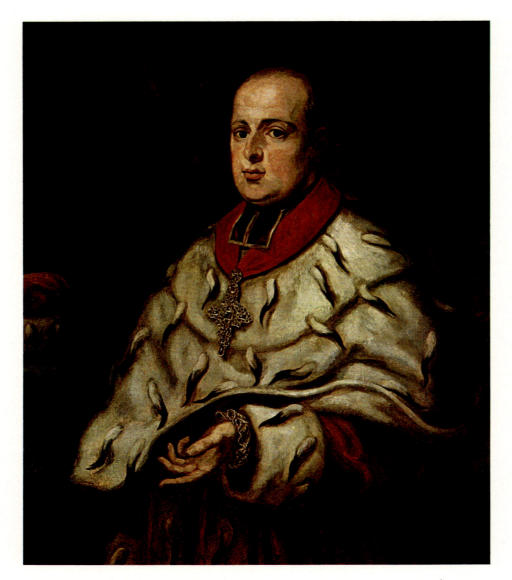

C. G. NEEFE.

10. Maximilian Franz, youngest brother of the Emperor Joseph II, as Elector and Archbishop of Cologne. Anonymous portrait in oils. Beethovenhaus Bonn.

In 1780 Maximilian Franz was chosen as Coadjutor to ensure his peaceful succession to Maximilian Friedrich as Elector and Archbishop. Since Maximilian Franz was no longer fitted for a military career because of a wound in the knee, it was decided that he should devote his life to the Church. He was very attached to the arts and especially to music, and during his reign a new and splendid life flourished at the Court in Bonn.

11. Christian Gottlieb Neefe (1748–1798). Engraved by Gottlob August Liebe from a drawing by Johann Georg Rosenberg. Gesellschaft der Musikfreunde, Vienna.

Neefe, a highly educated man and excellent musician, took over the direction of the National Theatre in Bonn in 1779 and was also the Court Organist. He was Beethoven's first important teacher.

12. The Breuning house on the Münsterplatz in Bonn. Watercolour by M. Frickel. Stadtarchiv Bonn.

The watercolour shows the house shortly before its demolition in 1896. Beethoven spent many happy hours in this house.

13. 'Drei / Sonaten / fuers / Klavier', WoO 47, called 'Die Kurfürstensonaten'. Title-page with the dedication to Elector Maximilian Friedrich. First edition; Gesellschaft der Musikfreunde, Vienna.

When these sonatas were published in 1783, Beethoven was not, as the title-page indicates, eleven years old, but already thirteen. Beethoven himself long believed that he had been born in 1772, because his father, in the manner of Leopold Mozart, reduced the age of his *Wunderkind* in order to create more of a sensation with him. The publisher of this first edition was Bossler in Speyer.

14. Helene von Breuning with her children. Anonymous silhouette dated 1782. Original owned by Rolf Wegeler, Coblenz. Photograph from the Beethovenhaus in Bonn.

Helene, widow of Court Councillor von Breuning, was Beethoven's motherly friend and adviser. After the death of her husband she lived with her children Eleonore, Christoph, Lorenz and Stephan in a handsome house on the Münsterplatz in Bonn; the Breuning house soon became a second home for Beethoven. The silhouette also shows Helene's brother, the Canon von Kerich.

15, 16. 'Variations / Pour le / Clavecin / Sur une Marche de / M.' Dresler', WoO 63. Title-page with the dedication to Countess von Wolff-Metternich and first page of music with the note 'Maestoso'. First edition. Beethovenhaus Bonn.

Written in 1782, this was Beethoven's first published composition; it was issued by Götz of Mannheim. Countess Wolff-Metternich, to whom this work was dedicated, was one of the leading ladies of Bonn court life.

17, 18. Christoph (1771–1841) and Stephan (1774–1827) von Breuning. Miniatures by Franz Gerhard von Kügelgen. Originals destroyed. Photographs Beethovenhaus Bonn.

Christoph, the eldest son, studied law abroad and later returned to Bonn to live. Stephan also studied law and came to Vienna in 1801. He remained a faithful friend of Beethoven's and was able to survive the composer's occasional fits of temper.

19. Maria Anna Wilhelmine, Freiin von Westerholt (1774–1852). Anonymous copy of a portrait
in oils. Beethovenhaus Bonn.

Beethoven was introduced to Maria Anna
Wilhelmine at the house of the Court Councillor's
widow Breuning. The young girl became
Beethoven's pupil and he soon fell in love
with her. Maria Anna later married a Freiherr
von Beverförde-Werries.

20. Franz Gerhard Wegeler (1765–1848).
Silhouette by Joseph Neesen. Photograph
Beethovenhaus Bonn.

After completion of his studies in medicine,
Wegeler settled in Coblenz as a doctor. He was
a friend of the Breunings and of Beethoven's,
and in 1802 he married Eleonore von Breuning.
In 1838 he wrote, together with Ferdinand Ries,
Biographische Notizen über Ludwig van Beethoven.

21. View of Augustusburg Castle in Brühl. Coloured engraving by Johann Ziegler from a drawing by Laurenz Janscha. Brühl Castle.

Not far from Bonn was Augustusburg Castle, the summer residence of the Electors of Cologne. The Electors took their musicians with them, and during the reign of Elector Maximilian Friedrich the band was led by Beethoven's grandfather. Beethoven's father was a good tenor and 'capabel vor die Violin'.

22. View of Aschaffenburg. Aquatint by Johann Jakob Strüdt. Freies Deutsches Hochstift, Goethemuseum, Frankfurt am Main.

In the autumn of 1791 a meeting of the Order of Teutonic Knights took place in Mergentheim, the capital of the Order, under the leadership of Grand Master Maximilian Franz. He took with him the court musicians; thus Beethoven went to Mergentheim and, with other members of the band, made an excursion to Aschaffenburg, to hear the pianist Abbé Sterkel, who lived in that town.

23. Abbé Johann Franz Xaver Sterkel (1750–1817). Anonymous engraving, c. 1810. Gesellschaft der Musikfreunde, Vienna.

Sterkel, then a man of some forty years of age, had studied theology but had then become a musician in the service of the Elector at Mainz. By the time Beethoven heard him, Sterkel had gained a considerable reputation as a composer and pianist: his playing was gracious, delicate and attractive.

24. View of Vienna from the Josephstadt. Coloured engraving by Carl Schütz. Antiquarian Gilhofer und Ranschburg, Vienna.

'This young genius deserves assistance to enable him to travel,' wrote Neefe in 1783. In the spring of 1787 the necessary funds were raised – possibly by the Elector himself – and Beethoven could travel to Vienna. The young man, now sixteen years of age, came to study with Mozart, who was then at the height of his fame and about to complete *Don Giovanni*.

25. Fragment of a Violin Concerto in C major, WoO 5. Autograph. Gesellschaft der Musik-freunde, Vienna.

The autograph, which may at one time have been complete, is written on German paper, and thus was probably composed while Beethoven was still in Bonn, before the end of 1792. In Vienna, Beethoven used the customary Italian paper with the characteristic three half-moons watermark.

26. Wolfgang Amadeus Mozart (1756–1791). Unfinished portrait in oils by Joseph Lange, *c.* 1790. Mozarteum, Salzburg.

This portrait was begun some two years after Beethoven's visit to Vienna. It was planned that Mozart become Beethoven's composition teacher. But Beethoven seems not to have made any lasting impression on the Mozart family, for Constanze Mozart never mentioned him later although he became very famous in Vienna. When Beethoven heard the news that his mother was seriously ill – she died shortly afterwards – he interrupted his studies with Mozart and travelled back to Bonn.

27. Ferdinand Ernst Gabriel, Count von Waldstein (1762–1823). Anonymous portrait in oils. Duchcov, Czechoslovakia.

This hitherto unknown oil portrait shows the Count during his youth, before his marriage in 1812. His two older brothers had no children, and in order to save the Waldsteins from extinction, Ferdinand married Maria Isabella Countess Rzewuska. With this beautiful and extravagant wife Waldstein soon spent his fortune and became penniless. Ferdinand died after his brother Franz von Paul Adam without knowing that he had meanwhile come into the family fortune.

28. Ferdinand Ernst Gabriel, Count von Waldstein. Anonymous silhouette from Beethoven's scrapbook. Österreichische Nationalbibliothek, Vienna.

Count Waldstein came to Bonn to serve his apprentice year as a Knight of the Teutonic Order under the Order's Grand Master, the Elector Maximilian Franz. Waldstein, a cultivated amateur musician, was one of the first who recognized Beethoven's genius, and gave him letters of recommendation for his trips to Vienna.

29. Emperor Joseph II as protector of the Freemasons. Anonymous Viennese engraving on stiff green paper. H. C. Robbins Landon, Buggiano Castello, Italy.

The Emperor Joseph (1741–90), eager to reform the conservative Austrian political and economic systems, was often regarded as an unofficial protector of the Freemasons. Joseph was not – as his father had been – a member of the Order. Beethoven was a Mason in his early years, as Carl Holz informs us.

48

The Court went in the summer to Augustusburg Castle in Brühl, which still exists today, and there Beethoven was often viola-player in the orchestra. The musicians themselves naturally cultivated chamber music, and many of the' members of the *Kapelle*, such as Franz Ries, the violinist, and Bernhard Romberg, the cellist, became Beethoven's firm friends as well as colleagues. Ries' son later became one of Beethoven's star pupils. Another friend was the horn-player Nikolaus Simrock, who later founded a famous publishing house in Bonn and published some of Beethoven's compositions.

Thomas Pennant describes Brühl:

[English original]
July 3 [1765].
... at two o'clock set out for Brühl, the palace where the Elector resides, about two miles out of the common road to Cologne. The outside has nothing to recommend it. The grand staircase is very magnificent; the sides are of mock marble enriched with the best stucco I ever saw; above is a circular gallery supported by very fine Caryatides. The Salle de Compagnie is fitted up in much the same manner, the stucco represented trophies, arms & ca, and is a noble room. In the Salle à Manger the sides of the ceiling and the middle are stuccoed and richly painted. In two other rooms there is fine Brussels Tapestry; in one it represents Landscapes, in the other Dutch feasts from Teniers. Chambre d'Audience, – its ceiling is remarkably elegant, partly stuccoed and finely painted. Between the stucco are small hunting pieces. Another room has a ceiling equally beautifull. The appearance of his electoral highness obliged me to retreat, so saw no more of this wing; the other contained only small apartments. The gardens are large, fitted with Basins spouting water, Parterres in all shapes & ca.

Pennant, *op. cit.*, p. 146.

21

Dr Franz Gerhard Wegeler on Beethoven's playing of chamber music:

Once Beethoven played [as a chamber musician] at a small gathering together with Franz Ries and the famous Bernhard Romberg, who was then still living, a new Trio by Pleyel, *a vista*. In the second part of the Adagio the players, although not together, did not get stuck; they played bravely on and finished happily together. As it was later discovered, two bars were missing from the piano part. The Elector was very much puzzled by this work of Pleyel's and had it repeated eight days later, whereupon the mystery was solved to the satisfaction of the Elector.

WRBN 15.

Carl Ludwig Junker gives an account of the Elector's orchestra in Bossler's Musikalische Korrespondenz, *23 November 1791:*

In every way the demeanour of these orchestra players [Electoral orchestra] is very good and respectable. They are persons of great elegance and their lives are exemplary. One could not wish for a greater discretion than I found here. In a concert the poor players were packed so close together, they were so surrounded and pressed by the audience that they could hardly play, and the sweat poured down over their faces. Nevertheless, they bore this all quietly and with composure; one could not see a single dissatisfied expression among them. At the court of a small prince such a situation would have given rise to impertinence after impertinence.

The members of this orchestra are almost all, without exception, still in the prime of their young lives and in excellent glowing good health. They are well educated and of good appearance. They present a striking picture when one takes into account the gorgeous livery which the Elector provides for them. This is red, richly embroidered with gold.

Heretofore, one was perhaps accustomed to think of Cologne as the land of darkness, wherein enlightenment had not yet set foot. Yet one will be of quite different mind when one arrives at the court of the Elector. Especially among the orchestra did I find men of considerable enlightenment and common sense.

The Elector, this most human and best of Princes, is not only, as is known, himself a player but also an enthusiastic lover of the musical arts. It seems almost as if he could never hear enough music. At the concert which I attended He was, and only He, the most attentive listener among the audience.

TDR I, 253. (Chaplain Junker was a composer and author.)

Carl Ludwig Junker writes about Beethoven's piano-playing on 23 November 1791:

13 I also heard one of the greatest players on the piano, the dear good Bethofen [sic], by whom some pieces appeared in the *Blumenlese* of Speier in 1783, which he had composed at the age of 11. As a matter of fact he did not appear at a public concert, perhaps because the instrument did not meet his requirements: it was a 'Grand' instrument by Spath; in Bonn he is used to playing only on a Stein. Nevertheless, I heard him improvise, which I infinitely preferred. In fact I was myself requested to give him a theme for variations. One can, I think, judge the virtuosity of this amiable, soft-spoken man from his well-nigh inexhaustible wealth of ideas, from the highly personal expressiveness of his playing and the skill with which he plays. I really do not know what he could possibly still lack in order to be a great artist. I have heard Vogler on the Fortepiano (I can pass no judgment on his organ playing, since I have not heard him on that instrument); I have heard him often, and heard him for hours on end and admired his extraordinary skill. But Beethoven is, apart from his skill, more eloquent, meaningful and expressive – in short, he speaks to the heart. He is thus as good a player of Adagios as he is of Allegros. Even the excellent players of this orchestra admire him: when he plays they are all ears. He is a most modest person and has no pretensions whatsoever. Nevertheless he claims that in the course of the journeys which his Elector has allowed him to undertake he has rarely found, among the best-known piano players, that which he believed to have the right to expect. His playing also differs so much from the customary way of handling a piano that it would seem as if he had wished to follow a completely individual path towards the goal of perfection which he has now reached.

TDR I, 251 f. Bossler's *Musikalische Korrespondenz.*

Letter from Nikolaus Simrock to Anton Schindler, about Beethoven's journey to Aschaffenburg and Mergentheim:

I remember that when we passed through Aschaffenburg many of the Electoral Court 22
musicians thought it seemly to call on Kapellmeister Sterkel and introduce Beethoven 23
to him. We were received in a very friendly manner and after a few courtesies the
Kapellmeister obliged us with one of his Sonatas with Violin accompaniment, which
Andreas Romberg undertook to play. Sterkel played in his individual, delicate and
very pleasing manner. Subsequently he asked Beethoven to play, and particularly
wished to hear him play his own variations on a theme by Righini, *Vieni Amore*,
which had been recently engraved in Mainz. He [Sterkel] insisted that they were
too difficult for him: he was unable to play them. Thereupon Herr Sterkel looked
through a pile of music but was unable to find his copy of the Variations. With
some difficulty we persuaded Beethoven to play them from memory. It seemed to us
as if the Kapellmeister was of the opinion that Beethoven had actually written
them but was himself perhaps unable to play them. Beethoven noticed this too. So
he sat down and played them to the astonishment of all those present from Bonn who
had never heard him play in such a manner. For he played them completely in the
manner of the Herr Kapellmeister with the utmost daintiness and brilliant lightness,
as if these difficult variations were really as light as Sterkel's own Sonata, and added a
couple of new variations for good measure. The Herr Kapellmeister was unbounded
in his praises and insisted that we visit him on our return journey. This we were
unable to do because of a lack of time.

In Mergentheim I only remember that he had written a Cantata [on the death of
Joseph II] which we rehearsed several times, but it was not performed at Court. We
all raised objections to the difficult passages which occurred; but he contended that
all the figures were quite unusual and that therein lay the difficulty. Father Ries, who
was conducting in Mergentheim, also expressed his opinion forcefully, and so the
Cantata was not produced at Court. We have never seen anything further of it.

TDR I, 246 f., 254. (Nikolaus Simrock was a French horn player in the Bonn Court orchestra; later he
became a musical publisher in Bonn. Beethoven went on this journey as a member of the Elector's musical
establishment in the autumn of 1791.)

Anton Schindler writes about Beethoven's youth:

Further or other more outstanding events in any detail regarding Beethoven's life
in his native city are not known to us. The long period of peace on the soil of Germany
lasted until the beginning of the 1790s. Musicians were bound to their duties at
the Courts, at all of which the fostering of music always took pride of place. The
concern with earning a livelihood, and also the urge towards further training and the
solitude that his budding genius required, the absence of all journalistic publicity
and other well-known methods of our present glorious age which transforms our
schoolboys into finished artists – it is in these and other internal and external factors
that we must seek the reasons why the youth of the composer, who was one day to
give his name to an era in German art, is so lacking in significant art-historical
incidents. So empty was it of miraculous and romantic anecdotes that the young

Beethoven cannot be compared with so many of our youthful prodigy geniuses who, at the same age, have already astonished the world with operas and symphonies.

Perhaps another reason for this paucity may lie in the fact that our young piano-player, organist and composer endeavoured, from his childhood onward, to be a man in the true meaning of the word and to achieve the most fundamental human principles, in complete antithesis to the musical demi-gods of our own day. And particularly it was his aspiration to achieve his highest task as a man, and from this task he never deviated. This is made clear in a passage from a letter of 29 June 1800 to Wegeler: 'This much I can tell you, that when you see me again I will be really great; not only as an artist but as a man. You will find me better, more fully developed, and if the prosperity of our fatherland has somewhat improved, then shall my art be directed towards the benefit of the poor. Oh happy moment, how fortunate I consider myself that I can contribute to this end, that I myself can bring this to pass!'

Schindler I, 15 f.

It was decided that Beethoven needed more expert guidance than was available in the provincial Court at Bonn, and in 1787 he was sent to Vienna to study with the great Mozart. Beethoven certainly met Mozart in Vienna and heard him play the piano, but it is doubtful whether Ludwig received any serious instructions from Mozart. He had been in Vienna only a few months when he heard that his mother was seriously ill; he broke off his stay in the Austrian capital and returned to Bonn where, in his own words, 'I found my mother still alive but in a wretched state of health' (TDR I, 200). His mother's death was a profound shock, all the more so as Ludwig saw his father Johann becoming a senile alcoholic. Beethoven was now, to all intents and purposes, head of the family and responsible for supporting his two younger brothers, Caspar Anton Carl (1774–1815) and Nikolaus Johann (1776–1848). After he finally moved to Vienna for good in 1792, Beethoven called his brothers there too, and for a time they helped him manage his rather complicated affairs, particularly in dealing with music publishers. Johann became an apothecary and lived in Linz; he later amassed a tidy fortune and bought a small estate at Gneixendorf near Krems on the Danube, where Beethoven visited him the autumn of 1826. The other brother, who became a banking clerk in Vienna, had a son, Carl, who was later to play an important and extremely unhappy rôle in Beethoven's life. Both brothers married wives of whom Beethoven violently disapproved. Beethoven's father Johann died in December 1792, a month after Beethoven had settled in Vienna.

24 *Caspar Risbeck describes Vienna in the late eighteenth century:*

Music is the only thing in which the nobility shows good taste. Many houses have their own special band of musicians, and all public performances indicate that this form of art is held in the highest esteem here. One can assemble four to five large orchestras, all of them unequalled. The number of actual virtuosos is small, but as regards orchestral musicians it would be hard to hear anything more beautiful in the whole world. I have heard thirty to forty instruments playing together, and all of them produce a tone so true, clean and distinct that one might have thought one was listening to a single unnaturally loud instrument. One stroke of the bow brings all the violins to life, and one breath all the wind instruments.... There are about 400 musicians here who organize themselves into regular associations and often work together undivided for many years.

Caspar Risbeck, *Briefe eines reisenden Franzosen über Deutschland an seinen Bruder zu Paris*, 2 vols, translated by K. R., 2nd corrected edition, 1784, vol. I, 275f. (Risbeck travelled through Germany and the Austrian Monarchy and stayed some time in Vienna, where he attempted to further his career as an actor.)

Johann Friedrich Reichardt describes the Viennese nobility:

The nobility were probably the most musical that has ever existed. The whole population took part in the happy art, and their lively spirit, their sensual, pleasure-loving character demanded variety and cheerful music on all occasions. What with the open-handedness of the Court and the nobility, the general prosperity of the people and the incredibly low prices of food, it was possible for a host of foreign artists to visit Vienna and to settle there, even for the rest of their lives, without any steady fixed engagement. In Berlin this would be possible at most for music teachers, particularly piano teachers, all of whom, however – and at that time rightly so – belonged to the school of Bach.

(Kapellmeister Reichardt visited Vienna in 1783 and published an account of his impressions in the *Allgemeine Musikalische Zeitung*, Leipzig, No. 41, 13 October 1813.)

Dr Gerhard von Breuning describes Beethoven's first visit to Vienna:

Beethoven arrived in Vienna during the winter of 1786–87 and was soon welcomed everywhere with open arms. He found an especially cordial reception from the best-known art-loving families of the aristocracy. Wegeler also soon arrived, in 1787, armed with particularly warm recommendations and subsidies from the Elector. He, like Beethoven, received an entrée into the circle of the celebrated professors and doctors of the Josephinum: Brambilla, Gerhard von Vering, Gottfried van Swieten, Hunczovsky, Adam Schmidt, Wilhelm Schmitt and many others.

Breuning 30.

Carl Czerny writes about Beethoven and Mozart:

In later years Beethoven also told me that he had often heard Mozart play and that, since in his day the invention of the Fortepiano was as yet in its infancy, Mozart had become used to playing in a manner suited to the more customary harpsichords, which was not at all suited to the Fortepiano. Afterwards I made the acquaintance of several people who had studied with Mozart and found that their way of playing fully bore out this observation.

Once, in my house, Beethoven saw the scores of the six Mozart Quartets. He opened the 5th in A [K. 464] and said 'That is a work! In it Mozart said to the world: "See what I could create if the time had come for you!"'

26

Czerny 14, 11. (Carl Czerny, the inventor of a famous piano method, was, in his youth, a pupil of Beethoven.)

Carl Holz tells Otto Jahn about Beethoven's visit to Mozart:

When he was a boy, Beethoven was taken to Mozart, who told him to play; whereupon he improvised. 'That is very pretty,' said Mozart, 'but studied.' Beethoven was vexed and asked for a subject on which he improvised in such a way that Mozart said to some friends, 'Watch out for him, he will have something to tell you.'

Kerst II, 185. (Carl Holz, because of his cheerful character, was a very welcome friend of Beethoven's. Otto Jahn, the great biographer of Mozart, also collected material on Beethoven, whose life he intended to write. But he died, in 1869, before he was able to begin his work.)

Cipriani Potter tells Alexander Wheelock Thayer about his meetings with Beethoven:

Potter also recalled several small particulars from the time of his meeting with Beethoven. He sometimes accompanied the Master on his walks in the country around Vienna. Beethoven would often stop, look about him and give expression to the pleasure which nature aroused in him. One day Potter asked him who, with the exception of himself, was the greatest living composer. Beethoven appeared to reflect for a moment, then he called out, 'Cherubini'. 'And who among dead Masters?' asked Potter further. Beethoven replied that he had formerly regarded Mozart as the greatest, but since he had become acquainted with Handel, he put him in the first place.

TDR IV, 56f. (Potter became Director of the Royal Academy of Music. He met Beethoven in 1817 in Vienna.)

29 *Carl Holz on the subject of Beethoven as a Freemason:*

Beethoven was a Freemason but, in his later years, not a practising one.

Kerst II, 187.

Caroline Pichler describes the Viennese Freemasons:

A characteristic feature of the reign of the Emperor Joseph II were the movements which flourished openly in the social world through the so-called secret societies. The order of Freemasons carried on its activities with an almost absurd publicity. Freemason songs were printed, composed and sung everywhere. Freemason insignia were worn as pendants on watches; ladies received white gloves from apprentices; several articles of fashion, such as the white satin muffs with blue-edged seams, representing mason's aprons, were known as 'à la franc-maçon'. Many men joined out of curiosity . . . Others had different motives. At that time, it was not unadvantageous to belong to this brotherhood, which had its members in every circle and had known how to entice leaders, presidents and governors into its bosom. For there, one brother helped the other . . . There were all sorts and varieties of masons . . . and during the last years of the reign of Joseph II they caused a great deal of mischief.

Caroline Pichler, *Denkwürdigkeiten aus meinem Leben*, Vienna 1844, I, 105. (Caroline Pichler, whose mother had been a secretary to the Empress Maria Theresa, wrote poetry and plays.)

Beethoven's most important patron in Bonn, apart from the Archbishop and Elector himself, was Ferdinand Ernst Gabriel, Count von Waldstein. He was one of those responsible for persuading the Elector to send Beethoven to Vienna the second time. A trained musician himself, Count Waldstein is said to have encouraged Beethoven in the art of extemporized variations on a given theme, something for which the young composer soon grew famous in Vienna's musical salons. As was often the case in relations between Beethoven and his patrons, some frightful quarrel must have occurred between them, for the conversation book of December 1819 quoted below shows that by then they were not even on speaking terms; but Beethoven immortalized their once happy relationship by dedicating to Waldstein one of his very greatest piano Sonatas (Op. 53).

It was now decided that Beethoven should study with Haydn, Mozart having died in December 1791. On his return journey from London in 1792, Haydn was shown a score of Beethoven's *Cantata on the Death of Joseph II*, and immediately accepted Beethoven as a composition pupil. Beethoven arrived in Vienna towards the middle of November 1792 and began to take lessons in counterpoint with Haydn who, however, being extremely busy with compositions for his second London journey, was an inattentive teacher. Nevertheless Haydn recognized that 'Beethoven will in time fill the position of one of Europe's greatest composers and I shall be proud to be able to speak of myself as his teacher . . .'. The rather humorous way Beethoven found to improve his badly corrected counterpoint exercises is detailed in the documents below: Beethoven first went to Johann Baptist Schenk and later, when Haydn returned to England in January 1794, Albrechtsberger took on the job of teaching Beethoven strict counterpoint. Ludwig also studied Italian vocal writing with Antonio Salieri. His first published compositions in Vienna, Op. 1, were three piano Trios, which came out in 1794.

Beethoven was soon famous in Vienna as a pianist and made his *début* playing the B-Flat Concerto Op. 19 at the Burgtheater on 29 March 1795. The subscription list of the Op. 1 Trios shows that barely two years after he had arrived in Vienna, Beethoven had gained a wide circle of patrons and admirers. Foremost among them was Prince Carl Lichnowsky, a pupil of Mozart's, in whose house Beethoven lived for a time in the mid 1790s; Beethoven dedicated Op. 1 to him and many other important works.

Dedication in Beethoven's album:

Dear Beethowen!

You are now going to Vienna in fulfilment of a wish that has for so long been thwarted. The *genius* of Mozart still mourns and weeps the death of its pupil. It has found a refuge in the inexhaustible Hayden, but no occupation; through him it desires once more to find a union with someone. Through your unceasing diligence, receive Mozart's spirit from the hands of Hayden.

Bonn, the 29th Oct. 792.

Your true friend Waldstein.   *27, 28*

Ludwig van Beethovens Stammbuch, facsimile edition with comments by Dr Hans Gerstinger, Bielefeld and Leipzig 1927.

Count Waldstein described by Anton Schindler:

Count Waldstein was a Knight of the German Order, the favourite and the constant companion of the young Elector. Later he became Commander of the German Order in Virnsberg and Chamberlain to the Emperor. He was not only a connoisseur of music but also a practising musician. As such, he was able to exercise a direct influence on the development of Beethoven's young talent. It was on his suggestion that Beethoven developed his ability to conceive and perform variations on an improvised theme, an art in which, during later years, he was unrivalled, let alone excelled, by any of his contemporaries . . . . To what extent Count von Waldstein already valued Beethoven's talent immediately following these first indications, and what a future he predicted for him, is apparent from a letter he wrote to the young composer, the contents of which are given [above, previous document]. From Wegeler, moreover, we learn that this true nobleman provided the young composer with several financial subsidies which, in order to spare Beethoven's sensitivity, were generally passed off as a small munificence from the Elector. It should also be recalled that Beethoven, when at the peak of his artistic career, openly expressed his gratitude to this patron, protector and fellow artist, by the dedication of his great Sonata in C Major, Op. 53, which was published in 1806.

Schindler I, 6.

From the Conversation book for December 1819 :

[Unknown person]
That is the inconvenience of public places. One is so exposed in everything. <u>Everyone</u> listens and eavesdrops.

Count Waldstein was also in the vicinity.

Does he live here?

Konv. N. I, 214. (Beethoven was obviously no longer on speaking terms with Waldstein.)

Baroness du Montet on Count Waldstein:

Count Ferdinand Waldstein is terribly in debt, and has been since he was the Finance Minister of the Elector of Cologne. He is a Knight of the German Order and was destined to enjoy a considerable income. A diplomat with no accreditation; a financier with no credit. He was in duty bound to celibacy on account of his vows, but he obtained a release from them and married (1812). Through mistaken calculations he ruined both himself and the witty and charming Countess Isabella Rzewuska. Count Waldstein, who possesses an unsurpassed intelligence, has not been able to establish his good reputation. Gifted with a righteous and noble heart and with exquisite ideas, he has not added anything to the glory of his name – he is merely a most amiable man.

Du Montet 174.

56

Christian Gottlob Neefe reports on Beethoven's second journey to Vienna:

In November of last year Ludwig van Beethoven, Assistant Court Organist and now unquestionably one of the foremost piano-players, went to Vienna at the expense of our Elector in order to perfect himself further, under Haydn's direction, in the art of composition.

Spazier's *Berliner Musik Zeitung* of 26 October 1793.

From Beethoven's notebook on his journey to Vienna:

Tip [Coblenz], because the fellow drove us through the middle of the Hessian Army where we were in danger of being beaten up, and drove like the devil – one small thaler.

TDR I, 271.

From Beethoven's album:

Friendship with the good
Grows long like the evening shadows
Until the sun of life goes down.
                    /Herder./

Bonn, 1 November 1792.   Your true friend Eleonore Breuning.

See! Oh friend, Albion calls you.
See! The shady grove, which entices the singer
hasten then without delay
over the surging sea
where a more beauteous grove offers you its shade
and a bard [Salomon] stretches out his hand to you in friendship,
who from our fields
fled to Albion's protection.
There let thy song ring loudly and victorious,
let it ring wildly through the grove, across the waves of the sea
to those fields
whence thou hadst fled with joy.

Bonn, 1 9 bre [Nov.] 1792.

                    Think of your friend
                    [Christoph] Ed. Breuning.

Beethovens Stammbuch, op. cit. (Albion refers to a plan for Beethoven to accompany Haydn to London, where the latter had gone with Salomon on a concert tour. This plan did not materialize.)

Serene Electoral Highness!

I humbly take the liberty of sending Your Serene Electoral Highness some musical works, *viz.* a Quintet, an eight-part Parthie, an oboe Concerto, Variations for the Fortepiano, and a Fugue, compositions of my dear pupil Beethoven, with whose care I have been graciously entrusted. I flatter myself that these pieces, which I may recommend as evidence of his assiduity over and above his actual studies, may be graciously accepted by Your Serene Electoral Highness. Connoisseurs and non-connoisseurs must candidly admit, from these present pieces, that Beethoven will in time fill the position of one of Europe's greatest composers, and I shall be proud to be able to speak of myself as his teacher, I only wish that he might remain with me a little while longer.

While we are on the subject of Beethoven, Your Serene Electoral Highness will perhaps permit me to say a few words concerning his financial status. 100 [Ducats] were allotted to him during the past year. Your Serene Electoral Highness is no doubt convinced that this sum was insufficient, and not even enough to live on; undoubtedly Your Highness also had his own reasons for choosing to send him into the great world with such a paltry sum. Under these circumstances and to prevent him from falling into the hands of usurers, I have in part gone bail for him and in part lent him money myself, with the result that he owes me 500 fl., of which not a Kreutzer was spent unnecessarily; which sum I would ask you to send to him here. And since the interest on borrowed money grows continually and is in any case very tedious for an artist like Beethoven, I think that if Your Serene Electoral Highness were to send him 1000 fl. for the coming year, Your Highness would earn his eternal gratitude, and at the same time relieve him of all his distress. For the teachers who are absolutely essential for him, and the display which is necessary if he is to gain admission into numerous salons, reduce this sum to such an extent that only the bare minimum remains. As for the extravagance which one fears will tempt any young man who goes into the great world, I think I can answer for that to Your Serene Electoral Highness; for a hundred circumstances have confirmed me in my opinion that he is capable of sacrificing everything without any restraint for his art. In view of so many tempting occasions, this is most remarkable, and gives every security to Your Serene Electoral Highness – in view of the gracious kindness that we expect – that your Highness will not be wasting any of your grace on usurers as far as Beethoven is concerned. In the hope that Your Serene Electoral Highness will continue his further patronage of my dear pupil by graciously acceding to this my request, I am, with profound respect,

Your Serene Electoral Highness'
most humble and obedient
Joseph Haydn.
Kapellmeister of Prince Nicolaus Esterházy.

Vienna, 23 November 1793.

The Collected Correspondence and London Notebooks of Joseph Haydn, ed. H. C. Robbins Landon, London 1959, 141 f.

Letter from Bartholomäus Ludwig Fischenich, Professor at the University of Bonn, to Charlotte von Schiller, 23 January 1793:

I am enclosing a musical setting of the *Feuerfarbe* and I would like to know your opinion of it. It is by a young man from here, whose musical talents are praised everywhere and whom the Elector has sent to Haydn in Vienna. He is also going to set Schiller's *Joy* with all the verses to music. I expect something perfect [from him] for, as far as I know, his ambitions are for the great and the sublime. Haydn has hitherto reported that he would turn over grand operas to him and would soon have to give up composing. Normally he does not bother with such trivialities as the enclosed [song], which he only composed at the request of a lady.

Ludwig Schiedermair, *Der junge Beethoven*, Leipzig 1925, p. 221. (*Feuerfarbe* = Op. 52, No. 2.)

Jahrbuch der Tonkunst von Wien und Prag, *1796, writes about Beethoven and Albrechtsberger:*

Beethoven, a musical genius, has chosen Vienna as his residence for the past two years. He is widely admired for the unusual velocity of his playing, and is astounding in the way he masters the most formidable difficulties with the greatest of ease. He seems already to have entered into the inner sanctuary of music, distinguishing himself for his precision, feeling and taste; consequently his fame has risen considerably. A living proof of his true love of art lies in the fact that he has put himself in the hands of our immortal Haydn in order to be initiated into the holy secrets of the art of music. The latter great Master, during his absence, has turned him over to our great Albrechtsberger. What cannot be expected when such a great genius places himself under the guidance of such excellent masters! There have already been several beautiful Sonatas by him, among which his latest [Op. 2] is regarded as particularly outstanding.

34

Kerst I, 30.

Anton Schindler relates Beethoven's reminiscences of Albrechtsberger:

About two or three weeks before Beethoven's death, it was necessary to find one of his works, which was said to be buried under a disorderly and untidy pile of music in the adjoining room. After Beethoven's brother had looked for it in vain, I tried to find it. In the course of this dusty work, my eye fell on a copy-book consisting of a few sheets written in a clear but unknown hand which, upon closer examination, proved to contain phrases worked out from various exercises in counterpoint. When I went to the sick-bed and asked him what these were, Beethoven answered: 'Oh, examples by Albrechtsberger which he had worked out for his pupils.' He kept the copy-book near him for several days and leafed through it once in a while, and also recalled with humorous comments the days long since past when he had occupied himself with such work.

32

Neue Zeitschrift für Musik, No. 16, 1851.

Letter from Albrechtsberger to Beethoven (15 December 1796):

My very best wishes for your name-day tomorrow. May God give you health and satisfaction and grant you much good fortune. My dear Beethoven, if you should happen to have an hour at your disposal, your old teacher invites you to spend it with him.

Stephan Ley, *Wahrheit, Zweifel und Irrtum in der Kunde von Beethovens Leben*, Wiesbaden 1955, p. 7.

Dolezalek to Jahn, 30 October 1852:

At that time, composers were inimical towards Beethoven, whom they did not understand and who had a sharp tongue. Dolezalek brought an article* about a quartet by Beethoven.
Albrechtsberger: 'Who is that thing by?'
Dolezalek: 'Beethoven.'
Albrechtsberger: 'Ah, don't have anything to do with him. He has learned nothing and will never amount to anything.'
Kotzeluch threw the C minor trio on the floor when he [Dolezalek] played it to him.

Kerst II, 191. (Johann Nepomuk Emanuel Dolezalek, a good musician, knew Beethoven when he was a young man and related his reminiscences of Beethoven to Otto Jahn on 30 October 1852.)

35   *Johann Schenk about his pupil Beethoven:*

In 1792, His Imperial Highness, Archduke Maximilian, Elector of Cologne, was pleased to send his protegé Louis van Beethoven to Vienna in order that he might study musical composition with Joseph Haydn. Towards the end of July [1793] the Abbé Gelinek informed me that he had made the acquaintance of a young man who displayed a rare virtuosity on the pianoforte, such as he had not heard since Mozart. At the same time he explained that Beethoven had begun to study counterpoint with Haydn more than six months before, but was still at work on the first exercise. He
82 also said that His Excellency Baron van Swieten had warmly recommended the study of counterpoint to him and often inquired how far he had progressed in his studies. On Beethoven's writing desk I came across a few phrases of the first exercise in counterpoint. After a cursory examination it was clear to me that in every tonality (short as these were) there were several mistakes. This tended to bear out the truth of Gelinek's above-mentioned remarks. Since I was now convinced that my pupil was ignorant of the primary rules of counterpoint, I gave him the universally known text-book by Joseph Fux, *Gradus ad Parnassum*, so that he might obtain a summary of the subsequent exercises. Joseph Haydn, who had returned to Vienna from London towards the end of the previous year, was engaged in harnessing his Muse to the

*German *Arbeit*, which means literally 'work', *i.e.* either an article about the quartet or, perhaps, a *Bearbeitung* (arrangement) which Dolezalek made.

60

composition of great new masterpieces. Taken up with these important endeavours, it was clear that Haydn could not easily occupy himself with teaching grammar. Now I was seriously anxious to be of assistance to one so eager to acquire knowledge. Before I began to teach him, however, I pointed out to him that our work together must forever remain a secret. In this regard, I ordered him to copy out once again every passage which I had corrected in my own hand, so that every time that Haydn examined it he would not notice the work of a strange hand. A year later, Beethoven came into conflict with Gelinek, the cause of which I have forgotten. It seems to me, however, that both sides were to blame. As a result of their dispute, Gelinek became angry and revealed my secret. Beethoven and his brothers made no secret of it . . . .

In about mid-May [1793] he informed me that he would shortly go to Eisenstadt with Haydn and would stay there until the beginning of winter. He did not yet know the day of departure. At the beginning of June I went to his house at the usual hour – but my good Louis was nowhere to be seen. He had left me the following little note which I transcribe word for word.

'Dear Schenk,

'I wish that I did not have to depart today for Eisenstadt. I would have liked to talk with you once more. In the meanwhile, you may count on my gratitude for the kindnesses you have shown me. I will make every effort to return them. I hope to see you again soon and to enjoy the pleasure of your company. Farewell and do not entirely forget

your
Beethoven.'

TDR I, 329ff. (Schenk wrote this document in summer 1830.)

Schindler describes Beethoven's meeting with Schenk:

One day in the spring of 1824, Beethoven was walking along the Graben with me, when we met Schenk. Beethoven was beside himself with joy at seeing once more this old friend of whom he had not heard for many years; he seized his hand and dragged him off to the nearby inn called *Zum Jägerhorn* and into the back room which had to be lit up even in the daytime. In order to remain undisturbed he closed the door. Then he began to open up all the secrets of his heart. After complaints about bad luck and description and discussion of misfortunes, events of the years 1793–94 were recalled. Upon which Beethoven broke out into loud laughter, remembering how they both had played a trick on father Haydn, who had never noticed anything. This scene was the occasion of my hearing for the first time about the unusual relationship which had existed between the two men. Beethoven, who at that moment stood at the summit of his art, overwhelmed the modest composer of the *Dorfbarbier* as well as the grand opera *Achmet und Almanzine* and several other *Singspiele,* and who lived by giving lessons, with the most fervent gratitude for the part he had played during his years of study and for his friendly devotion. The leave-taking of the two after that remarkable hour was moving, as if it were for life, and indeed so it was – Beethoven and Schenk never saw one another again after that day.

Schindler I, 31f.

From Ignaz Moscheles' diary:

[1808] How astonished I was one day when I saw at the home of Court Kapellmeister Salieri, whom I had not found at home, a note written in capital letters lying on the table which read 'The pupil Beethoven was here'. That made me think. A Beethoven can still learn something from a Salieri? How much more could I! Salieri had been the pupil and the warmest admirer of Gluck. Only he refused to recognize the value of Mozart and his works; that was well known. And yet I went to him, became his pupil, and was, for three years, his assistant at the Opera. On account of this, I received permission to visit every theatre without payment. It was a light-hearted and very stirring existence in my beloved Vienna.

Aus Ignaz Moscheles Leben, ed. by his wife, Leipzig 1872, p. 11. (Ignaz Moscheles, born in 1794, was the most famous pianist of his day.)

Carl Czerny describes Beethoven's piano-playing:

Clementi's manner is distinguished by the regular position of the hands, a firm touch and tone, clear fluent execution and a correct declamation, and also in part by great velocity and dexterity of the fingers.

Cramer's and Dussek's manner: beautiful *cantabile*; avoidance of all coarse effects; a surprising smoothness in the runs and passages as a substitute for fluency, which is less necessary in their works; also a beautiful legato linked to the use of the pedal.

Mozart's school: clear and markedly brilliant playing based more on staccato than legato; a witty and lively execution. The pedal is rarely used and never necessary.

Beethoven's manner: characteristic and passionate strength, alternating with all the charms of a smooth *cantabile*, is its outstanding feature.

The expressive means are often intensified to an extreme degree, especially as regards a humorous inclination. The piquant dominating manner is rarely employed. But for that reason total effects, partly by means of a full sounding legato, partly by a judicious use of the forte-pedal, etc., are more often applied.

Mozart's manner, which was so excellently perfected by Hummel, was more suited to the German Fortepianos which combine a delicate and shallow touch with a great clarity, and thus are best adapted for general use and for use by children.

Beethoven, who appeared around 1790, drew entirely new and daring passages from the Fortepiano by the use of the pedal, by an exceptionally characteristic way of playing, particularly distinguished by a strict legato of the chords, and thus created a new type of singing tone and many hitherto unimagined effects. His playing did not possess that clean and brilliant elegance of certain other pianists. On the other hand, it was spirited, grandiose and, especially in adagio, very full of feeling and romantic. His performance, like his compositions, was a tone-painting of a very high order and conceived only for a total effect.

Carl Czerny, *Vollständige theoretisch-praktische Pianoforte Schule*, Vienna n.d. Part III, Ch. 15. Kerst I, 63.

Wiener Zeitung of 1 April 1795:

On 29 and 30 March, in the Imperial Royal Court Theatre near the Burg, an oratorio   *38*
devised by Herr Kapellmeister Kartellieri, entitled *Joas, King of Judah,** was
performed at the regular large concert of the local *Tonkünstler-Gesellschaft* [Society
of Musical Artists] for the benefit of the widows' and orphans' fund.... As an inter-
mezzo, on the first evening, the celebrated Herr Ludwig van Beethoven reaped the
unanimous applause of the audience for his performance on the pianoforte of a
completely new concerto [in B-Flat, Op. 19] composed by him.

Ferdinand Ries describes Beethoven's relations with Haydn:

The three Trios by Beethoven (Op. 1) were to be performed for the first time before   *39, 40*
the art world at a soirée given by Prince Lichnowsky. The majority of artists and
music-lovers had been invited, in particular Haydn, whose verdict everybody was most
eager to hear. The Trios were played and immediately aroused great interest. Haydn,
too, said many good things about them but advised Beethoven not to publish the
third Trio in C Minor. This surprised Beethoven very much, inasmuch as he considered
it the best, just as today it is still the most popular and arouses the greatest enthusiasm.
Because of this, Haydn's remark made a bad impression on Beethoven and led him to
believe that Haydn was envious, jealous and badly disposed towards him. I must admit
that when Beethoven said this to me, I did not really believe it. I then took the
opportunity of asking Haydn himself. His answer, however, confirmed Beethoven's
remarks, inasmuch as he said that he had not believed this Trio would have been so
quickly and easily understood and so favourably received by the public.

WRBN 84 f.   (Ferdinand Ries had been Beethoven's pupil.)

Anton Schindler about Beethoven's relations with Haydn:

It is permissible, however, to be surprised by Haydn's opinion when one is acquainted
with his own Trios. As far as I am concerned I place the event in the long series of
misunderstandings of which there were, unfortunately, too many in Beethoven's life.

Schindler I, 54.

*Correctly: *Gioas, re di Giuda* by Casimir Antonio Cartellieri (1772 – 1807).

Baroness Du Montet describes Princess Lichnowsky:

In high Viennese society there were, at that time, a number of gentlemen and ladies who combined distinction with amiability ... Princess Lichnowsky, the beautiful ... Countess Kinsky and a few others. . . . But as a result of a peculiarity very widespread at that time among the high Austrian nobility, these highly-placed persons, in the truest sense of the word, were nearly all friends of the French Revolution, and hated the émigrés and the [French] aristocrats.

Du Montet 42.

Beethoven's *début* as an orchestral composer in Vienna took place on Sunday, 22 November 1795, St Cecilia's Day. Beethoven conducted Twelve Minuets (WoO 7) and Twelve German Dances (WoO 8) for the famous ball of the pension fund of the Society of Artists, for which Haydn and Mozart had composed most of their greatest dance music for orchestra. These masked balls were held at the Redoutensaal on the Josephsplatz in Vienna and usually, each year, two composers were asked to write the dances, one for the large room and one for the small room. Haydn had composed the Minuets and German Dances for the 1792 season and was probably responsible for getting Beethoven the commission in 1795. When Haydn returned from London in the late summer of 1795, he and Beethoven often appeared together at concerts, Haydn conducting and Beethoven playing the piano. Haydn launched three of his new Salomon Symphonies, composed in 1794 and 1795, at a concert in the Redoutensaal on 16 December 1795, and Beethoven played his Piano Concerto Op. 19. A few weeks later, on 8 January 1796, they again collaborated at such a concert in the Redoutensaal, this time for the benefit of the singer Maria Bolla. Beethoven was now becoming not only a successful pianist but a highly successful composer. Among the many Viennese publishers who clamoured to print his latest works was the distinguished firm of Artaria & Co. on the Kohlmarkt; Artaria had published many of Haydn's and Mozart's compositions and they immediately issued, for instance, the successful Minuets and German Dances that Beethoven had composed for the Redoutensaal.

Wiener Zeitung of 14 November 1795, No. 91:

37 The masked ball for the Pension Fund of the Society of Artists will be given this year on Sunday, 22 November, in the Imperial-Royal Ballroom. The music for the Minuet and German Dances for this ball will once again be in new arrangements. For the small ballroom the music has been composed by the master hand of Herr Ludwig van Beethoven as a token of his desire for solidarity between the various branches of the arts.

Wiener Zeitung of 16 December 1795, No. 100:

Musical Academy.

On Friday next, the 18th inst., Herr Kapellmeister Haydn will give a large musical academy in the small Ballroom, in which Mad. Tomeoni und Herr Mombelli will sing; Herr van Beethoven will play a concerto of his own composition on the Fortepiano; and three symphonies, not previously heard here, which Herr

Kapellmeister [Haydn] composed during his last visit to London, will be performed. Admission tickets may be obtained from Herr Kapellmeister Haydn at his residence on the Neuen Markt, in the Hoföbstlerisches Haus, third floor, at all hours.

New Music:

Artaria and Co. on the Kohlmarkt.

By Herr Ludwig van Beethoven; 12 new Minuets and 12 German Dances, in piano score. These were performed on the 22 November inst. on behalf of the Society of Artists at the masked ball in the Imperial-Royal Ballroom and, as is well known, were received with applause. This piano score has been arranged by the composer himself.

The price of the minuets is 45 Kreutzer, the German Dances 45 Kreutzer.

Ignaz Moscheles meets Beethoven at Artaria's:

One morning by chance I happened to be in the music shop of Domenico Artaria who, at that time, had just published some of my early attempts at composition, when a man entered with a short quick gait and slid through the crowd of ladies and professors, who were assembled there either on business or else to discuss musical affairs, without looking around, as if he wanted to remain unobserved, and went straight through to Artaria's private office at the far end of the shop. Artaria thereupon called me in and said, 'This is Beethoven,' and to the composer he said, 'This is the young man about whom I just spoke to you.' Beethoven nodded to me in a friendly way and said that he had heard a good report about me. To a few humble and respectful remarks which I stammered out, he made no reply and seemed only to wish to bring the conversation to a close. . . . I had observed Artaria talking very close to his ear. . . . I never missed Schuppanzigh's quartets, where Beethoven was often present, nor the delightful concerts in the Augarten where he conducted his own symphonies. I also heard him play a few times; this he did very rarely, sometimes in public, sometimes in private circles. The pieces I heard him play which made the most impression on me were the *Fantasia* with orchestra accompaniment and chorus, and the *Concerto in C Minor*. I made it a point to meet him in the rooms of two of his friends, Zmeskall and Zizius, through whose musical meetings Beethoven first found his way to the attention of the public. But instead of a closer acquaintance, I generally had to be satisfied with a distant greeting from him . . . .

In June 1814, when Artaria undertook to publish a piano score of Beethoven's *Fidelio*, he asked the composer if the preparation of it could be entrusted to me. Beethoven agreed under the condition that he must see the arrangement of each number before it reached the hands of the engraver. Nothing could have been more welcome to me for, in this way, I saw open to me the long desired opportunity of coming closer to the great man, and to derive advantages from his remarks and corrections. In the course of my frequent visits, the number of which I tried to increase by means of every possible excuse, he treated me with the most friendly consideration. Although his increasing deafness was the greatest hindrance to our

49, 50

69

intercourse, he nevertheless gave me many instructive suggestions and actually played such parts as he wished to have arranged for the piano in a particular way. I regarded it, however, as my duty not to put his friendliness to a proof and not to rob him of his valuable time through later visits. But I often saw him at Mälzel's where he used to go to discuss the various plans and models for a metronome which was in the last stages of completion, and also to negotiate over *The Battle of Vittoria* which he had written at Mälzel's suggestion.

TDR III, 431 f. (Dr Johann Zizius [1772–1824], professor of political science and teacher at the Vienna University, had many an evening of music, where the best artists played.)

> Beethoven now had a very wide circle of friends and colleagues. Among them was the famous actor Johann Heinrich Friedrich Müller, who lived in a big apartment-house complex called the Bürgerspital, next to the Kärntnerthortheater, one of Vienna's two principal theatres (the other was the Burgtheater, where Mozart had first conducted *Figaro* and Haydn was to conduct the first public performance of *The Creation* in 1798). In the Bürgerspital there also lived a Hungarian aristocrat, Nikolaus Zmeskall von Domanowecz, an excellent cellist who often participated in quartet parties and chamber music. He remained one of Beethoven's most faithful friends and the composer dedicated his Quartet in F Minor, Op. 95, to him. Later Zmeskall grew old and infirm, but it is touching to think that he was taken in a sedan chair to hear the first performance of the Ninth Symphony in 1824.

Carl Friedrich, Baron Kübeck von Kübau, describes how he made Beethoven's acquaintance at the actor Müller's house:

44
47

My aunt, who lived in the Bürgerspital, often visited a family who lived on the floor above her. The family was named M . . . . r [Müller]. The father had a great name as an artist; he was already very old and it seemed to me that he was always play-acting. There were two sons, of whom one was also an actor, but from what people said a very mediocre one; the other was a complete idiot. There were also daughters, of whom one was beautiful and married; the other was equipped with a somewhat too large nose but was very amusing. A lot of music-making went on there . . . . There was a new instrument, a Fortepiano manufactured by Herr Walter . . . . My aunt let it be known that I too knew how to play . . . . I played a couple of easy pieces from notes, but very indifferently, as the instrument was new to me . . . . The next time I came I found the hero of music, Herr van Beethoven. He was a small man with unkempt, bristling hair with no powder, which was unusual. He had a face deformed by pock-marks, small shining eyes, and a continuous movement of every limb in his body. He sat down at the Fortepiano and played in a masterly manner for half-an-hour to everyone's delight. Nina M . . . r, the jolly daughter of the artistic father, took it upon herself to embarrass me and introduced me to the great master as a young artist recently arrived from the provinces . . . . Beethoven looked at me with compassion, and his otherwise fierce countenance expressed visible appreciation of my embarrassment. He reproached Nina for her wantonness and said, 'We shall see if this childish youth has musical talent. But not today. Come to see me tomorrow, then I will drive everyone out of the room and we will have a try all by ourselves.' I went. It was 5 April 1796 . . . . He let me play a number of pieces for an hour. When we had finished he said to me, 'My dear fellow, you have no particular talent for music. Do not waste too much time on it. You do not lack, however, a certain facility or a strict training . . . . I can use you for a certain purpose and be of use to you at the same time. I teach a certain young person a few times a week. I can't do it more often, and that is not sufficient for her progress. Would you coach her daily in the pieces that I will then teach her to interpret? If so, I will recommend you.' I accepted his proposal with pleasure. On 8 April, Beethoven sent for me and took me to the place. The family consisted of father, daughter and governess. They were from Venice. The father had some secret business with the government and was, for the time being, settled in Vienna. He was a widower and was addressed as *Marchese*. His nose was a veritable promontory and stained with snuff. He spoke no German and his Latin was almost unintelligible. His name was M . . . .n. His daughter, addressed as Contessina, was named Julia, but was called Litta. She was 13 years old, had black eyes and a pale complexion . . . I had never before seen such a beautiful girl. She could speak only very broken German. The governess was born a Frenchwoman, Mademoiselle Marie Vedel, and spoke French, Italian, English and very fluent German. The Marchese turned me over to the governess who told me, through Herr van Beethoven, that I should come every day from 5 to 6 in the afternoon, and moreover that I should follow Herr van Beethoven's instructions to the letter, for which I would receive 20 florins monthly. . . . I should have liked to kiss Beethoven's hands, but he refused all thanks . . . .

On 10 March [1797] the governess told me that, because of political events, the Marchese could not remain in Vienna, and would flee to Prague. He had instructed her to pay me my fee for March. Beethoven had already given up [the lessons] in January. The man [Beethoven] was so much in demand everywhere, and gave lessons only out of kindness . . . .

Whoever sees Beethoven for the first time and knows nothing about him would surely take him for a malicious, ill-natured and quarrelsome drunkard who has no feeling for music . . . . On the other hand, he who sees him for the first time surrounded by his fame and his glory, will surely see musical talent in every feature of an ugly face . . . .

10 February[1801]. . . . How surprised I was this morning when I met Beethoven; He came towards me in his loping genius-gait and expressed his pleasure at seeing me again. We talked about all sorts of things . . . he embarked on his favourite subject, politics, which bores me very much. We took leave . . . .

Diaries of Carl Friedrich, Baron Kübeck von Kübau, published by his son, Max, Baron von Kübeck, 3 vols, Vienna 1919, 1, 9 f., 19, 24, 67. (Baron Kübeck von Kübau was an Austrian government official.)

Letter from Beethoven to Nikolaus Zmeskall von Domanowecz: 43

[Vienna 1798.]

My dear Baron Rubbish-driver,

Je vous suis bien obligé pour votre faiblesse de vos yeux. – Moreover, in future I refuse not to avail myself of the happy humour in which I sometimes find myself. For yesterday, because of your Zmeskall-Domanoveczish chatter, I became quite gloomy. The devil take you. I don't want to hear anything about your moral principles. Power is the moral strength of those who distinguish themselves above others, and it is also mine, and so if you start again today I will pester you to such an extent that you will find everything that I do is good and praiseworthy. (For I am coming to the *Schwan* though I'd prefer the *Ochs*; but that depends on your Zmeskalish-Domanoveczish decision.)

Adieu Baron Ba . . . . ron ron/nor/orn/rno/onr
(*voilà quelque chose* from the old pawnbroker)

TDR II, 115. Anderson 30.

Carl Holz on Zmeskall:

Zmeskall was a member of the Hungarian Chancellery and owned vineyards in Hungary. He was a somewhat dry man. Musical entertainments took place in his house.

Kerst II, 185.

Beethoven to Zmeskall (Dedication):

[September 1816]

Eleventh/ Quartet/ for/ two Violins, Viola and Violoncello/ dedicated/ to his friend/ Court Secretary/Nik: Zmeskall von Domanovetz/by/Ludwig van Beethoven/95th work/.

Letter from Beethoven on 16 December 1816 to Zmeskall:

Here, my dear Z, receive my affectionate dedication which I hope you will accept as a loving memento of our long friendship, and as a token of my esteem, and not consider it the end of what is now a long drawn-out thread (for you are one among my oldest friends in Vienna) . . . .

KHV 268.

From Beethoven's conversation book:

Joseph Czerny: Smeskall has been very ill in the last three months.

Unknown handwriting: Smeskall is unfortunately still ill and it seems that he will never be well again. He misses music very much.

Konv. N. book XXXIII, Autumn (November) 1819, 155 and book XXII, February 1820, page 56b.

30. Joseph Haydn (1732–1809). Portrait in oils by
Thomas Hardy, 1791. Royal College of Music, London.

At Christmas 1790, Haydn and the impresario Johann Peter Salomon
(a native of Bonn) stopped at Bonn on the way to London, and were
generously received by the Elector. Either at this time or later, in the
summer of 1792 (when on the return trip to Vienna), Beethoven was
introduced to Haydn.

31. View of Bonn from the Beul side of the Rhine. Anonymous coloured etching. Städtische Sammlungen, Bonn.

This drawing was probably made between 1792 and 1794, since French customs officers can be seen in the right-hand foreground. At that time the Elector had already left his dominions and the French Army had reached the Rhine. In July 1792, Beethoven had received permission from the Elector to go to Vienna to study with Joseph Haydn. In November he left Bonn forever.

74

33. Rondo for Pianoforte with Orchestra, WoO 6. Autograph. Gesellschaft der Musikfreunde, Vienna.

The page shows Beethoven's instructions to the copyist: 'Das Tempo I^{mo}♭♭♮6/8 muß in allen Stimmen wieder angezeigt werden' ('the tempo I^{mo}♭♭♮6/8 must be noted in all the parts'). It is believed that the Rondo served originally as the finale to the Piano Concerto in B flat, Op. 19.

◄ 32. Beethoven's contrapuntal studies. Autograph. Gesellschaft der Musikfreunde, Vienna.

When in 1794 Haydn went to London a second time, Johann Georg Albrechtsberger took Haydn's place in teaching counterpoint to Beethoven. The illustration shows corrections in Albrechtsberger's hand.

34. Johann Georg Albrechtsberger (1736–1809). Anonymous portrait in oils. Gesellschaft der Musikfreunde, Vienna.

Albrechtsberger was Court Organist and Kapellmeister at St. Stephen's Cathedral in Vienna. A famous musical theoretician, he was well fitted to give Beethoven a thorough training in counterpoint.

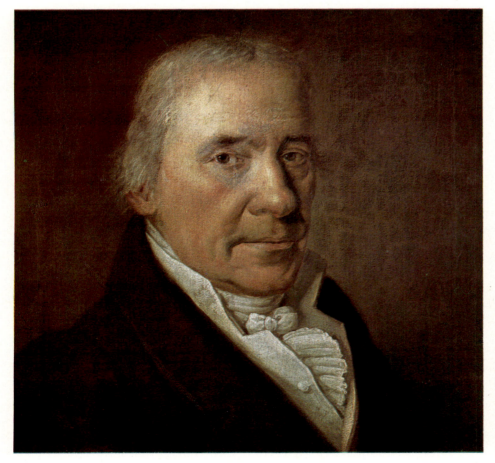

35. Johann Baptist Schenk (1753–1836). Anonymous portrait in oils. Gesellschaft der Musikfreunde, Vienna.

Dissatisfied with Haydn's teaching, Beethoven secured Schenk as his teacher. A popular operetta composer, Schenk did not wish to offend Haydn and went over Beethoven's contrapuntal studies with Haydn's corrections in such a secretive fashion that Haydn never realized that his own rather careless corrections were being subjected to a more severe scrutiny on Schenk's part.

36. Antonio Salieri (1750–1825). Anonymous portrait in oils. Gesellschaft der Musikfreunde, Vienna.

Antonio Salieri, Mozart's great rival and a favourite of the Emperor Joseph II and Viennese audiences, taught Beethoven operatic and vocal composition with particular reference to setting Italian texts.

37. Masked Ball in the great Redoutensaal in the Hofburg, Vienna. Engraving by Jos. Schütz, *c.* 1800. Prof. Hans Swarowsky, Vienna.

For the annual masked ball of the Pension Society for Vienna's Artists, Beethoven composed in 1795 his first orchestral works for Vienna: Twelve Minuets, WoO 7, and Twelve German Dances, WoO 8. He may have owed this commission to Haydn.

41. Carl Prince Lichnowsky (1756–1814). Anonymous portrait in oils. Hradec u Opavy, Czechoslovakia.

The Prince, who had been a pupil of Mozart's (the two had journeyed to Germany together), was a great admirer of Beethoven's. The composer lived for a time in the same house as the Prince and they both used the same servant. The Prince patiently overlooked Beethoven's eccentricities.

42. Marie Christiane, Princess Lichnowsky, née Countess Thun (1765–1841). Anonymous portrait in oils. Hradec u Opavy, Czechoslovakia.

The Princess, an excellent piano player, had also been Mozart's pupil.
She, too, was very understanding with Beethoven, who in turn revered her.

47. Johann Heinrich Friedrich Müller (1738–1815), famous actor in the Vienna Burgtheater (active from 1763 to 1801). Portrait in oils by Joseph Hickel. Portrait Collection of the Burgtheater, Vienna.

During the reign of Joseph II, Müller and his wife founded a famous school of actors, known as the 'Pflanzschule', which was designed to provide a steady stream of actors for the Imperial theatres in Vienna. The Müllers lived in a large apartment-house complex, called the Bürgerspital, and were friends of Beethoven's.

48. Carlo Artaria (1747–1808). Portrait in oils by J. Kreutzinger, c. 1780. Historisches Museum of the City of Vienna.

Carlo Artaria, doyen of the famous publishing house of Artaria & Co., soon recognized Beethoven's genius – and also the commercial success of his music. As quickly as 16 December 1795, Artaria published the Dances for the Redoutensaal.

49. Domenico Artaria (1775–1842) with his wife Teresa (1786–1844) and their son
August (1807–1893). Pastel by Johann Nepomuk Ender. Sturm family, Vienna.

50. The publishing house of Artaria & Co. on the Kohlmarkt in Vienna.
Engraved by Wett, drawn and coloured by A. Leithner. Sturm family, Vienna.

In 1770, Carlo Artaria and his cousin Francesco founded the house which became
famous as the leading Viennese music publisher. Haydn, Mozart, Beethoven and
many lesser-known composers appeared under their *impressum*.

51. Josepha Duschek (1754–1834). Engraving by Johann Friedrich August Clar from a painting by Haake, 1796. Národní Museum, Prague, Czechoslovakia.

Mme Duschek, the celebrated singer who had been hostess to Mozart in her Prague summer house, the Bertramka, soon became one of Beethoven's friends. She sang the first public performance of Beethoven's *Scena* 'Ah perfido!', Op. 65, at a concert in Leipzig on 21 November 1796.

52. View of Prague, 'as seen from Strahof Monastery or from West to East'. Coloured copper plate by Leopold Peuckert. Národní Museum, Prague, Czechoslovakia.

In the spring of 1796, Beethoven went with Prince Lichnowsky to Prague and enjoyed in that music-loving city the same success that Mozart had reaped some ten years earlier with *Le nozze di Figaro* and *Don Giovanni*.

53. The Clary Palace in Teplitz. Coloured engraving by Eduard Gurk. Teplice, Czechoslovakia.

In later years, Beethoven was often a guest in the Clary Palace; Teplice was a well-known spa in Bohemia.

54. View of Dresden. Coloured engraving from *Dresden mit seinen Prachtgebäuden und schönsten Umgebungen*, Dresden 1807/8. Freies Deutsches Hochstift, Goethemuseum, Frankfurt am Main.

Beethoven's great success in Prague seems to have induced him to continue his trip without Prince Lichnowsky and to give concerts in Dresden and Berlin.

55. Josephine Countess von Clary (1777–1828). Miniature
on ivory (9 × 7.5 cm), by Carl Joseph Alois Agricola. Countess
Clothilde Clam-Gallas, Vienna.

Josephine von Clary, who in 1797 married the music-loving Count Christian Clam-Gallas, was a well-
known amateur singer for whom Beethoven wrote 'Ah perfido!' ('dedicata alla Signora dè Clari . . .').

From the Diary of Count Zinzendorf:

[original French]
8 January 1796: This evening to the Concert in the small Redoutensaal.... The *46*
beautiful Madame Bolla sang in a very insignificant manner, and la Willmann indulged in some *tours de force* ....

HJB II, 50. (Carl von Zinzendorf noted in his diary all the social and artistic events in Vienna from the
time of the Empress Maria Theresa to that of Emperor Francis II.)

The Allgemeine Musikalische Zeitung *reviews Bolla's operatic debut in 1805:*

Mad. Bolla, who appeared therein [Fioravanti's opera *Die gebesserte Eigensinnige*]
for the first time, has a free and professional stage manner, and a handsome, effective
alto voice that somewhat resembles the tone of our Crescentini. Some of the ornamenta-
tion with which she richly provided her vocal pieces, as in the Italian manner, is
highly successful; she only occasionally misses a passage. She was successful and took
a curtsey.

Allgemeine Musikalische Zeitung, Leipzig, 7. Jahrgang, No. 43, 24 July 1805, p. 689.

Ferdinand Ries describes Beethoven's stubbornness:

Haydn had wished Beethoven to put 'Pupil of Haydn' on the title-page of his first
work. Beethoven did not want to do this because he had, as he said, taken some lessons
from Haydn but had never learned anything from him. (During his first visit to
Vienna he had received some instruction from Mozart but the latter had, as Beethoven
complained, never played to him.) Beethoven had also studied counterpoint with
Albrechtsberger and dramatic music with Salieri. I knew them all well; all three *34, 36*
thought highly of Beethoven, but they all were of one mind regarding his learning.
Each one of them said that Beethoven was always so stubborn and self-willed that he
had to learn from his own bitter experience what he had never been willing to accept
in the course of his lessons. Particularly Albrechtsberger and Salieri were of this
opinion: the dry rules of the former and the insignificant ones of the latter in dramatic
composition (following the old Italian school) meant nothing to Beethoven.

WRBN 86.

> Shortly after the Haydn-Bolla-Beethoven concert on 8 January 1796, Beethoven went on a
> journey to Prague in the company of Prince Lichnowsky (Mozart and Lichnowsky had made a
> similar trip some years before). This first big concert tour of Beethoven's was an enormous
> success, and after a brief return to Vienna he set out for Leipzig, Dresden and Berlin, where
> he gave concerts. In Prague, he composed the beautiful *scena* 'Ah, perfido!' for Josephine,
> Countess von Clary, who later married the famous musical patron of Prague, Christian
> Count Clam-Gallas. 'Ah, perfido!' (Op. 65), closely modelled on Haydn's *Scena di Berenice*
> (1795), was soon taken into the repertoire of Madame Josepha Duschek, one of Mozart's

friends and a brilliant dramatic soprano. In Berlin, Beethoven met the well-known pianist Friedrich Heinrich Himmel and played to Friedrich Wilhelm II, King of Prussia. There Beethoven composed the Cello Sonatas Op. 5 for Jean Louis Duport, a famous virtuoso cellist in the service of the King. In November 1796, we find Beethoven giving a concert in the handsome coronation city of Pressburg (now Bratislava, ČSSR) and writing home to his friend, the piano manufacturer Johann Andreas Streicher, about the concert and about the piano. The Fortepiano was now developing very quickly, its keyboard was being extended in both treble and bass, and an attempt was being made to increase its resonance and sonority. Beethoven, when he first came to Vienna, used to play on pianos made by Anton Walter, then the leading piano manufacturer, who had also supplied Mozart's beautiful instrument (now in the Mozarteum in Salzburg) as well as instruments for Eszterháza Castle (one is now in the Haydn Museum in Eisenstadt).

Letter from Beethoven to his brother Nikolaus Johann:

Prague, 19 February [1796]

Dear Brother,

I must write to you so that you will at least know where I am and what I am doing. In the first place, things are going well with me, very well indeed. My art wins me friends and renown. What more can I want? And this time I will earn quite a lot of money. I shall remain here for another few weeks, and then go to <u>Dresden</u>, <u>Leipzig</u> and <u>Berlin</u>. It will be surely at least six weeks before I return. I hope that you will enjoy your stay in Vienna more and more. But have a care for the whole tribe of bad women. Have you already been to see <u>cousin Elss</u> [?]. You can write to me here once more, if you want to and have the time.

P[rince] Lichnowsky will soon return to Vienna. He has already departed from here. In case you should need money, you may make bold and go to him, for he still owes me. And now, I hope that your life may be ever happier, and I would like to contribute something to it. Farewell, my dear brother, and think sometimes of your true and faithful brother,

L. Beethoven.

Greet brother Caspar [heavily crossed out, but later underlined].
My address is: Im goldenen Einhorn auf der Kleinseite

Address: To be delivered to my brother Nicolaus Beethoven care of the Apothecary by the Kärnthner Thor.

Herr von Z[meskall] will be so kind as to give this letter to the wig-maker who will forward it.

KAL 19 f. (Cousin Elss may very well be related to Emmerich Joseph Philipp Johann Nepomuk Count Eltz [*recte*], at that time Envoy at the Court of Saxony, to whom Beethoven brought some letters in Dresden. See p. 91.)

Advertisement in the Leipziger Zeitung *of 19 November 1796:*

On Monday 21 November Mad[ame] Duschek from Prague will give a great vocal concert in the Theater am Randstädter Thore. The programme will include *Die Lehrstunde* [The Lesson], an Ode by Klopstock. Conversation between two nightingales, mother and daughter, on the fundamentals of musical art, music by Neumann [J. G. Naumann] sung by Mad[ame] Duschek and Dem[oiselle] Neefe; further an Italian Scena [*Ah! Perfido*] composed for Mad[ame] Duschek by Beethoven, and a few pieces by Mozart.

[In Beethoven's handwriting on the cover of a copy of *Ah! Perfido, spergiuro* revised by him]:
Une grande Scène mise en musique par L. v. Beethoven à Prague 1796.

[On the first page is written]:
Recitativo e Aria composta e dedicata alla Signora Contessa Di Clari Da L. v. Beethoven.

TDR II, 11

55

Karl August Varnhagen von Ense describes Friedrich Heinrich Himmel:

Kapellmeister Himmel, that dissolute eccentric who now lives almost perpetually in a state somewhere between being drunk on champagne and cheerless sobriety, was heard on the Fortepiano at the Golizin house, and at Clary's, and later in a concert. His playing, according to the verdict of connoisseurs, is by no means overshadowed by the latest great development in this field of the arts.

57

TDR III, 273. (Varnhagen, the fiancé of Rachel Levin, was a great admirer of Beethoven.)

Letters from August von Schall to the Elector Maximilian Franz:

[Dresden, 24 April 1796]
Young Beethoven arrived here yesterday. He had letters from Vienna to Count Elz. He will play at Court and go on from here to Leipzig and Berlin. He is reputed to have improved immensely and to compose well . . . .

[Dresden, 6 May 1796]
Beethoven was here for about eight days. Everyone who heard him play on the clavier was delighted. With the Elector of Saxony, who is a connoisseur of music, Beethoven had the privilege of playing accompaniments for one and a half hours. His Electoral Highness was exceptionally satisfied and presented him with a gold snuff-box. Beethoven has left Dresden for Leipzig and Berlin. He expressly requested me, when I had time and opportunity, to lay his homage most respectfully at your Serene Electoral Highness's feet and to beg for your Gracious further favour . . . .

Hans Volkmann: *Beethoven in seinen Beziehungen zu Dresden*, Dresden 1942, p. 24. (August von Schall was the Marshal of the Court of the Elector Maximilian Franz. He had already shown much interest in Beethoven in Bonn and recommended him to his cousin in Dresden, the Envoy of the Elector Palatine, Count Carl Theodor von Schall, so that he might smooth his path in Dresden.)

Ferdinand Ries describes Beethoven's visit to Berlin:

56 He performed a few times at Court (for King Friedrich Wilhelm II), where he also
played the two Sonatas with obbligato Violoncello, *Opus* 5, which he had com-
58 posed for Duport (the first violoncellist of the King) and himself. On taking
leave he received a gold box filled with *louis d'or*. Beethoven told me with pride that
it was no ordinary box, but one of the kind which are presented to Ambassadors.

WRBN 109.

57 *Ferdinand Ries writes about the pianist Friedrich Heinrich Himmel:*

He [Beethoven] went around Berlin a good deal with Himmel, about whom he said
that he had quite a pretty talent but nothing further. His piano-playing was elegant
and pleasant, but he was in no way comparable to Prince Louis Ferdinand. He paid
the latter what he considered to be a great compliment when he once told him that
he did not play in a royal or princely manner, but like a capable pianist. He had a
row with Himmel for the following reason. When they were together one day,
Himmel asked Beethoven to improvise, which Beethoven did. Afterwards, Beethoven
insisted that Himmel should do the same. Himmel was foolish enough to let himself
be persuaded. After he had been playing for quite a long time, Beethoven said,
'Now, when are you going to begin in earnest'? Himmel thought he had been performing wonders, considering how much he had played already. He jumped up, and they
both became offensive. Beethoven said to me, 'I thought that Himmel had only been
preluding for a little'.
    Later, it is true, they did become reconciled. But Himmel could only forgive,
he could never forget. For a while they exchanged letters until Himmel played a mean
trick on Beethoven. The latter always wanted to hear the latest news from Berlin.
This bored Himmel, who finally wrote him one day that the latest novelty was the
invention of a lantern for the blind. Beethoven ran around with the news of this
novelty; everyone wanted to know how this could actually be. He therefore wrote off
immediately to Himmel that it was maladroit of him not to have sent further explanations about the lamp. As a result of the unrepeatable answer he received, not only did
all correspondence come forever to an end, but all the ridicule which it contained
recoiled on Beethoven, who was foolish enough to show it here and there.

WRBN 110.

59 *Letter from Beethoven to Johann Andreas Streicher in 1796:*

Dear Streicher!
    The day before yesterday I received your Fortepiano which has truly turned out
excellently. Anyone else would try to keep it for himself, while I – have a good
laugh – I would have to lie if I did not tell you that in my opinion it is too good for
me. And why? Because it deprives me of the freedom of creating my own tone.

Nevertheless, this should not prevent you from making all your Fortepianos in the same way; there can be but few people who have such whims as I do.

My Academy will take place on Wednesday the 23rd of this month. If Stein wants to come he will be most welcome; he can certainly find lodgings for the night with me.

With regard to the sale of the Fortepiano, I had given the matter thought before you did, and I will also make every effort to carry it out. I thank you kindly, my dear S[treicher], for your kindness in being so obliging to me. I only hope that I may be able to return this kindness in some way and that, without my having to tell you, you are convinced how very much I hope that the merits of your instruments will be recognized both here and everywhere, and that you will always be fond of me and will always regard me

as your affectionate and warm friend
Beethoven.

Pressburg, the 19th November
Anno 96 Post Christum Natum.

Many kind greetings to your wife and to the bride and bridegroom.
[Address] A Monsieur de Streicher, Musicien très renommé a Vienne; to be delivered on the Landstrasse, at the Rote Rose.

Sonneck 182. Anderson 17. (Streicher, a friend of Schiller, married Nanette Stein and took over her long-established piano factory.)

Ferdinand Ries describes Beethoven's pride:

Beethoven obtained an engagement for me as piano-player to Count Browne. The latter spent some time in Baden bei Wien, where, in the evenings, I often had to play Beethoven's things, partly from notes and partly from memory, to an assembly of rabid Beethovenians. I was here able to observe the fact that for most people the name alone is sufficient for them to judge everything in a work as either beautiful and perfect, or mediocre and bad. One day, tired of playing from memory, I played a March just as it came into my head, without any further intention. An old Countess, who literally plagued Beethoven with her devotion, went into raptures of admiration because she imagined that it was a new piece by him. In order to have some amusement at her expense and that of the other enthusiasts, I hastened to assure them that this was so. Unfortunately, the next day Beethoven himself came to Baden. That evening, no sooner had he come into Count Browne's room than the old lady began to rave about the truly inspired and wonderful March. One can imagine my embarrassment. Knowing quite well that Beethoven could not stand the old Countess, I quickly took him into a corner and whispered to him that I had only wanted to amuse myself over her inanity. To my good fortune, he took the affair in good spirits, but my embarrassment grew as I had to repeat the March, which came off much worse since Beethoven was standing next to me. He then received extravagant panegyrics on his genius, which he listened to with perplexity and growing wrath until it was finally all resolved by a great peal of laughter. Later he said to me, 'Look here, my dear Ries!

63

Those are the great connoisseurs who want to judge every bit of music ever so correctly and severely. Just give them the name of their favourite: that's all they need!'

This March, nevertheless, had a happy outcome. Count Browne immediately commissioned from Beethoven the composition of three Marches for four hands (Opus 45) which were dedicated to the Princess Esterházy.

Beethoven composed a part of the second March while at the same time (which is still incomprehensible to me) coaching me in a Sonata which I was to play that evening at a small concert at Count Browne's. I was also due to play the Marches with him.

While this performance was going on, young Count P . . . ., standing in the doorway leading to the next room, was talking so loudly and freely to a beautiful lady that Beethoven, after several unsuccessful attempts to obtain silence, wrenched my hand away from the piano in the middle of my performance, leaped up and said quite loudly: 'I do not play for such swine.' Every effort to lead him back to the piano was in vain. He would not even allow me to play the Sonata. And so the music ended, to the general ill-feeling.

WRBN 90 ff.

Ferdinand Ries describes Beethoven's absent-mindedness:

Beethoven was very forgetful about some things. Once he received from Count Browne, in return for the dedication of the *Variations in A Major*, No. 5, on a Russian song, the gift of a fine riding horse. He rode it a few times, but soon forgot about it and, what was even worse, forgot about feeding it. His servant, who soon noticed this, began renting out the horse for a fee, to his own advantage, and, in order not to draw Beethoven's attention, for a long time did not give him a bill for the fodder. Finally, to Beethoven's great surprise, a very large bill was presented which suddenly made him aware once more not only of the horse but also of his negligence.

WRBN 120 f. (The work in question is WoO 71.)

59 *Johann Friedrich Reichardt on Streicher's pianos, 7 February 1809:*

Streicher has abandoned the softness of the other Viennese instruments, with their too delicate touch and bouncing rolling action, and on Beethoven's advice and request has given his instruments a more resisting touch and elastic action, so that the virtuoso who executes with strength and meaning has more control of his instrument in sustaining and carrying, in the striking and releasing [of the keys]. He thereby gives his instruments a stronger and more varied character, so that they should satisfy every virtuoso, who doesn't seek merely a light brilliance in his playing, more than any other instrument. . . .

Reichardt I, 311.

Letter from Beethoven to Johann Andreas Streicher, about 1796:

Most excellent Streicher!

I really must beg your pardon for being so late in answering your very obliging letter. If I tell you that I was prevented from doing so by the pressure of my almost overwhelming work, I assure you that I am not telling you a lie. Your little pupil, my dear St., apart from drawing a couple of tears from my eyes by her playing of my Adagio, has aroused my admiration. I wish you every good luck; you are fortunate in being able to display your understanding through the medium of such talent. And I am happy that this dear talented child has you for a master. Honestly, I assure you that this is the first time I have felt pleasure in hearing my Trio. Truly this will decide me to write more for the piano than heretofore. Even if only a few people understand me I will be satisfied. Undoubtedly, the manner of playing the piano is as yet the least developed form of instrumental playing. One often imagines one is listening to a harp, and I am happy, my dear friend, that you are one of the few who realize and feel that one can also sing on the piano, so long as one has feeling. I hope that the time will come when the harp and the piano will be regarded as two completely different instruments. For that matter, I think you may allow the girl to play everywhere. Between ourselves, she will put certain of our commonplace and conceited hurdy-gurdy grinders to shame.

One more thing: Would you take it amiss, my very good St., if I too have a small share in her training? That is, if I take an interest in her progress. For, while not wanting to flatter you, I cannot think of anything better to tell her than that you should oversee her and her progress, and encourage her on my behalf. Now, farewell, my dear St., and continue to be my friend, as I am entirely

your true friend,
L. v. Beethoven.

I hope to be able to visit you soon; then I will give you the number of my lodgings. Give my greetings to your dear wife.

Sonneck 183. Anderson 18.

One of Beethoven's colleagues was Ignaz Schuppanzigh, an excellent violinist who was to play the first performances of all Beethoven's string quartets and many of his other pieces of chamber music. Beethoven's circle of patrons was also growing rapidly. Among them was Johann Joseph, Prince von Schwarzenberg, at whose winter palace on the Mehlmarkt Haydn's *Creation* was first performed in 1798 and where Beethoven's very popular Septet Op. 20 was first heard. Another excellent patron was Johann Joseph, Prince von Liechtenstein, whose beautiful wife (née Landgravine Fürstenberg) was a pupil of Beethoven's, and to whom Beethoven dedicated the lovely Piano Sonata Op. 27, No. 1. Still another interesting patron and pupil of Beethoven's was Anna Luisa Barbara (Babette), Princess Odescalchi, née Countess von Keglevics de Buzin, to whom Beethoven dedicated, among other things, his Piano Concerto in C, Op. 15. He gave concerts at the Odescalchis', including a performance of the Septet, about which he writes to Zmeskall. The year that Haydn finished his *Creation*, 1798, saw the publication of Beethoven's *Sonate pathétique*, Op. 13, a landmark in Beethoven's *œuvre* and in the history of the piano as well. In the seven years since Mozart's death, the piano had already been enlarged considerably, and if it was by no means the powerful instrument of Beethoven's maturity, it was nonetheless capable of dynamic gradations not hitherto found in anything except Haydn's late London sonatas (a group of composers and pianists in London, such as Muzio Clementi and J. B. Cramer, were enlarging the piano's range and scope quite independently of the Viennese school).

65, 66   *Carl Czerny describes the violinist Schuppanzigh:*

Among Beethoven's friends Schuppanzigh was exceptionally noteworthy.

One would not have imagined, when seeing this short, fat, pleasure-loving young man (whom Beethoven only referred to as his Falstaff), that he should be possessed of so fine and ingenious a spirit. As one of the best violin-players of that time, he was unrivalled in quartet playing, a very good concert artist and the best orchestra conductor of his day.

Since he himself was not a composer, he was not swayed by any form of egotism from following Beethoven with unshakable faithfulness, and using every aspect of his performing ability to ensure that Beethoven's works might be presented to the public in all their greatness and beauty. Moreover, no one knew how to enter into the spirit of this music better than he: in fact, such a friend was of the greatest usefulness to Beethoven.

Czerny 12.

Johann Friedrich Reichardt writes about the Schuppanzigh Quartet:

Vienna, 10 December 1808.

Today I must tell you about the very fine quartet of Herr Schuppanzigh, a good violinist, which has opened a subscription series for the winter under the patronage
137   of Count von Razumovsky, the former Russian Envoy at the Imperial Court in Vienna. Performances will take place every Thursday from twelve to two in a private house. Last Thursday we heard it for the first time. Actually, there was not a large assembly there, but one consisting of very zealous and attentive music-lovers. And that is the proper public for this finest and most intimate of all musical associations.

This quartet was on the whole very well put together, although some people claim that last year, together with Kerr Kraft, this was even more the case. Herr Schuppanzigh has an individual piquant way of playing which is very suitable to the humorous quartets of Haydn, Mozart and Beethoven; or perhaps, rather, it resulted from a measured whimsical reading of those masterpieces. He executes with clarity, though not always absolutely cleanly, the most difficult passages, which the local virtuosi seem to avoid altogether. He also accents very correctly and significantly. His *cantabile* is often truly singing and moving. He also leads his well-picked colleagues skilfully and truly in the spirit of the composer; but he often disturbs me on account of the damnable habit, which has crept into use here, of beating time with his foot, even when it is not necessary, often out of sheer habit and often only to reinforce a *forte*. In general one rarely hears a *forte* here, or even a *fortissimo*, without the leader's pounding violently with his feet.

Reichardt I, 162, 164.

Carl Holz describes Schuppanzigh to Otto Jahn:

Schuppanzigh was a small, very corpulent man: he was always merry and very much   *65, 66*
given to material pleasures, Beethoven's 'Falstafferl'. Once, after a lively party, he
took Beethoven to a girl; after which he did not dare to show his face at Beethoven's
for weeks.

Kerst II, 186.

Ignaz von Mosel describes Schuppanzigh's performance of Beethoven's music:

Schuppanzigh, who understood so perfectly how to interpret Haydn's and Mozart's
ideas, was perhaps even more qualified to perform Beethoven's compositions. The
inspired composer soon realized this and chose him as his favourite interpreter. No
sooner had his creativeness given forth, no sooner was the music copied, than Beethoven
would give him his works to perform, first in the house of the music-loving Prince
Lichnowsky, then later at von Zmeskall's, the Royal Hungarian Court Secretary,
a universally admired art connoisseur and Beethoven's trusted friend, who gave the
most interesting morning concerts, to which the élite of the art world thronged.
In addition to Beethoven's quartets, his piano works were played there by a brilliant
lady, who is still living [Ertmann?], with a perfection unequalled since that time.
The early flowering of Mayseder's talents first found recognition in that circle and it
was there that he developed that union of taste and elegance which are the characteristics of his playing.

Allgemeine Wiener Musikzeitung, No. 124, 1843. (Ignaz von Mosel was a composer and writer on music in
Vienna, and a friend of Beethoven.)

Beethoven's dedication to Prince von Schwarzenberg: *61*

[March 1801]
GRAND QUINTET/for the/Fortepiano/with Oboe, Clarinet, Bassoon and Horn/
or/Violin, Viola and Violoncello/Composed and dedicated/to his Highness My Lord
the Reigning Prince of Schwarzenberg &. &./by LOUIS VAN BEETHOVEN/Opus 16/
[1:] 151 [r:] f3″ / in Vienna, T. Mollo and Co./Leipzig, Industrial Bank/Frankfurt,
Gayl and Hedler.

KHV 37.

Countess Thürheim on Prince and Princess von Schwarzenberg: *60, 61*

Joseph Joh. Nep. [Schwarzenberg], brother of the Field Marshal and victor of
Leipzig Karl Schwarzenberg, married in 1794 Pauline Princess Arenberg . . . Princess
Schwarzenberg was burned to death at a ball in Paris which her husband gave on the

occasion of the marriage of Marie Louise to Napoleon. The temporary ballroom in the then Rue de Montblanc caught fire and the Princess, who was searching for her daughter, later Princess Schönburg-Hartenstein, died in the flames. The daughter was rescued.

Thürheim IV, 186 ff.

Dolezalek on Beethoven's Septet:

The Septet was first performed at Prince Schwarzenberg's and was much admired. 'That is my Creation' [said Beethoven, with reference to Haydn's oratorio *The Creation*, which had also been performed for the first time in the Schwarzenberg palace].

Kerst II, 192.

Dr Franz Wegeler writes about Beethoven's dislike of playing in society:

Later, when Beethoven had already achieved a high position in Vienna, he expressed a similar, if not even more violent, aversion to being asked to play at social gatherings; every time this happened he would lose all his cheerfulness. On several occasions he came to me in a gloomy and ill-humoured mood, complaining that people forced him to play even if the blood was burning under his fingernails. Gradually a conversation would develop between us, in the course of which I would try to calm him down. When my aim had been satisfactorily achieved, I would let the conversation drop and sit down at my desk, and Beethoven, if he wanted to go on talking to me, would be obliged to sit on the chair in front of the piano. With an uncertain hand, and often still turned around, he would pick out a few chords from which, little by little, would develop the most beautiful melodies. Alas, why did I not understand more about it! Once, in order to obtain some manuscript from him, I had, to all intents and purposes accidentally, left music paper on the stand. He wrote on it, but in the end it was folded and placed in his pocket! All that was left to me was the permission to laugh at myself.

About his playing I could say nothing, or only very little, and that, as it were, in passing. He would then leave quite relaxed and would always come back again with pleasure. Nevertheless, this aversion remained with him and was often the source of the bitterest quarrels with his best friends and patrons.

WRBN 19 f.

64 *Ferdinand Ries writes about the Quintet Op. 16 :*

In the last Allegro there is, in several places, a pause before the theme begins again. In one of these, Beethoven suddenly began to improvise, taking the Rondo as a theme, entertaining himself and the others for quite a while. This, however, did not at all entertain the accompanying musicians; they became quite indignant and Herr Ramm actually furious. It was truly comical to see these gentlemen waiting every moment for their entrance, put their instruments continuously to their mouths, and then quietly put them down again. Finally, Beethoven was satisfied and led into the Rondo once more. The whole company was delighted.

WRBN 79 f.

Ferdinand Ries on Beethoven and the Princess Liechtenstein:

One evening I was due to play at Count Browne's a Sonata by Beethoven (A Minor, Op. 23), a work not often heard. Since Beethoven was present and since I had not practised this Sonata with him, I declared that I was ready to play any other Sonata but not that one. People turned to Beethoven, who finally said, 'Surely you will not play it so badly that I will not be able to listen to it.' So I was obliged to play it. As usual, Beethoven turned pages for me. In a jump in the left hand, where one particular note must be brought out, I went completely astray and Beethoven tapped me on the head with one finger. Princess L[iechtenstein], who sat leaning on the piano facing me, watched this with amusement. When I had finished playing, Beethoven said, 'Very good. You did not need to study the Sonata with me first. The finger was just meant to prove my attentiveness.' Later Beethoven had to play, and chose the D Minor Sonata [Op. 31 No. 2], which had just appeared. The Princess, who was expecting that Beethoven would surely make a mistake somewhere, now placed herself behind him while I turned the pages. At bars 53 and 54, Beethoven missed the beginning and instead of going down two notes and then two more, struck with his whole hand all the crotchets (3–4 notes at the same time) while descending; it sounded as if a piano were being cleaned out. The Princess gave him several not exactly gentle slaps on the head with the observation, 'If the pupil gets one finger for one wrong note, the Master must be punished with the whole hand for making bad mistakes.' Everyone laughed, and Beethoven first. He started again and played wonderfully. Particularly the Adagio he played inimitably.

63

67

WRBN 92

Dedication to the Princess Liechtenstein:

67

Sonata quasi una Fantasia/ for the Clavicembalo or Piano-forte/ Composed and dedicated to her Highness the Princess Johann Liechtenstein/born Landgravine Fürstenberg/ – by – / Louis van Beethoven/ Opus 27 No. 1 / In Vienna at Gio. Cappi, St. Michael's Square No. 5 [r:] 1 f.30/878 . 879 [March 1802].

KHV 66.

What the *Sonate Pathétique* was in the hands of Beethoven (although he left something to be desired as regards clean playing), was something that one had to have heard, and heard again, in order to be quite certain that it was the same already well-known work. Above all, every single thing became, in his hands, a new creation, wherein his always *legato* playing, one of the particular characteristics of his execution, formed an important part. In his lessons, Beethoven taught: always place the hands on the keyboard so that the fingers do not rise any more than is strictly necessary, for only with this method is it possible to create a tone and to learn how to 'sing'. He hated staccato playing, especially in the execution of passages; he called it 'finger dance' or 'leading the hands into the air'. The pieces which I myself heard Beethoven execute were, with few exceptions, always quite free of tempo limitations: a *tempo rubato* in the truest sense of the word, according to the demands of the contents and situation, without, however, the slightest tendency to caricature. It was the clearest and most comprehensible declamation, in the utmost degree, as perhaps can only be elicited from his works.

His older friends, who carefully followed the evolution of his spirit in every aspect, assure [me] that he developed this style of execution in the first years of the third period of his life, and that he turned completely away from his earlier manner of playing with fewer *nuances*. From this it is clear that his urge towards discovery had already found the ways and means to open up with confidence the portals of the mystery to both laity and initiated.

He wanted the quartets to be performed in the same manner as the sonatas, for they paint states of mind similar to the majority of his sonatas.

Kerst II, 32.

Ignaz Moscheles on the Sonate Pathétique:

At this time I heard from some of my fellow pupils that a young composer had arrived in Vienna who wrote the most extraordinary stuff, which no one could either play or understand; a Baroque music in conflict with all the rules. This composer's name was Beethoven. When I went back to the circulating library in order to satisfy my curiosity about the eccentric genius who bore that name, I found Beethoven's *Sonate Pathétique*. That was in 1804. Since my pocket money did not suffice to buy it, I secretly copied it out. The novelty of the style fascinated me, and I was seized by such an enthusiastic admiration of it that I went so far as to forget myself and tell my teacher about my new discovery. This gentleman reminded me of his instructions and warned me against playing or studying eccentric productions before I had developed a style based on more respectable models. Without paying heed to his instructions, however, I laid Beethoven's works on the piano, in the order of their appearance, and found in them such consolation and pleasure as no other composer ever vouchsafed me.

TDR II, 146.

The Sonata was composed for her by Beethoven when she was still a girl. He had the whim — one of many — since he lived across from her, of coming to give her lessons clad in a dressing-gown, slippers and a peaked nightcap.

TDR II, 52.

Beethoven's dedications to Countess von Keglevics:

[October 1797]
GRAND SONATA/ for the Harpsichord or Piano-Forte/ composed and dedicated/ to Mademoiselle the Countess/ BABETTE DE KEGLEVICS/ by/ Louis van Beethoven/ Opus 7/ in Vienna at Artaria and Co./ [l.:] 713. [r.:] f. 1. 30

[March 1801]
GRAND CONCERTO/ for the Forte-Piano/ with two Violins/ two Violas/ Bass and Violoncello, two Flutes/ two Oboes, two Clarinets, two Bassoons, two Trumpets, and Timpani/ composed and dedicated to Her Highness, the Princess/ Odescalchi née Countess Keglevics/ by/ LOUIS VAN BEETHOVEN/ Opus 15/ in Vienna at T. Mollo and Co./[l:] 153. Leipzig at the Industrial Bank [r:] f. 4, 30/ Frankfurt at Gayl and Hedler.

KHV 16, 34.

Letter from Beethoven to Zmeskall:

[Vienna, about 1801]
I write to you, my dear Music Count, on the best paper I have, that you will be so kind as to play the Septet tomorrow at Odescalchi's. Schindleker is not in town, the whole performance would have to be abandoned if you do not play and I would certainly fall under the suspicion of having been remiss about something.

Therefore, I beg you, dear M.G. [Musikgraf] not to fail me in this favour. You will surely be treated with the greatest consideration. Prince Odescalchi will   70 write to you personally tomorrow morning.

The rehearsal is tomorrow morning at eleven o'clock. I will send you the score so that you can look over the solo in the last Minuet which, as you know, is the most difficult. Eppinger will play the violin.

— I await you —
Your Bthvn.

KAL 80. Anderson 56.

Beethoven's oldest Viennese patron, Prince Carl Lichnowsky, had a younger brother, Count Moritz, also a pupil of Mozart's, who soon became not only a staunch patron but also a firm friend; the friendship lasted the whole of Beethoven's life. Altogether it is significant how Beethoven managed to be on terms of near equality with the Austro-Hungarian aristocracy; this was partly because they thought that the 'van' in Beethoven's name denoted nobility and thus considered him one of theirs, but also because Beethoven always insisted on being treated as an intellectual equal. It should be stressed that, at this period in Beethoven's life, towards the end of the eighteenth century, he presented a well-manicured appearance and dressed very neatly in the style of the period; he was also an interesting talker, and, unlike most musicians of the period, fascinated by politics. He also must have had considerable personal charm, such as a later letter to Count Moritz (1814) well illustrates.

76   *Anton Schindler about Count Moritz von Lichnowsky:*

Even higher stood his [Carl Lichnowsky's] brother Count Moritz Lichnowsky, also Mozart's pupil, who must be described as the most faithful companion of Beethoven during his whole life.

Schindler I, 21.

Letter from Beethoven to the publisher Breitkopf und Härtel:

Vien [na], 8 April 803

. . . You would certainly do me a very great favour if you would omit completely the dedication to Abbé Stadler on the Grand Variations [Op. 35] and in place of that print the one which I quote, namely dédiées, etc. A Monsieur le Comte Maurice

76, 41   Lichnowski [sic]. He is the brother of Prince Lichnowski and he has recently granted me an unexpected favour. Otherwise, I would have no other opportunity at present of doing something agreeable for him.

KAL III. Anderson 72.

Beethoven's dedication to Count Moritz von Lichnowsky:

[June 1815]
SONATA/for the/PIANO-FORTE/dedicated to/the Noble Count/MORITZ VON LICHNOWSKY/by/Ludw. van Beethoven/90th work/ [l.:] No. 2350. Property of the author [r.] Price [left blank and handwritten]/Vienna at S. A. Steiner.

KHV 249.

Letter from Beethoven to Count Moritz von Lichnowsky:

Baden, 21 September 1841 [1814]

Worthy and esteemed Count
        and friend,
    Unfortunately I received your letter only yesterday. Many thanks for thinking of me and also all good wishes to the honoured Princess Christiane [Thun-Lichnowsky].

Yesterday, I took a beautiful walk in the Brühl with a friend and in the course of our amicable conversation you were a frequent subject and lo! yesterday evening on arriving home I found your good letter. I see that you are constantly overwhelming me with kindnesses. As I should not like you to imagine that any step I have taken was dictated by a new interest or, indeed, anything of that sort, I hasten to tell you that a Sonata of mine will shortly appear which I have dedicated to you. I had wanted to surprise you, for this dedication has been long destined for you. But your letter of yesterday obliges me to reveal it to you now. There is no need of any new motive for me to express openly my feelings for your friendship and goodwill. But by anything resembling, even in the slightest, a gift you would cause me much distress because then you would have completely misunderstood my intention. Anything of that kind I can only refuse.

I kiss the hands of the Princess (in gratitude) for her remembrance and goodwill towards me. I have never forgotten to what an extent I am indebted to you, even though an unfortunate event resulted in a situation in which I was not able to express it as I should have wished . . . .

> Farewell,
> my honoured friend
> and regard me as
> ever worthy of your goodwill –
> your
> Beethoven.

I kiss the hands of the beloved Princess C. a thousand times.

KFR 209. Anderson 498.

In 1798, Beethoven made another successful concert trip to Prague where he played the Piano Concerto in B Flat, Op. 19, perhaps with the revised finale that we know today rather than the original Rondo (WoO 6). It is also considered possible that he gave at Prague the first performance of the Piano Concerto in C, Op. 15, which, despite its earlier opus number, is the later of the two works.

It was now fashionable to pit Beethoven against leading piano virtuosi such as Joseph Wölffl. The piano was becoming the most popular instrument not only among the aristocracy but also the bourgeoisie; almost every educated person in Vienna could play the instrument.

Beethoven's first big public concert in Vienna took place on 2 April 1800, and included the first performance of the First Symphony and perhaps the Viennese première of the Piano Concerto in C, Op. 15. The Symphony was dedicated to Baron Gottfried van Swieten, one of those in Vienna who immediately recognized Beethoven's enormous talents. The concert also included the now famous Septet, dedicated to the Empress Marie Therese herself. Emperor Francis was never an admirer of Beethoven, but so long as Marie Therese was still alive, Beethoven managed to preserve a tenuous connection with the Royal and Imperial house. The concert, which took place at the Burgtheater, was a decided success: Beethoven was now, after Haydn, the leading composer in Vienna.

Johann Wenzel Tomaschek about Beethoven's piano-playing:

In 1798, when I began my studies in jurisprudence, Beethoven, the giant among pianists, came to Prague. . . .

I heard Beethoven in his second concert. Neither his playing nor his compositions made the same powerful impression on me [as did the first]. This time he played the Concerto in B flat which he had just composed in Prague. Then I heard him for the third time at Count C . . . [Clary? Clam?] where, in addition to the graceful Rondo from the A major Sonata, he improvised on the theme *Ah vous dirai je Maman*. This time I followed Beethoven's artistic achievement. I admired particularly his powerful and brilliant playing, but I did not overlook his often daring leaps from one motive to another, whereby the organic connection and a gradual development of ideas is lacking. Such flaws often weaken his most grandiose musical works which he has conceived with his exultant talents. Not infrequently the unsuspecting listener is jolted violently out of his state of joyful transports. The most important thing in composition for him seems to be the unusual and original. This is also corroborated by his answer to a lady who recently asked him if he 'often went to Mozarts operas'. He replied that he 'did not know them and did not care to listen to other people's music since he did not wish to lose his own originality'.

75

TDR II, 73. (Tomaschek was a Czech composer.)

Letter from Ignaz Pleyel to his family about Beethoven:

[1805, original French]
Finally, I have heard Beethoven; he played a Sonata of his own composition and Lamare accompanied him. He has great execution, but he has no training and his execution has no finish; that is, his playing is not clean. He has much fire but he pounds a bit too much. He overcomes diabolical difficulties but he does not do them quite neatly. Nevertheless, his improvising gave me much pleasure. He does not improvise coldly like Woelfl [sic]. He plays anything that comes into his head and there is nothing he does not dare. Sometimes he does quite astounding things. Moreover, he should not be regarded as a pianist because it is very difficult to be a composer and performer at the same time.

77

O. Commettant, *Un nid d'autographes,* 2nd edition, Paris 1886, p. 92. (Ignaz Pleyel was a pupil of Haydn.)

77 *Johann Wenzel Tomaschek writes about the pianist Joseph Wölffl in his autobiography:*

Not long afterwards [March 1799] Wölffl came to Prague. His fame as an extraordinary pianist, which had been spread abroad through various newspapers, made all the music-lovers in the city curious as to his artistic ability. Whosoever wished to see him or speak to him had to look for him at the Blaue Weintraube, where he was busy all day long around the billiard-table. Despite his artistic billiard playing, he managed to lose more than six hundred gulden to the marker, so that Wölffl gave him a share in the proceeds of the concert. The concert took place in a theatre where a large audience was assembled. Wölffl played a Concerto of his own composition with unparalleled cleanliness and precision, which — on account of the immense stretch of his hands – no one else could perform. Then he played Mozart's *Fantasia in F Minor* published in Breitkopf's edition for four hands, exactly as it is printed without leaving out a single note. Nor in any way, in his execution, did he shorten the value of the notes as the so-called romantics of our times love to do, who then imagine that they can smooth everything out again by making an appalling confusion of sounds by raising the dampers. As I said, he played this piece of music without any mishaps. Then he improvised, weaving in the theme *Wenns Lieserl macht*, and brought the concert to an end with several very beautiful and brilliant variations. A hearty applause was granted to this (in his own way) unique virtuoso. He is a pianist, six feet tall, whose fingers, monstrously long, can encompass a thirteenth without any strain and, moreover, so thin that all his clothes flap on him like a scarecrow. Yet he overcomes difficulties which, for other pianists, would be impossibilities, with a somewhat weak but pleasant touch, and does not lose the quiet composure of his body. He often plays whole sections in a moderately fast tempo with only one finger, as in the Andante of the Mozart *Fantasia*, where he binds together the section in which the tenor voice goes on for a long time in semiquavers. Such a pianist can certainly be regarded as unique in his own way.

TDR II, 67 f.

Samuel Appleby writes about Dragonetti and Beethoven:

Beethoven had heard that his new friend could play violoncello music on his own gigantic instrument. One morning, as Dragonetti was calling on him in his room, he   73
expressed a wish to hear a Sonata. The double-bass was sent for, and the Sonata Op. 5, No. 2 was chosen. Beethoven played his part with his eyes fixed on his fellow-player. When, in the finale, they came to the arpeggios, he broke out in such an excitement of pleasure that at the end he jumped up and threw his arms around both the instrument and the player.

TDR II, 76. (Appleby, whose father, Thomas Appleby, was Director of a Concert Society in Manchester, played the violin and was, from his earliest youth, a follower and admirer of Beethoven.)

Ferdinand Ries on John Cramer:

Among piano players he [Beethoven] praised only one person as an excellent player: John Cramer. All the others were worth nothing to him.   74

WRBN 99.

Anton Schindler recalls Cherubini's and Cramer's opinions:

I take this opportunity of recording the information on Beethoven's second period, provided by Cherubini and Cramer. The opinions of these two high authorities on the

Master's piano-playing follow. The terse and waspish Cherubini characterized it with one word: crude. The gentleman Cramer chose to object less to the crudeness of the execution than to the unreliability in the repetition of one and the same work: one day it would be spirited and full of characteristic expression; the next day, however, it might be fitful and unclear to the point of confusion. For this reason, some of his friends once expressed the wish to hear several works, some of them still in manuscript, performed by Cramer in public. This touched a very sensitive side of Beethoven. Jealousy was aroused which, according to Cramer, was followed by strained relations on both sides.

Schindler II, 232.

John Cramer's widow speaks of Beethoven:

Cramer's widow tells us a pretty anecdote. At a concert in the Augarten, both artists were walking around listening to a performance of Mozart's Concerto in C Minor [Köchel 491]. Beethoven suddenly stood still and drew the attention of his companion to the exceptionally simple, yet so beautiful motive which appears towards the end of the piece, and exclaimed 'Cramer! Cramer! We'll never be able to do anything like that.' And where the motive is repeated and worked up to a climax, Beethoven, moving his body to and fro, indicated the rhythm and in every possible way expressed his ever growing pleasure until it reached a pitch of enthusiasm.

TDR II, 78.

The Allgemeine Musikalische Zeitung *reviews Beethoven's concert on 2 April 1800:*

Finally, Herr Beethoven was able for once to obtain the use of the theatre, and this was the most interesting Academy held for a long time. He played a new concerto of his own composition which contains many beautiful things, namely the first two movements. Then a septet by him was performed; it is written with a great deal of taste and feeling. He then improvised with mastery, and at the close a symphony of his composition was performed, which revealed much art, novelty and wealth of ideas. But there was too much use of wind instruments, so that it sounded more like a wind-band than an orchestra. Perhaps we might do some good if we make the following observations on the subject of this Academy. The orchestra of the Italian Opera showed to very poor advantage. First: quarrels regarding the conductors. Beethoven believed, and rightly, that rather than Herr Conti no one could be better trusted to conduct than Herr Wranitzky. The gentlemen did not want to play under him. The shortcomings of this orchestra, already denounced above, were therefore even more evident, especially since B.'s composition is hard to play. In the accompaniments they did not take the trouble to consider the soloist. Of delicacy in accompanying, of following the sequence of the feelings of the solo player and so forth, not the slightest trace. In the second part of the symphony they were so condescending that they did not even follow the beat, so that it was impossible to get any life into their playing, especially in the woodwinds. In such cases, of what avail is their skill? – which one does not in the least wish to deny to the majority of the members of this Association. What significant effect can even the most excellent composition achieve?

TDR II, 172.

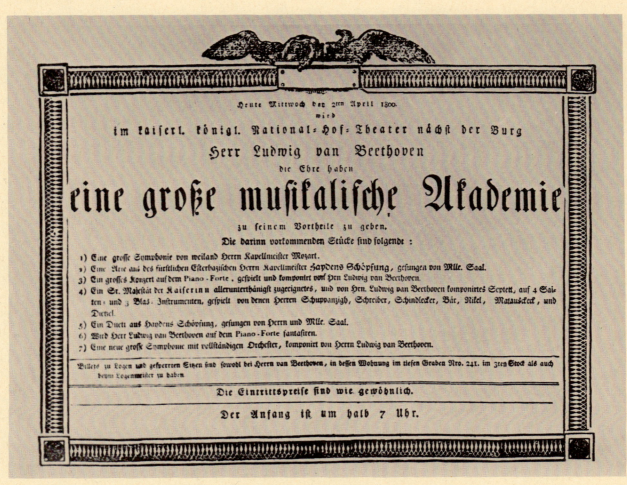

Placard of Beethoven's Benefit Concert at the Burgtheater in Vienna on 2 April 1800.

Johann Nepomuk Emanuel Dolezalek reports on the Emperor Francis I:

The Emperor Francis did not wish to hear anything about Beethoven's music: 'There is something revolutionary in that music!'

Kerst II, 192.

Letter from Georg August Griesinger to the publishers Breitkopf und Härtel:

29 May 1801

... On the 24th the Empress sang *The Seasons*, on the 25th *The Creation* under   84

H[aydn]'s direction but only in the presence of her family. According to H[aydn],
she has much taste and expression, but a weak organ. . . .

HJB III, 23. (Griesinger, the Saxon Chargé d'affaires at the Viennese Court, acted as intermediary for
Breitkopf and Härtel with Beethoven and Haydn.)

84   *Beethoven's dedication to the Empress Marie Therese:*

SEPTET/ for / Violin, Viola, Clarinet, Horn Basson / Violoncello and Double-bass/
composed and dedicated to Her Majesty/MARIE THERESE/Roman Empress/Queen
of Hungary and of Bohemia etc., etc./ BY /LOUIS VAN BEETHOVEN/ Opus 20/
PART I [II]/In Vienna at Hoffmeister & Co./In Leipzig at Hoffmeister and Kühnel/
at the Bureau of Music [r.:] Price, 1 Rth 8 Ggr.

KHV 49.

Countess Josephine von Deym writes to her sister, Therese von Brunsvik:

[21 December 1801]

. . . at one of Schuppanzigh's concerts he was particularly enchanted by a septet of
Beethoven's which he thought to be the *non plus ultra* in composition as well as in
execution . . .

La Mara, *Beethoven und die Brunsviks*, nach Familienpapieren aus Therese Brunsviks Nachlass, Leipzig
1920, p. 39. (The Countess refers to her brother Franz who was then her frequent guest in Vienna; about the
Deym family and the Brunsviks see pp. 159–60, 193–95.)

Cipriani Potter about Beethoven:

Once, when he, Potter, told Beethoven of the effect which the Septet had at that time
on him, Beethoven said, more or less: 'In those days I did not know how to compose.
Now, I think I do know.' On this, or on a similar occasion, he said, 'Now I shall
write something better' – and soon after appeared the B-Flat Sonata, Opus 106, the
work of the year 1818.

TDR IV, 57. (Potter was numbered among Beethoven's admirers.)

82, 83   *Letter from Baron Gottfried van Swieten to Beethoven:*

[undated]

To Herr Beethoven, in the Alstergasse No. 45, care of Prince Lichnowsky.
    If next Wednesday you are not prevented, I should like to see you, with your
nightcap in your pocket, at my house at half-past-eight in the evening. Please do not
fail to give me an answer.

Swieten.

From Beethoven's diary
[October or November 1793] :
Ate yesterday evening at Swieten's – tip of a 17th; to the porter for opening the door,
4 Kreutzer.

TDR I, 360.

Anton Schindler writes about Beethoven's obstinacy:

Beethoven very often ran his head against the wall .... Even van Swieten's understanding advice and admonitions often went unheeded. He, who had been his sponsor
in high society, had to be satisfied if the capricious artist consented to appear at his
musical evenings. Emancipation from all the conventions of the drawing-room seems
to have been one of his early obsessions, although his personal relations, in particular
his close connections with the élite of the musical world who, overlooking his social
shortcomings, regarded him as one of themselves, should have been sufficient grounds
for him to lay such aspirations aside, at least for a short time.

Schindler I, 23.

From Jahrbuch der Tonkunst, *Prague 1796* :

[Gottfried, Baron van Swieten] should also be regarded as a patriarch of music. His
taste tends generally towards the grandiose and the sublime. He himself, many years
ago, wrote twelve beautiful symphonies. When he attends a concert, our semi-
experts do not take their eyes off him in order to read from his expressions (which,
however, may not always be sufficiently revealing for certain persons) what sort of
judgment they should pass on the performance in question. Every year he gives a few
very large and magnificent concerts where only compositions of the old masters are
performed. He particularly loves the style of Handel, whose large choral works are
generally performed [on these occasions]. During the last Christmas festivities (1794)
he gave a concert of this sort at Prince Paar's where an oratorio by this composer
was performed.

Gottfried van Swieten writes about himself:

Insofar as music is concerned, I have returned altogether to those times when it was
considered necessary to study an art soundly and thoroughly before practising it. In
this conviction I find nourishment for both spirit and heart: and this gives me strength
when I have been cast down by further evidence of the decline of the arts. My com-
forters are, above all, Handel and the Bachs and, along with them, those few masters
of our present day who, following with a firm tread the path of those examples of
truth and greatness, promise to reach their goal, or have already reached it.

Allgemeine Musikalische Zeitung. Leipzig, No. 16, 3 January 1799.

Carl Czerny writes about his first meeting with Beethoven:

I still remember how one day Gelinek told my father that he had been asked that evening to compete with a foreign piano-player at a reception. 'We must make mincemeat out of him,' added Gelinek. The next day my father asked Gelinek for the outcome of the previous day's dual.

'Oh,' said Gelinek quite subdued, 'I'll never forget yesterday evening! Satan himself is hidden in that young man. I have never heard anyone play like that! He improvised on a theme which I gave him as I never heard even Mozart improvise. Then he played some of his own compositions which are in the highest degree remarkable and magnificent. He can overcome difficulties and draw effects from the piano such as we couldn't even allow ourselves to dream about.'

'Eh,' said my father, 'and what is the man's name?'

'He is', answered Gelinek, 'a small, ugly, black and wild-looking young man whom Prince Lichnowsky brought here a few years ago from Germany in order to have him study with Haydn, Albrechtsberger and Salieri; his name is Beethoven' . . .

I was about ten years old when I was taken to Beethoven through the kind offices of Krumpholz. It was the winter of 1799–1800. How I was overjoyed and terrified on the day when I was to meet the esteemed master! Even today [1842] every moment of it is still fresh in my memory. On a winter's day, my father, Krumpholz and I walked from the Leopoldstadt, where we still lived, into the city, to the so-called Tiefer Graben [the name of a street], climbed up, as if in a tower, to the fifth or sixth floor, where a rather grubby-looking servant announced us to Beethoven and then showed us in. A very barren-looking room, papers and clothes strewn all over the place, a few boxes, bare walls, hardly a single chair save for a rickety one by the Fortepiano, a Walter, at that time the best make. In this room were gathered six to eight persons, including both the brothers Wranitzky, Süssmeyer, Schuppanzigh and one of Beethoven's brothers.

Beethoven himself was dressed in a jacket of some shaggy dark grey cloth and trousers of the same material, so that he immediately reminded me of Campe's *Robinson Crusoe**, which I had just then read. The coal-black hair cut *à la Titus* stood up around his head. His black beard, unshaven for several days, darkened the lower part of his already dark-complexioned face. Also I noticed at a glance, as children are wont to do, that his ears were stuffed with cotton-wool which seemed to have been dipped in some yellow fluid. Yet at that time not the slightest sign of deafness was apparent. I had to play something immediately, and since I was too shy to begin with one of his own compositions, I played Mozart's great C Major Concerto [K. 503] which begins with chords. Beethoven was immediately attentive; he came close to my chair and played with his left hand the orchestra part in those sections where I had only accompanying passages. His hands were very hairy and his fingers, especially at the tips, very broad. He expressed himself as being satisfied, so I made bold and played the *Pathétique* Sonata which had then just appeared, and finally the *Adelaide* which my father sang with his very good tenor voice. When I had finished, Beethoven turned to my father and said, 'The boy has talent. I will teach him myself and accept him as my pupil. Send him to me a few times a week. Before anything else, obtain for him

*The German writer Joachim Heinrich Campe (1746–1816) wrote a version of *Robinson Crusoe* based on Defoe.

Emanuel Bach's handbook on the proper way to play the clavier, so that he can already bring it with him the next time he comes.'

In the first lessons, Beethoven gave me scales in every key, showed me the only proper position of the hands and of the fingers and particularly the use of the thumb, then unknown to the majority of players, rules whose complete scope I mastered only at a much later time.

Then he went over the exercises of the handbook with me and drew my special attention to *legato* of which he himself was an unequalled master and which, at that time, all other pianists believed to be impossible to obtain on the Fortepiano. At that time, dating still from Mozart's days, the clipped and *staccato* way of playing was the fashion.

Czerny 10 f. (Paul [1756–1808] and Anton [1761–1819] Wranitzky were both composers; so was F. X. Süssmayer [*recte*], a former pupil of Mozart's.)

Beethoven was never entirely free from ill health; the latest generation of Beethoven scholars believes that he probably caught syphilis, and in any case he was always subject to intestinal disorders, sometimes of considerable severity. But towards the end of the eighteenth century, Beethoven began to discover something much more frightful, namely that he was losing his hearing. Gradually, indeed, Beethoven became stone deaf over the years, and it can be imagined how the awareness of this increasing deafness affected him. From the psychological standpoint it is interesting to observe that at the very depth of his misery, when he was writing the 'Heiligenstädter Testament' of 1802, he was composing the brilliant and energetic Second Symphony; this should be something of a warning to those who will insist on seeing a constant parallel between Beethoven's life and his music. We do not need to go so far as W. H. Auden in condemning Beethoven's letters, but it is obvious that his music always existed on a higher level, often isolated from his physical and mental agonies.

Letters from Beethoven to Dr Franz Gerhard Wegeler in Bonn:

Vienna, 29 June [1801]

My dear, good Wegeler,
. . . You want to know about my situation: Well, on the whole it is not so bad. Since last year Lichnowsky, however difficult it will be for you to believe it when I tell you, who was always and still is my warmest friend (there have been small misunderstandings but have these not further cemented our friendship?), has placed at my disposal a fixed sum of 600 Florins on which I may draw so long as I do not obtain a suitable appointment. My compositions bring in a considerable amount, and I can truthfully say that I receive more offers of commissions than I can possibly accept. Moreover, for every composition I have six or seven publishers and could have more if I should want them. People no longer bargain with me: I state my price and they pay. So you see that this is an agreeable state of affairs. For example, I see a friend in need, and if the state of my purse will not allow me to help him out on the spot, I have only to sit down at my desk and in a short time help for him is forthcoming. I have also become more economical than formerly. If I should settle here permanently it would certainly soon be possible for me to obtain one day each year for a concert; I have already given a few. Only that jealous demon, namely my bad health, has thrown a mean spoke in my wheel; in the past three years my hearing has become increasingly

weaker. It appears that my abdomen which, as you know, was already at that time [in Bonn] in a wretched state, has become worse here. I have been constantly plagued by colic and hence by a fearful fatigue. This appears to have been the original cause of my deafness. Frank wanted to build up the tone of my body by means of strong tonic medicines, and my hearing with almond oil. But Prosit! it did me no good whatever. My hearing became even worse and the digestive trouble remained the same. This went on all last year until the autumn when sometimes I was reduced to utter despair. Then a medical asinus recommended cold baths for my condition; a more intelligent one suggested the usual tepid Danube baths. These worked wonders. I improved, but my deafness persisted or even worsened. This winter I was really wretched. I had fearful colics and I again relapsed completely into my former state. This went on until about four weeks ago, when I went to Vering, since I began to think that this condition might call for a surgeon and, anyway, I always had confidence in him. He succeeded in almost checking the violent diarrhoea. He prescribed the tepid Danube baths into which I must pour a flask of strengthening substances. He gave me no medicines until about four days ago when he prescribed four pills daily for the stomach and an infusion for my ear. I must say that now I find myself stronger and better. Only my ears hum and buzz continuously day and night. I can tell you that I lead a miserable existence. For the past two years I avoid almost all social intercourse because it is impossible for me to say to people: 'I am deaf.' If I practised any other profession it would be easier, but in my profession this is a terrible condition. My enemies, and their number is not small – what would they not say! To give you an idea of this remarkable deafness, I can tell you that at the theatre I must find a place very close to the orchestra in order to understand the actors. If I am a little way distant I cannot hear the upper notes of the voices or of the instruments. In conversation it is remarkable that there are people who have never noticed this. Since I am often given to periods of distraction, people attribute my deafness to this. Sometimes, if someone speaks in a low voice, I can barely understand; I hear the sounds but not the words. If anyone shouts it is unbearable. What is to become of me, heaven only knows. Vering says that I will undoubtedly improve, even if I am not completely cured. I have cursed my fate many times already. Plutarch has shown me the way to resignation. I shall, if it is at all possible, challenge my fate, although there will be moments when I shall be God's most unhappy creature. I beg you to tell no one of this condition of mine, not even Lorchen. What I tell you is a secret which I entrust to your keeping. I should like you to correspond with Vering about this. If my condition goes on like this, I will come to you next spring. Rent a house for me in some beautiful place in the country and then I will become a peasant for half a year. Perhaps that will change things. Resignation! What a wretched means of escape, and yet that is the only thing left to me. You will surely forgive me if I unload on you the troubles of your friend, when you are yourself in a sorrowful condition of your own. Steffen Breuning is here at present and we see each other almost daily. It does me so much good to revive the old feelings of friendship . . . .

87   [I send] you the portrait . . . of your ever good and affectionate Beethoven; it is being published by Artaria who has often, like many others, including art shops, requested it from me.

KAL 45 ff. Anderson 51.

56. Friedrich Wilhelm II, King of Prussia (1744–97). Engraving by Jakob Adam from a painting by Anton Graff, 1793. Österreichische Nationalbibliothek, Vienna.

Friedrich Wilhelm, a gifted cello player and highly educated musician, was a major musical influence in Berlin. Haydn and Mozart had written string quartets for him. Friedrich Wilhelm at once appreciated Beehoven's gifts and attempted to keep him in Berlin.

57. Friedrich Heinrich Himmel (1765–1814). Engraving by Johann Friedrich Bolt from a painting by Lauer, 1803. Gesellschaft der Musikfreunde, Vienna.

Himmel owed his musical education to the generosity of the Prussian King. He was a first-rate pianist whose only rival in Berlin was the King's cousin Prince Louis Ferdinand, himself a gifted composer.

58. Jean Louis Duport (1749–1819). Engraving by Eleonore Lingée from a drawing by Charles Nicolas Cochin the Younger. Österreichische Nationalbibliothek, Vienna.

This fine cellist was in the service of King Friedrich Wilhelm and played together with Beethoven in a concert in Berlin.

59. Johann Andreas Streicher (1761–1833). Portrait in oils by Johann Ender, *c.* 1820. Historisches Museum of the City of Vienna.

Streicher and his wife Nanette, née Stein, were intimate friends of Beethoven's, who often asked Nanette's advice in household matters. Streicher, who took over the celebrated piano firm of his wife, was as early as 1796 supplanting Walter's instruments in Beethoven's opinion. Later he constructed for Beethoven a piano which had 'more strength and importance', as the composer Johann Friedrich Reichardt wrote.

60. Schwarzenberg Palace on the Mehlmarkt. Anonymous coloured engraving, *c.* 1825. Historisches Museum of the City of Vienna.

At the end of the seventeenth century, Prince Ferdinand Eusebius Schwarzenberg began the construction of the palace; the main part of the building was completed by 1704, together with the summer palace at the foot of the Belvedere Gardens on what is now known as the Schwarzenbergplatz. Behind the town house, reached by a narrow street, was the Bürgerspital.

61. Joseph Johann Prince von Schwarzenberg (1769–1833). Anonymous portrait in oils, copy of a painting by A. F. Oelenhainz. Hluboká, Czechoslovakia.

In Schwarzenberg's Vienna winter palace Beethoven's Septet Op. 20 was performed for the first time. Prince Schwarzenberg had his own orchestra and performed several works of Beethoven in his various palaces and castles.

62. View of Pressburg. Coloured engraving by Joseph and Peter Schaffer, 1787. Antiquarian Gilhofer und Ranschburg, Vienna.

Beethoven returned from Berlin to Vienna, highly satisfied with his artistic and material successes. In November 1796 he gave a concert in Pressburg, at which he played the piano, but about which no details have as yet been discovered.

63. Johann Georg, Reichsgraf von Browne-Camus (1767–1827). Engraving by Sebastian Mansfeld. Historisches Museum of the City of Vienna.

Beethoven found a generous patron in the Russian Count and dedicated a number of works to him as well as his wife. Johann Georg gave Beethoven a saddle-horse when the composer dedicated to him the Twelve Variations on a Russian Dance from Wranitzky's *Das Waldmädchen* (1797 [WoO 71]).

Heute Donnerstag den 6ten April 1797.

Hat Herr Ignaz Schuppanzigh die Ehre in der Himmelpfortgasse in dem Saale des Herrn Hoftraiteurs Jahn,

Eine grosse musikalische Akademie

zu seinem Vortheile zu geben.

Folgende Stücke werden dabei aufgeführt.

1. Eine grosse Sinphonie von Herrn weil. Mozart.
2. Eine Arie, gesungen von der Madame Willmann, komponiert vom Herrn Ludwig van Beethoven.
3. Ein Konzert auf der Violine, gespielt vom Herrn Ignaz Schuppanzigh.
4. Eine Arie, gesungen vom Herrn Lodecaſs, komponiert vom Herrn Sarti.
5. Ein Quintet auf dem Fortepiano mit 4 blasenden Instrumenten akompagniret, gespielt und komponiert vom Herrn Ludwig van Beethoven.
6. Variazionen auf der Violine, gespielt vom Herrn Ignaz Schuppanzigh.
7. Eine Schlußsinphonie.

Der Eintrittspreis ist 2 fl.

Der Anfang ist um 7 Uhr.

64. Programme of a large *Akademie* (concert) in the *Jahnschen Saal* (Jahn's concert room) held on 6 April 1797, for the benefit of the violinist Ignaz Schuppanzigh. Gesellschaft der Musikfreunde, Vienna.

In this concert Beethoven played the piano part in the first public performance of his Quintet Op. 16 in E flat. The Quintet was dedicated to Prince Joseph Schwarzenberg.

65, 66. (*Left*) Ignaz Schuppanzigh (1776–1830). Lithograph by Bernhard Edler von Schrötter. Gesellschaft der Musikfreunde, Vienna. (*Right*) Caricature of the violinist Schuppanzigh, printed in 1810 by Adamel. Gesellschaft der Musikfreunde, Vienna.

Schuppanzigh was an excellent solo violinist who also liked to direct orchestral performances. In 1798 and 1799 he conducted the orchestra in the summer concerts given in the Augarten which Mozart and Martin had begun some years earlier. Schuppanzigh's corpulence induced Beethoven to tease him unmercifully; in 1801 Beethoven wrote for him a short vocal piece with the title 'In Praise of the Fat Man', WoO 100.

67. Josepha Princess von Liechtenstein, née Landgravine von Fürstenberg (1776–1836). Portrait in oils by Angelika Kauffmann. Galerie Liechtenstein, Vienna.

The young Princess was Beethoven's pupil and a highly gifted pianist. Beethoven dedicated to her the lovely and poetic Sonata Op. 27 No. 1.

68. Anna Louisa Barbara (Babette) Princess Odescalchi, née Countess Keglevics de Buzin (?–1813). Anonymous portrait in oils. Principe Livio Odescalchi, Rome.

Countess Babette Keglevics took piano lessons from Beethoven before her marriage in 1801. Beethoven dedicated to her variations for piano on Salieri's aria 'La stessa, la stessissima' from his opera *Falstaff* (WoO 73), and the Piano Sonata Op. 7. Shortly after her marriage Beethoven dedicated to her his Piano Concerto in C, Op. 15.

69. Johann Joseph Prince von Liechtenstein (1768–1836). Portrait in oils by Johann Baptist Lampi the Elder. Galerie Liechtenstein, Vienna.

Prince Liechtenstein also kept a private orchestra and was first cousin to Beethoven's patron Count Waldstein.

70. Innocenzo Prince d'Erba Odescalchi (1778–1831). Anonymous portrait in oils. Principe Livio Odescalchi, Rome.

Prince Innocenzo came from the old Roman aristocratic family Odescalchi; he owned a palace in Pressburg (Bratislava) and spent the winter months in Vienna.

71, 72. Sonate pathétique, Op. 13. Title-page of the first edition, and first page of the music. Gesellschaft der Musikfreunde, Vienna.

The autograph of this epoch-making sonata, dedicated to Prince Carl Lichnowsky, has disappeared. From a sketch it is assumed that the last movement was originally conceived for more than one instrument, perhaps for a sonata for violin and piano. The 'Pathétique' was printed by Hoffmeister in Vienna, and immediately reprinted by the Viennese publisher Eder.

74. Jean Baptiste Cramer (1771–1858). Anonymous engraving. Gesellschaft der Musikfreunde, Vienna.

Cramer, son of the famous violinist Wilhelm Cramer, received his musical education in England, where his father led the celebrated Professional Concerts. Jean Baptiste came to Vienna in 1799, at which time he came into contact with Beethoven, who generously admitted Cramer's excellence in the art of pianoforte playing. Indeed, Beethoven asserted that Cramer's clean attack and great accuracy of execution surpassed his own and Beethoven always preferred Cramer's attack to that of any other pianist.

73. Domenico Dragonetti (1763–1846). Study by Francesco Bartolozzi. British Museum, London.

Dragonetti met Beethoven in 1799, during a concert trip which took the Italian artist from Venice to London and during which he stayed a few weeks in Vienna. Dragonetti was one of the world's greatest virtuosi on the double bass, which he played not only with great bravura but also with considerable subtlety. His art of playing the unwieldy instrument made a lasting impression on Beethoven.

75. The Clam-Gallas Palace in Prague. Papier maché relief. Countess Clothilde Clam–Gallas, Vienna.

Beethoven's former pupil, the Countess Clary, married Count Christian Clam-Gallas, and the composer played in their house when he visited Prague again in 1798.

76. Moritz Count Lichnowsky (1771–1837). Anonymous portrait in oils. Hradec u Opavy, Czechoslovakia.

Count Lichnowsky, younger brother of the Prince and, like him, an excellent piano-player, was also a staunch friend of Beethoven's and was to prove of great assistance to the composer, especially after the death of Prince Carl. Beethoven dedicated to Count Moritz the Fifteen Variations with a Fugue in E flat ['Eroica', Op. 35], and the Piano Sonata in E Minor, Op. 90.

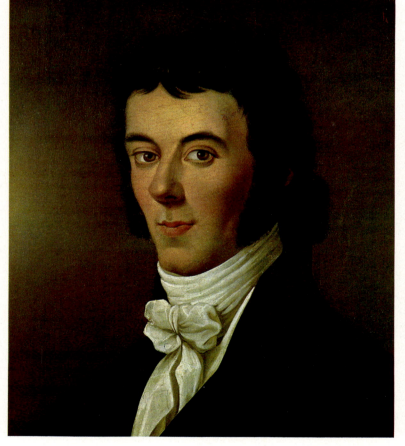

77. Joseph Wölffl (1772–1812). Anonymous portrait in oils. Gesellschaft der Musikfreunde, Vienna.

Wölffl, born in Salzburg, and a pupil of Leopold Mozart's, appeared in public as a pianist for the first time at the age of seven. His success as a performer was almost rivalled by the success of his compositions. During a soirée at the house of Freiherr von Wetzlar (who had been a friend of Mozart's), Wölffl and Beethoven were pitted against each other in the art of improvisation; the listeners found it hard to decide which of the musicians was the more successful. Wölffl showed his respect for Beethoven by dedicating to him the Piano Sonata Op. 7, which was praised in the *Allgemeine Musikalische Zeitung* of 1799.

78, 79. (*Above*) Michaelerplatz in Vienna, with the old Burgtheater. Coloured engraving by Carl Postl, 1810. Galerie Liechtenstein, Vienna. (*Below*) The interior of the Burgtheater. Print from a coloured engraving, *c.* 1830; from *Denkmäler des Theaters*. Historisches Museum of the City of Vienna.

In what was then called the 'K.K. National-Hof-Theater' Beethoven gave his first public benefit concert on 2 April 1800.

80. Ludwig van Beethoven. Engraving by Johann Neidl from a drawing by Gandolph Ernst Stainhauser von Treuberg. 1800: Vienna, published by Cappi. Beethovenhaus Bonn.

Mentioned in Beethoven's letter of 19 January 1801 to Wegeler as available 'at Artaria's'; at one time Cappi had been in business with Artaria.

81. Symphony No. 1 in C major, Op. 21. Title page with the dedication to Baron Gottfried van Swieten. First edition. Gesellschaft der Musikfreunde, Vienna.

The First Symphony was begun in 1799, using earlier sketches, and completed at the beginning of 1800. It was dedicated to Baron van Swieten and first printed by Hoffmeister in Vienna. Beethoven conducted the first performance at the Burgtheater on 2 April 1800.

82. Baron Gottfried van Swieten (1733–1803). Silhouette by Pierre Gonord, 1781. Reproduction H. C. Robbins Landon, Buggiano Castello, Italy.

Baron van Swieten, son of Maria Theresa's private physician, was from 1777 director of the Imperial and Royal Court Library. A composer whose symphonies — said Haydn — 'were as stiff as the Baron himself', Van Swieten had learned to love Bach and Handel's music when in the diplomatic service in Berlin; when he returned to Vienna, he became the friend and patron of Haydn and Mozart. He wrote the librettos of Haydn's *Creation* and *Seasons*, but he also appreciated Beethoven's genius from the very first and received by way of thanks the dedication of Symphony No. 1 in C, Op. 21.

83. The National Library on the Josephsplatz in Vienna. Coloured engraving by Carl Schütz, 1780. Historisches Museum of the City of Vienna.

Baron van Swieten also had a flat in this building, and often asked Beethoven to 'bring his nightcap' so that he could spend the night and play Bach's *Wohltemperiertes Klavier* to van Swieten, when the last guests had left. Our engraving shows the Josephsplatz before 1807, when a monument to the Emperor Joseph II, which still stands, was put up in the middle of the square. The Redoutensaal was in the rear of the building on the right-hand side.

84. Marie Therese, Empress of Austria (1772–1807). Portrait in oils by Joseph Kreutzinger. Kurt Stümpfl, Vienna.

Marie Therese, a granddaughter of the Empress Maria Theresa, was born a Princess Bourbon. Her father, Ferdinand IV, King of Naples and the Two Sicilies, had married Maria Carolina—of all Maria Theresa's daughters, the one most like her mother. Marie Therese was highly musical and had a trained soprano voice. Beethoven dedicated the Septet, Op. 20, to her.

85. Carl Ferdinand Amenda (1771–1836). Portrait in oils by Johann Samuel Benedictus Grüne. Beethovenhaus Bonn.

In the year 1798, Amenda, a young theologian from Kurland, arrived in Vienna and soon made Beethoven's acquaintance, playing first violin in a quartet by the composer; although Amenda left Vienna a year later, the friendship continued for many years.

86. String Quartet in F major, Op. 18 No. 1. Manuscript. Title-page of the first violin part with Beethoven's autograph dedication to Amenda. Beethovenhaus Bonn.

This manuscript shows an earlier chronological arrangement of the six Quartets contained in Op. 18: the present no. 1 was then no. 2. The first edition shows other changes as well compared to the text as found in this copy for Amenda.

87. Ludwig van Beethoven. Engraving by C. F. Riedl, possibly from a drawing by Gandolph Ernst Stainhauser von Treuberg. 1801: Leipzig, Bureau de Musique. Beethovenhaus Bonn.

88. Ludwig van Beethoven. Anonymous wax relief, attributed to Joseph Nikolaus Lang, 1815/18? Historisches Museum of the City of Vienna.

From the Historisches Taschenbuch *(1802):*

Although little happened, insofar as Vienna and her excellent composers are concerned, in the field of theatrical music, much else has otherwise been achieved in this art, which has reached a very high level. Particularly in the field of instrumental music, this year has been fortunate in a number of very successful works which have also been very well performed by both virtuosos and amateurs.

The Austrian composers showed the greatest diligence in instrumental composition and one may assert that the most successful of these works virtually leave all other contemporary works far behind. Father Haydn has given us in his Opus 77 three new quartets*. They reveal his simple effortless greatness as much as do his *Creation* or the heavenly *Seven Words:* the richest harmonies are at the service of the most beautiful melodies which, in their light flow, soon dance away with wanton high-spiritedness, or rise to rich, intimate and uninhibited heights. Beethoven wrote his First Symphony in C Major, a masterpiece which does honour alike to his powers of *81* invention and to his musical erudition. Equally beautiful and remarkable are its plan and its formal development. In it reign such a clear and luminous order, such a flow of agreeable melody and such a rich but never overwhelming instrumentation, that this symphony has every right to a place alongside those of Mozart and Haydn.

Hist. Tb. II, 198 ff.

Beethoven's dedication to Carl Amenda: *85, 86*

Dear Amenda. Accept this Quartet as a small token of our friendship. Every time you play it remember the days we spent together and at the same time how truly devoted to you was, and always will be

Your true and affectionate friend,
Ludwig van Beethoven.
Vienna, 1799, 25 June.

KAL 40.

Letter from Beethoven to Carl Amenda:

[Vienna. About summer 1799]
Today I received an invitation to Möthling [Mödling] in the country. I have accepted *198* it and am leaving this very evening for a few days there. This invitation was all the more welcome to me since my heart, broken as it is, would have suffered even more; although the main tempest has already spent itself, I am still not certain how my plan of resistance will succeed. Yesterday I received a proposal for a journey to Poland in September: travel and living expenses would not cost anything. Moreover I could amuse myself in Poland and there is also money to be earned there. Farewell,

---

*Correctly: two quartets. The third remained unfinished and was later published as Op. 103.

my dear A. and let me have news of you, from your stopping places en route, and also when you have reached your native land. Have a good journey and do not forget

Your Bthvn.

KAL 39. Anderson 32.

Countess Josephine von Deym writes to her sisters:

[Vienna, 10 December 1800]

. . . Yesterday we had music to honour the Duchess. I had to play and was, moreover, responsible for all the arrangements and supposed to see that everything went off well. We opened all the doors and everything was illuminated. I assure you, it was a splendid sight. Beethoven played the Sonata with violoncello, I played the last of the three violin Sonatas [Op. 12] accompanied by Schuppanzigh who, like all the others, played divinely. Then Beethoven, that real angel, let us hear his new Quartets [Op. 18], which have not been engraved yet, and are the greatest of their kind. The famous Kraft played cello, Schuppanzigh first violin. You can imagine what a treat it was for us! The Duchess was enchanted and everything went famously.

La Mara, *op cit.*, p. 14. (The Duchess Julia von Giovane, née Freiin von Mudersbach, lived at the Deyms' house in the Rotenturmstrasse. For the Deym family, see pp. 159 ff.)

85   *Letter from Beethoven to Carl Amenda in Mirben (Courland):*

Vienna, 1 July [1801]

My dear, my good Amenda, my kind-hearted friend, I received and read your last letter with intense feelings of emotion and with pain and pleasure at the same time. What can I compare with your faithfulness and your affection for me? Oh, how wonderful it is that you have always been so good to me. Indeed, I know that your friendship is precious to me above all others. You are no <u>Viennese friend:</u> no, you are one of those whom my own native land is wont to produce. How often I would have you near me, for your Beethoven lives a very unhappy life in conflict with nature and with the Creator. Many times have I cursed Him for subjecting His creatures to even the slightest jeopardy, which often crushes and destroys the most precious blossom. For you should know that my most precious gift, <u>my hearing,</u> has much deteriorated. I already noticed the symptoms when you were with me, but I kept silent. Now my condition is much worse, and whether or not it can be cured is yet to be determined. This condition is apparently connected with the state of my stomach. As far as my digestion is concerned I am almost completely recovered, but whether my hearing will improve, I have hopes, but faint ones; such diseases are the hardest to cure. . . . The affair of my hearing, <u>I beg you to keep as a great secret to be entrusted to no one whoever it may be.</u> Write to me often. Your letters, however short, bring me comfort, and do me good. I await a letter from you soon again, my dear friend. Do not hand on your quartet to anyone because I have altered it a great deal, since I have only now learned how to write quartets, as you will see when you receive them. And now, farewell, my dear good friend. If you should think that there is anything that I might do for you here, naturally it goes without saying, you should tell first of all

Your true and most devoted
L. v. Beethoven.

KAL 42. Anderson 53. (Amenda came to Vienna as tutor to the children of Prince Lobkowitz.)

The Allgemeine Musikalische Zeitung *reports on the Augarten Concerts, 1804:*

The second subscription of our Augarten Concerts opened in a very brilliant fashion . . . The concert began with Beethoven's great Symphony in D Major, a work full of new and original ideas, of great vigour, effective instrumentation and erudite development. It would undoubtedly gain, however, by the curtailment of a few sections as well as the sacrifice of certain far too unusual modulations. This Symphony was followed by a Concerto by Beethoven in C Minor . . . . This Concerto without doubt belongs among Beethoven's most beautiful compositions. It is worked out in a masterly fashion. Herr Ries, who took the solo part, is, at present, Beethoven's only pupil and his most fervent admirer. He had prepared the piece entirely under the direction of his teacher and gave proof of a very smooth expressive execution as well as unusual polish and sureness, overcoming with ease the most extraordinary difficulties. *89*

Allgemeine Musikalische Zeitung, Leipzig, No. 46, 15 August 1804.

> Ferdinand Ries, son of the first violin of the Bonn orchestra, came to Vienna to study with Beethoven. He later collaborated with Beethoven's old friend Wegeler in writing a short biographical sketch of his experiences with Beethoven which give many interesting eyewitness accounts of the composer.
>   One of the most famous pianists of that time was Mozart's pupil Johann Nepomuk Hummel, who later became Haydn's successor as Kapellmeister of the Esterházy band in Eisenstadt. Hummel played in Mozart's manner, as might be expected, which was in many respects widely different from that of Beethoven.

Ferdinand Ries describes Beethoven as a teacher:

Beethoven gave me his beautiful Concerto in C Minor (Op. 37) while still in manuscript, so that I might appear with it for the first time in public as his pupil. In fact I am the only person who appeared under this guise during his lifetime.

   Besides myself he recognized only the Archduke Rudolph as a pupil. Beethoven *138* himself conducted, and probably no concerto was ever so beautifully accompanied. We had two main rehearsals. I had begged Beethoven to compose a cadenza for me, which he refused to do and directed me to write one myself which he would then correct. Beethoven was very satisfied with my composition and made very few changes. Only there was an extremely brilliant and difficult passage in it which he liked but which seemed to him to be rather risky; he therefore told me to write another one. Eight days before the performance he asked to hear the cadenza again.

I played it and bungled the passage. He advised me again, albeit somewhat unwillingly, to change it. I did so, but the new one did not satisfy me. So I practised the other one diligently without, however, being too certain of it. In the public concert, during the cadenza, Beethoven sat down quietly. I could not persuade myself to choose the easier one. When I boldly began the difficult one, Beethoven made a violent start with his chair. But nevertheless it came off perfectly and Beethoven was so pleased that he cried 'Bravo' aloud. This electrified the whole audience and immediately assured me of a standing among the artists. Later, when he expressed his satisfaction over my performance, he added, 'Obstinate you certainly are! If you had bungled the passage I would have never given you another lesson!'

WRBN 113.

90   *Carl Czerny describes the playing of Johann Nepomuk Hummel:*

The perfection of the Fortepiano, in which the Viennese instrument-makers particularly excelled, soon gave the younger talents, who were still perfecting themselves, the opportunity either to discover or to develop further a new way of handling this instrument; namely the brilliant manner of playing which (around 1814) was characterized by a very marked staccato touch, an absolute cleanliness in mastering the greatest difficulties and by an extremely pleasing elegance and propriety of the decorative passages. Through the art of a Hummel, Meyerbeer, Moscheles, Kalkbrenner and others, it soon was recognized as the favourite and most satisfactory [school of playing].

The peculiar characteristics of this school are: complete mastery over all difficulties; the utmost velocity; delicacy and grace in the manifold decorations; the most perfect clarity calculated to a nicety for every type of ambience and a proper declamation which can be appreciated by everyone, combined with elegance and good taste.

Kerst I, 64 f.

The Ofner und Pesther* Taschenbuch *of 1800 writes about Beethoven:*

91, 92   Today [7 May] Academy of Herr Beethover [sic] and Herr Punto . . . Who is this Beethoven? Such a name is not known in German musical history. Punto is, of course, very well known . . . Three weeks before his [Punto's] concert in Ofen-Pesth, Punto appeared in Vienna in a concert in partnership with a certain Beethoven.

The Ungarische Kurier *of 1800 reports on the festivities in honour of the birthday of the Archduchess Alexandra Pavlovna**, wife of the Palatine Joseph, which took place from 3 to 7 May:*

3 May [in Pesth]: Carousel – on the same evening [in Ofen] performance of a play *Die seltsame Audienz* [The Unusual Audience] [author and performers not given].

*Ofen-Pesth: today's Budapest.   **Alexandra Pavlovna – daughter of the Russian Tsar Paul I and sister of Alexander I.

5 May: In Pesth, theatrical performance. A ballet by the Vienna Imperial Royal Court Ballet Master Muzzarelli was performed.

6 May: The citizens of Pesth gave a ball in honour of the Princess. After the ball there was a gala banquet.

7 May: [As the closing event of the festivities] Carousel, after which a concert was given in the theatre, at which a famous musician by the name of Beethoven drew the attention of all those present by his artistic playing on the Fortepiano.

Deutsche Musiker Zeitung, official journal of the Union of German Musicians, 1927, no. 38, p. 840.

The Allgemeine Musikalische Zeitung *reports on the concert given by Punto and Beethoven at the Burgtheater on 18 April 1800:*

The famous Punto is at present in Vienna. Recently he gave a concert in the Hoftheater in which there was a sonata for Fortepiano and hunting horn, composed by Beethoven and performed by him and Punto, which was such a success and pleased so much that, despite the new theatre rules which prohibit repetitions and loud applause, the virtuosi were nevertheless persuaded by the very loud applause which greeted them when the piece was finished to start at the beginning and play the whole thing through once again. 92

Allgemeine Musikalische Zeitung, Leipzig, No. 40, 2 July 1800.

From the diary of Count Zinzendorf:

[original French, 30 January 1801]:
The grand concert for the benefit of the wounded in the large *Redoutensaal* . . . Punto's hunting horn could not be heard at the back of the hall.

Programme of the concert on 30 January 1801:

A Sonata on the Pianoforte, composed and played by Herr van Beethoven and accompanied on the [French] horn by Herr Punto . . . .

HJB II, 59.

Wiener Zeitung of 7 February 1801, No. 11:

The recently announced Musical Academy for the benefit of wounded in the Imperial-Royal Army took place on 30 January inst. to the great pleasure of all the audience . . . . Herr v. Beethoven played on the pianoforte a sonata of his own composition which was accompanied by Herr Punto on the French horn. Both fully came up to the expectations which the public cherish for these masters of their art.

Countess Josephine von Deym writes to her sisters:

[2 May 1801]

Recently we also had a charming concert here: Punto, Beethoven, Schuppanzigh, Zmeskall. You can imagine that something good would come out of that. Punto plays really delightfully. They all lunched with us, and then we made music all the afternoon: the Sonata by Beethoven with the horn. Then the new Quintet with piano [Op. 16] and lots of other beautiful things. Punto talked a lot about you and said, or rather paid me the compliment, that I was very like you. He is leaving, or has already left, for Prague.

La Mara, *op. cit.*, p. 17.

Kapellmeister Friedrich Starcke tells Music-Director Gassner in Karlsruhe about Beethoven:

At that time, in 1812, Beethoven lived on the Mölker Bastei. After breakfast, which consisted of very good coffee (which Beethoven habitually prepared himself in a glass machine), Starcke begged for a breakfast for heart and soul, and Beethoven improvised in three different styles – first in *legato*, second in *fugato*, in which a subject with semiquaver was worked out divinely and in the most wonderful fashion, and thirdly in a chamber style, wherein Beethoven was able to combine the greatest difficulties with his particular fancy.

Starcke, in order to show his respect for Beethoven, had had his horn brought and proposed playing the F Major Sonata [Op. 17] with him. Beethoven accepted with pleasure. But it happened that the Fortepiano was tuned exactly a half-tone too low. Starcke said he would tune his horn half a tone down; Beethoven objected, remarking that this would spoil the effect; he himself would rather transpose half a tone higher (that is, to play in F sharp instead of F natural). They began and Beethoven played admirably well: the passages rolled so clearly and beautifully that one would never have guessed he was transposing. Beethoven also praised Starcke, telling him that he had never heard the Sonata with such feeling, he found the pianissimo particularly excellent. The whole was a breakfast fit for the gods.

Kerst I, 240.

Ferdinand Ries recalls Beethoven's duel with Steibelt:

93 When Steibelt arrived in Vienna armed with his great Parisian reputation, many of Beethoven's friends were worried for fear he might injure Beethoven's reputation.
94 Steibelt did not call on him. They first met one evening at Count Fries' where Beethoven played for the first time his new Trio in B-Flat for piano, clarinet and violoncello (Opus 11). In this work the pianist cannot show himself off to any great advantage. Steibelt listened to it with a certain air of condescension, paid a few compliments and felt himself certain of victory. He played a Quintet of his own composition, improvised and also made a great effect with his *tremulandos* which, at that time, constituted a great novelty. Beethoven could not be induced to play any

134

more. Eight days later there was another concert at Count Fries. Steibelt again played a quintet with much success and in addition (and this was quite evident) had prepared a brilliant improvisation, choosing as a theme the subject of the variations of Beethoven's Trio. This outraged not only Beethoven's supporters but also the composer himself. He now had to seat himself at the piano in order to improvise. He went in his usual, I must say ungracious, manner to the instrument as if half lunging towards it, grabbing, as he passed, the violoncello part of Steiblet's quintet, placed it (intentionally?) upside-down on the music stand and from the opening notes drummed out a theme with one finger. Offended and stimulated at the same time, he improvised in such a manner that Steibelt left the room before Beethoven had finished. He refused ever to meet him again; in fact he made it a condition that Beethoven should not be invited anywhere where his company was requested.

WRBN 81f.

Carl Czerny describes Beethoven's improvisation in Cock's London Musical Miscellany, *1852:*

[English original]
His improvisation was most brilliant and striking – in whatever company he might chance to be he knew how to achieve such an effect upon every listener, that frequently not an eye remained dry, while many would break out into loud sobs, for there was something wonderful in his expression in addition to the beauty and originality of his ideas and the spirited style of rendering them. After ending an improvisation of this kind, he would burst into loud laughter and banter his hearers on the emotion he had caused in them. 'You are fools' he would say. Sometimes he would feel himself insulated by these indications of sympathy. 'Who can live among such spoiled children' he would cry and only on that account (as he told me) he declined to accept an invitation, which the King of Prussia gave him after one of the extempory performances above described.

TDR II, 14.

Letters from Georg August Griesinger to Court Councillor Böttiger in Dresden, on the subject of Count Fries: 94–96

Vienna, 25 September 1811.
Countess Fries had prepared an entertainment for her husband on the day of St Maurice at Lengbach, where I stayed for a few days. Since Fries, however, only returned from Styria yesterday, richer by a beautiful manor which he had purchased there, the feast at Lengbach will therefore be celebrated tomorrow and I cannot possibly fail to honour this charming and precious friend with my presence . . . .

Vienna, 1 September 1819.
. . . Yesterday the solemn burial of Countess Fries took place in Vöslau. The procession first moved to the neighbouring church in Gainfahrn . . . where every step   95

reminded me of the happiest hours. Count Fries left today with his children for Styria. Seclusion, occupation and smiling surroundings are the most effective cure after such a shock . . . .

Vienna, 13 December 1826.

. . . The beautiful Vöslau has been acquired by the banker Baron Geimüller for 91,000 Florins Convention money, without the farmlands, which are worth about 30,000 Florins. The Fries Palace in the city went to the banker Sina for 388,000 Florins Convention money. This entire sum goes to the creditors and not a penny to the children.

Autograph. Sächsische Landesbibliothek, Dresden.

Baroness du Montet writes about Count Fries:

On that evening [at the reception given by the Marquis of Marialva in the Augarten in 1817] Countess Fries, née Princess Hohenlohe, wore a necklace and tiara of almost monstrous pearl drops. These pearls were a part of the purchase price which the widow of King Murat paid to Count Fries for a country estate. The entailed estate of Count Fries was of an absolutely incalculable value . . . Add to that his flourishing banking house . . . all that has vanished . . . his beautiful and virtuous wife died several years before he did. It was possible to keep the state of affairs from her, but was the Count able also to keep his indiscretions secret from her? A French actress, a small, yellow-complexioned and ugly slut, Mademoiselle Lombard . . . was the evil spirit who fastened herself on to the Count . . . . One of his daughters became a governess . . . .

Du Montet 146.

Förster's reminiscences of Beethoven and the Razumovsky Quartet:

He remembered Beethoven very clearly and had seen him often, from earliest childhood until he entered the military service as a cadet, that is, from 1803 to 1813. That Beethoven, after Albrechtsberger had retired, regarded Förster as the leading teacher of counterpoint and composition in Vienna, is known well enough from other sources and is fully confirmed by the information given by his son. On Beethoven's advice Förster had that short *Introduction to Ground Bass* printed in 1805 which was published by Breitkopf & Härtel and was especially recommended by the *Allgemeine Musikalische Zeitung* of 15 October 1808. A few years later Count Razumovsky requested Beethoven to teach him musical theory and particularly quartet composition. Beethoven would not accept him personally as a pupil, but urgently recommended his friend Förster who was thereupon appointed. The son remembers that the Count's carriage used to come at the appointed hour two or three times a week to take his father to the Palace in the Landstrasse suburb. The evening hours had been chosen [for these lessons]: Frau Förster often made use of the carriage and visited her friend Frau Weiss, the wife of the viola player, while their husbands were busy with Razumovsky. In those years Förster's house was the favourite gathering place of the most capable composers and amateurs. Among these were Beethoven, Nikolaus van Zmeskall, 'a somewhat stiff gentleman with a shock of white hair', Ignaz Schuppanzigh, 'a small fat man with a big paunch', Franz Weiss, 'tall and gaunt', Joseph Linke the lame violoncellist, Heinrich Eppinger the Jewish amateur violinist, the young Joseph Mayseder, J. N. Hummel and others whose names Herr Förster can no longer remember.

43

65, 66

90

These quartet meetings used to take place regularly on Sunday mornings and Thursday evenings. In those years Beethoven often spent other evenings with Förster, and the conversation generally turned to matters of musical theory and composition. In spite of the considerable difference in their ages (22 years), their friendship was intimate and sincere. The older man not only admired and valued the genius of the younger but also respected him as a man, and spoke of him not just as a great composer but, in spite of his rough and unfriendly, nay even uncouth, manner, as an honourable and noble character. Finally, we come to the fact that in later years Beethoven recommended Förster as his 'old master' to pupils. The supposition that Beethoven studied quartet composition with Förster is not in the least fanciful or unnatural; similarly, he took instruction in counterpoint from Albrechtsberger and in operatic composition from Salieri.

TDR II, 184 f. (The son of the well-known composer Emanuel Aloys Förster related, when an old man, his reminiscences of Beethoven to Thayer.)

Förster's son describes Beethoven as a piano teacher:

He remembered that Beethoven, of his own accord, gave him piano lessons, but that in order to have them he had to get up at 6 o'clock in the morning and run down the cold stairs, and that as a child of barely six years. Once, he came screaming back up again because his teacher had beat him on the fingers with one of those iron or steel needles with which the coarse jackets worn by the working classes are knitted.

Kerst I, 71.

Cipriani Potter recalls Beethoven and Förster:

Beethoven advised him [Potter] to take a teacher, as he himself did not give lessons, but wanted to look over all his work. When Potter asked him whom he would recommend as a teacher, Beethoven said, 'I have lost my Albrechtsberger, and have no confidence in anyone else.' On Beethoven's recommendation, however, Potter took lessons from Förster, with whom he studied for so long that his teacher finally said to him he had studied enough and now only needed practical work in composition. When Potter told this to Beethoven, the latter answered that one can never cease to

97

In 1800, the beautiful young Giulietta, Countess Guicciardi, took Viennese society by storm. She became Beethoven's pupil and he fell in love with her. The match was, of course, hopeless because of the difference in their ranks, but the beautiful countess has been immortalized as the recipient of perhaps the most famous piano sonata ever written, the so-called 'Moonlight' Sonata in C-sharp Minor, Op. 27, No. 2. Giulietta married a third-rate composer of ballets, Robert Count von Gallenberg, and the couple thereafter left Vienna to settle in Naples, where, incidentally, Countess Gallenberg carried on a love affair with Prince Hermann von Pückler-Muskau. Her marriage with Gallenberg was, in any case, a disastrous failure. Part of the desperation of the 'Heiligenstädter Testament' is certainly the result of Beethoven's broken love affair with Countess Giulietta.

Countess Josephine von Deym writes to her sisters:

[January 1801]

102 . . . Julie Guicciardi is creating a furore here. They refer to her only as the beautiful Guicciardi, and you know that she understands how to capitalize on it. She is intimate with the Gallenbergs.

La Mara, *op. cit.*, p. 14.

Letter from Beethoven to Dr Franz Gerhard Wegeler:

Vienna, 16 November [1801]

. . . I am now living a more agreeable life, inasmuch as I go about more among my fellow men. You can hardly imagine how empty, how sad my life has been for the past two years. My weak hearing haunted me everywhere, like a ghost, and so I avoided people. I must have appeared like a misanthrope, and yet I am so far from being one. This change has been brought about by a lovable charming girl who loves me and whom I love. So after two years I enjoy a few happy moments and this is the first time I feel that marriage could bring happiness with it. Unfortunately she is not of my class – and now – I naturally could not marry – I must somehow keep going as best I can . . . .

KAL 53. Anderson 54. (Count Wenzel Robert von Gallenberg, born 20 December 1783, married the Countess Julia (Giulietta) Guicciardi on 3 November 1803 and took her to Naples, where he was engaged to write ballet music.)

Beethoven's Dedication to Countess Guicciardi:

104 **Sonata** quasi una **Fantasia** for the Cembalo or Piano-Forte/composed and dedicated/to Mademoiselle Countess/**Giulietta Guicciardi**/by/Luigi van Beethoven/Opus 27, No. 2/ In Vienna care of Gio. Cappi on St. Michael's Square No. 5 . . . . [March 1802]

KHV 67.

Letter from Prince Hermann von Pückler-Muskau to Countess Gallenberg:

[original French]   26 February 1810 Strasbourg

I am still here, my dear Julie, and as happy as I can be away from you. Three beautiful women who resemble you make my sojourn here quite pleasant . . . . Moreover, those ladies, it seems to me, do not appear to be ignorant of what is agreeable to women, namely, to be mistresses in their own house . . . . The husbands naturally fall into that category of horned animals [i.e. cuckolds] and, if by chance one comes across one who constitutes an exception to the rule, that is a case of what naturalists term a freak of nature . . . . Farewell, my well beloved Julie, love me always a little and remember that you have no better friend than me in the whole world . . . .

Anton Schindler's sister, Frau Egloff, speaks to Ludwig Nohl:

She [Countess Gallenberg] was not happy. What woman could be, with a husband like that. She lived always a very retired life in the same house with her husband, by whom she had several children, but they saw each other only at the table.

A. Chr. Kalischer, *Beethoven und Seine Zeitgenossen: Beethoven's Frauenkreis*, Berlin 1909, I, 184 ff.

From Beethoven's conversation books:

February 1823
[original partly French]
[Beethoven:] I was very much loved by her, far more than her husband ever was – [there follows a cancelled passage] – he was really more her lover than I was. But from her I heard about his poverty and I found a rich man who gave me 500 florins to help him out.

[Beethoven:] He was always my enemy and that is the reason why I did him all the good that I could.

[Schindler:] Whereupon he also said to me, 'He is an intolerable man', undoubtedly out of sheer gratitude. But, Father, forgive them, for they know not what they do!

Madame the Countess?

Was she rich?

She has a pretty face, down to here!

Mons. G[allenberg].

Is it a long time since she was married to Mons. de Gallenberg?

[Beethoven:] She was born Guicciardi.

She was already his wife before [she went to] Italy, and she came to see me in tears, but I spurned her.

Hercules at the crossroads.

If I had wanted to spend my strength and my life in this manner, what would have been left over for the nobler better part?

Konv. Sch. II, 363. Autograph in the Berlin State Library.

Countess Giulietta Gallenberg speaks to Otto Jahn about Beethoven (1852):

Beethoven was her teacher. He allowed her to play his compositions, but was exceedingly severe with her until the interpretation was correct to the very last tiny detail. He insisted on a light touch. He himself was often violent, throwing the music around and tearing it up. He refused payment, although he was very poor. But he would accept linen, under the pretext that the Countess herself had sewed it. He also taught Countess Odescalchi and Baroness Ertmann. His pupils either went to him, or he came to them. He did not like to play his own compositions, but he would improvise. At the slightest disturbance he would get up and go away. Count Brunswick, who played the violoncello, adored him, as did also his sisters Therese and Countess Deym. Beethoven had given the Rondo in G [Op. 51, No. 2] to Countess Gallenberg Guicciardi, but asked for it back because he had to dedicate something to Countess Lichnowsky, and then dedicated to her the Sonata [Op. 27, No. 2]. Beethoven was very ugly, but noble, sensitive and cultured. Most of the time he was shabbily dressed.

68, 124

117

118, 120

TDR II, 307. (For Princess [*recte*] Odescalchi and Baroness Ertmann, see pp. 101 and 195ff.)

Beethoven's Will written at Heiligenstadt:

105

    For my brothers Carl and [Johann] Beethoven.

O ye men, who consider or declare me to be hostile, obstinate or misanthropic, how unjust you are to me, for you do not know the secret cause of that which makes me seem so to you. My heart and my soul, since my childhood, have ever been filled with tender feelings of good will: I was even ready to perform great deeds. But consider that for six years now I have been afflicted with an incurable condition, made worse by incompetent physicians, deceived for year after year by the hope of an improvement and now obliged to face the prospect of a permanent disability [cancelled word] (the healing of which may take years or may even prove to be quite impossible). Born with an ardent, lively temperament and also inclined to the distractions of society, I was, at an early age, obliged to seclude myself and to live my life in solitude. If, once in a while, I attempted to ignore all this, oh, how harshly would I be driven back by the doubly sad experience of my bad hearing; yet it was not possible for me to say: speak louder, shout, because I am deaf. Alas, how would it be possible for me to admit to a weakness of the <u>one sense</u> that should be perfect to a higher degree in me than in others, the one sense which I once possessed in the highest perfection, a perfection that few others of my profession have ever possessed. No, I cannot do it. So forgive me if you see me draw back from your company which I would so gladly share. My misfortune is doubly hard to bear, inasmuch as I will surely be misunderstood. For me there can be no recreation in the society of others, no intelligent conversation, no mutual exchange of ideas; only as much as is required by the most pressing needs can I venture into society. I am obliged to live like an outcast. If I venture into the company of men, I am overcome by a burning terror, inasmuch as I fear to find myself in the danger of allowing my condition to be noticed. So it has been for this last half year which I have spent in the country. Advised by my sensible physician to spare my hearing as much as possible, he [only: erased] to a certain extent encouraged my natural disposition: although sometimes torn by the desire for companionship, I allowed myself to be tempted into it. But what a humiliation when someone standing next to me could hear from the distance the sound of a flute whereas <u>I heard nothing</u>. Or, someone could <u>hear the shepherd singing</u>, and that also I did not hear. Such experiences brought me near to despair, it would have needed little for me to put an end to my life. It was <u>art</u> only which held me back. Ah, it seemed to me to be impossible to leave the world before I had brought forth all that I felt destined to bring forth. So I endured this miserable existence – miserable indeed. For I have so sensitive a body that even a slight change can transport me from the highest to the most wretched states. <u>Patience</u> – it is said – is what I must now choose as my guide. This I have done – and I hope that my resolution will remain firm until the implacable Parcae are pleased to break the thread. Perhaps my condition will improve, perhaps it will not. I am obliged – when only in my twenty-eighth year – to become a philosopher, and that is not easy, and for an artist it is harder than for any other. Almighty God, Thou lookest down into my innermost being; Thou knowest that the love of mankind and the desire to do good dwell therein. Oh men, when you once shall read this, reflect then, that you have wronged me, and let some unfortunate be comforted that he has found one like himself who, in the face of all the obstacles which nature has placed in his path, has yet done all that lay in <u>his</u> power to be numbered among the ranks of worthy artists and men – You, my brothers Carl and [Johann], as soon as I am dead, if Professor Schmid be still alive, request him in my name to describe my malady, and let him attach this written document to the report of my ailment [an illegible word: erased], so that, as far as possible, the world will be reconciled with me after my death. At the same time I hereby declare both of you to be [my: crossed out] the heirs of my small estate (if such it can be termed), divide it justly, bear with and help each other. What harm you have done to me, that, you know, has long since been forgiven. I thank you, my brother Carl in particular, for the affection which you have shown me in these latter times. My wish is that [I: crossed out] you may lead a better life and one more [full of: crossed out] free of care than mine. Recommend <u>virtue</u> to your [after: crossed out] children: that alone, and not money, can ensure happiness. I speak from experience: it was virtue which sustained me in my misery; next I thank my art that I did not end my life by suicide. Farewell – love each other. I thank all my friends, in particular <u>Prince Lichnowski</u> and <u>Professor Schmidt</u>. I wish the instruments from Prince L. to be preserved by one of you, but no of bread and butter, cold meats and wine. In a friendly way he invited everybody to help themselves, which they did even with both hands, so that everone was once again in a good humour. Then the Prince requested that the oratorio be tried out once more, so that if might come off well in the evening and Beethoven's first work of this kind be presented to the public in a worthy manner. So the rehearsal began again.

WRBN 76.

From the Diary of Joseph Carl Rosenbaum:

Tuesday 5 April 1803. I went to see Fuchs where we talked about the performance of Bethowen's cantata *Christ on the Mount of Olives* today which is sure to come off poorly since Braun is giving the *Creation* in the B[urg] Th[eatre] with both orchestras for *78, 79* the benefit of poor theatre folk.

Wednesday the 6th... I spoke to Willmann at the Lusthaus about Bethowen's concert. He praised it, although I heard the opposite opinion from everyone else. Eberl told me that in yesterday's concert Bethowen did not come up to the justifiable expectations of the public and that nothing was really worthy of a great master.

HJB V, 107.

Anton Schindler writes about Beethoven's Christ on the Mount of Olives:

The composer agreed with all this, inasmuch as in later years he declared without reserve that it was a 'mistake' to have treated the part of Christ in a modern operatic manner. The fact that the work remained unperformed after its first performance, as well as the unusually drawn-out delay before its appearance in print (about 1810), would indicate that the author was not particularly satisfied with the work and probably made considerable changes in it.

Schindler I, 91.

Among the many virtuosi of one kind or the other passing through Vienna, a particularly interesting man was George Polgreen Bridgetower, the mulatto son of Prince Nicolaus I Esterházy's personal page, August. Beethoven wrote the A Major Violin Sonata, Op. 47, for Bridgetower in 1803, but afterwards they got into a row over a girl and Beethoven dedicated the Sonata to Rodolphe Kreutzer.

Beethoven's dedication to George Polgreen Bridgetower: *108*

Autograph of the 'Kreutzer-Sonata' in A Major, Op. 47:
'Mulattick Sonata. Composed for the mulatto Brischdauer, great lunatick and mulattick composer.*

Betty Matthews, 'George Polgreen Bridgetower', *The Music Review*, February 1968, p. 22.

*'Sonata mulattica. Composta per il Mulatto Brischdauer gran pazzo e compositore mulattico'.

Monday the 16th [May 1803]... in the evening with Kuhnel and Tomasini in the W[ieden] Th[eatre]. *Lodoiska* by Cherubini... there I met for the first time the mulatto (son of the Negro August who served as footman in the household of Prince Niklas*) Bridgtower (Brischdauer), first violinist of the Prince of Wales, and invited him for dinner tomorrow.

Tuesday 24 May 1803 ... Concert of the violinist Bridgtower in the Augarten at 12 o'clock noon ... it was not very full but a select audience.

HJB V, 110. (Bridgetower and Beethoven played the 'Kreutzer' Sonata.)

Note in Bridgetower's copy of the Sonata in A Major, Op. 47:

[original English]
When I accompanied him in this concerted Sonata, in Vienna, I altered, during the repeat of the first part of the Presto, the run of bar 18 of the Pianoforte part of this movement in the following way:

He leaped out of his seat, embraced me and said once more, 'My dear boy'. Then he held down the open pedal during this run on the note of C until the ninth bar.

Beethoven's expression in the Andante was so chaste, always a characteristic of the execution of his slow movements, that everyone unanimously insisted that the passage be repeated twice.

George Polgreen Bridgetower.

TDR II, 396.

Mercure de France reviews Bridgetower's first appearance in a Concert spirituel *on 13 April 1789 in Paris:*

[original French]
A curious debut which aroused much interest was that of M. Bridge-Tower, a young Negro from the colonies, who played several concertos for the violin with a neatness,

*Prince Nicolaus Esterházy ('The Magnificent'), died 1790.

(that is, a letter once a year from me) I hope he will know nothing about it. I hear all the time that you are constantly improving your fortunate position and that pleases me very much indeed. Give my greetings to all your family and all those others whom you think would appreciate my greetings. Please give me an early reply.

Beethoven.

Kal 143. Anderson 99. (The letter deals with the 'Kreutzer' Sonata.)

1804 is the year of the *Eroica*, the work which, more than any other except Beethoven's own Ninth, changed the history of the symphony. Its huge size – twice the length of any Haydn or Mozart symphony – and vast complexity made it more than problematical for many of Beethoven's contemporaries. Up to now, with very few exceptions, Beethoven's compositions had been almost unmitigatedly successful; with the *Eroica*, Beethoven began to move forward faster than many of his contemporaries could comprehend. Yet even the most difficult of Beethoven's compositions, such as the last String Quartets, always had their staunch admirers among what was becoming known as the Beethoven 'clique'. And such an astute critic as Haydn's biographer, Georg August Griesinger, summed up public opinion in his usually perspicacious way when writing to the publishers Breitkopf & Härtel after the first public performance in 1805. Much of the autograph was completed in Döbling. Beethoven originally intended to dedicate the Symphony to Napoleon but, as the documents show, he became furious when Napoleon crowned himself Emperor and tore up the dedication; later, Beethoven conceived a furious dislike of all things French.

The history of the *Eroica* involves another of Beethoven's patrons: Franz Joseph Max, Prince von Lobkowitz, for whom Haydn had written the Quartets Op. 77. Lobkowitz's private orchestra played the first performances of many Beethoven compositions in the first fifteen years of the nineteenth century.

110, 111   *Title-page of the first edition of the* Eroica *(October 1806):*

SINFONIA EROICA/for two Violins, Viola, two Flutes, two Oboes, two Clarinets/ two Bassoons, three Horns, two Trumpets, Kettle-drums and Bass/composed/to celebrate the memory of a great Man/and dedicated to his Most Serene Highness the Prince of Lobkowitz/ by /Luigi van Beethoven/Op. 55 /No. 3 of the Symphonies/ In Vienna/at the Bank of Arts and Industry in the Hohenmarkt No. 582 /[l.:] 512 [r.:] F9.

KHV 129. (The price, in the earliest copies, is written in by hand.)

Note regarding the particular length of the work, on the first violin part:

[original Italian]
This symphony being purposely written much/longer than is usual, should be performed nearer/the beginning rather than at the end of a concert and/shortly after an overture, an aria and a/concerto: so that if heard too late it will not/lose for the listener already tired out by/previous performances, its own/proposed effect./The part of the third horn is arranged/in such a manner that it can be played equally/on the first horn or on the second.

KHV 129.

152

Dr Andreas Bertolini tells Otto Jahn on 22 September and 4 November 1852 about the origins of the Eroica:

The first idea for the Eroica Symphony came to Beethoven from Bonaparte's expedition to Egypt; the rumour of Nelson's death in the Battle of Aboukir occasioned the Funeral March.

Kerst II, 194. (Dr Bertolini was Dr Malfatti's assistant and Beethoven's friend and medical adviser.)

Christoph Kuffner tells Music Director Krenn about Beethoven's opinion of the Eroica:

Court Councillor Kuffner told Music Director Krenn that he had lived with Beethoven in Heiligenstadt and had often gone with him to Nussdorf to eat fish at the inn *Zur Rose*. Once, when Beethoven was in good humour, Krenn asked which of his symphonies was his favourite, and he answered pleasantly, 'Eh, Eh, the Eroica.' Krenn, 'I would have thought the C Minor.' Beethoven, 'No, the Eroica.'

Kerst II, 196. (The poet Christoph Kuffner had been a friend of Beethoven.)

From the periodical, Der Freimüthige, *No. 83, 26 April 1805:*

One party, Beethoven's most special friends, contend that this particular symphony [No. 3, *Eroica*] is a masterpiece, that this is exactly the true style for music of the highest type and that if it does not please now it is because the public is not sufficiently cultivated in the arts to comprehend these higher spheres of beauty; but after a couple of thousand years its effect will not be lessened. The other party absolutely denies any artistic merit to this work. They claim that it reveals the symptoms of an evidently unbridled attempt at distinction and peculiarity, but that neither beauty, true sublimity nor power have anywhere been achieved either by means of unusual modulations, by violent transitions or by the juxtaposition of the most heterogeneous elements – when, for example, a Pastorale in the grandest style is developed through violent rents in the basses, by three horns and other similar tricks, a certain, but not desirable, originality can be achieved without much effort. But the creation of something beautiful and sublime, not the production of something merely unusual and fantastic, is the true expression of genius. Beethoven himself, in his own early works, has proven the truth of this statement. The third, very small party stand in the middle. They concede that there are many beautiful things in the symphony, but admit that the continuity often appears to be completely confused and that the endless duration of this longest and perhaps most difficult of all symphonies is tiring even for the expert; for a mere amateur it is unbearable. One wishes that H[err] v[an] B[eethoven] would use his recognized great talent to present us with works similar to his first two Symphonies in C and D, to his agreeable Septet in E flat, the spirited Quintet in D Major [C Major?] and others of his early compositions which will always assure B. a place among the foremost instrumental

less generous Emperor took him at his word, since he could hardly refuse a reward after such brilliant successes, but in order to whittle down the reward, acceded to his request insofar as he lent a considerable sum of money to the trustee of the young Prince Lobkowitz at a low rate of interest. In this manner the Lobkowitz fortunes were enabled to recover during the long trusteeship and the present Prince, who is more economical but less generous than his father, once again enjoys a large fortune.

Thürheim I, 137 f.

The Vaterländische Blätter *about Prince Lobkowitz:*

In the reigning Prince of Lobkowitz we admire a bass voice of rare beauty, in tonal quality as well as range and delivery.

Die Vaterländischen Blätter für den Österreichischen Kaiserstaat, Vol. I, 51, Vienna 1808.

Georg August Griesinger recalls his meeting with Beethoven:

When we were both young, I still an Attaché and Beethoven only renowned as a pianist but little known as a composer, we met at Prince Lobkowitz's. A gentleman who regarded himself as a great connoisseur in the arts began a conversation with Beethoven which turned on the position in life and the ambition of poets.

'I should like', said Beethoven with a pleasant frankness, 'to be relieved of all bargaining and haggling with publishers and find one who would decide to assure me a fixed annual income for the rest of my life, for which he would have the right to publish everything that I compose; nor would I be indolent in composing. I think that Goethe has such an arrangement with Cotta and, if I am not mistaken, Handel's London publisher had one with him.'

'My dear young man,' the gentleman said reprovingly, 'you should not complain; you are neither a Goethe nor a Handel, nor is it likely that you will ever be; such spirits are no longer born.'

Beethoven gritted his teeth, threw a derisive glance at the gentleman and said nothing further to him. Later he expressed himself rather violently about the effrontery of the man.

Prince Lobkowitz tried to bring Beethoven back to a more amiable mood and said in a friendly way, when the conversation turned on that same man, 'My dear Beethoven, the gentleman did not mean to offend you. It is a well known fact that most people do not want to believe that one of their younger contemporaries can achieve as much in the arts as the older ones, or those who are dead or who already have made a name for themselves.'

'Unfortunately true, Serene Highness,' answered Beethoven, 'but I do not like or want to have anything to do with people who refuse to believe in me because I have not yet achieved a wide fame for myself.'

At that time many people used to shake their heads and say that Beethoven was

116

arrogant and conceited. If they had been able to see into the future they would have regarded that gentleman as impudent.

Kerst I, 86 f.

Letter from Beethoven to Ferdinand Ries:

[Oberdöbling, Summer 1803]

You will undoubtedly already know that I am here – go to Stein and find out if he cannot let me have an instrument here – to be paid for – I am afraid to have mine brought here. Come out here this evening at about seven o'clock. My lodgings are at Oberdöbling No. 4, on the <u>left side</u> of the street where one goes down the hill   *114*
to Heiligenstadt.

Beethoven.

KAL I, 110. Anderson 80.

Letter from Beethoven to Ferdinand Ries:

[Baden, *c.* 20 July 1804]

. . . Now, I beg you, my dear Ries, as soon as you have received this letter, go to my brother, the apothecary, and tell him that I am about to leave Baden in a few days and   *115*
that he should rent lodgings for me in Döbling as soon as you have spoken to him. I nearly returned today; I cannot stand this place and I am tired of it. For heaven's sake insist that he engage the rooms at once because I want to settle in Döbling immediately . . . .

Your friend
Beethoven.

KAL 134. Anderson 93.

Friedrich Starcke, in his Memoirs, describes his visit to Beethoven:

Starcke had Beethoven's sympathy, he was the piano-teacher of his nephew Karl and was often invited to mid-day dinner at Beethoven's. Particularly remarkable was one mid-day meal at Döbling (1820 or 21). Beethoven at that time had summer lodgings in Unter-Döbling. Starcke visited him often. Once he found only the cook at home. Starcke left his compliments and promised to make an appearance in the afternoon. 'When Beethoven came home he asked the cook where I had gone to; she could not tell him because she did not know. Beethoven guessed that I would be eating at the inn called *Zum Finger* (because we often met there) and found me, in the summer-house, at the soup course. The waiter wanted to serve the beef, but Beethoven sent it back and said to me, "You'll eat your beef in an hour at my house." We walked to-gether as far as the chapel of St John and there we stopped' (Beethoven had already told Starcke earlier that, as a boy, he had played the organ). Starcke being at that time on friendly terms with Herr von Albert, to whom this church belongs, it was easy to get the keys of the church and of the organ. Making use of this golden opportunity, Starcke asked Beethoven to give him some spiritual food before dinner, on the organ.

Beethoven was willing enough and played for almost half an hour. This organ programme consisted of two Preludes, the first one *con amore* with an agreeable registration (Beethoven's hearing was at that time still a condition which enabled him to hear this *piano* on the organ), the second consisted of *fugato* movements: it was a feast of joy for Starcke.

Kerst I, 242.

Ferdinand Ries writes about the Eroica:

110, 111
105

In 1803 Beethoven composed his third symphony (now known as the *Sinfonia eroica*) in Heiligenstadt, a village about one and a half hours from Vienna. When he was composing, Beethoven often had some particular object in mind although he frequently laughed and roared over musical painting, particularly in its more trumpery aspects. Sometimes even *The Creation* and *The Seasons* suffered thereby; not that Beethoven would belittle Haydn's greater qualities, in fact he meted out the highest praise on many choruses and other things of Haydn. In this symphony Beethoven had Buonaparte in mind, but this was when he was First Consul. At that time Beethoven held him in the very highest esteem and compared him with the greatest of the Roman Consuls. Not only I myself but several of his closest friends had seen this symphony, already in full score, lying on his table; at the head of the title page was the word 'Buonaparte' and quite at the foot was written 'Luigi van Beethoven', but no other word. Whether or how the intervening gap was to be filled out I do not know. I was the first person who brought him the news that Buonaparte had declared himself Emperor. Thereupon he flew into a rage and cried out, 'He too is nothing but an ordinary man! Now he will trample underfoot all the Rights of Man and only indulge his ambition: he will now set himself on high, like all the others, and become a tyrant!' Beethoven went to the table, seized the title-page from the top, tore it up completely and threw it on the floor. The first page was written out anew and it was now that the symphony received the title *Sinfonia eroica*. Later Prince Lobkowitz bought this composition from Beethoven for his own use for a few years and it was

116

given in his palace several times. Here it once happened that Beethoven, who was himself conducting, in the second part of the first Allegro where it goes on for so long in half-notes on the off-beat, threw the orchestra out to such an extent that they had to start again from the beginning. In the same Allegro Beethoven has a wicked trick

117

for the horn; a few bars before the theme comes in again complete, Beethoven lets the horn indicate the theme where the two violins still play the chord of the second. For someone who is not familiar with the score this always gives the impression that the horn player has counted wrong and come in at the wrong place. During the first rehearsal of this symphony, which went appallingly, the horn-player, however, came in correctly. I was standing next to Beethoven and, thinking it was wrong, I said,

'That damned horn player! Can't he count properly? It sounds infamously wrong!'
I think I nearly had my ears boxed – Beethoven did not forgive me for a long time.

WRBN 77 ff.

Carl Czerny writes about the Eroica:

The so-called harmonic irregularities which are to be found in Beethoven's works can
be explained and justified on aesthetic and effective grounds, but they are suitable
only in those passages where Beethoven used them. It would be most foolhardy to
attempt to derive from them new rules for other composers. Moreover, such passages are by no means numerous in Beethoven's music and do not detract in the least
from its greatness. In two or three cases it would be, on the contrary, desirable to
eliminate them, namely, in the *Eroica*, the entrance into the theme [1st movement,
2nd part]. [There follow two bars of the score before the recapitulation with the E
flat theme in the horn part.]

Czerny 22.

Letter from Georg August Griesinger to Breitkopf und Härtel:

[13 February 1805]

. . . This much I can, however, assure you; that the Symphony has been heard at
Academies at Prince Lobkowitz's and at an active music-lover's named Wirth, with
unusual applause. That it is a work of genius, I hear from both admirers and detractors
of Beethoven. Some people say that there is more in it than in Haydn and Mozart,
that the Symphony-Poem has been brought to new heights! Those who are against it
find that the whole lacks rounding out; they disapprove of the piling up of colossal
ideas . . . . Eight days later a new Symphony by Eberl was given at Wirth's and
fourteen days later one by Kanne . . . . Kanne himself attended the burial of his
symphony.

Der Bär – Year Book of Breitkopf und Härtel for the year 1927. Wilhelm Hitzig, *Aus den Briefen Griesingers
an Breitkopf und Härtel entnommene Notizen über Beethoven*, p. 32.

Among Beethoven's most intimate friends were the young members of the Brunsvik family.
With Franz Count von Brunsvik Beethoven was actually so intimate that they used the 'Du'
form when addressing each other. Countess Therese was a faithful friend to Beethoven
throughout her life, and with Countess Josephine, Beethoven's friendship gradually grew
into something much deeper; he wanted very much to marry her in the winter of 1805, and
it was probably only his rather insecure economic situation that prevented her from agreeing
to the match. The Brunsviks, and also Count Joseph Deym (Josephine's husband till his
death in 1804), appear again and again throughout Beethoven's life. Giulietta, Countess
Guicciardi, was also a cousin of the young Brunsviks.

119 *Letter from Beethoven to Franz von Brunsvik:*

My friend, I cannot accept your refusal. I let <u>Oliva</u> depart alone on your account. I must have someone trustworthy with me if my everyday life is not to become a burden. I expect you at latest by the 12th of this month, perhaps even the 15th of this month, but unquestionably. This is a supreme command. It cannot be refused without the severe retribution and punishment; it must be followed unconditionally.

And now, keep well, my trusted friend, for we pray God to keep you under His merciful protection.

Given this morning immediately on rising from the coffee table.

Vienna, 4 July [1811]   Beethoven.

Since I do not know by what means you came into possession of the portrait,* do your best to bring it with you. We shall easily find a sympathetic artist to copy it, on the basis of friendship.

TDR III, 270. Anderson 318.

118 *From the Memoirs of Therese von Brunsvik:*

I was extremely weak and delicate, with a deformed spinal column. At the age of three this was combined with the so-called English disease. The nervous system in particular remained delicate.

107, 120 ... When we were in Vienna for those 18 remarkable days, my mother wished to obtain for her two daughters, Therese and Josephine, the priceless musical instruction of Beethoven. As Adalbert Rosti, a school-friend of my brother assured us, Beethoven could not be induced to accept a simple invitation. However, if Her Excellency would 98 take the trouble to climb the three flights of the spiral staircase in St Peter's Square and pay a call on him, he [Rosti] would vouch for success. And so it turned out. Taking my Beethoven Sonata with Violin and Violoncello accompaniment under my arm like a girl going to school, we went in. The immortal and adored Louis van Beethoven was most friendly and as courteous as he knew how to be. After a little small talk *de part et d'autre* he sat me down at his out-of-tune piano and I started right in, singing the violin and violoncello accompaniment, and managed to play quite well. This delighted him to such an extent that he promised to come daily to the Hotel *Zum Erherzog Carl* – at that time called *Goldene Greifen.* This was the last year of the previous century, in May. He came regularly and moreover often stayed, instead of an hour, from 12 o'clock until 4 or 5 o'clock and did not tire of holding down and bending my fingers, which I had been taught to raise and hold flat. This noble man must have been very pleased; for during all the sixteen days he did not miss a single one. We did not even feel hungry until 5 o'clock. My good mother hungered with us – but the Hotel people were much outraged – for at that time it was not customary to eat mid-day dinner at 5 o'clock in the afternoon.

TDR II, 304, and *'Beethoven,' dreizehn unbekannte Briefe an Josephine Gräfin Deym geb. v. Brunsvik*, ed. Joseph Schmidt-Görg, Bonn 1957, p. 7.

*The portrait could be the one of Therese Brunsvik found among Beethoven's effects. This possibility is strengthened by a letter of 2 February 1811 from Therese to her sister Josephine, reproduced below, p. 193.

89. Ferdinand Ries (1784–1838). Anonymous portrait in oils (by Möller, *c.* 1814?). Beethovenhaus Bonn.

Ferdinand Ries was the son of Bonn court musician Franz Anton Ries, first violin in the Elector's orchestra, who had given lessons to the young Beethoven. Now the rôle was reversed, and Beethoven became the teacher of Ferdinand, who studied piano with the master from 1801 to 1805. Later, Ferdinand Ries, together with Franz Gerhard Wegeler, published the famous *Biographische Notizen über Ludwig van Beethoven.*

90. Johann Nepomuk Hummel (1778–1837). Anonymous portrait in oils. Gesellschaft der Musikfreunde, Vienna.

An excellent pianist and a well-known composer, Hummel had been a pupil of Mozart's. After an extended concert tour which took him as far as London, Hummel returned to Vienna, where he soon made Beethoven's acquaintance. Hummel's pearly, brilliant and perhaps faintly superficial piano playing made an enormous impression on the Viennese public, and indeed, as a pianist, Hummel became a serious rival of Beethoven's.

91. View of the city Ofen and Pest (now Budapest). Coloured engraving, drawn and engraved by Joseph and Peter Schaffer.
Chlumec, Czechoslovakia.

Beethoven made a concert tour to Budapest in the company of the famous horn-player Wenzel Punto. Punto was a frequent guest of the aristocratic family of von Vegh, who had a hospitable house in Vereb and maintained a private string quartet. It is reported that Beethoven gave a concert with Punto in 1800 and both were subsequently expected at Vereb; but only Punto arrived, having had a difference of opinion with Beethoven.

92. Wenzel Punto (1746–1803). Engraving, partially etched, by Simon Charles Miger, from a drawing by Charles Nicolas Cochin the Younger, 1782. Österreichische Nationalbibliothek, Vienna.

Wenzel Punto, whose real name was Johann Wenzel Stich, was an excellent horn-player whom Mozart had admired and who taught Beethoven a great deal about the technique of his difficult instrument.

162

93. Daniel Steibelt (1765–1823).
Lithograph by Alfred François
Lemoine. Österreichische National-
bibliothek, Vienna.

Steibelt, another rival of Beethoven's
as a piano virtuoso, achieved considerable success in Prague with a concert
early in 1800 which brought him in
the respectable sum of 1800 Gulden.
At one point Steibelt engaged a girl to
accompany him on the tambourine,
which instrument excited the admiration and curiosity of Prague female
society. It is reported that, with his
tambourine-playing colleague, Steibelt
made a tidy profit on the side by giving
lessons on that instrument and by sell-
ing the actual tambourines themselves.
Steibelt's compositions were at one
time highly appreciated.

94. Soirée in the palace of Moritz Count von Fries in Vienna. Drawing by J. Fischer, 1800.
Historisches Museum of the City of Vienna. The original disappeared in 1945; from a
photograph in possession of H. C. Robbins Landon, Buggiano Castello, Italy.

163

95. Therese Countess von Fries, née Princess Hohenlohe-Waldenburg-Schillingsfürst (1779–1819). Pastel by Anette von Eckhardt after a drawing by C. Vogel, Vienna 1813. Chlumec, Czechoslovakia.

96. Moritz Count von Fries (1777–1826). Pastel by Anette von Eckhardt after a drawing by C. Vogel, Vienna 1813. Chlumec, Czechoslovakia.

Count Fries, an artistically minded member of a famous banking house, led a hospitable salon with his beautiful wife in their palace on the Josephsplatz. Fries was famous not only for his picture gallery and antiquities but also for his concerts and balls. Beethoven dedicated to him a whole series of works. By 1820, Count Moritz had gone through his huge inheritance; his palace and collections were sold by auction, but the income from this sale was not sufficient to cover the debts.

97. Emanuel Aloys Förster (1748–1823). Anonymous portrait in oils. Gesellschaft der Musikfreunde, Vienna.

Beethoven took lessons with Förster, who was a good composer, and whose string quartets Beethoven particularly admired; he used to refer to Förster affectionately as his 'old master'.

98. Petersplatz in Vienna. Coloured engraving by Carl Schütz, c. 1800. Historisches Museum of the City of Vienna.

About 1802, Beethoven took a flat on the Petersplatz. In 1852, Carl Czerny wrote: '... Beethoven lived somewhat later (about 1802) on the Petersplatz ... *vis-à-vis* my present flat on the fourth floor. ...'

165

102. Giulietta Countess Guicciardi, later Countess von Gallenberg (1784–1856). Anonymous miniature on ivory (6.3 × 8 cm). Found after Beethoven's death among his effects. Collection Dr. H. C. Bodmer, Beethovenhaus Bonn.

Beethoven came to know the young girl about 1800 at the Brunsvik house: Giulietta was a cousin of the young Brunsviks. In 1801, the seventeen year-old girl became his pupil; she remembered much later that he had been a very severe teacher and had not permitted any kind of sloppiness. Beethoven fell passionately in love with what he called that 'enchanting girl' and when, after the master's death, this miniature portrait was found in his desk drawer, her name was – quite erroneously – soon connected with the letters to the 'Immortal Beloved'. The conversation books show that Beethoven was profoundly shocked by Giulietta's marriage.

103. Ludwig van Beethoven. Miniature on ivory (6.5 × 5.4 cm) by Christian Horneman, signed and dated 'Horneman 1803'. Collection Dr. H. C. Bodmer, Beethovenhaus Bonn.

This miniature portrait, which Beethoven sent his friend Stephan von Breuning as a token of good will after an argument between the two friends, is the first that shows Beethoven as a mature man who, famous and something of a lion in Viennese society, was nearing the end of his career as a performing artist. His deafness had not yet isolated him from society, and at this period in his life he appeared well-dressed and elegant in the glittering salons of the Viennese aristocracy.

108. George Polgreen Augustus Bridgetower (1779–1860). Drawing by Henry Edridge. British Museum, London.

Bridgetower was the son of the Negro August, the personal page of Prince Nicolaus I von Esterházy. Bridgetower studied composition with Haydn and became a virtuoso on the violin. He went to London, played at the Haydn-Salomon concerts, and became a member of the Prince of Wales' orchestra, receiving in 1802 leave of absence to visit his German mother in Saxony. He used the opportunity to give concerts in Dresden and Vienna. Beethoven, with whom he soon came to be on friendly terms, wrote for him the Sonata for Violin and Piano in A major, Op. 47, which was later dedicated to Rodolphe Kreutzer.

109. Rodolphe Kreutzer (1766–1831). Engraving by C. T. Riedel from a drawing by Antoine Paul Vincent, 1809. Gesellschaft der Musikfreunde, Vienna.

Beethoven made the acquaintance of the violinist and composer Kreutzer in 1798 at the house of General Bernadotte, at that time the French Ambassador to Vienna. It is believed that Kreutzer never even played the famous Sonata which still bears his name.

110, 111. Symphony No. 3 in E flat, Op. 55, entitled by Beethoven ▶ 'Sinfonia Eroica'. Title-page of the manuscript score, which contains many corrections and additions in Beethoven's hand. (*Below*) Beginning of the second movement. Gesellschaft der Musikfreunde, Vienna.

The autograph is lost. The manuscript here reproduced is a copy which Beethoven used for conducting. Underneath the title is the remark in Beethoven's handwriting 'Nb. 1 in the first violin part, the other instruments will also occasionally be entered'. Under the title 'Sinfonia grande' was written 'intitolato Bonaparte', but this was scratched out by Beethoven when he learned that Napoleon had crowned himself.

Sinfonia grande
Louis van Beethoven
Sinfonia
Op: 55

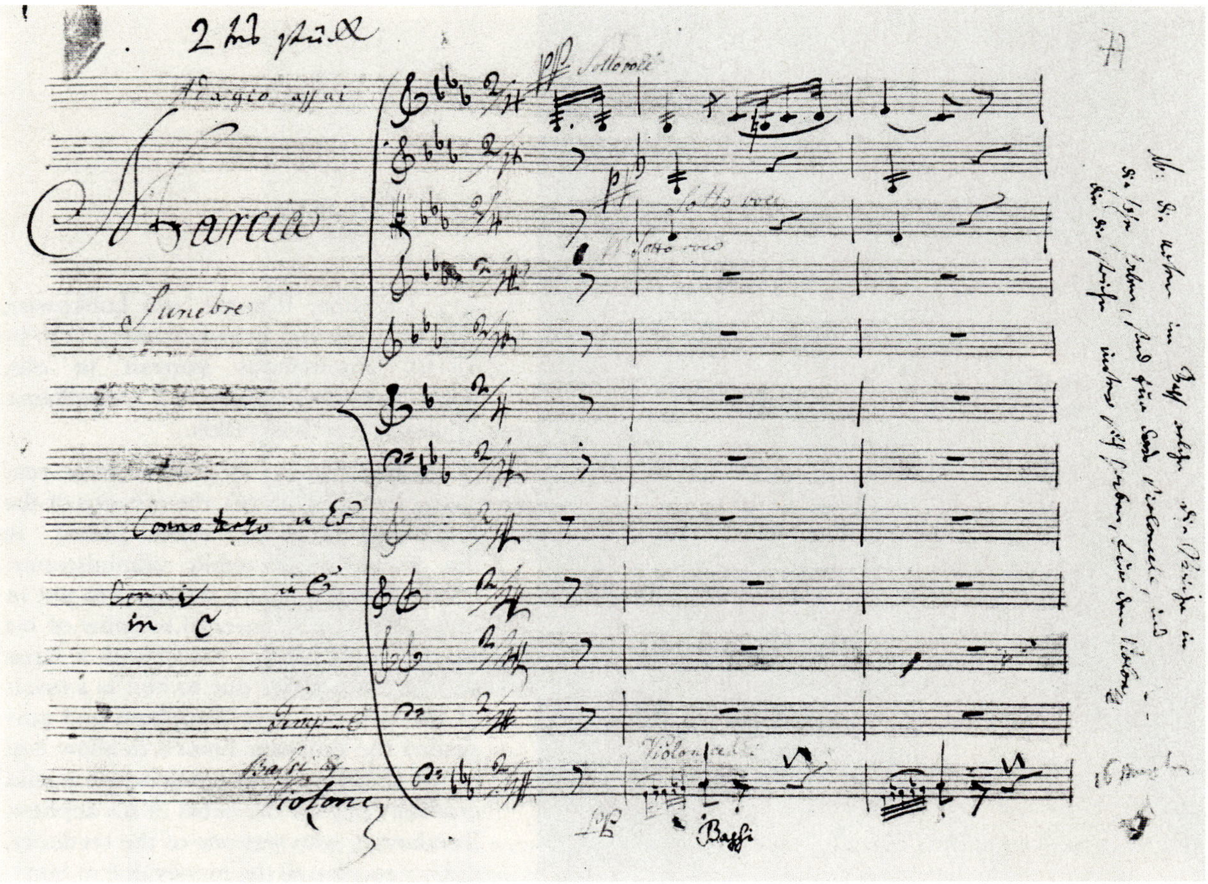
Adagio assai
Marcia
funebre
sotto voce
Violoncelli
Bassi

116. The Lobkowitz Palace on the Lobkowitzplatz. Coloured engraving by Vincenz Reim. Historisches Museum of the City of Vienna.

The 'Eroica' Symphony was given its first performance in the Lobkowitz Palace. When Prince Louis Ferdinand of Prussia visited Lobkowitz, the German Prince-*cum*-composer heard a performance of this work, and was so impressed by it that he had the symphony repeated twice.

118. Therese, Countess von Brunsvik (1775–1861). Portrait in oils by Johann Baptist Lampi the Elder. Beethovenhaus Bonn.

In 1799 the widowed Countess Brunsvik brought her two daughters Therese and Josephine to Vienna, where they were to be presented to society. At that time the two girls took piano lessons from Beethoven for about a fortnight and – as Therese von Brunsvik wrote later in her memoirs – 'there began an intimate and warm-hearted friendship for Beethoven that lasted as long as he lived.'

119. Franz Count von Brunsvik (1777–1849). Portrait in oils by Heinrich Thugut. Historisches Museum of the City of Vienna.

Beethoven's friendship with Count Franz, who was seven years younger than the composer, was so intimate that they addressed each other in the 'Du' form—something much rarer then in German than today. Beethoven dedicated to Brunsvik the Piano Sonata in F minor, Op. 57 ('Appassionata'), and the *Fantasie für Klavier*, Op. 77. Schindler writes about Brunsvik that he had a particularly subtle appreciation of Beethoven's art and that Beethoven in his turn was fully aware of this, which explains the dedication of these two masterpieces.

◄ 117. Page from the manuscript score of the 'Sinfonia Eroica'. Gesellschaft der Musikfreunde, Vienna. (*See Plate 110.*)

The famous horn dissonance in the first movement, just before the recapitulation.

179

139. Symphony No. 4 in B flat, Op. 60. First page of the first movement in autograph. Staatsbibliothek, Preussischer Kulturbesitz, Musikabteilung, Berlin.

This symphony was largely written down in the late summer and autumn of the year 1806 at the Lichnowsky Castle of Grätz. The page shown contains a remark in Beethoven's hand: 'All the abbreviations must be written out when the score is copied.'

140. Programme of the concert held on 23 December 1806 in the Theater an der Wien. Österreichische Nationalbibliothek, Vienna.

At this concert, given for the benefit of the violinist Franz Clement, occurred the first performance of the Violin Concerto in D, Op. 61, which Beethoven wrote expressly for the young musician. Franz Clement (1780–1842) was a Viennese who, like Mozart, had toured Europe as a *Wunderkind* before he became the first violinist of the Theater an der Wien.

Letter from Therese von Brunsvik to her sister Josephine von Deym, on 2 February 1811:

I too have received through Franz a memento of our noble Beethoven which gives me pleasure. I do not mean his Sonatas, which are very beautiful, but a short note which I shall copy for you immediately.

'Even without intention, the better people think of one another, and this is also the case between you and me, worthy and honoured Therese. I am still indebted to you and must express my heartfelt thanks for your beautiful picture. And if I accuse myself as a debtor, so must I soon appear in the guise of a beggar inasmuch as I beg of you, when you feel the spirit of painting within you, to draw anew that small drawing, which I was so unlucky as to lose. It was an eagle looking at the sun; I cannot forget it. But I pray you, do not believe that I think of myself in that guise, although such thoughts have been ascribed to me. But many people like to look upon heroic scenes and derive pleasure from them, without any feeling of kinship with them. Farewell, worthy Therese, and think sometimes about your truly devoted friend

Beethoven.'

Therese von Brunsvik to her sister on 23 February 1811:

What I beg of you, beloved Josephine, is that picture which you could bring to life once again better than anyone. . . .

We await no other answer to our supreme command than Yes/Yes/Yes!/ six times as fast as lightning – otherwise our wrath will reach you as far as Ofen.

The other news regarding the return journey, you will receive soon.

TDR III, 270 f. Anderson 295.

From the diary of Joseph Carl Rosenbaum:

Monday 18 April [1803] . . . After 7 o'clock Stessel and I went to the Müller Art   *123*
Gallery which was lit up by Winger's thermo lamps . . . . He [Count Deym, the   *122*
owner of the gallery] assured me that 22 lamps were burning in the gallery, and led
me to the furnace from which the light is fed by means of pipes to all the rooms.
From 6 o'clock to 10 o'clock in the evening this lighting consumes 1 Florin 30
Kreutzer worth of wood, or thereabouts.

HJB V, 108.

Letter from Beethoven to Countess Josephine von Deym: *107, 120*

[Winter 1805]

. . . Yes, it is true that I am not as active as I should have been – but an inner un-
happiness has for a long time robbed me of my usual buoyancy, ever since my feelings

of love for you, desirable J., began to spring up within me, and this increased further. When we are once more together undisturbed, then you shall be told all about my real suffering and of the struggle which has gone on within me for some time between life and death. A fact which for a long time made me doubt whether there can be any happiness in life on this earth – now it is not half as desperate. I have won your heart. Oh, I know for certain what this will mean to me; my activity will increase once again and – and this I promise you by all I hold highest and most precious, in a short time I will be there, worthier of myself and of yourself. Oh, if only you would be willing to establish my happiness through your love – to increase it. Oh beloved J. it is not a desire for the opposite sex which draws me to you, No, you, your whole self with all your characteristics, have fettered all my feelings, my entire sensitivity, to you. When I came to you I had made the firmest decision not to allow even the tiniest spark of love to light up within me. You overwhelmed me, whether you did it willingly or unwillingly? – That question J. could surely answer for me some day. Oh Heavens, what more could I not tell you – how I think of you – what I feel for you – but how weak, how poor in spirit is this language – at least mine.

For a long, long time may our love last. It is noble – based so much on mutual respect and friendship – indeed the very similarities in so many things – in thinking and in feeling. Oh let me hope that your heart will long beat for me. Mine can only cease beating for you when it no longer beats at all – beloved J. keep well. But I also hope that you may be a little happy through me. Otherwise I would be – selfish.

'Beethoven', dreizehn unbekannte Briefe . . ., op. cit., p. 17 f.

Draft of a letter from Countess von Deym to Beethoven, presumably written in the winter of 1804 or 1805:

The closer association with you, my dear Beethoven, during these winter months left impressions in my innermost self which neither time – nor any other circumstances – will ever destroy. Whether you are happy or unhappy? Would you say to yourself – also – whether you – in this regard, through control – or by giving free rein – would lessen or increase your feelings.

My own spirit which, in any case, was enthusiastic for you even before I knew you, received nourishment from your inclination. A feeling which lies deep within my heart and is not capable of expression, made me love you. Before I met you your music made me enthusiastic for you – the goodness of your character, your inclination towards me increased my enthusiasm – this prerogative which you granted me, the pleasure of being with you, could have been the greatest jewel of my life if you loved me less sensually. Because I cannot satisfy this sensual love you are angry with me – I would have to destroy sacred bonds if I were to give heed to your desires. Believe me – that the fulfilment of my duties causes me the greatest suffering – and that surely the motives which guide my conduct are noble.

Ibid., p. 24 f.

From the diary of Therese von Brunsvik:

[4 February 1846]
... Beethoven! It seems like a dream that he was the friend, the intimate of our
house – a stupendous spirit! Why did not my sister J., as the widow Deym, accept *120*
him as her husband? She would have been happier than she was with St[ackelberg].
Maternal love caused her to forego her own happiness.

[12 July 1817]
Josephine must suffer remorse on account of Luigi's sorrow – his wife! What could
she not have made of this Hero!

Ibid., pp. 27, 36.

Vienna's fashionable society included, as we have seen, many pianists so expert that they
could be, and indeed were, considered professional. One of the most brilliant was Dorothea
Baroness von Ertmann, the wife of an Austrian army officer. Baroness Dorothea became a
specialist in performing Beethoven's piano music, and theirs was an intimate friendship
which at one point may actually have become something more: the latest research indicates
that, of all the known candidates, Baroness Dorothea seems most likely to have been the
recipient of the famous letters to the 'immortal beloved'. Her piano-playing was greatly
admired by her contemporaries, and there is also an interesting account by Felix Mendelssohn-
Bartholdy of her life in Milan after Beethoven's death. Whether or not Baroness von Ertmann
really is the 'immortal beloved' it is clear that Beethoven was always very much attracted by
pretty women, and we have a sympathetic description of Beethoven's love affairs by Ferdinand
Ries. Some of these fashionable ladies even wanted to borrow Beethoven's portrait from him
while they were staying in Vienna, as we know from a letter Beethoven wrote to the painter
Joseph Willibrord Mähler.

Johann Friedrich Reichardt writes about Baroness von Ertmann:

Vienna, 7 February 1809
As it happens, there also lives in this Bürgerspital a great music lover and connoisseur, *43*
and a great friend and admirer of Beethoven, Herr von Zmeskal. He is also a good *44*
violoncello player. A new quartet has been established in his apartments on Sunday
mornings, which played together for the first time last Sunday. After a difficult quintet
by Beethoven had been performed well, we had the good fortune to hear a great
Fantasia by Beethoven [Sonata Op. 27, No. 2] played by Frau von Ertmann (wife of *124*
Major von Ertmann), with such great power, spirit and perfection that it left us all
enchanted. It is not possible to hear anything more perfect on this perfect instrument.
It was a beautiful Streicher Fortepiano which was made to sound like an entire
orchestra. ... The previous evening I had already had the fortune to hear Frau von
Ertmann at a large reception at her brother-in-law's. But this gathering was more
an occasion for the dancing which was to follow and which the numerous handsome
young people awaited with impatience. So she purposely chose only agreeable and
short pieces in order to satisfy the curiosity of the large company. But she played
even those pieces with a precision and elegance which reveal a great mastery. But in

that marvellous Fantasia which seemed to me to be in C sharp minor, she developed the same qualities to the fullest extent and to an astounding degree. I do not recall ever having heard anything greater or more consummate. This great artistic talent is not, however, a native of this country. Frau von Ertmann was born a Graumann from Frankfurt-am-Main, but has lived now for several years in this artistic country and has derived her greatest benefit from her closeness to Beethoven.

Reichardt I, 309 ff.

Felix Mendelssohn-Bartholdy writes about Baroness von Ertmann:

Milan, 14 July 1831

She [Baroness von Ertmann] told me that when she lost her last child, Beethoven was at first unable to come to her house any more. Finally he invited her to come to him, and when she came he sat at the piano and merely said: 'We will now converse in music,' and played for over an hour and, as she expressed it, 'He said everything to me, and also finally gave me consolation.'

TDR II, 415. (The famous composer, in the course of his journey to Italy, had called on the Baroness, whose husband, now a General, was stationed in Milan, and admired her piano-playing.)

Antonie von Arneth speaks of Baroness von Ertmann to Alexander Wheelock Thayer on 25 December 1864:

After the funeral of her [Baroness Ertmann's] only child she could not find tears. . . . General Ertmann brought her to Beethoven. The Master spoke no words but played for her until she began to sob, so her sorrow found an outlet and comfort.

TDR III, 583. (Antonie Adamberger, the popular Viennese actress, later married Joseph von Arneth. She played the part of Klärchen in Goethe's *Egmont*, to which Beethoven composed the music.)

Anton Schindler writes about the Baroness von Ertmann:

Without Frau von Ertmann, Beethoven's piano music would have vanished much sooner from the repertoire in Vienna. For it was this lady, at once tall, beautiful and with refined taste, who from purely altruistic motives entertained a love of higher things and who opposed the emergence of a new approach towards composition and playing fostered by Hummel and his neophytes. Beethoven thus had double reason to honour her as a priestess of music: he used to call her his 'Dorothea-Cecilia'. Another key to her success in reproducing music at the highest level was that Frau von Ertmann, characteristically, never placed anything on her music stand that did not suit her personality.

Schindler I, 242.

Letter from Beethoven to Dorothea von Ertmann:

Vienna, 23 February 1816
[correctly 1817]

My dear, treasured Dorothea-Cecilia!

You must often have misjudged me in cases when I have appeared to oppose you. Much of this was due to circumstances, especially in the earlier days, when my idiom was less recognized than it is now. You know the protestations of the unbidden Apostles who made shift with means quite different from the Holy Gospel – I would not wish to be counted among their number – Receive now what has often been promised to you* and what you may take as a token of my admiration for both your artistic talent and your own person. . . . I hope to hear soon from you how the Muses flourish in Sankt Pölten** and whether you still have esteem for your

admirer and friend
L. v. Beethoven.

All best wishes to your worthy husband and consort.

TDR IV, 18. Anderson 764.

Letter from Beethoven to Tobias Haslinger:

[Vienna, January 1817]

. . . By chance I have hit upon the following dedication:

Sonata for the Pianoforte
or – Hammerklavier
composed and
dedicated to
Baroness Dorothea Ertmann
née Graumann
by
Ludwig van Beethoven

for the new Sonata [in A Major, Op. 101, February 1817, published by S. A. Steiner in Vienna].

TDR III, 630. Anderson 742.

Ferdinand Ries describes Beethoven's relations with women:

Beethoven very much enjoyed the company of women, especially those with pretty young faces, and generally, if we happened to see a pretty girl, he would turn around, ogle her pointedly with his eyeglass and laugh or grin when he noticed that I had

*Evidently a reference to the Sonata in A Major, Op. 101 (*Hammerklavier*).
**At that time Baron von Ertmann's regiment was stationed in Sankt Pölten in Lower Austria.

been watching him. He was frequently in love, but generally not for very long. Once when I chaffed him about his conquest of a beautiful lady, he admitted that she had captivated him more thoroughly and for longer than anyone else – namely for seven whole months.

One evening I went to see him in Baden in order to continue my lessons. There I found a beautiful young lady sitting with him on the sofa. Since it seemed to me that my arrival had been inopportune, I started to go away again immediately. But Beethoven held me back and said, 'Play to us for a while.'

He and the lady remained sitting behind me. I had been playing for a long time, when Beethoven suddenly called out: 'Ries, play something amorous!' Then a little while later: 'Something melancholy!' Then, 'Something passionate,' and so forth.

From what he told me I gathered that he must have offended the lady to some extent and that he now wanted to humour her. Finally he jumped up and shouted, 'Those are all things I wrote!' I had, as it happens, played parts of his own compositions, linked together only with short connecting passages, but this seemed to have pleased him. The lady soon went away and, to my great astonishment, Beethoven did not know who she was. I now found out that she had arrived shortly before me in order to make Beethoven's acquaintance. We soon went out after her in order to find out where she lived and what her position might be. We could still see her a long way off (it was bright moonlight), but suddenly she vanished. We walked up and down in the neighbouring beautiful valley, talking about all sorts of things for another good hour-and-a-half. As we went home, however, Beethoven said, 'I must find out who she is and you must help me.' A long time afterwards I met her in Vienna and found out that she was the mistress of a foreign Prince. I reported my discovery to Beethoven but I never heard anything further about her, either from him or from anyone else.

WRBN 117 ff.

Letter from Beethoven to the painter Joseph Willibrord Mähler:

[Vienna, c. 1804]

Dear Mähler,

I do beg of you, as soon as you have finished using my portrait, to return it to me as soon as possible. If you should still need it I would ask you, please, at least to make haste with it. I have promised a foreign lady, who saw the portrait in my room, to give it to her during her stay here for a few weeks. You will understand that I cannot resist such charming overtures. It is understood, of course, that a portion of the delightful favours which may be vouchsafed me by this means will not pass you by.

All yours Bthvn.

KAL 145. Anderson 107.

Franz Grillparzer describes Beethoven's appearance:

At that time he was still slim, dark and, in contrast to his later habits, very elegantly dressed. He wore glasses, which I noticed particularly, because in later times he no longer made use of this aid for short-sightedness.

FRBS I, 27.

The invasion of Vienna by Napoleon's troops in 1805 coincided, most unfortunately, with the première of Beethoven's only opera, *Fidelio*. To find a good libretto for a German opera had always been a serious problem for composers. Both Mozart's *Abduction from the Seraglio* and *The Magic Flute* are markedly inferior to the Da Ponte libretti (of which, incidentally, Beethoven did not approve – he thought the subjects frivolous); and Beethoven had very definite ideas concerning the ethic and moral standards of the libretti suitable in his eyes for an operatic subject. After the disastrous reception in 1805, Beethoven revised the opera in 1806, when it was much more successful; he again worked over the whole opera for the next performance in 1814, and after that *Fidelio* was an unqualified success. Again, many people, such as Joseph Carl Rosenbaum, found that the music was 'pretty, artistic and difficult'; but the public gradually caught up with Beethoven's unfettered fantasy.

Louis Schlösser writes about the first performance of Fidelio: *127*

Napoleon's headquarters were [in 1805] in Schönbrunn; the French military filled the rooms at the Opera House. Was it imaginable that the ethical purity and chaste beauty of a work, whose language they could not even understand, could awaken a sympathetic echo from guests who were accustomed to more frivolous fare?

Kerst II, 4. (Kapellmeister Schlösser came in 1822 to Vienna, and visited Beethoven. He wrote his Memoirs for the periodical *Hallelujah*, No. 20/21, 4th year, 1885.)

From the Diary of Joseph Carl Rosenbaum:

[20 November 1805]

At the [Theater] an der Wien the first performance of Beethowen's Grand Opera *155*
Fidelio or *Conjugal Love* in 3 Acts; freely [adapted] from the French by Jos. Sonnleithner . . . . In the evening I went to the Th. W. to hear Louis Beth.'s opera . . . . The *131*
opera contains pretty, artistic and difficult music, a boring, not very interesting book. It was not a success, and the theatre was empty.

HJB V, 129.

Georg Friedrich Treitschke reports on Fidelio: *128*

From the distance the thunder of war was rolling towards Vienna and this robbed audiences of the serenity necessary for the enjoyment of a work of art. Particularly in view of this situation, everything possible was done to enliven the sparsely filled house. *Fidelio* was thought to be a trump card, and so the opera opened on 20 November under stars which were in no way propitious. Only the women's parts could be satisfactorily cast with Mlles Milder and Müller; the men left all the more to be *186*
desired.

TDR II, 481. (Georg Friedrich Treitschke, a libretto writer and stage director, later revised the text of *Fidelio* for Beethoven.)

Criticism of Beethoven's Fidelio (*by August von Kotzebue?*):

The entry of the French into Vienna was an experience to which, at first, the Viennese could not become accustomed, and for a few weeks a most unusual silence reigned. The Court, the courtiers and most of the great landowners had left; instead of the usual ceaseless rattle of coaches lumbering through the streets, one rarely heard so much as a simple cart creeping by. The streets were peopled mainly with French soldiers who, on the whole, maintained good discipline. In the city itself almost exclusively officers were quartered; the other ranks were billeted in the outskirts. It was only natural that people gave little thought to entertainment; the difficulty of obtaining provisions was very great, and the fear of possible collisions and unpleasant encounters kept the majority of men and women at home. The theatres were also quite empty at the beginning, and only after a while did the French begin to attend them; and it is still they who comprise the greater majority of the spectators.

Recently little of importance has been given. A new opera by Beethoven, *Fidelio*, or *Conjugal Love*, did not find favour. It was performed only a few times, and immediately following the first performance it played to quite empty houses. Moreover, the music falls far below the expectations to which connoisseurs and music-lovers consider themselves entitled. The melodies and characterization, in spite of many felicities, lack that happy, striking, overwhelming expression of passion which, in Mozart's and Cherubini's works, moves us so irresistibly. The music has some attractive passages but it is very far from being a perfect or even a successful work. The text, translated by Sonnleithner, consists of one of those liberation stories which have come into fashion since Cherubini's *Deux Journées*.

TDR II, 488 f. *Der Freimüthige*, 26 December 1805.

Joseph August Röckl speaks about the revision of Fidelio:

It was December 1805, the Oper an der Wien and both Court Theatres were at that time under the management of the *intendant* Baron Braun, the Court banker. Herr Meyer, Mozart's brother-in-law and the stage manager of the Oper an der Wien came to me and invited me to an evening party at the palace of Prince Carl Lichnowsky, the great protector of Beethoven. *Fidelio* had been performed a month previously at the Theater an der Wien, unfortunately just after the French military occupation when the Inner City was cut off from the suburbs.

The whole theatre was filled with Frenchmen, and only a few of Beethoven's friends ventured out to hear the opera. These friends were gathered at Prince Lichnowsky's in order to persuade Beethoven to give his consent to the changes which had to be made in the opera in order to overcome the heaviness of the first act. The necessity for these improvements had already been recognized and determined between them. Meyer had prepared me for the impending storm which would burst when Beethoven was told that three entire numbers would have to be cut from the first act.

The company consisted of Prince Lichnowsky and the Princess his wife, Beethoven and his brother Caspar, [Stephan] von Breuning, [Heinrich] von Collin the poet, the actor Lange (another brother-in-law of Mozart's), Treitschke, Clement the conductor of the orchestra, Meyer and myself. Whether Kapellmeister v. Seyfried was present or not I can no longer remember for certain, although I think he was.

I had come to Vienna only a short time before, and it was here that I met Beethoven for the first time. Since the whole opera had to be gone through, we went to work immediately. Princess Lichnowsky played the piano from the large orchestra score and Clement, who sat in a corner of the room, accompanied the whole opera from memory on his violin, playing all the solos of the various instruments. Since Clement's uncanny memory was a matter of common knowledge, no one but myself was in the least astonished at this feat. Meyer and I made ourselves useful by singing, to the best of our abilities, he (a bass) the lower and I in the higher parts of the opera. Although Beethoven's friends were fully prepared for the coming battle they had never before seen him in *such* a fury. Without the pleas and tears of the very delicate and gentle Princess, who was a second mother to Beethoven, and recognized as such by him, his united friends would probably have had difficulty achieving any success whatever in this undertaking, which seemed to them besides a very doubtful proposition. But after their united efforts, which lasted from seven o'clock to after one at night, the sacrifice of three numbers was accepted. And worn out, hungry and thirsty, as we prepared to restore ourselves with a lavish supper, no one was in a happier or merrier mood than Beethoven. If I had seen him first in his wrath, now I saw him in a good humour. When he saw me sitting opposite him busy dealing with a French dish, he asked what I was eating. I answered that I did not know. Thereupon he roared out in his leonine voice, 'He eats like a wolf, without knowing what! Ha! Ha! Ha!'

TRD II, 492 ff. (Joseph August Röckl sang Florestan in *Fidelio*. He related his experience to Alexander W. Thayer on 26 February 1861.)

Letter from Joseph Sonnleithner to State Councillor von Stahl on 3 October 1805: 131

You will eternally oblige Her Majesty the Empress, the public which is noticeably abandoning the theatre because it cannot be served according to its wishes and has waited for a long time for an opera by Beethoven, and the theatre whose duty is always to fulfil as far as possible the desires of the high authorities.

It is true that a Minister abuses his powers, but only to indulge in a private revenge – in Spain – in the 16th century – moreover he is punished, punished by the Court and he is confronted with the heroism of womanly virtue . . . .

Carl Glossy, *Zur Geschichte der Theater Wiens*, Vienna 1915, Vol. I, p. 83. (On 5 October the performance was authorized by the censors 'after a few changes in the more problematical sections.')

Grillparzer describes a visit by Beethoven to Sonnleither:

At Sonnleithner's, there were gathered together Cherubini, Beethoven and Vogler. They all played; Vogler being the last and playing endlessly, so that in the meantime the company went in to dine. Beethoven was full of attention and respect for Cherubini.

Kerst II, 49.

The Vienna correspondent of the Zeitung für die elegante Welt *reports on 10 May 1806 on Sonnleithner's text for* Fidelio:

106, 155   Beethoven's opera *Fidelio* appeared in a new version at the Theater an der Wien. The revision consists of condensing it from three into two acts. It is incomprehensible how the composer could be willing to try to bring this vapid pot-boiler by Sonnleithner to life with beautiful music. As a result, . . . the effect of the whole cannot possibly be of the kind which the composer must have set out to create, for the inanity of the spoken parts entirely or very nearly wipes out the beautiful effect of the sung parts.

TDR II, 505.

132   *Baron de Trémont on Beethoven's reactions to Napoleon:*

At the Imperial Court in Vienna he was regarded as a republican. Far from patronizing him, the Court never attended the performance of even a single one of his compositions. Napoleon had been his hero as long as he remained First Consul of the Republic. After the battle of Marengo he worked on his hero-symphony (*Eroica*) with the intention of dedicating it to him [Napoleon]. The symphony was completed in 1802 when it began to be rumoured that Napoleon wished to be crowned and then to subject Germany to his rule. Beethoven tore up his dedication and transferred his hatred to the French nation which had bowed beneath the yoke. Nevertheless, the greatness of Napoleon interested him a great deal and he often talked about it with me. In spite of his poor opinion of Napoleon, I realized that he admired Bonaparte for having risen so high from such humble origins. This appealed to his democratic ideas. One day he said to me 'Would I be obliged to pay homage to your Emperor if I came to Paris?' I assured him that it would not be necessary for him to do so, so long as he was not commanded. 'And do you think that I would be summoned?' 'I have no doubt you would be if Napoleon knew who you were, but you have heard from Cherubini how little he understands about music.'

    This question led me to think that, in spite of his convictions, it would have flattered him if he had been decorated by Napoleon. Human pride bows down in the face of flattery.

Kerst I, 139 f. *Mercure Musical*, 1906, No. 9. (Baron de Trémont, a French official, was in Vienna during the French occupation and visited Beethoven.)

Beethoven's opinion of Napoleon:

Even with that Bastard I made a mistake.

Kerst II, 192.

Anton Schindler writes about Beethoven's overture to Fidelio:

The first overture composed for *Fidelio* begins:

[Leonore I]

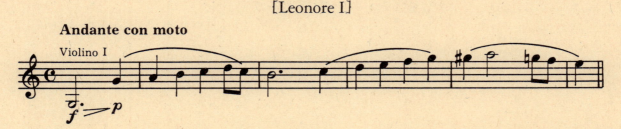

As soon as he had completed it, the composer had no great opinion of this work. His friends agreed. A trial reading of it with a small orchestra was then held at Prince Lichnowsky's. Its content was declared to be unsuited for an introduction. Neither the idea, the style nor the character met with the approval of the Areopagus assembled in judgment. It was therefore discarded. The publisher, Steiner & Company, immediately acquired the publishing rights. It appeared in print only during the *fourth* decade [of the 19th century] and figures in the Catalogue as the *last* work of our master [Op. 138].

The overture which then followed, also in C major, was actually performed with the opera in 1805; the Allegro movement begins:

[Leonore II]

An essential part of this theme was fated always to be drowned out by the woodwinds.

The figure, previously heard on the violins, which the violoncello begins:

alternates with this:

and both are immediately given to the winds and played antiphonally between them, while the first violins (viola doubling an octave lower) repeat the rising figure which has already appeared at the beginning of the movement.

(See score from p. 52 to 57)

Instead of eliminating this obstacle (31 bars) to a good performance, Beethoven found it advisable to revise the whole [overture], since he was already occupied in revising other parts of the opera. He kept both the motives of the introduction and of the Allegro, but to enrich the sonority of the latter he had it played by the violins and violoncellos together. On the basis of what he had already written [Leonore II] he built a new structure with the introduction of several new ideas. With this altered overture, the revised opera opened again in March 1806.

This newly reconstructed overture had, however, been so greatly expanded that the experts considered it too long as the introduction to an opera; and according to various sources this was also the opinion of the composer himself. Moreover, the majority had declared themselves unequivocally in favour of the *first* version because the main ideas were expressed more succinctly, and more characteristically as an opera overture, whereas the second version could be regarded as a concert overture. All this, added to the fact that not only the wood-winds but also the strings, particularly in the running passages at the end (actually marked *Presto* in the revised version), could not perform to the satisfaction of the composer, led to the composition of a fourth overture (in E major) for the revival of the opera in 1814.

[Fidelio]

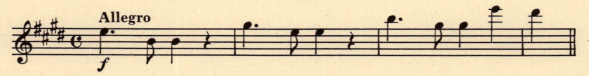

This presented the orchestra with no difficulties. But the character of this overture is the least adapted to opera: it is much more in the nature of a concert overture. The master could easily drive one mad.

The publication of the *revised* overture in C major [Leonore III] was soon entrusted to Breitkopf and Härtel in 1810. Since then it has become the declared favourite of all orchestras. Now that their techniques have improved (here and there, alas, sometimes degenerating into mere virtuosity!), it enables them to show off their ability.

Schindler I, 127 ff.

The poet Ignaz F. Castelli discusses the public's reaction to Beethoven's music:

The giant Beethoven appeared with his gigantic creations. But the instrumentalists were unable to play them and the public did not understand them. How often during a performance of a superb symphony by this master did I have to hear: 'This is utter nonsense,' and see (particularly during the last movements of a symphony) the hall emptied as fast as if a downpour of rain had fallen from heaven; and yet it was not water but pure spirit. Beethoven even had to withdraw that superb, greatest of masterpieces, the overture to the opera *Leonore* because it was declared to be unplayable.

Now instrumentalists have studied all these masterpieces through and through. Yes, they know every last note by heart and they perform these compositions with all possible precision. And so the public, too, has learned to understand and to admire them.

I. F. Castelli, *Memoiren meines Lebens, Gefundenes und Empfundenes, Erlebtes und Erstrebtes*, edited by Dr Josef Bindtner, Munich 1913, Vol. I, 241.

Ferdinand Ries discusses Beethoven's waywardness:

Etiquette and all that goes with it was something that Beethoven never learned and never wanted to learn; thus his behaviour often caused great embarrassment to the *suite* of the Archduke Rudolph when Beethoven first attended him. They attempted to force him to learn what formalities he had to observe. But this he found insupportable. He did, however, promise to improve, but – that was as far as it went. Finally one day he burst in on the Archduke in a state of exasperation because he was again being, as he put it, tutored. He declared outright that he most certainly had all possible respect for the Archduke's person, but that the stringent instructions and regulations which were being imparted to him every day did not concern him. The Archduke laughed pleasantly over this occurrence and gave orders that Beethoven should be allowed to go his own way without hindrance: that was the way he was.

138

Kerst I, 95 f.

Letter from Xaver Schnyder von Wartensee to Nägeli in Zurich, 17 December 1811:

I was extremely well received by Beethoven and already have been several times to see him. He is a most unusual man. Great thoughts float through his mind which he can only express through music. Words are not at his command. His whole culture is very neglected and, apart from his art, he is rough but honest and without pretensions. He says straight out what is on his mind. In his youth, and even now, he has had to struggle with disappointments. This has made him suspicious and grim. He rails against Vienna and would like to leave. 'From the Emperor down to the last shoe polisher,' he says, 'the Viennese are all a worthless lot.' I asked him if he took pupils. No, he answered, that was tiresome work. He only has one who gives him a lot of trouble and whom he would glad to be rid of, if only he could. 'Who is he, then,' I asked. 'The Archduke Rudolph.'

Kerst I, 166. (Schnyder, a Swiss composer, came to Vienna in 1811 and made Beethoven's acquaintance.)

From the Diary of Fanny Giannastasio del Rio:

At that time, Beethoven gave lessons to the brother of the Emperor Francis, the Archduke Rudolph. I once asked him if he played well. 'When he feels strong enough,' was the answer, given with a smile. He also once told me laughingly that he raps him on the fingers, and once when His Highness wanted to put him back in his place, Beethoven, to indicate his justification, pointed with his finger to a certain line of a poet – it was Goethe, if I am not mistaken.

Kerst I, 215 f. (Fanny Giannastasio's father kept a school in Vienna attended by Beethoven's nephew Carl.)

Louis Schlösser reminisces about Beethoven's relations with the aristocracy:

After he [Beethoven] had drawn his hand across his forehead he replied, 'In my earlier years I had made up my mind to leave Vienna; there were determining reasons which had nothing to do with my profession. Then there were also requests for me from abroad, namely from England and from Kassel, which would have assured me a much higher income, and this would have carried much weight in my situation. When my Imperial patron and pupil, the Archduke Rudolph, heard of my decision he was fearfully upset. "No, No," he cried out, "that must never happen! You shall never leave the place made sacred before you by Mozart and Haydn! Where in the world will you find a second Vienna? I will speak to my brother the Emperor Francis, I will speak to Esterházy, to Liechtenstein, to Palffy, Lobkowitz, Karoly, to all the Princes, so that they may guarantee you a permanent subsidy sufficient to relieve you of all concern for your future existence."'

Kerst II, 11 f. (For Schlösser, see p. 199. Palffy probably Prince Joseph Franz. Karoly probably Count Joseph Karoly von Nagy-Karoly.).

One of Beethoven's most important patrons was Andreas Cyrillovich Prince Razumovsky, Russian Ambassador to the Austrian Court, for whom he wrote his famous 'Razumovsky' Quartets, Op. 59. The success of these great and revolutionary String Quartets induced the Prince to form a regular quartet.

Shortly before Beethoven began work on the 'Razumovsky' Quartets, he took on as a pupil the Archduke Rudolph von Habsburg, the youngest brother of Emperor Francis I, to whom Beethoven dedicated a series of masterpieces ranging from the 'Archduke' Trio in B Flat, Op. 97, to the *Missa Solemnis*.

137   Baroness du Montet describes Prince Razumovsky:

I found the Prince aged and depressed. His extravagant magnificence has ruined him .... During the Congress of Vienna, when the Emperor of Austria was discussing the prince with the Tsar Alexander, he called him 'King of one of his suburbs'.... He is a great gentleman who commands respect and is generally most amiable. His presence and appearance are imperious; he radiates pride in all things; pride in his birth, his rank and his honour... in his bearing, in his speech... in short he is proud in all things .... Sometimes he is downright haughty .... This nobleman was afflicted a few years before his death with the decay of his mental and physical faculties.

Du Montet 150 f.

Anton Schindler writes about the Razumovsky Quartet:

Count Razumovsky was also a practising musician and, to sum him up appropriately in a few words, the chief upholder of the Haydn tradition in instrumental music. Alternating with Prince Lichnowsky, he would also gather the . . . musicians in his palace to perform quartet music, in which he himself played second violin. Soon, however, he decided on another course, which was to give his circle a higher significance: he placed a permanent Quartet under a life-long contract. This was the first and only example of its kind in Austria. Not that other rich art-lovers did not follow this example, establishing permanent quartets in their households; indeed there were several. But none of them did what the Russian Maecenas did, namely to provide these artists with pensions for the rest of their lives.

This model Quartet was composed of the following artists: Schuppanzigh, I Violin; Sina, II Violin; Weiss, Viola; Linke, Violoncello. Under the name 'The Razumovsky Quartet,' they achieved not only a European fame but also a place in the history of music. Nevertheless they never made a single concert tour, a fact in many ways most regrettable, for they would have established standards for the *authentic* performance of classical works, which in our time are sadly lacking.

We have just named Count Razumovsky as the upholder of the Haydn tradition of quartet music. How can this be explained? Very simply: Haydn had revealed to this art-lover [Razumovsky] that *fine* sensitivity necessary to the understanding of many of those particular qualities in his quartets and symphonies which are neither superficial nor conveyed through the usual [musical] symbols. Since these things had eluded other artists, he undertook to acquaint the Count with his hidden intentions so that he might then transmit them to the performing musicians. This fact is of *great* importance in understanding the true qualities of the Razumovsky Quartet, especially as far as Beethoven's quartet-music is concerned; a contributory factor was the youth of the four players, which made it necessary for them to seek instruction from older and more experienced musicians.

Count Razumovsky was one of the first to determine the path of the new musical constellation. Having established his permanent Quartet, he, more than any other of Beethoven's patrons, became closely bound to the composer's future development. For in fact, Razumovsky's Quartet became equally Beethoven's Quartet: it was as if this noble patron had engaged them exclusively for this purpose; they were placed at his complete disposal.

Schindler I, 37 ff.

Schindler on Beethoven and Prince Razumovsky:

There [at Razumovsky's] the master was the object of general attention on the part of all foreigners, for it is in the nature of things that creative genius, particularly when combined with a certain heroic element, attracts the attention of all the nobility. Can we not term it a form of heroism when we consider the composer's struggles against prejudices of every kind: against the traditionalists on account of his art,

135

asked Beethoven if he also knew the violin.' Weiser, who was also at table, 'saw at once how this outraged the artist . . . Beethoven did not deign to answer his interlocutor.' Weiser could not attend the rest of the dinner since, as Director of the Troppau Hospital, he had to make a professional call there. He heard the rest of the story from Beethoven himself. When the time came for Beethoven to play, he was nowhere to be found. He was looked for. The Prince wanted to persuade him – to cajole him – into playing. No use. An unpleasant, even vulgar, scene took place. Beethoven immediately had his things packed, and hastened, despite the pouring rain, on foot to Troppau, where he spent the night at Weiser's. It was because of the rain that the Sonata in F Minor Op. 57, the *Appassionata*, which Beethoven was carrying *129* with him was damaged by water . . . . Weiser tells further that the next day it was difficult, without the Prince, to get a passport to return to Vienna. Finally it was procured. Before he left, Beethoven wrote a very self-willed letter to Lichnowsky which is supposed to have read as follows: 'Prince! What you are, you are by circumstance and by birth. What I am, I am through myself. Of princes there have been and will be thousands. Of Beethovens there is only one . . .' Unfortunately, it seems that the march from Grätz to Troppau induced a considerable worsening of Beethoven's deafness. An exaggerated tradition even tells us that Beethoven's deafness was the result of the chill.

T. von Frimmel, *Ludwig van Beethoven*, 4th edition, Berlin 1912, p. 44. (Frimmel quotes a report written by Prince Lichnowsky's personal physician.)

Aloys Fuchs tells Jahn about the performance of the C Major Mass at Troppau:

In the year 1811, Beethoven was a guest of Prince Lichnowsky at his estate of Grätz near Troppau. A performance of the [C Major] Mass took place in Troppau for which everyone was pressed into service. The local *Turnermeister* was put on the kettledrum; in the 'Sanctus' Beethoven himself had to show him the beat. The Mass was rehearsed three afternoons. After the performance Beethoven improvised on the organ for half-an-hour, to the greatest astonishment of everyone.

Kerst II, 196. (Aloys Fuchs later became a bass singer in Vienna. In this performance he sang the soprano part.)

Letter from Stephan von Breuning to Dr Franz Wegeler, October 1806:

. . . Beethoven is at present at Prince Lichnowsky's in Silesia and will not return until the end of the month. His present situation is not the best, since his opera has had only a few performances, due to the cabals of his opponents, and has therefore not earned him any money. His humour is mostly very melancholy, and to judge from his letters, his stay in the country has not cheered him up . . . .

TDR II, 518.

Ignaz Ritter von Seyfried describes Beethoven's musical jokes:

When he [Beethoven] was not in the proper mood, it required many and repeated requests even to get him to a pianoforte. Before he began to play, he would strike the keys with the flat of his hand, run over them with one finger, and in general indulge in all kinds of tomfoolery and laugh heartily all the while at his own antics.

TDR II, 519.

Letter from Beethoven to the publishers Breitkopf und Härtel:

Grätz – on   *130*
the 3rd of the Hay Month [July], 1806
Because I have had rather a lot to do and on account of the short journey here I could not answer your letter right away . . . . as soon as I know your opinion on this matter – – – you can have from me 3 violin quartets, a new Piano Concerto, a new   *139*
Symphony . . . .

[written inside the cover.] N.B. I am at present here in Silesia, and will stay as long as the autumn lasts – with Prince Lichnowsky – who sends his greetings – – – My address is: L.v. Beethoven, Troppau.

KAL 169 f. Anderson 134.

Letter from Beethoven to Count Franz von Oppersdorff:

[Vienna, March 1808]
That you should have run off, beloved friend, without giving me an inkling about your departure, has truly hurt me very much. Perhaps something about me has annoyed you, but surely not of my volition. Today I have too little time to write more to you, I only add that your symphony [No. 5] has been ready for a long time and I shall   *150–153*
now send it to you by the next post. You may add 50 Florins, for the copies which I had made for you cost at least 50 Florins. In case you do not want the symphony, please let me know at the latest before the next post day. If, however, you will accept it, then you will do me a great pleasure if you would send me as soon as possible the 300 Florins which are still due to me. The last movement of the symphony has three trombones and flautino – and not 3 timpani, but will make more noise than 6 timpani, and better noise at that. I am still treating my poor innocent finger and on that account I have not been able to go out for 14 days. All good wishes – and let me hear something from you my very dear Count – things are not going well for me.
In haste,
your most devoted,
Beethoven.

A Monsieur le comte d'Oppersdorf, Troppau (in Silesia)

TDR III, 11 f. Anderson 166. (Count Franz von Oppersdorff, a great music-lover, had his own personal orchestra in Oberglogau (Poland) and made Beethoven's acquaintance at Prince Lichnowsky's Grätz Castle.)

Letter from Beethoven to Count Franz von Oppersdorff:

Vienna, the 1st November 1088 [1808]

My good Count!

You will regard me in an unfavourable light, but necessity has obliged me to give the symphony I wrote for you, and another one as well, to someone else. But rest assured that you will get the one destined for you quite soon. I hope that you have been well all this time, and also your wife, to whom please give my best regards. I am living just below Prince Lichnowsky, if you should ever do me the honour of visiting me in Vienna, in care of Countess Erdödy. My circumstances are improving – without needing to call on people who treat their friends with flails. – Also I have been called to the conductorship for the King of Westphalia and it is quite possible that I shall accept this call.

My best wishes to you, and think sometimes of your devoted friend

Beethoven.

149, 154

162

KAL 239 f. Anderson 178.

Letter from Beethoven to the publishers Breitkopf und Härtel:

139

. . . I cannot yet give you the symphony I promised because a distinguished gentleman has taken it from me. I have, however, the right to publish it in half a year – . . . moreover, rest assured that I always prefer, and will continue to do so, to transact business with your firm rather than with any of the others.

With regards,
devotedly yours,
L.v. Bthvn.

Vienna, 18 November 1806.

KAL 176 f. Anderson 137.

Title-page of the first edition of Symphony No. 4 with a dedication to Count von Oppersdorff:

[original French]

139

IVth SYMPHONY/ for 2 Violins, Viola, Flute, 2 Oboes, 2 Clarinets/ 2 Horns, 2 Bassoons, Trumpets, Timpani/ Violoncello and Bass/ Composed and Dedicated/ to Count Oppersdorff/by LOUIS VAN BEETHOVEN/ 60th Work/[l:] 596. [r.:] 9 f./ At Vienna and Pesth at the Bureau of Arts and Industry.

KHV 144.

In 1806, Beethoven was persuaded to write his only Violin Concerto, Op. 61, for Franz Clement, leader of the orchestra in the Theater an der Wien. The first performance took place at Clement's benefit concert on 23 December 1806. Later, the famous pianist and composer Muzio Clementi, who was now in the publishing business in London, came to Vienna and made Beethoven's acquaintance. He persuaded Beethoven to rewrite the Violin Concerto for piano, which Beethoven did, adding a fascinating cadenza in the first movement for piano and timpani solo, and dedicating the work to the wife of his old friend Stephan von Breuning, Julie (née von Vering). Clementi's letter to his partner Collard of 22 April 1807 amusingly describes his successful attempts to secure the English rights for various Beethoven compositions, and it is interesting to realize that many of Clementi's Beethoven editions are in fact the first, preceding those on the Continent – for example, the 'Emperor' Concerto, Op. 73.

Johann Nepomuk Möser writes in the Wiener Theaterzeitung, *1806:* *140*

The excellent violinist Klement also played, besides other beautiful pieces, a Violin Concerto by Beethhofen, which on account of its originality and many beautiful parts was received with exceptional applause. Klement's genuine art and gracefulness, his power and assurance on the violin – which is his slave – called forth the loudest *bravos*. As regards Beethhofen's Concerto, the verdict of the experts is unanimous, allowing it many beauties, but recognizing that its scheme often seems confused and that the unending repetitions of certain commonplace parts could easily prove wearisome. . . . This concerto was generally well liked, and Klement's cadenzas exceptionally well received.

TDR II, 538. (Johann Nepomuk Möser was an Austrian official as well as an art critic.)

Ferdinand Ries on Beethoven and Clementi:

When Clementi came to Vienna Beethoven wished to call on him at once; but his *141* brother put it into his head that Clementi should call first. Clementi, although much older, would probably have done this anyway, if some gossip about it had not arisen. So it came about that Clementi was in Vienna for a long time without Beethoven's knowing him except by sight. We often ate mid-day dinner at the same table at the Swan; Clementi with his pupil Klengel (1783–1852), and Beethoven with me. Everyone knew who everyone else was, but neither spoke to the other, or even greeted each other. The two pupils had to follow their masters, probably because each was under the threat of losing his lessons, which for me, at least, would certainly have been irrevocable, since with Beethoven there was never any compromise.

Kerst I, 95.

Anton Schindler writes about Beethoven's library:

His music library was very skimpy. Of his own works there was only a small number. Of the old Italians he knew no more than was generally known in his time – nothing beyond the collection of short pieces by Palestrina, Nanini, Vittoria and others, which Artaria had printed for Baron von Tucher around 1824. Those were there. There was not a note by Joseph Haydn or Cherubini. Of Mozart, a part of the score of *Don Giovanni* and many sonatas. He had almost all Clementi's sonatas. He had the greatest admiration for these and placed them in the front rank of works dedicated to beautiful piano-playing; he also loved them for their beautiful, pleasing and fresh melodies, and for the consistent, and therefore easily fathomable, form of all the movements. For Mozart's piano music he had little liking. Therefore, the master based the musical upbringing of his beloved nephew for several years almost exclusively on Clementi's Sonatas. This did not please Carl Czerny, at that time the nephew's teacher, who did not hold them in such esteem.

Schindler II, 182.

Notice in the Wiener Zeitung *of 10 August 1808:*

[original French]
143 Concerto for the pianoforte with large orchestra accompaniment, arranged from his 1st Concerto for Violin and dedicated to Madame de Breuning, Opus 61.

141 *Letter from Muzio Clementi to the publisher F. W. Collard, London:*

[original English]
Messrs. Clementi & Co., No. 26 Cheapside, London.
Vienna, April 22d, 1807.

Dear Collard:

By a little management and without committing myself, I have at last made a compleat conquest of that haughty beauty, Beethoven, who first began at public places to grin and coquet with me, which of course I took care not to discourage; then slid into familiar chat, till meeting him by chance one day in the street — 'Where do you lodge?' says he; 'I have not seen you this long while!' — upon which I gave him my address. Two days after I found on my table his card brought by himself, from the maid's description of his lovely form. This will do, thought I. Three days after that he calls again, and finds me at home. Conceive then the mutual ecstasy of such a meeting! I took pretty good care to improve it to our house's advantage, therefore, as soon as decency would allow, after praising very handsomely some of his compositions: 'Are you engaged with any publisher in London? — 'No' says he. 'Suppose, then, that you prefer me?' — 'With all my heart.' 'Done. What have you ready?' — 'I'll bring you a list.' In short I agreed with him to take in mss. three quartets, a symphony, an overture and a concerto for the violin, which is beautiful, and which, at my request he will adapt for the pianoforte with and without additional keys; and a concerto for the pianoforte, for all which we are to pay him two hundred pounds sterling. The property, however, is only for the British Dominions. To-day sets off a courier for London through Russia, and he will bring over to you two or three of the mentioned articles.

Remember that the violin concerto he will adapt himself and send it as soon as he can . . . .

TDR III, 26.

Julie was a pupil of Joh. Schenk, the composer of the *Dorfbarbier* [The Village 35
Barber], of *Weinlese* [The Vintage] and other music (whose appearance clad in
buckram breeches and a Spencer worn over his tail-coat still floats before my eyes).
Since she was a good pianist and even attempted small compositions (which I treasure),
it was natural that Beethoven soon took a double interest in the talented eighteen-
year-old wife of Steffen. He played four-hand duets with her and, what is more, he
honoured her artistic ambitions by dedicating his own pianoforte arrangement of the
Violin Concerto, Op. 61 (dedicated to Stephan) to 'Julien von Breuning née von
Werin' (correctly Vering).

Breuning 41.

Beethoven was always very interested in the theatre and wrote some excellent 'incidental'
theatrical music, such as that for Goethe's *Egmont*. One of the finest of his pieces in this
category was the overture to *Coriolan* by Heinrich Joseph von Collin, which Beethoven wrote
in 1807.

Johann Friedrich Reichardt on the Overture to Coriolan: 142, 144

Vienna, 10 December 1808

I also attended an amateur concert, which started the winter season, but its external
arrangements were nearly the death of me, in spite of the fact that the company was
most agreeable. Three rather small rooms were filled with a larger crowd than I have
ever seen here of listeners of all social classes, as well as an equally large number of
musicians. They were so crammed that I could neither breathe nor hear. Luckily my
sight was not impaired as well, for there was a goodly number of very pretty and
elegant ladies present, some of whom sang very nicely. But even some very good
things by Beethoven, Romberg, Paer and others could achieve no effect; the blare of
trumpets, kettledrums and all manner of wind instruments was quite deafening in
those narrow rooms. Nevertheless, I did manage to hear something absolutely perfect,
which was completely suited to the conditions and was therefore all the more a treat.
This was a Neapolitan guitar player .... This was appropriate for both the room and
the audience, who were delighted. But they did not seem to notice that the whole
pleasant impression was once more destroyed by Beethoven's overwhelming, gigantic
Overture to Collin's *Coriolan*. My brain and my heart almost burst from the hammer
blows and shrillness within the narrow rooms, especially as everyone tried with all his
might to increase the noise in view of the fact that the composer was present. It gave
me great pleasure to see dear Beethoven being much fêted, particularly because he
has the unfortunate, hypochondriac whim that everyone here persecutes and despises
him. His highly obstinate character may well scare off many of the kind-hearted and
gay Viennese. And even among those who recognize his great talent and achievement,
there are few who have enough humanity and subtlety to offer the sensitive, easily
aroused and suspicious artist the means to grasp the pleasant side of life, so that he
might happily accept it and find in it his satisfaction as an artist. It really upsets me

very deeply when I see this basically good and remarkable man looking gloomy and suffering, although I am convinced, on the other hand, that his best and most original works can only be produced when he is in a stubborn and deeply morose state of mind. Those people who are able to enjoy his works should never lose sight of this and not let themselves be put off by his outward peculiarities and rough edges. Only then can they be his true and sincere admirers.

Reichardt I, 174 ff.

144   *Johann Friedrich Reichardt describes Heinrich von Collin:*

Vienna, 30 November 1808

I have made a very interesting and, for me, highly important acquaintance with the poet Collin. Herr von Seckendorff, who has been here for a year and will stay on, and who takes a most friendly interest in me, had announced my arrival to him and I called on him. Since he works all day as a Court Secretary in the Imperial War Chancellery, I went in the evening in order to be sure to find him at home and alone. In this I was successful. The noble author of *Regulus* and *Coriolan* is an imposing man of spirit and understanding. He received me with all the Austrian candour and friendliness, which I like so much in this dear land, and with such ease of manner that from the very first he became a very dear and worthy friend. Even his completely Austrian manner of speech surprised me as little as his outward appearance which, apart from his light blue, truly gifted artist's eyes, suggests at first sight an honest sturdy burgher rather than a tragic poet. He seemed to take a liking to me too and had the kindness to read me a beautiful and powerful opera libretto. It was *Bradamante*, after Ariosto . . . .

Reichardt I, 118.

Caroline Pichler describes Heinrich von Collin:

. . . Such an unpretentious, simple, amiable conduct would hardly be associated with so distinguished a talent. This open heartiness was combined with a thorough understanding, an excellent knowledge of affairs (he was a civil servant, at that time a clerk or secretary in the Court Chamber) and a high classical culture.

Caroline Pichler, *Denkwürdigkeiten aus meinem Leben*, Vienna 1844, II, p. 52.

Among the many Haydn forms which Beethoven intended to stay clear of was the large-scale Mass. Haydn, after he had returned from London, had written six great Masses for the name-day of Princess Hermenegild Esterházy, and now that he was no longer able to compose, Prince Nicolaus II Esterházy asked Beethoven to compose a Mass for Eisenstadt. Through Haydn, Beethoven had long been in touch with the Esterházy family and had dedicated some marches to Princess Hermenegild. The new Mass was ready in 1807 and Beethoven went to Eisenstadt to conduct the first performance. The Mass in C Major, Op. 86, did not find favour, and Prince Nicolaus even went so far as to describe it as 'unbearably ridiculous and detestable', certainly not a tribute to that famous Prince's taste and discernment.

Anton Schindler on Beethoven's religious ideas:

Beethoven was brought up in the Catholic religion. The whole course of his life proves that he was truly religious at heart. The fact that he never discussed religious matters or the dogmas of the various Christian churches, or expressed his opinions about such questions, was one of his peculiar characteristics. It can be stated with relative certainty, however, that his religious views were based far less on faith in the Church than on Deism. Without any specific theory, he acknowledged God in the world, as well as the world in God. The theory for this he found constituted in the whole of nature, and that often-cited book, Christian Sturm's *Betrachtungen der Werke Gottes in der Natur*, as well as the teachings created out of the philosophic systems of the Greek sages, seem to have been the signposts he followed along this path. It would be difficult to assert the opposite if one had observed how he absorbed the significant contents of these writings into his inner life.

Kerst II, 26 f. Schindler II, 161.

Letter from Beethoven to Prince Nicolaus Esterházy: *145, 146*

Most Serene and Most Gracious Prince!
Since I have been told that you, my Prince, have inquired after the Mass which you commissioned me to write for you, I allow myself the freedom, most Serene Prince, to inform you that you will receive it at the latest by the 20th of August. This will allow sufficient time to perform it on the name-day of Her Serene Highness the Princess. Unusually advantageous offers were made to me from London, and since, unfortunately, a benefit day in the theatre did not come off, I was obliged to accept them gladly. This delayed the completion of the Mass, although I would have wished to present it to Your Serene Highness in person. Then I was struck down with a head condition which at the beginning prevented me from working at all and still only permits me to work very little. Since people are only too glad to misconstrue everything I do to my disadvantage, I submit for Your S[erene]H[ighness]'s perusal a letter from my physician. May I add that I shall deliver the Mass to you with much trepidation, as your S.H. is accustomed to the performance of the inimitable masterpieces of the great Haiden [sic].

Most Serene, Most Gracious Prince,
With respect,
your devoted and humble
Ludwig van Beethoven.

Baden, 26 July [1807].

Anderson 150.

Letter from Dr Schmidt, Beethoven's physician, to Beethoven:

Vienna, 22 July 1807

I was, my dear friend, at first convinced that your headache was caused by gout, and I am still of this opinion since the tooth was extracted. Your pains will be eased but they will not cease in Baden, nor will they in Rodaun, for the *Boreas* is your enemy. Therefore leave Baden, or, if you want to try out Rodaun for 8 days, put a spurge-laurel poultice on your arm straightaway. We can expect nothing more from bleeding, but you will be helped by taking the baths, working little and sleeping, eating well and drinking spirits in moderation.

Greetings and friendship,

In haste. Yours, Schmidt

Letter from Prince Nicolaus Esterházy to Beethoven:

Most esteemed Herr van Beethoven!
I perceive with much pleasure from your letter from Baden that I can entertain the agreeable hope of receiving a Mass from you before the 20th of this month. This fulfilment will give me all the more pleasure since I expect a great deal from it. Your expressed anxiety about a comparison with Haydn's Masses has only increased the value of your work. I wish you, moreover, the speediest recovery of your complete good health and remain with all esteem

Your most eager,
Nicolaus Prince Esterházy.

Eisenstadt the 9th August 8o̅7 .

Letter from Prince Nicolaus Esterházy to his Vice-Kapellmeister Johann Fuchs:

To my Vice-Kapellmeister Johann Fuchs.
My Vice-Kapellmeister will have to explain to me the reason why my contracted female singers are not always present at the *Musique*? On this very day I noticed, to my extreme displeasure, that at the rehearsal of the Beetovish [sic!] Mass only one of the five contraltos was present. This matter should have been under the control of the Vice-Kapellmeister and I herewith charge him with the duty of insuring strictly that all the members of my *Musique* and singing establishment are present not only at tomorrow's performance of the Beethovish [!] Mass, but also that in no case shall anyone be absent from his duties without a sufficient reason. I hold my Vice-Kapellmeister, as the appointed head, personally responsible for the maintenance of discipline and the avoidance of anything contrary to the established service and will call him to account.

Eisenstadt on the 12th September 1807.

Prince Esterházy

Note by Johann Nepomuk Hummel:

N.B. Herr Beethoven gave the following to the local copyist, which was to be used for the concert he intended to give; for two parts of a concerto, of which he took away the

1st violin part, together with three duplicate parts of a symphony, 53 sheets... 8 florins and 50 kreutzer.

Eisenstadt on the 12th Oct., 1807.

Johann Nep. Hummel, Konzertmeister

Letter from Prince Esterházy to Countess Henriette von Zielinska:

[original French]

... Beethoven's Mass is unbearably ridiculous and detestable, and I am not convinced that it can ever be performed properly. I am angry and mortified. Gulistan [an opera by Dalayrac] was well played. This is our news.

Johann Harich, *Beethoven in Eisenstadt*, special supplement from the *Burgenländische.Heimatblätter*, Eisenstadt 1959, 21st year, No. 2, p. 173 ff.

E.T.A. Hoffmann reviews Beethoven's Fifth Symphony in the Allgemeine Musikalische *150–153 Zeitung, July 1810:*

This reviewer has before him one of the most important works of the master whose position in the first rank of composers of instrumental music can now be denied by no one. So imbued is he with the subject at hand that he hopes that no one will take it amiss if he oversteps the boundaries of run-of-the-mill reviewing in an attempt to put into words the profound feelings which this composition has stirred within him. When one considers music as an independent art, one should always mean instrumental music which, avoiding all assistance, any interference from any of the other arts, exclusively expresses its own individual artistic essence. It is the most romantic of all the arts – in fact one might almost say the only purely romantic one ... Haydn and Mozart, the creators of the newer instrumental music, first revealed this art to us in the fullness of its glory. He who looked upon it filled with love and who penetrated its innermost substance is – Beethoven. Although the instrumental compositions of all three masters breathe the same romantic spirit which lies precisely in the same intimate ability to comprehend the individual essence of this art, the nature of their compositions differs markedly. In Haydn's compositions the expression of a youthful, light-hearted spirit is dominant. His symphonies lead us into an infinite green grove, in a cheerful, gaily coloured throng of merry people. Mozart leads us into the depths of the spiritual world. Fear grips us, but without torment; it is more a foreboding of the eternal.... Beethoven's instrumental music also opens up to us the world of the immense and the infinite. Glowing rays of light blaze through the dark night of this world and we are made conscious of gigantic shadows which surge up and down, gradually closing in on us more and more and annihilating everything within us, except the torment of endless longing.... Beethoven is a pure romantic and because of this a truly musical composer. That may be the reason why he is less successful in vocal music (which does not allow undefined longings, but represents only those passions, expressed through words, which are experienced as if in the realm of the eternal), and his instrumental music rarely appeals to the crowd.... Beethoven bears deep within his nature the romantic spirit of music, which he proclaims in his works with great genius and presence of mind. Your reviewer has never felt this so clearly as in this particular symphony which, more than any other of his works, unfolds Beethoven's romantic spirit in a climax rising straight to the end and carries the listener away irresistibly into the wondrous spirit world of the infinite . . . . Beethoven has retained the usual sequence of movements in this symphony; in their fantasy they appear to be linked one to the other. The whole work storms past some people like an ingenious rhapsody; but the soul of every sensitive listener will surely be deeply and intimately seized right up to the final chord by an enduring feeling which is exactly that inexpressible prophetic longing. Indeed, for a while after the final chord he will not be able to step out of that wonderful realm of the spirit where torment and joy, expressed in sound, embrace him. Apart from the construction, the instrumentation, etc., it is especially the inner relationship of the individual themes to one another which produces a unity that preserves the listener's mood. In Haydn's and Mozart's music this unity prevails everywhere. It becomes clearer to the musician, when he discovers a ground-base common to two different movements, or when it is revealed to him by the linking together of two movements. But a deeper relationship, which cannot be demonstrated by these means, often speaks only from the spirit to the spirit. And it is this relationship which dominates the two Allegro movements and the Minuet and gloriously proclaims the master's thoughtful genius. This reviewer believes he can express his verdict on this glorious artistic creation of the master in a few words by saying that it is conceived with genius, carried out with profound thoughtfulness, and expresses in the highest degree the romantic spirit in music.

In 1808, Beethoven had lodgings with a charming and delightful member of the Austro-Hungarian aristocracy, Anna Marie Countess Erdödy, who lived separated from her husband. A gifted pianist, Countess Erdödy gave musical dinner parties, a description of which has come down to us from the distinguished German critic and composer, Johann Friedrich Reichardt.

149, 154   *Letter from Beethoven to Countess Erdödy:*

[Vienna, March 1809]

My dear Countess,

I have been in the wrong, that is true. Forgive me. It is certainly not deliberate wickedness on my part if I have caused you pain. Only since yesterday evening have I known exactly how things stand and I am very sorry that I behaved as I did – read your note in cold blood and judge for yourself whether I deserved that, and whether you are not paying me back with it six-fold, considering that I offended you unintentionally. Please send my note back today and write a single word to say you are fond of me again. I suffer endlessly over this. If you do not do this, I can do nothing if things go on like this – I await your forgiveness.

KAL 259. Anderson 207.

Letter from Beethoven to Countess Erdödy:

To Countess Marie Erdödy, née Nizky –
Everything good and beautiful to my beloved, honoured and treasured friend,

from your true
and admiring friend,
L.v. Beethoven.

In haste, 19 Dec. 1819.
I shall soon come in person.

TDR IV, 174. Anderson 986.

Johann Friedrich Reichardt writes about Countess Erdödy:

Vienna, 30 November 1808.

I have also sought out and visited the good Beethoven. People pay so little attention to him here that no one could tell me where he lives, and it entailed quite a lot of trouble on my part to locate him. Finally I found him in a large, desolate and lonely apartment. At first he looked as dark as his own lodgings, but soon became more cheerful and even seemed as pleased to see me again as I was heartily glad to see him. He also told me a lot of things which were important for me to know, all in a very frank and agreeable manner. His is a powerful nature, like a cyclops in appearance but at the same time very intimate, hearty and good. He lives and spends a good deal of time with a Hungarian Countess Erdödy who lives in the front part of the large house. But he has become quite estranged from Prince Lichnowsky who lives in the upper part of the same house, although some years ago they were on very intimate terms. I wanted also to call on the Prince, who is an old acquaintance of mine, and on his wife, the daughter of the delightful Countess von Thun, to whom I owe the greatest part of my pleasure during my first visit to Vienna. But I found neither of them at home, and I soon found out that the Princess lives a very retired life.

5 December 1808.

I was invited to another most agreeable dinner by means of a very friendly note from Beethoven, who had not been able to reach me in person. It was given by his hostess, Countess Erdödy. I was so deeply touched there that my pleasure was nearly ruined. Imagine a very pretty, small, delicate woman of twenty-five who had been married at the age of fifteen, had contracted an incurable illness at the time of her first confinement, and in the ten years since then has not been able to remain out of bed for more than two or three months. And yet she has given birth to three healthy and charming children who are as close to her as burs. The only pleasure left for her is music and she plays even Beethoven's music quite well, hobbling from one Fortepiano to the other on her still very swollen feet. Withal she is so cheerful, so friendly and kind, that it frequently made me very sad during the otherwise so very pleasant dinner among six or eight good musical souls. And then we got the temperamental Beethoven to the Fortepiano as well. He improvised for a good hour from the depths of his artistic feelings, ranging from the highest heights to the deepest depths of the celestial art, with mastery and versatility, so that ten times at least tears came to my eyes. At the end, I could find no words to express my deep-felt rapture. I hung around his neck like an ardently emotional child, and again was childishly pleased that he and the other enthusiastic souls also seemed to enjoy my Goethe songs.

Reichardt I, 124f., 147f.

Baron de Trémont describes a visit to Beethoven:

I betook myself to the unapproachable composer, and when I had reached his door, I thought that I had chosen the wrong day. Since I was making an official call, I was wearing undress state uniform. Besides, he unfortunately lives on the ramparts, and since Napoleon had ordered their destruction, a mine had been placed under his windows.

His neighbours pointed out his apartment to me. 'He is at home', they told me 'but at the moment he has no servants, because he changes them all the time. It is doubtful whether he will open.' I rang three times and was about to leave again when a very ugly man, visibly in a bad temper, opened and asked what I wanted. 'Do I have the honour to address Herr Beethoven?' I asked. 'Yes, Sir, but I must warn you', he answered in German, 'that I understand very little French.' I understand German no better, Sir, but my embassy is limited to delivering a letter from Paris to you, from Herr Reicha.'

He looked at me, took the letter and allowed me to enter. His apartment consisted, I think, of only two rooms. The first contained an enclosed alcove with his bed, but was so small and dark that he must have dressed in the second room, or salon. Imagine the dirtiest and most disorderly room possible. There were water stains on the floor: a rather ancient pianoforte on which the dust struggled for supremacy with sheets covered with handwritten or printed notes. Underneath – I do not exaggerate – an unemptied chamber pot. Next to it was a small walnut table which had become accustomed to having writing materials spilled on it. There was a large number of quills encrusted with dried ink, compared to which the proverbial pens provided by inns would have seemed excellent. The chairs nearly all had straw seats and were covered with clothes and dishes filled with the remains of last night's supper. Balzac or Dickens could continue this description for two pages and would need the same again to describe to you the outward appearance of the famous composer. Since I am neither Balzac nor Dickens, I limit myself to saying: I was at Beethoven's.

I barely spoke broken German, but I understood it somewhat better. He did no better with French. I expected him to read the letter and dismiss me, and feared that our acquaintance would end there. I had seen the bear in his pit; that was more than I could hope. I was therefore most surprised when he went on looking at me, placed the letter, unopened, on the table and offered me a chair – and was even more

222

startled when he began to chat with me. He asked me about my uniform, my office, my age and the purpose of my journey, whether I was a musician, whether I would have to stay on in Vienna. I replied that the letter from Reicha would more or less answer all his queries, and, moreover, explain it a good deal better than I would be able to do.

'No, no, tell me', he said, 'but slowly, since I am very hard of hearing. I will understand you.' I made incredible efforts to express myself, while he went about it with the best of wills. It was the most peculiar mixture of bad German and bad French. In a word: we understood each other, the visit lasted nearly three-quarters of an hour, and I had to promise him to come again.

I went away prouder than Napoleon when he entered Vienna: I had conquered Beethoven.

Kerst I, 134 ff.

Beethoven had meanwhile been composing many masterpieces which needed to be presented to the public, and on 22 December 1808, at the Theater an der Wien, he gave a stupendous evening in which the world heard for the first time the Fifth Symphony, the Sixth Symphony, the Choral Fantasy, the Piano Concerto in G, Op. 58, and several movements of the Mass for Princess Esterházy, Op. 86.

Ferdinand Ries describes Beethoven's concert on 22 December 1808:

Beethoven gave [on 22 December 1808] a large concert in the Theater an der Wien at which were performed for the first time the C Minor and Pastoral Symphonies as well as his Fantasia for Piano with orchestra and chorus. In this last work, at the place where the last beguiling theme appears already in a varied form, the clarinet player made, by mistake, a repeat of eight bars. Since only a few instruments were playing, this error was all the more evident to the ear. Beethoven leaped up in a fury, turned around and abused the orchestra players in the coarsest terms and so loudly that he could be heard throughout the auditorium. Finally, he shouted 'From the beginning!' The theme began again, everyone came in properly, and the success was great. But when the concert was finished the artists, remembering only too well the honourable title which Beethoven had bestowed on them in public, fell into a great rage, as if the offence had just occurred. They swore that they would never play again if Beethoven were in the orchestra, and so forth. This went on until Beethoven had composed something new, and then their curiosity got the better of their anger.

Kerst I, 96.

Johann Friedrich Reichardt describes the concert on 22 December 1808:

Vienna, 25 December 1808.
During this past week, when the theatres were closed and the evenings were taken up with musical performances and concerts, my eagerness and resolution to hear everything caused me no small embarrassment. This was particularly the case on the 22nd,

because the local musicians gave the first of the season's great musical performances in the Burgtheater for the benefit of their admirable Society for Musicians' Widows; on the same day, however, Beethoven also gave a concert for his own benefit in the large suburban theatre, consisting entirely of his own compositions. I could not possibly miss this and accepted with heartfelt gratitude Prince Lobkowitz's kind invitation to take me with him in his box. There we held out in the bitterest cold from half-past six until half-past ten, and experienced the fact that one can easily have too much of a good – and even more of a strong – thing. I, no more than the extremely kindly and gentle Prince, whose box was in the first tier very near to the stage, on which the orchestra with Beethoven conducting were quite close to us, would have thought of leaving the box before the very end of the concert, although several faulty performances tried our patience to the utmost. Poor Beethoven, for whom this concert provided the first and only small profit that he had been able to earn and retain during this whole year, had encountered a great deal of opposition and very little support both in its organization and performance. The singers and the orchestra were assembled from very heterogeneous elements. Moreover, it had not even been possible to arrange a complete rehearsal of all the pieces to be performed, every one of which was filled with passages of the utmost difficulty. You will be amazed [to hear] all that was performed by this fertile genius and untiring worker, in the course of four hours.

Reichardt I, 205.   Kerst I, 132 f.

Louis Spohr describes Beethoven conducting:

Seyfried, to whom I expressed my astonishment at this extraordinary method of conducting, told me about a tragi-comical incident which took place during Beethoven's last concert in the Theater an der Wien [1808].

Beethoven was playing a new piano concerto of his, but already at the first *tutti*, forgetting that he was the soloist, he jumped up and began to conduct in his own peculiar fashion. At the first *sforzando* he threw out his arms so wide that he knocked over both the lamps from the music stand of the piano. The audience laughed and Beethoven was so beside himself over this disturbance that he stopped the orchestra and made them start again. Seyfried, worried for fear that this would happen again in the same place, took the precaution of ordering two choirboys to stand next to Beethoven and to hold the lamps in their hands. One of them innocently stepped closer and followed the music from the piano part. But when the fatal *sforzando* burst forth, the poor boy received from Beethoven's right hand such a sharp slap in the face that, terrified, he dropped the lamp on the floor. The other, more wary boy, who had been anxiously following Beethoven's movements, succeeded in avoiding the blow by ducking in time. If the audience had laughed the first time, they now indulged in a truly bacchanalian riot. Beethoven broke out in such a fury that when he struck the first chord of the solo he broke six strings. Every effort of the true music-lovers to restore calm and attention remained unavailing for some time; thus the first Allegro of the Concerto was completely lost to the audience. Since this accident, Beethoven wanted to give no more concerts.

Louis Spohr, *Selbstbiographie, 1860–61*, new edition, Brunswick 1954, p. 200 f. (English transl. London 1865). Kerst I, 174. (The composer Spohr lived in Vienna from 1812 to 1816 and knew Beethoven during those years.)

141. Muzio Clementi (1746–1832). Engraving by Edward Scriven from a painting by James Lonsdale, 1819. Gesellschaft der Musikfreunde, Vienna.

Clementi persuaded Beethoven to re-write the Violin Concerto in D as a piano concerto, in which form it was published by Clementi and his partners in London; Beethoven added a new and interesting cadenza in which there appear solo timpani.

142. Overture to *Coriolan*, Op. 62. First page of the autograph. Beethovenhaus Bonn.

The first performance of the overture took place at an amateur concert in Vienna, during December 1807. At the top of the page is the title in Beethoven's own hand: 'overtura [Zum Trauerspiel, these words later cancelled] composta de L. v. Beethoven 1807.'

143. Julie von Breuning, née von Vering (1791–1809).
Anonymous portrait in oils, attributed to Joseph Willibrord
Mähler. Historisches Museum of the City of Vienna.

Julie von Vering married Beethoven's friend from Bonn,
Stephan von Breuning, in April 1808. She was a pupil of
Johann Baptist Schenk and a talented pianist; Beethoven
used to improvise on the piano for hours at the Breunings'.

144. Heinrich Joseph von Collin (1772–1811). Portrait in oils by Joseph Lange, *c.* 1800. Historisches Museum of the City of Vienna.

The well-known Austrian poet Heinrich von Collin, author of many patriotic songs such as the 'Wehrmannslieder' of 1809, which encouraged the Viennese to war-like fervour in the Napoleonic era, wrote the tragedy *Coriolan*, performed for the first time at the Burgtheater in 1802. Joseph Lange (Mozart's talented brother-in-law, whose portraits are realistic and well-drawn) was in the title rôle.

145. Bergkirche in Eisenstadt.
Lithograph by A. L. Jung from
a drawing by Michael Mayer,
1840. Haydnmuseum, Eisenstadt.

In 1807, Prince Nicolaus II
Esterházy ordered a new Mass
from Beethoven to celebrate the
name day of his wife. Beethoven,
aware that the Prince was used
to Haydn's Masses, had some
reservations, but overcame them
and wrote his Mass in C, Op. 86,
for the Princess Hermenegild.
The Mass was first performed
with Haydn's orchestra and choir
at the Bergkirche but was not
particularly successful, and
Beethoven, rather offended, soon
left Eisenstadt.

146. Esterházy Castle in Eisenstadt. Coloured steel plate engraving by C. Rorich,
from a drawing by Ludwig Rohbock. Haydnmuseum, Eisenstadt.

Beethoven had planned to hold an 'Academy' (concert) in Eisenstadt, and some of
the new music had actually been copied for it; but the concert did not take place,
probably because of the cool reception given to the new Mass.

147. Ludwig van Beethoven. Pencil drawing by Ludwig(?) Schnorr von Carolsfeld, *c.* 1808. The original has disappeared. Reproduction H. C. Robbins Landon, Buggiano Castello, Italy.

Underneath the portrait is the following note in an unknown hand: 'By the old Direktor Schnorr von Carolsfeld from Dresden in the year 1808 or 1809 in a sketchbook of the Malfatti family in Munich. Owned by Frau von Gleichenstein née Malfatti in Freiburg i. Br[eisgau].' Beethoven was an intimate friend of the Malfatti family; he was particularly attracted to one of the daughters, the beautiful Therese, and officially asked her hand in marriage. The family disapproved of the idea.

148. Maria Hermenegild Princess Esterházy, née Princess von Liechtenstein (1768–1845). Portrait in oils by Angelika Kauffmann, dated Rome, 1795. Galerie Liechtenstein, Vienna.

After Haydn's return from England in 1795, it became a tradition in Eisenstadt to celebrate the Princess's name day, which occurred in September, with the performance of a big Mass for solo voices, choir and orchestra in the Bergkirche. Haydn composed his last six Masses for this event, and finished the series in 1802 with the *Harmoniemesse*. Prince Nicolaus II Esterházy commissioned other composers to write such masses when Haydn was no longer able to compose. It is thought that Beethoven owed his commission of 1807 to Haydn.

149. Anna Marie Countess Erdödy, née Countess Niczky (1779–1837). Miniature on ivory (7 × 9 cm). Collection, Dr H. C. Bodmer, Beethovenhaus Bonn.

This miniature was found after Beethoven's death in his desk, and thus Countess Erdödy has been put forward as the 'Immortal Beloved' (which she emphatically was not). But Beethoven was warmly attached to the sympathetic Anna Marie, who was a semi-invalid; she was separated from her husband and her salon was one of Vienna's most brilliant. At one point Beethoven shared lodgings with her. He used to call her his 'father confessor'.

Sheet 1

Sheet 2

Sheet 4

150–153. Symphony No. 5 in C minor, Op. 67. Trio. Violoncello and basso parts of the original performance material. Gesellschaft der Musikfreunde, Vienna.

The four sheets here reproduced show the trio of the Fifth Symphony in its original state; at the first performance this movement had the unusual length of 611 bars. The Symphony was first performed on 22 December 1808 at an 'Academy' held in the Theater an der Wien, which included only music by Beethoven. Apart from the Fifth and Sixth ('Pastoral') Symphonies, Beethoven conducted several movements from the Mass for Princess Esterházy, Op. 86, the Choral Fantasy, Op. 80, and the Piano Concerto in G, Op. 58. Many critics found the concert too long, and perhaps this may explain the cut in the Scherzo, which in its present state is about half the original length. Sheet 3 was sewed shut, so that in the revised version the player cut from line 2, bar 2 of Sheet 2, right across to Sheet 4, line 3 (marked 'Vi-de').

Sheet 3

154. Anna Marie Countess Erdödy with her husband Count Peter Erdödy. Anonymous family picture — reproduction H. C. Robbins Landon, Buggiano Castello, Italy.

Dr Stephan Ley discovered the painting in Vienna at Baroness Skrbensky's, a great-granddaughter of Countess Erdödy. The picture was destroyed in 1945, and Baroness Skrbensky was killed.

233

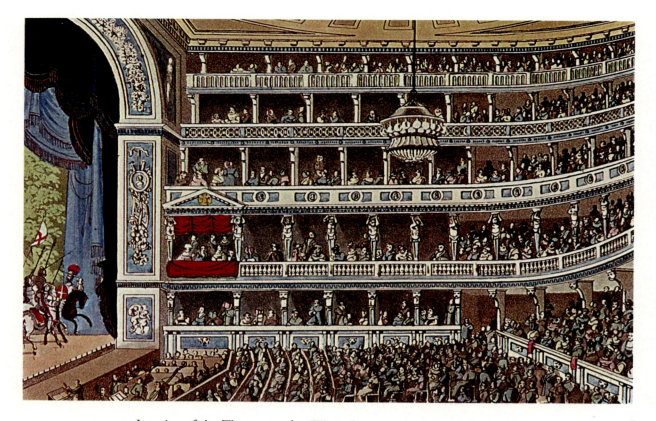

155. Interior of the Theater an der Wien. Anonymous coloured engraving, 1825. Historisches Museum of the City of Vienna.

The famous concert of 22 December 1808 took place here. *(See also plate 106.)*

156. Symphony No. 6 in F major, Op. 68. First movement. First violin part of the original performance material. Gesellschaft der Musikfreunde, Vienna.

This page contains corrections in Beethoven's own hand. The Symphony was completed at Heiligenstadt in 1808. In one of his notebooks Beethoven wrote: 'Anyone who has even a faint idea of life in the country can imagine what the author wishes without the descriptive titles.'

157. Ludwig van Beethoven. Portrait in oils by Isidor Neugass, *c.* 1806.
The so-called Beethoven portrait of the Brunsvik House. Mme Françoise
de Cossette, Paris.

Isidor Neugass, who had painted Haydn's portrait (now in Eisenstadt),
made two portraits of Beethoven, of which only one is signed 'peint par
Neugass Wienne 1806'. This signed and dated portrait was formerly owned
by Prince Lichnowsky in Grätz Castle and is now in possession of the
Lichnowsky descendants in South America. This is the first reproduction
of either in colour.

158. Caroline Marie Princess Kinsky, née Freiin von Kerpen (1782–1841), with her sons Rudolph and Joseph. Reproduction from an anonymous etching, dated 1827. Palais Kinsky, Vienna.

The Princess lost her husband suddenly when a horse threw and killed him in 1812; the complicated Kinsky financial affairs, in addition to the national catastrophe of the Austrian state bankruptcy, forced her to hold up payments to Beethoven until Prince Ferdinand's estate could be put in order.

159. Freiherr Ignaz von Gleichenstein (1778–1828). Pencil
drawing. Frau von Gleichenstein, Kiechlingsbergen, Germany.

Gleichenstein, a government official, was a talented amateur cellist
and a friend of Beethoven's from 1797; he was one of the few
among Beethoven's friends whose relationship remained uncloud-
ed by any major differences. Beethoven dedicated his Cello
Sonata in A, Op. 69, to Gleichenstein.

160. Concert at the Malfattis'.
Anonymous oil painting. Frau von Gleichenstein, Kiechlingsbergen, Germany.

In the centre are the two daughters of Jakob von Malfatti (*left-hand corner*): Therese at the piano and her sister Anna. Behind Therese, to the left, her mother and to the right Dr Giovanni von Malfatti, who was Beethoven's doctor for a time and attended him on his deathbed. Far right, Mathias von Malfatti, the grandfather of the two girls. To the left of Mathias in the background, are two more of his sons; and in the right-hand corner a young cousin of the girls. The Malfatti family came from Lucca. In 1795 Giovanni Malfatti settled in Vienna and soon became a popular doctor. His brother Jakob owned an estate in Wolkersdorf where the family spent the summers; in the winter they returned to Vienna. Beethoven was introduced to this music-loving family by their friend Ignaz von Gleichenstein.

161. Anna Freifrau von Gleichenstein, née von Malfatti (1792–1869?). Anonymous portrait in oils. Frau von Gleichenstein, Kiechlingsbergen, Germany.

Anna, eleven months younger than her sister Therese, married Ignaz von Gleichenstein in 1811 and from 1813 lived in Breisgau.

238

162. Jerome Bonaparte, King of Westphalia (1784–1860). Portrait in oils by Antoine Jean Gros. Arenenberg Castle, Switzerland.

Jerome Bonaparte, Napoleon's younger brother, offered Beethoven a yearly income of 600 Ducats, with 150 Ducats for travelling expenses, if he would go to Kassel, where Jerome Bonaparte's court was in residence. The composer was to conduct concerts there and occasionally to play for Jerome personally. Beethoven was very tempted by this offer of a regular income, and to keep him in Vienna, the Archduke Rudolph, together with Princes Lobkowitz and Kinsky, offered the master a contract in 1809 which was to provide him with an assured regular yearly income.

163. Ferdinand Bonaventura Prince Kinsky (1781–1812). Anonymous portrait in oils. Chlumec, Czechoslovakia.

Of the annual 4000 Gulden which Archduke Rudolph and Princes Lobkowitz and Kinsky guaranteed to Beethoven, Prince Kinsky agreed to contribute 1800 Gulden. Beethoven dedicated to Prince Kinsky his Mass in C, Op. 86, originally written for Princess Esterházy, but which had received a very cool reception at Eisenstadt.

164. The city walls at the Burgbastei damaged by French sappers. Gouache by Franz Jaschke, 1809. Historisches Museum of the City of Vienna.

At the end of May 1809, French troops took Vienna after a large-scale night bombardment and began systematically to destroy Vienna's fortifications. Joseph Haydn died on 31 May 1809 at the beginning of the French occupation.

165. Playbill of the performance of Goethe's *Egmont* on 15 June 1810 at the Burgtheater. Theatersammlung der Österreichischen Nationalbibliothek, Vienna.

Goethe's tragedy *Egmont* was performed from May, but the first performance with Beethoven's incidental music took place on 15 June.

One leaves it to the listener to determine the situations [in the] Sinfonia Caracteristica — or reminiscences of country life. . . .
All painting, if carried too far in instrumental music, is lost – Sinfonia Pastorale. Whosoever has retained only an inkling of country life can think for himself, without too many headings, what the author wants – Even without description one will recognize the whole more as feeling rather than as tone-painting.

TDR III, 98.

From the Allgemeine Musikalische Zeitung *of 25 January 1809 :*

Programme of the Concert of 22 December 1808:
Pastoral Symphony (No. 5)*, more an expression of feeling than painting.
1st piece. Agreeable feelings awakened in man by his arrival in the country.
2nd piece. Scene by a stream.
3rd piece. Merrymaking of country folk. There arises
4th piece. a thunderstorm; wherein occur
5th piece. Charitable thoughts combined with thanks to the Deity after the storm.

Anton Schindler discusses the Pastoral Symphony:

The Pastoral, as well as the **C Minor** Symphony, were written in Heiligenstadt, in the   *105*
place already familiar to the reader from the events of 1802. This village, lying on the right bank of the Danube, was in those years the customary summer resort of our master. Only many years later did he choose places to the south of the capital city, such as Hetzendorf, Mödling or Baden, as his Tusculum, the latter two towns being recommended by his doctors on account of their thermal baths.

In the second half of April 1823, a period of many tribulations and reverses, Beethoven one day proposed a holiday expedition to the north side where he had not set foot for ten years. We decided to go first to Heiligenstadt and its charming surroundings, where he had put so many musical works to paper, and where he had also made many studies of nature. The sun was shining as in summer and the country-side was already clad in its best spring finery. After we had seen the baths of Heiligenstadt with their adjoining gardens and other pleasant sights, and reminisced the while about the works which he had created there, we continued our excursion to the Kahlenberg in the direction of Grinzing. As we walked along the pleasant grassy valley between Heiligenstadt and Grinzing, which is traversed by a softly murmuring brook flowing rapidly down from the nearby hills, shaded in places by tall elm trees, Beethoven frequently stopped and, filled with happy feelings of rapture, let his gaze wander over the beautiful landscape. Then he sat down in a field, leaning against an elm, and asked me if any yellow-hammers were to be heard in the upper branches

*The Pastoral Symphony was originally No. 5, while the C-Minor Symphony was originally No. 6.

of these trees. But all was quiet. Thereupon he said, 'This is where I composed the scene by the stream and the yellow-hammers up there, and the quails, the nightingales and the cuckoos round about composed with me.' To my question as to why he had not introduced the yellow-hammers into the scene, he reached for his sketch-book and wrote:

'That is the lady composer up there,' he said, 'and does she not play a more important rôle than the others? For *them*, it is only a game' . . . .

The Viennese music-lovers of that time had guessed fairly easily, without explanations by the composer, his intentions in this movement [Third Movement, 'Merrymaking of the Country Folk by a Stream']. They apparently recognized, in the form of the first part in three-four time, a version of Austrian country dance music, if not almost a parody of it such as a Beethoven could have written . . . .

The Pastoral Symphony! As the painter completes each element and brings the whole into a united picture, so also did Beethoven in this tone painting. It begins peacefully enough in the foreground; the manifold parts are always resolved quietly. After the terrifying and fearsome depiction of the thunderstorm, the background again resolves itself peacefully, and when in the final measures the distant note of the hunting horn is heard, we feel as if we were in the great concert hall of nature. Praise be to thee, exalted master!

Schindler I, 153 ff.

Letter about Beethoven from Stephan von Breuning to Dr Franz Wegeler, from Vienna:

[13 November 1804]

. . . The friend, who remained from the years of my youth here, is still often the cause of my being obliged to neglect the absent ones. You would not believe, my dear Wegeler, what an indescribable and, I might say, ghastly effect the loss of hearing has had on him. Imagine to yourself what the feeling of being a victim of misfortune can do to his vehement character, namely reserve, mistrust, often towards his best friends, and indecision in many things. On the whole, with only a few exceptions when he gives expression to his original spirit, to be with him is truly an effort, wherein one can never trust oneself. From May until the beginning of this month we lived in the same house, and on the very first days I took him into my room. He had hardly been with me when he came down with a very serious passing illness, bordering on the fatal, which finally turned into a continuous intermittent fever. (His chronic tendency to liver malfunction from old times is still noticeable.) Worry and nursing rather took it out of me. Now he is quite well again. He lives on the *Bastei*, while I live in a house recently built by Prince Esterházy in front of the Alser barracks. Since I keep house for myself, he has his meals with me every day.

Breuning 38f. (The sentence within parenthesis was added by Dr Gerhard von Breuning, Stephan's son.)

Never adept at managing his own finances, Beethoven began seriously to worry about his future. He had no steady income, and Mozart's death in dire poverty was obviously a spectre that haunted Vienna for many years after. Now there came a glowing offer from Napoleon's brother, Jerome Bonaparte, King of Westphalia at Cassel. It would have meant a regular yearly income of 600 gold ducats, and Beethoven accepted early in January 1809. His Viennese friends and patrons were aghast, and Countess Erdödy, as well as another intimate friend of Beethoven's, Baron Ignaz von Gleichenstein, worked out a contract for which undoubtedly the Archduke Rudolph was responsible. Under the terms of this contract, dated 1 March 1809, Beethoven was provided with a yearly income of 4000 gulden, guaranteed by the Archduke, Prince Lobkowitz, and another distinguished patron, Ferdinand Bonaventura, Prince Kinsky. As a result of the Napoleonic Wars, and because Prince Lobkowitz and Prince Kinsky soon died (Kinsky in 1812 and Lobkowitz in 1816), Beethoven's financial position was only temporarily improved. But Princess Kinsky proved to be honourable as well as generous, as did the Lobkowitz estate; Beethoven was therefore never really penniless, though he never had much money after the Congress of Vienna in 1815.

Letter from Beethoven to the publishers Breitkopf und Härtel:

Vienna, 7 January 1809

... I have at last been obliged by intrigues, cabals and underhanded actions of all kinds to abandon the last remaining German part of my fatherland. His Royal Majesty, the King of Westphalia [Jerome Bonaparte] has offered me the post of *162* Kapellmeister with a yearly stipend of 600 gold ducats. I have today sent by post my assurance that I will accept, and now await the decree of my appointment, following which I will make my travel preparations which should take me through Leipzig – therefore, in order that my journey may be more brilliant for me, please, if this is not otherwise disadvantageous to you, do not make any of my works known until Easter ...

With my respects,
your devoted servant,
Beethoven.

[Written on the back of the envelope]:
Please do not make any definite public statement about my appointment in Westphalia until I write to you that I have received the decree. May things go well with you and please write to me soon – we will discuss my compositions in Leipzig – a few hints could be dropped in the Musikalische Zeitung about my departure from here, and perhaps a dig or two, since no one has ever wanted to do anything here to my advantage – –

KAL 245 ff.   Anderson 192.

Letter from Beethoven to Baron Ignaz von Gleichenstein: *159*

[Vienna, February 1809]

It is probably too late to do anything today – I have been unable to get back your written statement from the A[rchduke] until this minute, because his H[ighness] wanted to add a few more items and buts and whereas's. I beg of you to see that the whole refers to the true practice of my art as is proper to me, for then you will have written fully what is in my heart and my head. The introduction states what I receive in Westphalia, 600 # in gold, 150 # travel expenses and for that I must conduct only the concerts for the King, which are short and actually infrequent. I am not even bound to conduct an opera of my composition. From all this it is clear that I can entirely fulfil the most important aspects of my art, to write great works – and also have an orchestra at my disposal . . .

N.B. We must have the document by 12 noon tomorrow, because we must go to Kinsky's at that time – I hope to see you today.

163

KAL 241. Anderson 195. (# = ducat.)

Letter from Beethoven to Baron Ignaz von Gleichenstein:

[Vienna, February 1809]

149, 154 Countess Erdödy thinks that you should draw up a plan with her, whereby, if she is approached, as she believes she undoubtedly will be, she will be in a position to negotiate.

Your friend,
Lu. Beethoven.

If you had time this afternoon, it would give the Countess pleasure to see you.

KAL 255. Anderson 198.

Contract between Beethoven and his patrons:

[stamp of 4 gulden]

Contract.

The daily demonstrations which Herr Ludwig van Beethoven gives of his extra-ordinary talent and genius as a musical artist and composer have aroused the desire that he may surpass the great expectations warranted by the experiences heretofore achieved.

Since, however, it has been demonstrated that only a man as free from cares as possible can devote himself to one profession excluding all other occupations, and thus be enabled to create great and sublime works ennobling the arts, therefore the undersigned have come to a decision to place Herr Ludwig van Beethoven in the position wherein his most pressing requirements will not be of embarrassment to him, nor in any way inhibit his powerful genius.

They accordingly bind themselves to pay him the yearly fixed sum of 4000 (four thousand) gulden, in the following proportions:

His Imperial Highness, the Archduke Rudolph	Fl. 1500	*138*
The Noble Prince Lobkowitz...	„ 700	*112*
The Noble Prince Ferdinand Kinsky	„ 1800	*163*
Total	Fl. 4000	

upon which Herr Ludwig van Beethoven can draw half-yearly from each of these noble contracting parties in the amount of his contribution, upon release of a receipt therefor.

The undersigned are also willing to continue this annual subsidy until Herr Ludwig van Beethoven obtains an appointment which will pay him a stipend equivalent to the above stated amount.

In the event that such an appointment should not come about, or that Herr Ludwig van Beethoven, through unfortunate circumstances or old age, should be prevented from practising his art, the partners grant him this stipend for the rest of his natural life.

In return, however, Herr Ludwig van Beethoven binds himself to reside in Vienna where the noble contracting parties reside, or to fix on another city situated within the hereditary dominions of His Austrian Imperial Majesty, and to leave such a residence only for stated periods as may be dictated by reason of business or in connection with the encouragement of art, after informing the noble contracting parties of such intended departure, and obtaining the approval thereof.

     Thus presented, in Vienna, on 1 March 1809.

[seal] [signed]   Rudolph,
                Archduke.

[seal] [signed]   Prince von Lobkowitz,
                Duke of Raudnitz.

[seal] [signed]   Ferdinand Prince Kinsky.

[This document bears the following words written in Beethoven's hand:]

Received
on 26 February 1809
from the hands
of the Archduke
Rudolph K. H.

TDR III, 125. (K. H. means Königliche Hoheit.)

Dedications by Beethoven to Caroline Princess Kinsky: *158*

[October 1810]
SIX SONGS/ with Pianoforte accompaniment / set to music / and dedicated / to Her Serene Highness / the Princess v. Kinsky, née Kerpen / by L. v. BEETHOVEN/. Property of the Publisher/[l.:] Opus 75. [r.:] Price 1 Rthlr/Leipzig/at Breitkopf & Härtel.

[October 1811]
THREE SONGS / by Göthe [sic] / with Pianoforte accompaniment / set to Music / and dedicated / to the Princess von Kinsky, née Countess v. Kerpen / by / Ludwig v. Beethoven / [l.:] Opus 83. Property of the publisher. [r.:] 12 gr./ at Breitkopf & Härtel in Leipzig.

[April 1816]
To Hope/FROM TIEDGE'S URANIA/set to music/ for solo voice with accompaniment of the Pianoforte / and / dedicated / TO HER SERENE HIGHNESS / THE PRINCESS von KINSKY née COUNTESS von KERPEN/ by Ludw. van Beethoven/ Opus 94. [l.:] No. 2369. property of the publisher. – [r.:] Price/Vienna, at S. A. Steiner und Comp.

KHV 202, 224, 266.

Letter from Beethoven to the publishers Breitkopf und Härtel:

Vienna, 28 January 1812

... if the 3 songs by Göthe [Op. 83] have not yet been engraved, please make haste with them. I want very much to give them to the Princess Kynsky [sic], one of the prettiest, plumpest women in Vienna. And the songs from Egmont, why are they not out yet? In fact why not the whole of E? Out with them, out, out . . . .

KFR 56. Anderson 345.

Letter from Beethoven to Caroline Princess von Kinsky in Prague:

Vienna, 30 December 1812

Your Serene Highness!

158, 163   The unhappy event – which removed His Serene Highness, the Prince von Kinsky, your late most noble consort, from his fatherland, from your own dear family and from so many others whom you so generously support, and which has filled with deepest sorrow all those who are sensitive to what is great and good – has also affected me in a way that is as singular for me as it is painful. The bitter duty of self-preservation obliges me to lay before Your Serene Highness a humble request which, being justified, will provide the excuse for having to trouble Your Serene Highness at a time when so many important matters require your attention. Allow me, Serene Highness, to lay this matter before you.

It will undoubtedly be known to Your Serene Highness that when in the year 1809, I received a call to Westphalia, His Serene Highness the Prince von Kinsky, your late noble husband, jointly with His Imp. Highness the Archduke Rudolph and His Serene Highness the Prince von Lobkowitz, offered to guarantee me a life-long annual stipend of four thousand gulden, if I were willing to give up that appointment and to remain in Austria. Although even at that time this sum was in no way equivalent to what would have been guaranteed to me in Westphalia, my preference for Austria, as well as my recognition of the great generosity of this proposal, did not allow me a moment's hesitation before accepting it. The share of this stipend, which His Serene Highness the Prince von Kinsky underwrote, was in the amount of 1800 fl. which since 1809 I have received in quarterly instalments from the Prince's Exchequer . . . .

Since at that time His Serene Highness Prince von Kinsky was in Prague, in May of this year I arranged for Herr Varnhagen von Ense, an officer of the Vogelsang Regiment, to present to His Serene Highness a humble petition requesting that His Serene Highness' share of 1800 fl. might, like that of the other noble guarantors, be paid in redemption bonds. Herr von Varnhagen reported as follows, as per his letter, of which the original still exists:

'Yesterday I had a satisfactory conversation with Prince Kinsky. Expressing the highest praises of Beethoven he immediately agreed to his requests and will pay him arrears from the time that the redemption bonds were introduced, and will pay him all future amounts in this currency. The cashier was given the necessary instructions and Beethoven can draw the whole amount here when passing [through Prague] or, if he prefers, in Vienna, as soon as the Prince has returned there.

Prague, 9 June 1812.'

As I passed through Prague a few weeks later on my journey to Töplitz [Teplitz], *172, 173* I presented myself to the Prince and received from him the confirmation of his consent to all the details of this arrangement. His Serene Highness declared, moreover, that he fully agreed with the justice of my request and found it in every way most fair. Since I was not able to delay in Prague until this matter could be completely settled, His Serene Highness was graciously pleased to give me an account of 60 Ducats which, according to his statement, should be equivalent to 600 fl. in Viennese currency . . . .

I therefore place my humble request to receive the arrears of my stipend in redemption bonds and to instruct the Princely Exchequer that future payments be made to me in the same currency; in the hands of Your Serene Highness and convinced of your sense of justice, I await a favourable decision to my request.

Your Serene Highness's
Most Obedient
Ludwig van Beethoven.

KFR 108 ff. Anderson 393.

Statement and receipt from the Kinsky disburser's office:

First statement from 4 November 1812 to the end of December 1813, from the guardianship of the minor Rudolph Prince Kinsky on behalf of Prince Ferdinand *158* Kinsky's estate.

Page 28, section 'Concerning certain payments for the estate'. Attachment No. 194: 'Item No. 2. Owed to Ludwig van Beethoven according to the document of 1 March 1809 a guaranteed annual income of 1800 gulden from the terms of which he is to receive the just sum, hereby receipted, in Viennese currency of 1020 gulden 48 Kreuzer for the period from 1 December 1810 to and including 3 December 1812, as specified in attachment No. 194.'

Receipt.

No. 82 .

Praes, 2 March 1827.

Receipt for the sum of two hundred and forty gulden Convention Coin from 1 September 1826 to 1 March 1827, the semi-annual delayed income which the recipient is due according to the decision of the Imperial Royal Bohemian Provincial Court dated Prague 18 January 1815 No. Exhib. 293, recognized as justly belonging to me and containing the annual sum of 1200 gulden Viennese currency (or 480 gulden Convention Coin) from the Princely Rudolph disbursal office in Prague; received in cash and in full and herewith acknowledged by receipt.
Vienna, 25 February 1827.
J. e. 240 fl. C. Mz.

[Signed] Ludwig van Beethoven.

Living at No. 200 in the Alservorstadt, 25 February 1827.

[Signed] C. Santner, Parish Priest.

Beethovenjahrbuch, edited by Theodor von Frimmel, Munich 1909, II, pp. 30, 43 f.

Among Beethoven's circle of acquaintances in Vienna was the Malfatti family from Lucca. Dr Giovanni von Malfatti was a famous physician, and Beethoven fell in love with his niece Therese. Her younger sister Anna married Beethoven's intimate friend, Ignaz von Gleichenstein, in 1811. When the Malfattis refused to allow Therese to marry Beethoven, the composer broke off relations, and it was not until Beethoven lay dying that Dr von Malfatti came to see his former patient.

160   *Letter from Beethoven to Therese von Malfatti:*

[Vienna, 1 May 1810]

You receive here, honoured Therese, what I promised you, and had there not been certain weighty obstacles, you would have received still more, if only to show you that I always do more for my friends than what I promise them – I hope, and have no doubt, that you are agreeably occupied as well as entertained – the latter not too much, so that we too may be remembered. It would be laying too much stress on you, or setting my worth too high, if I were to apply to you the saying, 'People are united not only when they are together; the distant one and even the departed one is here with us'. Who would wish to apply such a saying to the flighty T[herese] who treats everything in life so lightly? . . . .

Please commend me to the goodwill of your father [and] your mother, although I have as yet no right to claim this and likewise to your cousin M. And now all good wishes to you, honoured T. – I wish you everything good and beautiful in life. Remember me and with fondness – forget the madman – rest assured that no one can desire you to have a merrier and happier life than I do and even when you do not take any interest

in your devoted servant and friend
Beethoven.

TDR III, 209. Anderson 258.

Dr Franz Gerhard Wegeler recalls Beethoven's intention to marry:

It appears, to be sure, that Beethoven once in his life had the intention of marrying, after having often had love affairs, as the saying goes. This intention was evident to many persons, who, like me, read his letter of 10 May [actually 2 May] 1810, wherein Beethoven requested me to obtain for him his baptismal certificate. He said he would repay me for all the expenses, including the cost of travel from Coblenz to Bonn. There follow explicit instructions that in my search for the certificate I should take good care to obtain the right one. I found the solution to this puzzle in a letter from my brother-in-law St. v. Breuning written three months later. In this he said, 'Beethoven tells me at least once a week that he will write to you: personally I think that *his marriage plans have come to nought*, and so he does not feel the urgency of thanking you for obtaining the baptismal certificate.' Beethoven at the age of 39 had consequently not yet abandoned the idea of marriage.

TDR III, 211 f.

Schindler writes about Beethoven's reconciliation with Malfatti:

[In December 1826] Beethoven remembered his former friend, Dr Malfatti, who had *160* become a very celebrated physician, from whom he had been estranged twelve years before and to whom he had not addressed a single word since then. He now placed all his hopes for recovery on this man. But Malfatti would not listen to the master's appeal which I transmitted to him, and coldly turned it down. I made a second and even a third attempt to arouse his compassion for the ailing composer. Finally, I succeeded in persuading him to grant the patient the pleasure of a visit, as if he were making a call to the sick-bed of a stranger. At Malfatti's expressed desire this visit was to take place in the presence of the physician in charge of the case. This, however, was not in accordance with Beethoven's wishes: he wanted to see his former friend alone and to effect a reconciliation. A white lie achieved its aim. Malfatti appeared but did not find his colleague; instead he found the open arms of the remorseful friend who begged forgiveness. All the past was forgotten. From that day onward, Malfatti came almost every day together with Wawruch to [Beethoven's] bedside.

Schindler II, 135.

Dr Bertolini writes about Beethoven's friendship with the Malfattis and with other ladies:

In the company of his intimate friends, Beethoven was extremely cheerful and uninhibited, full of jocose ideas, particularly at a ball given in honour of Malfatti in 1815, for which he had composed a cantata (on a text by Bondi, now in the possession of Miss Belville in London) . . . .

Beethoven generally had a 'flame', la Guiccardi [sic], Frau von Frank, Bettina [von] Brentano. But he also often had 'affairs' which did not always turn out very well for him.

Kerst II, 193. (The Cantata was *Un lieto brindisi*, WoO 103.)

From Beethoven's conversation books, autumn 1820 :

160 Bernard [?]: The Drossdick [born Therese Malfatti] –
Yesterday at Frau von S. I sat alone next to a young lady. She also talked about Frau v. Dr. because the other day she had sat next to Weissenbach and me at the theatre. Dr. S. was also there. She gave me to understand that it is only when her husband is present that she is unwilling to flirt. It seems as if she is not at all as Weissenbach has described her. S. also says that she was only trying to humbug W.

It seems that she doesn't love her husband. I heard from Frau von Janischek that she is not a homebody and that this summer she was not with her husband, so one can't be too careful.

Kerst II, 260. (Bernard was editor of the *Wiener Zeitung* and a confidant of Beethoven.)

Julius Franz Borgias Schneller writes about Baron Ignaz von Gleichenstein:

159 Baron Ignaz von Gleichenstein belonged to an old noble family from the Breisgau. He was one of the most delightful men whom the writer of this biographical sketch has ever known. He was distinguished by a clear understanding, practical sense, an upright disposition in all things and a passionate love for all that is good and beautiful. His life and his actions were, in the spirit of that old Greek saying, like a glass house into which everyone can see and look through at all times. Married to
161 a Fräulein [Anna] Malfatti, of the same family as the celebrated physician, he [Gleichenstein] had at his side one of the most perfect of ladies, as regards both body and soul. The goodness of the father and the charm of the mother were reproduced once again in their children.

TDR II, 558. (Schneller had been a school friend of Gleichenstein and was later Professor of History in Linz and Graz. His tragedy *Vitellia* was performed in Vienna in 1805.)

Letter from Beethoven to Baron Ignaz von Gleichenstein:

[Vienna, summer 1808]

Pour Monsieur de Gleichenstein.

Here, my dear friend, is your letter to Winter – First of all it says that you are a friend of mine – second, what you are, namely an Imperial Royal Court Secretary – third, that you are no connoisseur of music, but that nevertheless you are a lover of everything beautiful and good – In consideration of this, I have asked the Kapellmeister, in the event that anything by him is to be performed, to give you the opportunity of hearing it. Here you have a hint to show rather eagerly that you have an interest in his work – this belongs to the political sciences of which your friend understands but little. Perhaps it may be of use for other purposes in Munich – and now, farewell, my dear friend – have a happy journey – and think occasionally of me – greet the little brother,

Your true friend
Beethoven.

TDR III, 117. Anderson 173. (Peter von Winter was a successful composer of operas. His *Das unterbrochene Opferfest* [The Interrupted Sacrifice] was for many years in the operatic repertoire in Vienna.)

In May 1809, Napoleon again invaded Vienna at the head of the French troops; but this time, Vienna resisted and Napoleon bombarded the city. Haydn died peacefully on 31 May, while Beethoven was composing the 'Emperor' Concerto. Napoleon set up headquarters in Schönbrunn Palace and a concert was given there in his honour, to which Beethoven was not invited.

Ferdinand Ries writes about Beethoven during the bombardment: 164

[Beethoven fled to the Rauhensteingasse and] spent most of the time in the cellar with his brother Caspar, where he covered his head with pillows in order not to hear the cannon.

WRBN 121. TDR III, 138.

Friedrich Anton Schönholz describes the occupation of Vienna by the French in 1809:

... When the city was already in the hands of the enemy, people still did not feel safe and hid their best things in those houses which had obtained a *sauvegarde* .... When the people noticed that the battalions, instead of attacking people's purses with their bayonets, were setting up bivouacs in the main squares and that the soldiers, half-naked, were washing their bodies and their shirts in the fountains, the fear of plunder vanished and people dared ... to go out into the streets again ....

Within a few hours everyone was all over the place and before one could imagine . . . the hot sausage vendors were making their rounds.

Friedrich Anton von Schönholz, *Traditionen zur Charakteristik Oesterreichs*, introduced with commentary by Gustav Gugitz, Munich 1914, I, 194 ff.

While Beethoven was getting over his love affair with Therese von Malfatti, he was consoled by the friendship of the vivacious Bettina von Brentano, with whom Goethe was also on friendly terms.

168   *Letter from Bettina von Brentano to Prince von Pückler-Muskau (1810):*

People were astonished to see me arrive hand in hand with Beethoven at a reception of more than forty people who were seated at tables. He took his place without ceremony, spoke but little because he is deaf; twice he took his notebook out of his pocket and wrote down a couple of figures in it. After dinner the whole company climbed up to the top of the tower of the house in order to look at the view. When they had all gone down again and he and I were alone, he took out his notebook, looked over it, wrote and erased things in it and then said to me, 'My song is finished.' He sat down by the window and sang the whole song out into the open air. Then he said, 'It sounds well, doesn't it? It belongs to you, if you like it. I wrote it for you. You incited me to it, I read it in your eyes as if it had all been written down . . .'

A lady from the upper ranks of society, one of the foremost pianists, performed one of his sonatas. After he had listened to her for a while, he said, 'That's nothing.' He sat down at the piano himself and played the same sonata; it was superhuman.

TDR III, 219 f. (Bettina Brentano, the half-sister of Beethoven's friend Franz Brentano, and wife of Ludwig Joachim von Arnim, maintained a considerable correspondence with Prince Pückler-Muskau, a great admirer of beautiful women. The Prince also boasted of the friendship of Countess Giulietta Guicciardi.)

In 1810, Beethoven wrote his remarkable incidental music to Goethe's *Egmont*, which was first performed together with the play at the Burgtheater in Vienna on 15 June 1810. Klärchen was played by Antonie Adamberger, who has left an interesting memoir of her first meeting with Beethoven. We also learn, from a letter about *Egmont* from Griesinger to Breitkopf & Härtel, that Beethoven was seriously thinking of following Haydn's footsteps and going to England. But nothing ever came of Beethoven's many plans to visit London. The *Egmont* music, which contains not only the famous overture but many highly original and impressive numbers, was a great public success.

166   *Antonie Adamberger speaks to Ludwig Nohl of her meeting with Beethoven:*

Antonie Adamberger, daughter of the well-known Viennese tenor of Mozart's time, was born in Vienna on 31 December 1790. She lost her parents at an early age and was obliged to support several younger brothers and sisters. So she became an artist

at the age of 14. Thereupon the poet Heinrich von Collin took over her training and _144_
let her study Goethe's *Iphigenia*. Her first part was Aricia in Racine's *Phaedra* (in
Schiller's version). The most kindly and extravagant Prince Lobkowitz also took an _112_
interest in her. In his house there were all kinds of trial readings, which were attended
by Count Schönborn, Deinhardstein, Count von Breuner and others. Among them
she also saw Beethoven.

While the first rehearsals were being held of Goethe's *Egmont*, in which she was _165_
given the part of Klärchen because the other actresses were too uneducated for the
rôle, Beethoven went to see her about the composition of her songs. He asked her if
she could sing? 'No.' – 'Well then, how can you play Klärchen?' – 'As well as I can,
and if the audience hiss, I shall have to put up with it.' – Beethoven threw out his
hands in astonishment and laughed out loud. Then she went to the piano. There lay
her father's scores: Haydn's *Creation*, Weigel's *Schweizerfamilie* and *Waisenhaus*.
Beethoven asked if she sang anything from these? Yes, she answered, from what she
had been able to hear from her father. Then Beethoven noticed 'Ombra adorata'
from Zingarelli's *Romeo* lying there. 'Can you sing that too?' – 'Yes.' –

He sat down and accompanied. She sang. He did not praise her, he did not criti-
cize, but said at the end: 'Yes, you can sing: I will compose the songs.'

'Shortly thereafter he brought them, sang them for me and accompanied me on the
piano. Apart from this I had no further personal contact with him', – thus she
ended her story, but added, in answer to my inquiry: 'The two Malfatti daughters _160, 161_
were the most beautiful girls in Vienna at that time. At the concert of Collin's
Wehrmannslieder in the Redoutensaal they both sat next to me with their mother.'

Ludwig Nohl, *Beethoven*, Leipzig 1877, p. 59. Kerst I, 140 f. (Ludwig Nohl visited Antonie von Arneth née
Adamberger in 1867 and talked about Beethoven with her. He published her recollections in his *Beethoven*
in 1877.)

Carl Czerny writes about Beethoven's music for the theatre:

When it was decided to stage Schiller's *Tell* and Goethe's *Egmont* in the city theatres,
the question arose as to who should compose the music. Beethoven and Gyrowetz
were chosen. Beethoven very much wanted to be given *Tell*. But a number of intrigues
were started, with the purpose of assigning to him the *Egmont* which was (so they
believed) less adapted to musical treatment. He proved, nevertheless, that he could
compose masterly music even for this drama, and to this task he brought all the
power of his genius.

TDR III, 154.

Letter from Georg August Griesinger to the publishers Breitkopf und Härtel:

[Vienna, 20 June 1810:] Beethoven is toying with the sensible idea of going to England;
but he cannot say anything about it in public. There he would soon make himself
talked about much more than here. An overture of his composition, as well as music

165 for the entr'actes to Goethe's *Egmont*, were performed with great success last week at the Burgtheater. He gives lessons in composition to the Archduke Rudolph and lives most of the time in Schönbrunn.* Thompson, in Edinburgh, is very pleased with the Scottish songs which Beethoven arranged for him, and has paid him very handsomely for them. Nevertheless, I know that Beethoven has not yet collected a draught from Thompson which has been deposited with a local banker: perhaps he is trying to raise his demands, because he doesn't need the money.

Der Bär, Yearbook of Breitkopf und Härtel for the year 1927, Leipzig 1927. *Aus den Briefen Griesingers an Breitkopf und Härtel entnommene Notizen über Beethoven*, by Wilhelm Hitzig, p. 33.

The Brentano family was related by marriage to Johann Melchior von Birkenstock, a famous collector, in whose house Beethoven met Bettina von Brentano. Franz von Brentano had married Antonie von Birkenstock in 1798 and they became intimate with Beethoven. In 1812, Beethoven wrote a delightful Trio in one movement (WoO 39) for their daughter Maximiliane, who was then ten years old. Later Beethoven dedicated to her the towering Piano Sonata Op. 109.

168   *Letter from Bettina von Brentano to Johann Wolfgang von Goethe:*

[Vienna, 15 May 1810]

An enormous bunch of lilies of the valley fills my small room with its fragrance. I am happy in this small narrow chamber in the old tower from which I can overlook the whole Prater. Trees and trees of majestic appearance, beautiful green lawns. Here *167* I live in the house of the late Birkenstock,** in the midst of two thousand copper engravings, as many drawings, hundreds of funeral urns and Etruscan lamps, marble vases, antique fragments of hands and feet, paintings, Chinese costumes, coins, collections of stones, and of marine insects, telescopes, numberless maps, plans of old buried empires and cities, artistically carved walking-sticks, valuable documents and finally the sword of Charlemagne. All this surrounds us in a motley confusion, and is supposed to be shortly put in order, so nothing can be touched or moved; [what with] the chestnut alley in full bloom and the rushing Danube which carries us across on its surface, one simply cannot stand being in the art gallery . . .

TDR III, 213.

Letter from Beethoven to Anton Ignaz von Baumeister, the Private Secretary of Archduke Rudolph:

[Vienna, Wednesday, 3 July 1811]

I beg you urgently to send me the musical material left behind by our gracious Lord – at the same time I am sending you the titles of two old works which would be

---

*This is incorrect. Beethoven probably went to Schönbrunn a good deal to give the Archduke his lessons, but he did not live there.
**Johann Melchior von Birkenstock, father-in-law of Franz von Brentano, died in 1809.

suitable for the Archduke's library. Although the auction of the Birkenstock library and paintings has not yet taken place, Herr and Frau Brentano (née Birkenstock), who live in the Landstrasse on the Erdbeergasse [Erdberggasse], would nevertheless let the Archduke have these works. Since I told the Archduke about them when he was here, speak yourself to the owners about this, if you think it advisable, as I personally do not know how old works of this kind are sold.

170, 171

Your most devoted servant
Beethoven.

KFR 24. Anderson 316.

Dedications to Maximiliane von Brentano:

Vienna, 26 June 1812. For my little friend Maxe/Brentano, to enliven her/piano-playing . . . l v Bthvn.

169

Some ten years later he dedicated another sonata to Maximiliane, who in the meanwhile had become a young lady and whose playing of the piano had matured markedly:

SONATA /for the Pianoforte / composed and / dedicated to / Fräulein Maximiliana Brentano/by/LUDWIG van BEETHOVEN/[l.:] Opus 109. Property of the publisher. [r.:] Price 1 Rth/ [l.:] No. 1088/ Berlin / in Schlesinger's Book and Music Shop/ Vienna/at Artaria & Co, Cappi & Diabelli, Steiner & Co.

KHV 482, 312. (Maximiliane was the daughter of Franz von Brentano.)

Letter from Beethoven to Maximiliane von Brentano:

Vienna, 6 December 1821

A dedication!!! – Now, this is not one of those which are abused wholesale. It is the spirit which holds together the noble and better people on this globe and which time can never destroy. This is the spirit which speaks to you now and which still brings back to me the years of your childhood as well as your beloved parents, your most excellent and intelligent mother and your father, so truly endowed with good and noble qualities, always concerned with the well-being of his children. At this moment I am in the Landstrasse – and see you all before me. And while I think of the wonderful qualities of your parents, I have not the least doubt that you are inspired to be like them, and will be more so with each passing day. The memory of a noble family can never be erased from my heart. May you sometimes think kindly of me.

My most heartfelt good wishes. May heaven forever bless you and all of yours.

Devotedly and eternally,
Your friend
Beethoven.

Beethovens Briefe, ed. Albert Leitzmann, Leipzig 1912, p. 175 f. Anderson 1062.

Herr von Brentano on the friendly relations between Beethoven and his family:

The friendly relations of Beethoven with the Brentano family of Frankfurt/Main concern:

171   Frau Antonie Brentano, née Birkenstock, born in Vienna 28 May 1780, married there on 23 July 1798, died in Frankfurt/Main on 12 May 1869, and her

170   husband Herr Franz Brentano, merchant, later Juryman and Senator of the Free City of Frankfurt, born in Frankfurt 17 November 1765, died there on 28 June 1844.

These relations had their origin in the friendly intercourse between Beethoven and

167   Imperial Aulic Councillor Johann Melchior von Birkenstock of Vienna, born in Heiligenstadt im Eichsfeld 11 May 1738, married 1 March 1778 to Carolina Josepha von Hay, widower since 18 March 1788, died in Vienna 30 October 1809;

which had existed since the time when Frau Brentano visited her father in Vienna, whence she had moved with her older children in 1809 for a long period because her father, Aulic Councillor von Birkenstock, had been seriously ill for some time. This relationship continued also after the death on 30 October 1809 of Aulic Councillor von Birkenstock, during the three years that the Brentano family lived in Vienna. Beethoven was a frequent guest in the Birkenstock, later Brentano, house, where he attended the quartet-playing of the excellent Viennese musicians and where he often gave pleasure to his friends with his wonderful playing. The Brentano children sometimes brought fruit and flowers to his apartment; in return he would regale them with sweets, and he treated them with the greatest friendliness.

TDR III, 216. (This ancient Italian family hardly made use of their title.)

Carl Czerny writes about Beethoven and the Brentano children:

Today Court Councillor Witteschek/: who knew Beethoven well:/told me that in the year 1814, B:/who could then still hear fairly well:/very often went to the Brentano-Birkenstock house, and that once one of the members of the family, an eight-year-old girl, whom he had been teasing, in a fit of childish caprice suddenly emptied a bottle of ice-cold water over his head, when he was overheated. From then on, there developed the diseased condition which led to his complete deafness.

Note by Schindler: This occurrence dates back to the year 1812, when Frau von Brentano-B[irkenstock] visited Vienna for the last time with her little daughter (now Frau von Blattersdorf, [wife of] the former Minister of Baden), as she herself told me. To ascribe such consequences to a dousing with cold water is not acceptable, since B[eethoven] was able to hear music quite well for some years after that, and also in 1814 himself played his new Trio Opus 97 in public twice. This little Brentano-B[irkenstock] is the 'little friend' to whom B. dedicated one or two of the little Rondos.

A. Schindler.

Czerny 18.

166. Antonie Adamberger (1790–1867). Miniature on ivory (6.5 × 5 cm) by
Jaquet. On the back is a note in old handwriting: 'A. A. Wien 1809'. Freies Deutsches
Hochstift, Goethemuseum, Frankfurt am Main.

The young actress played the rôle of Klärchen in the performance of *Egmont* in
1810 which included Beethoven's music.

167. Johann Melchior von Birkenstock (1738–1809). Portrait in oils by Heinrich Friedrich
Füger. On the reverse side of the picture is the rather confusing note: 'Painted after his [Birken-
stock's] death, given to the daughter of the artist.' Achim von Brentano, Winkel, Germany.

Birkenstock was a famous collector and music-lover. It was in
his house at Erdberg that Beethoven met Bettina von Brentano.

168. Elisabeth (Bettina) von Brentano (1785–1859). Drawing by Ludwig Emil Grimm, *c.* 1809. Freies Deutsches Hochstift, Goethemuseum, Frankfurt am Main.

Bettina von Brentano came from a wealthy and artistically-minded Frankfurt family; she came to Vienna to visit her half-brother Franz von Brentano who was married and lived in that city. Bettina was young, gay and slightly hysterical, but she amused Beethoven and helped him to get over his unsuccessful love affair with Therese von Malfatti.

169. Trio in one movement, B flat, for piano, violin
and violoncello (WoO 39). Autograph. First page of
music. Beethovenhaus Bonn.

Beethoven wrote this little trio on 26 June 1812 for Maximiliane,
the ten-year-old daughter of his friends Franz and Antonia von
Brentano; he wrote on the autograph that it was to 'encourage her
in her piano-playing'. The work was not published until after
Beethoven's death.

170. Franz Dominik Maria Joseph von Brentano (1765–1844). Portrait in oils by Joseph Carl Stieler, 1808. Achim von Brentano, Winkel, Germany.

In 1798, Franz von Brentano married Antonia von Birkenstock, and since the young Viennese girl did not really feel at home in Frankfurt, the young couple moved to Vienna, where they looked after Antonia's father. They were close friends of Beethoven's and continued to write each other even after the Brentanos had moved back to Germany.

171. Antonia Josepha von Brentano, née von Birkenstock (1780–1869). Anonymous miniature (8.4 × 7.4 cm). Achim von Brentano, Winkel, Germany.

Beethoven dedicated to Antonia, his friend 'in good and bad times', the Diabelli Variations, Op. 120.

172, 173. View of Bad Teplitz. Anonymous watercolour. (*Below*) The spring at Bad Teplitz. Anonymous coloured print. Teplice, Czechoslovakia.

In August 1811 Beethoven took a six weeks' cure in Bad Teplitz. He was there alone at the beginning, because his friend Count Brunsvik was not able, as had previously been arranged, to accompany him; but later his young friend Franz Oliva joined him. In Teplitz Beethoven became acquainted with a large group of interesting people among them Karl August Varnhagen von Ense, Elise von der Recke, the poet Christoph August Tiedge, Rahel Levin, and many others.

174. Rahel Levin (1771–1833). Plaster of Paris relief medallion after Christian Friedrich Tieck, 1796. The original was probably bronze or marble. Freies Deutsches Hochstift, Goethemuseum, Frankfurt am Main.

Rahel Levin, who had a famous salon in Berlin, came with her fiancé, Karl August Varnhagen von Ense, to Teplitz in the year 1811, and soon made Beethoven's acquaintance.

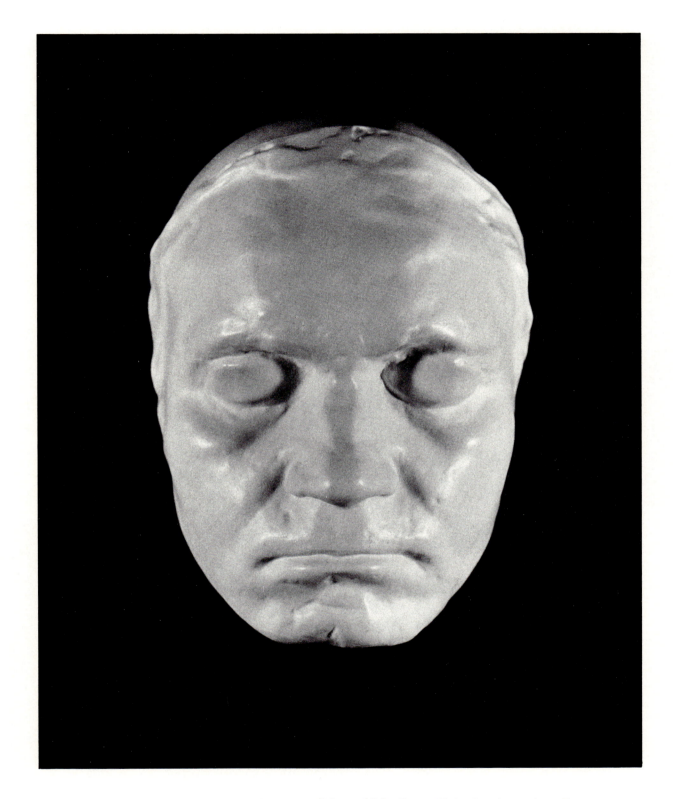

175. Ludwig van Beethoven. Plaster cast ('life mask') by Franz Klein. Beethovenhaus Bonn.

In 1812 Beethoven's friend, the piano-maker Johann Andreas Streicher, commissioned the sculptor Franz Klein to do a bust of Beethoven. Klein first made a plaster mask of Beethoven's face, which was accomplished with considerable difficulty because Beethoven imagined that he would suffocate; the composer seems to have ruined the first attempt. The second was, however, eminently successful. The Beethovenhaus in Bonn owns two copies of this mask, one contains a certificate by the painter Ludwig Cramolini and his colleague Castelli, and purports to be the original; the second came to the Beethovenhaus in 1890 from the publisher E. H. Schroeder in Berlin. (*See also plate 178.*)

176. Amalie Sebald (1787–1846).
Pastel by Dorothea Stock. Historisches Museum
of the City of Vienna.

Amalie Sebald, a talented singer, was a member
of the famous Berlin *Singakademie* and in 1811
accompanied Countess Medem (Elise von der
Recke) to Teplitz. She and Beethoven were
much attracted to each other and a correspondence
exists: enough to have encouraged Beethoven
biographers to include her as a candidate for the
'Immortal Beloved' which, of course, she was not.

177. Johann Wolfgang von Goethe (1749–
1832). Portrait in oils, *c.* 1808, by Franz
Gerhard von Kügelgen. Freies Deutsches Hochstift, Goethemuseum, Frankfurt am Main.

During his second sojourn in Teplitz, in 1812,
Beethoven met Goethe, whom he had admired
all his life. The elegant and polished Goethe
evidently did not enjoy Beethoven's abrupt
manners.

178. Ludwig van Beethoven. Bronze bust by Franz Klein. Beethovenhaus Bonn.

Using the mask of 1812 as his model, Franz Klein made what is prob-
ably the most accurate representation of Beethoven's features.
In Vienna there are three other copies of the mask, of which one was
given by Klein to Johann Streicher, who later passed it on to Anton
Dietrich when the latter was preparing his Beethoven bust. From
Dietrich's estate it passed into the possession of the *Bildhauersocietät*
(Society of Sculptors) and later to the artist Zumbusch and finally
to Anton Rainbauer, from whom the Historisches Museum of the
City of Vienna acquired it.

179. Symphony No. 8 in F major, Op. 93. Timpani part of the original performance
material. Gesellschaft der Musikfreunde, Vienna.

The page shows a cancellation in Beethoven's hand and suggests that he rewrote
the ending of the Symphony. The work was first performed on 27 February 1814
in the large Redoutensaal in Vienna, together with other music by the composer.

IOHANN VAN BETHOFEN APOTHEKER ZUR KRONE.

180. Visiting card of Johann van Beethoven's apothecary shop. Aquatint etching by Karl Russ. Signed on the right leg of the chair 'Rusz'. Oberösterreichisches Landesmuseum, Linz.

The apothecary shop 'Zur goldenen Krone' was locally known as the 'Wasserapotheke' ('Apothecary Shop on the Water'), since it was at the Danube.

181. View of Linz from across the river at Urfahr. Coloured copper plate engraving by Johann Ziegler from a drawing by Ferdinand Runk. Stadtmuseum, Linz.

In October 1812, Beethoven travelled from Bohemia to Linz, to visit his brother Johann. Johann put his brother in a large room with a view over the Danube, the dock and the pleasant surrounding hills. Here Beethoven finished the autograph of his Eighth Symphony. Johann was at that time living with a local girl called Therese Obermayer (later his wife), of whom Beethoven strongly disapproved.

182. View of Karlsbad. Coloured engraving by Friedrich Wilhelm Rothe, from a drawing by Johann Gottfried Jentsch. Freies Deutsches Hochstift, Goethemuseum, Frankfurt am Main.

Beethoven was again in Bohemia, taking the baths, in the summer of 1812. On 5 July he arrived in Teplitz after a very difficult journey; it had rained and his carriage had broken down on the muddy roads. On 6 July he wrote the first of three famous letters to the 'Immortal Beloved', who at that time was in K. (= Karlsbad). Research has not yet been able to reveal the name of the lady to whom these letters were written. From the police list of Karlsbad we may note that, among the possible candidates, Beethoven's friend, the Baroness von Ertmann, was there at that time (without her husband, Major – later General – von Ertmann). (See Plate 124).

183. Ludwig van Beethoven. Portrait in oils by Johann Christoph Heckel, 1815. Library of Congress, Washington.

Heckel's portrait of Beethoven dates from 1815, when Beethoven was at the height of his fame. For many years it remained in private hands and had only been reproduced very imperfectly; its recent rediscovery and sale proved to be one of the sensations of post-war Beethoveniana. The sessions for the portrait took place in the pianoforte salesrooms of J. A. Streicher.

Fidelio.

184. *Wellingtons Sieg oder die Schlacht bei Vittoria* ('Wellington's Victory or The Battle at Vittoria'), Op. 91. Title-page of the first edition for pianoforte. Stadtbibliothek, Vienna.

The first edition was issued by Sigmund Anton Steiner in Vienna. When the news of Wellington's victory at Vittoria reached Vienna, Johann Nepomuk Mälzel (1772–1838), the inventor of the metronome and the 'Panharmonika', suggested to Beethoven that he celebrate the occasion by writing a piece for Mälzel's newly invented instrument. Beethoven agreed and 'Wellington's Victory' was so successful that the composer undertook a version for symphony orchestra, in which form it became the major public success of Beethoven's career.

185. A scene from *Fidelio* as illustrated in the *Wiener Hoftheater Almanach* for the year 1815, 12. Jahrgang, edited by Franz Castelli and published by Wallishauser, Vienna. Stadtbibliothek, Vienna.

For the revival of his opera *Fidelio*, Beethoven wrote a new overture, the fourth, and the one now in general use. Treitschke reworked the text once again, shortened and improved it, and in this new form – the one in which it has come down to us – the opera was launched on 23 May 1814, and proved to be an enormous success.

270

186. Anna Pauline Milder, later Hauptmann (1785–1838). Copper plate engraving by David Weiss from a drawing by Sigmund Perger. Historisches Museum of the City of Vienna.

This famous soprano, born in Constantinople, had a rich and beautiful voice about which Haydn once said: 'My dear child! You have a voice the size of a house!' Beethoven wrote the rôle of Fidelio (Leonore) for her; she sang the part at the 1814 revival, although another soprano, Hönig, had studied the part. One day before the première she yielded to Milder.

187. Ground-plan and façade of the Pasqualati House in Vienna. Coloured Indian ink drawing, 1786. Historisches Museum of the City of Vienna.

Between 1804 and 1815 Beethoven frequently lived in rooms in the house owned by Freiherr Johann Baptist von Pasqualati zu Osterberg. The house still stands on the Mölkerbastei, but it then commanded a view over the hills round about Vienna. Pasqualati, the son of one of Empress Maria Theresa's personal physicians, helped Beethoven with business affairs and in particular with the dispute over his nephew Carl.

made him unsociable and his pecularities which, due to his isolation, grew ever sharper, made the limited intercourse with whomever he happened to meet by accident difficult and short. He had, however, seen Rahel* a few times during his lonely walks in the castle gardens and he had noticed her facial expression, which in certain aspects recalls his own. An amiable young man called Oliva, who accompanied him as a faithful friend, easily arranged an introduction. What Beethoven obstinately refused, even when insistently requested; what on one fearful occasion a Prince tried to oblige him to do, attempting by physical force to make him play to his guests; what no violence could bully him into doing, he now granted gladly and generously. He sat down at the Fortepiano and played his still unknown newest compositions, or else engaged in free improvisation. To me, the man meant even more than the artist, and since an intimate friendship sprang up between Oliva and myself, I was with Beethoven almost daily. I was able to engage in closer relations with him through his eagerly expressed hope that I might procure or adapt texts for dramatic compositions. That Beethoven has a violent hatred for the French and is very German in his feelings is well known, and this also brought us close to one another.

Kerst I, 167. K. A. Varnhagen von Ense: *Denkwürdigkeiten*, II, p. 344.

Letter from Beethoven to Amalie Sebald:

For Amalie von Sebald.

Teplitz, 16 September 1812

I a tyrant? Your tyrant! Only a misunderstanding could let you say such a thing, even if this judgment of yours did not indicate a disagreement with me! I don't blame you on this account, on the contrary, it would be fortunate for you. Even yesterday I did not feel very well, and since this morning my condition is worse. Something indigestible is the cause of it and apparently my irritable nature is affected as much by what is bad as by what is good. But do not apply this fact to my moral nature. People say nothing; they are just people. They only see themselves in others, and that is actually nothing. Away with it. The good and beautiful needs no [other] people. It is there, with no other assistance, and that seems to be the basis of our understanding. Farewell, my dear Amalie. If this evening the moon seems to me to be brighter than the sun during the day, you will have the smallest of all the smallest men with you.

Your friend,
Beethoven.

TDR III, 331. Anderson 382.

Letter from Amalie Sebald to Beethoven, after 17 September 1812, with a note by Beethoven:

My tyrant demands an accounting – here it is:
One chicken – 1 fl. W. W. [Vienna currency]

*Rahel Levin, who was later (27 September 1814) married to Varnhagen. (Otto Verdrow, *Rahel Varnhagen*, Berlin 1900, p. 113)

The soup – 9 kr.
I hope from my heart that they satisfied you.

[in Beethoven's writing]
Tyrants do not pay, but this bill must still be receipted, and that you could do best if you were to come in person. N.B. with the bill to your mortified tyrant.

TDR III, 333. Anderson 387.

Friedrich Johann Rochlitz writes about Beethoven and Goethe:

'So you know the great Goethe, do you?' I nodded, and strongly. 'I know him too,' he went on, throwing out his chest, and his features revealed pure pleasure. 'I met him at Karlsbad [actually Teplitz], God knows how long ago. At that time I was not so utterly deaf as now, but already I heard little enough. What patience the great man showed me! What did he not do for me!' He told many anecdotes and most delightful details. 'How happy it made me at that time! I would have let myself be killed for him – ten times over. At that time, when things were still going well for me, I was working on my music to his *Egmont* and it was successful, was it not?' I made all the gestures I knew to express my pleasure. Then I wrote out that this music was not only performed every time *Egmont* was given, but also almost every year in concert, with a sort of illustration, generally consisting of those scenes from the play to which his music referred. 'I know, I know,' he cried. 'Since that summer in Karlsbad I read Goethe every day – that is, when I read at all. He killed Klopstock for me. You are surprised? You laugh. Oh, because I have read Klopstock?... But Goethe, he lives, and we should all live with him. That's why his works allow themselves to be set to music. No one is better to set to music than he is. I do not like writing songs . . .'

177

Friedrich Johann Rochlitz, *Für Freunde der Tonkunst*, Leipzig 1824-32, vol. IV (1832), 355 f. Kerst I, 285 f. (Rochlitz was the editor of the *Allgemeine Musikalische Zeitung* in Leipzig. He met the composer in Vienna in 1822.)

Letter from Johann Wolfgang von Goethe to his friend Carl Friedrich Zelter:

[2 September 1812]
I met Beethoven in Töplitz [Teplitz]. His talent astounded me; but unfortunately he is a quite intractable person, which in fact is not unjustified if he finds the world detestable; but as a result, of course, he does not make things more enjoyable either for himself or for others. He is much to be forgiven and also to be pitied, since he can hear nothing. This is perhaps less harmful to the musical than to the social part of his life. And being by nature laconic, he feels this defect twice as much.

Kerst I, 169. (Zelter was the director of the Berlin *Singakademie*.)

From Johann Wolfgang von Goethe's diary:

20 July [1812] . . . in the evening went with Beethoven to Bilin.

21 July . . . evening at Beethoven's. He played delightfully.

Letter about Beethoven from Goethe to his wife, 19 July 1812:

I have never before seen a more comprehensive, energetic or intense artist. I understand very well how strange he must appear to the outside world.

Kerst I, 169.

Xaver Schnyder von Wartensee writes about Beethoven in the Schweizerische Musikzeitung und Sängerblatt:

Beethoven never played in Schnyder's presence either. The young musician complained of this to a certain Herr von Bonora, a member of Beethoven's circle, who told him that Beethoven never played when coaxed. One had to get him to the piano by trickery. 'You will have noticed,' said Bonora, 'that Beethoven has the habit of pacing up and down the room during a conversation. His piano always stands open. If you pace up and down with him, speak to him about anything at all, except about music. As you pass the piano, play a note as if by chance, pretend to be surprised, and say, "Why, Herr van Beethoven, this key has a slow action." Beethoven will go to the piano, test the key by striking it several times, then the fifth, then the third. Later he will add the bass to the chord. Then bring him a chair; he will sit down and continue testing the "dead" key in all manner of chords. In this way he begins to improvise without even noticing it, and you are afforded a rare pleasure. This ruse never fails; I have often used it myself with great success.'

Kerst I, 165.

178 *Anton Schindler on Beethoven's appearance:*

Beethoven could not have been much more than 5 feet 4 inches tall, Viennese measure. His body was thick-set, with large bones and a strong muscular system; his head was unusually large, covered with long, unkempt, almost completely grey hair, giving him a somewhat savage aspect, enhanced even more when his beard had grown to an immoderate length, which was quite often the case. His forehead was high and broad, his brown eyes small, almost retreating into his head when he laughed. They could, however, suddenly become unusually prominent and large, either rolling and flashing – the pupils almost always turned upwards – or not moving at all, staring fixedly ahead

276

when one or another idea took hold of him. When that happened, his whole appearance would suddenly and conspicuously alter, with such a noticeably inspired and imposing look that his small figure would loom before one as gigantically as his spirit. These moments of sudden inspiration often befell him in even the most jovial company, but also in the street, which generally attracted the close attention of passers-by. Only his gleaming eyes and his face showed what was going on inside him; he never gesticulated with his head or his hands, except when leading an orchestra. His mouth was well formed, the lips even (it is said that when he was young the lower lip was somewhat prominent), the nose rather broad. With his smile a most benevolent and amiable air spread over his whole face; this was of special benefit when he conversed with strangers, for it encouraged them. His laughter, on the other hand, often burst out immoderately, distorting the intelligent and strongly marked features; the huge head would swell, the face would become still broader, and the whole effect was not seldom that of a grimacing caricature. Fortunately, it always passed quickly. The chin had a longish cleft in the middle and at both sides, which gave it the shape of a mussel-shell and a special peculiarity of its own. His complexion was yellowish, but this was less obvious due to his being so much out of doors, particularly during the summer; then his full cheeks took on a fresh red and brown coloration.

Schindler, *Beethoven*, 2nd ed., 1845, p. 269. Kerst II, 19 f.

Letters to the 'immortal beloved':

Morning of 6 July [1812]

My angel, my all, my other self, just a few words today and that in pencil (yours); only tomorrow will I know for certain where I am to stay, a worthless waste of time and such – why this deep sorrow when necessity speaks? Can our love exist other than by sacrifices, by not desiring everything? Can you help it that you are not all mine, that I am not all yours? Oh God, look at the loveliness of nature and calm your spirit about what has to be – love demands everything, and perfectly rightly, that is how it is with me about you, with you about me – except that you forget so easily that I must live for me and for you. If we could be united, you would feel this pain as little as I. The journey was terrible – I did not arrive here until 4 in the morning. There were not enough horses, so the post coach took another route, but what a terrible one. At the second-last station they warned me against travelling at night and tried to frighten me about a forest, but that only tempted me – – – and I was in the wrong. The coach had to go and break down on such a terrible road, for no reason, just a country road. Without the postillions I had, I would have been held up completely on the way. The same thing happened to Esterházi, who took the normal route with 8 horses, as happened to me with four – however, it was partly enjoyable for me, as it is every time I survive something that turns out well. And now quickly from externals to more intimate things. We will surely see one another soon; today, too, I cannot tell you the observations I have been making during the past few days about my life – – – if our hearts were always close to one another I would probably not make any. My heart is full of things to tell you – oh – there are moments when I feel that speech is

Georg Friedrich Treitschke on the revision of the libretto of Fidelio:

Beethoven was asked for permission to perform the opera, and he consented with great selflessness, with the stipulation that many changes would have to be made in the opera. He suggested my humble self for this work. I had earned his friendship some time before and my twofold office of opera poet and stage-manager made his wish *131* a precious duty for me. With the permission of Sonnleithner I first set to work on the dialogue, rewrote it almost completely, as concisely and to the point as possible. This being a requisite in an opera with spoken dialogue . . . .

One evening at about seven o'clock, Beethoven came to see me. After talking about this and that, he asked how things were going with the aria. I had just finished it and handed it to him. He read it, ran up and down the room mumbling and humming as he was wont to do, instead of singing, and then opened up the piano. My wife had often asked him to play, in vain. Today he placed the text before him and began wonderful improvisations which, alas, no magic could record for posterity. From these he seemed to be conjuring up the motive of the aria. The hours passed, but Beethoven went on improvising. Supper, which he had meant to take with us, was served, but he would not let himself be distracted. Much later he embraced me and, passing up the meal, hastened home. The next day the wonderful composition was ready . . . .

On 22 May the dress rehearsal took place but the promised new overture was still in the pen of the creator.

TDR III, 410, 411, 425.

Joseph August Röckel tells Alexander Wheelock Thayer about Beethoven and Prince Lichnowsky:

When he [Beethoven] invited Röckel to visit him, he added that he would give his servant special instructions to admit him at any time, even in the mornings when he was working. It was agreed that if Röckel were admitted and found that Beethoven was very busy, he would go through his room to the adjoining bedroom. (Both rooms *187* were on the fourth floor of the Pasqualati house on the Mölker Bastei, and commanded a full view over the Glacis.) There he would wait a certain length of time. If the composer did not appear, Röckel was to leave again quietly. One morning, on his first visit, it so happened that at the front door Röckel saw a carriage in which a lady *41* was sitting. When he arrived at the fourth floor, there was Prince Lichnowsky arguing with the servant. He wished to be admitted, but the servant declared he could admit no one because his master was busy and had left strict orders to admit no one at all. Röckel, however, who did have permission, told Beethoven that Lichnowsky was outside. Though in bad humour, he [Beethoven] could not go on refusing to admit the Prince. Lichnowsky and his wife had come to invite Beethoven for a drive, and in the end Beethoven consented; yet even as he entered the carriage, Röckel observed, his face bore a dour expression.

Kerst I, 120. TDR II, 565.

Anton Schindler about Prince Lichnowsky:

...Prince Lichnowsky was in the habit of visiting his protégé quite often in his *41* study. They mutually agreed that neither was to take any notice of the other's presence, so that the master would not be disturbed. The Prince, after saying 'Good Morning', would leaf through a manuscript, observe the master at work for a while, and would then depart with a friendly 'Adieu'. Even so, Beethoven felt himself disturbed by such a visit, and from time to time he would lock the door. Not taking this amiss, the Prince would descend the flights of stairs. When the servant, who also worked as a tailor, was sitting in the anteroom, his Serene Highness would keep him company and tarry until the door opened and he could give the Prince of the musical art a friendly greeting.

Schindler I, 188.

Because of his deafness, Beethoven was now just able to play his own chamber music in public: the well-known pianist Ignaz Moscheles was present when Beethoven gave his new 'Archduke' Trio, Op. 97, and made some interesting notes about Beethoven in this period.

Ignaz Moscheles about Beethoven in 1814: *188, 190*

11 April, 1814. At a musical entertainment at the *Römischer Kaiser* given at noon, I heard a new Trio* by Beethoven in B-Flat Major played by himself. How many compositions are unjustifiably marked with the little word 'new'. But never a composition by Beethoven, and surely not this one, which is completely original. Apart from the spirit, his actual playing gave me less satisfaction, because it was neither clean nor precise, yet I could still notice many traces of a once great virtuosity, which I had long recognized in his compositions.

[1814.] I went early to see Beethoven. He was still in bed. On this day he was in an exceptionally good humour, jumped out of bed and, quite as he was, went and stood by the window, which overlooked the Schottenbastei, to look through the arrangements of the pieces.** Quite naturally all the dear street urchins gathered under the window, until he exclaimed: 'Those damned boys, what do they want?' I pointed smilingly at him. 'Yes, yes, you are right,' he said, and quickly put on a dressing gown.

When we came to the last great duet 'Namenlose Freude', I wrote the text: 'Ret=terin des Gat=ten'; he crossed it out and wrote: 'Rett=erin des Gatt=en'; for it is impossible to sing the consonant 't'. Underneath the last piece I had written: '*fine* with God's help'. He was not at home when I brought it to him. When he sent it back to me, he had written underneath: 'O Man, help thyself.'

Kerst I, 162 f.

*The 'Archduke' Trio, Op. 97, dedicated to Archduke Rudolph.
**See p. 69.

Höfel saw Beethoven frequently at Artaria's, and when his work was fairly well advanced, he asked him to sit for him once or twice. The request was willingly granted, and at the appointed time the engraver appeared with his plate. Beethoven placed himself in the desired position, and sat still for perhaps five minutes, then he suddenly jumped up, ran to the piano and began to improvise, much to Höfel's discomfiture. The servant tried to help him out, assuring Höfel that he could now sit near the instrument and work at leisure, for the master had completely forgotten him and did not even realize any more that anyone was in the room. This Höfel did. He remained at work as long as he needed, and then left without Beethoven's taking the least notice. The result was satisfactory, since only two sittings of less than one hour each were required.

Kerst I, 180.   TDR III, 437 f.

Beethoven was passionately fond of the countryside and spent almost every summer in one of the little towns surrounding Vienna, such as Heiligenstadt, Döbling, and later Baden or Mödling. We have slightly disturbed the chronology here by printing a document from Ferdinand Ries's memoirs on the subject of Beethoven at Baden sometime around 1804.

Ferdinand Ries relates his first experience of Beethoven's deafness to Heinrich Friedrich Ludwig Rellstab:

[*c.* 1804]

89   One morning in the summer, when Beethoven lived in Baden, I [Ries] arrived to take a lesson. When I entered the house, I heard him improvising in his room. In order not to disturb him, I remained listening at the door and noticed that, strictly speaking, he was not really improvising but that he was rhapsodically going over isolated passages, seemingly casting them now in one way and then in another. After a few moments he rose from the instrument and opened the window. I went in. He greeted me in a very cheerful voice and said: 'We won't have a lesson today. Instead let us take a walk together, the morning is so beautiful.' Beethoven took a particular pleasure in wandering along lonely, often pathless, ways through the forests, valleys and mountains. We set out happily together and soon found ourselves in lonely woods
197   on the beautiful mountain slopes of Baden. I observed that Beethoven was much absorbed in private meditation and that he was humming to himself; I knew from experience that at such moments he was in the most powerful throes of creation and so I took good care not to disturb him but walked along with him in silence. In some isolated phrases which he was humming to himself, I thought I recognized a similarity to what he had been playing in his room. It was evident that he was engaged on a major work. After having walked for about an hour, we sat down to rest in the grass. Suddenly, from the slope on the other side of the valley, the sound of a shawm was heard, whose unexpected melody under the clear blue spring sky, in the deep solitude of the woods, made a remarkable impression on me. Since Beethoven was sitting next to me I could not refrain from calling his attention to it: sunk deep in thought he had heard nothing. He listened, but I observed from his expression

that he did not hear the sounds, although they continued. It was then that for the first time I was convinced his hearing was impaired. Previously I had had the same impression; but since in the early stages this condition came and went periodically, as it did even later, I had thought that I was mistaken. This time, however, there was no doubt whatever in my mind about it. The sounds continued so bright and clear that it was not possible to miss even a single note: yet Beethoven heard nothing. In order not to sadden him, I made believe that I too could not hear anything any more. After a while we set out again, the tones accompanying us for a long time on our solitary way through the woods, without Beethoven's taking the least notice of them. The sweet fascination which these tones had exercised on me at first now turned into a profound sadness. Almost without realizing it, I walked along silently, sunk in sad thoughts, at the side of my great master, who, as before, occupied with his own inner meditations, continued to hum indistinguishable phrases and tones, and to sing aloud. When after several hours we returned home, he sat down impatiently at the piano and exclaimed: 'Now I shall play something for you.' With irresistible fire and mighty force he played the *Allegro* of the great F Minor Sonata.* The day will *129* forever remain unforgettable to me.

Kerst I, 106 f. Heinrich Friedrich Ludwig Rellstab, *Aus meinem Leben,* Berlin 1861, II, p. 257. (Rellstab, from Berlin, whose father was a publisher, came to Vienna in 1825.)

> During the last fifteen years of his life, one of Beethoven's principal Viennese publishers was the firm of Steiner & Co. Between the composer and the publishers there existed a cordial relationship, and the men gave themselves military titles. Beethoven was the 'Generalissimus', Steiner was the 'Lieutenant-General', etc.

Letter from Sir Julius Benedict to Alexander Wheelock Thayer:

Honoured Sir! As I promised you, I will try to recall the impressions which I received when I first met Beethoven in Vienna in October 1823. He was then living in Baden, but he came to town regularly once a week and never failed to call on his old friends Steiner and Haslinger, whose music shop was at that time located in the Paternoster- *191, 192* gässchen, a little street which no longer exists, between the Graben and the Kohl- markt.

If I am not mistaken, when I saw Beethoven for the first time it was in the morning. Blahetka, father of the pianist, called my attention to a stocky man with a very red face, small penetrating eyes, bushy eyebrows, clothed in a very long coat which reached almost to his ankles, who entered the shop around twelve o'clock. Blahetka asked me: 'Who do you think that man is?' I exclaimed immediately: 'It must be Beethoven!' Despite the extreme redness of his cheeks and his quite careless appearance, I saw an expression in his small penetrating eyes which no painter could possibly portray. It was an expression of nobility and melancholy combined. As you can well imagine, I paid attention to every word which he spoke. He took a small book out of his pocket and began a conversation which, of course, remained almost incomprehensible to me, because he simply answered the questions which Messrs. Steiner and Haslinger wrote down in pencil.

*Op. 57, 'Appassionata,' begun in 1804 and completed two years later.

On this occasion I was not presented to him, but a few weeks after, on the second occasion, Herr Steiner introduced me as a pupil of Weber...

TDR IV, 462 f. Kerst II, 63 f. (Sir Julius Benedict, born at Stuttgart, was a pupil of Weber. In 1835 he settled in London and was knighted in 1871.)

251 *Anselm Hüttenbrenner speaking to Alexander Wheelock Thayer:*

Beethoven came every week a couple of times to the publishing house Steiner & Co., in the mornings between eleven and twelve o'clock. There a group of composers
222 gathered almost every morning and exchanged musical opinions. Schubert accompanied me several times. We enjoyed Beethoven's pithy and often sarcastic observations, especially when they were about Italian music.

TDR III, 582. Kerst I, 207. (Hüttenbrenner, a friend of Schubert's, was a musician.)

From the diary of Dr Carl von Bursy:

Vienna, 1 June [1816]
Beethoven came out of the room next door to meet me. It was difficult and unnatural for me to pay the master of my art only a polite and impersonal compliment. I should have liked to seize his hand and press on it a kiss of the deepest veneration....

Small, rather stocky, hair combed back with much grey in it, a rather red face, fiery eyes which, though small, are deep-set and unbelievably full of life. Beethoven,
85 especially when he laughs, has a great resemblance to Amenda. He asked after him [Amenda] and showed feelings of true friendship for him. 'He is a truly good man,' said he. 'It is my misfortune that all my friends are far away and here I am alone in this hateful Vienna.' He asked me to speak loudly to him because at the moment he again has great difficulties with his hearing, and for that reason wants to go to Baden this summer and be in the country. In general he has not been in good health for some time and has not composed anything new.... [They discussed a libretto which Amenda had sent to Beethoven.]

I shouted into his ear that for such tasks one must certainly have plenty of time and inspiration. 'No,' said he, 'I never do anything straight through without pause. I always work on several things at once, and sometimes I work on this one and sometimes on that one.' He misunderstood me very often and had to use the utmost concentration, when I was speaking, to get my meaning. That, of course, embarrassed and disturbed me very much. It disturbed him, too, and this led him to speak more himself and very loudly. He told me a lot about his life and about Vienna. He was venomous and embittered. He raged about everything, and is dissatisfied with everything, and he curses Austria and Vienna in particular. He speaks quickly and with great vivacity. He often banged his fist on the piano and made such a noise that it echoed around the room. He is not exactly reserved; for he told me about his personal affairs and related much about himself and his family. That is precisely the *signum diagnosticum* of

288

hypochondria. I was rather pleased with this hypochondria, because I learned so much about his life from his very lips. He complains about the present age, and for many reasons. Art no longer occupies a position high above the commonplace, art is no longer held in such high esteem and particularly not as regards recompense. Beethoven complains of bad times in a pecuniary sense. Can one believe that a Beethoven has grounds for such complaints?

'Why do you stay in Vienna when every foreign potentate would be glad to give you a place at his court or next to his throne?' 'Certain conditions keep me here', said he, 'but everything here is mean and dirty. Things could not be worse. From top to bottom everything is shabby. You can't trust anyone. What is not written down in black and white, no one will honour. They want your work and then pay you a beggar's pittance, not even what they agreed to pay. . . .'

His lodgings are pleasant and look out over the green *Bastei*. The rooms are well appointed and decently furnished. A bedroom opens out of the entrance hall, on the other side is a music room with a closed piano in it. I saw very little music, there were a few sheets of music paper on the desk. Two good oil portraits were on the wall, a man and a woman.

Petersburger Zeitung, 1854, Nos. 78 and 79.   Kerst I, 198 ff. (Dr Carl von Bursy was a friend of Amenda's and came with his recommendation to see Beethoven in 1816.)

Louis Schlösser describes Beethoven's appearance in about 1822:

A few weeks later we met on the Kärnthnerstrasse; with his sharp eye he had seen me first. He came up to me and took my arm with the following words: 'If you have time, come with me to the Paternostergässel to Steiner's (the music shop of Steiner & Haslinger), and I will read him the riot act; these publishers always have every kind of subterfuge up their sleeves. When it comes to publishing my compositions, they would just as soon avoid doing this until after my death because they could make more money out of them; but I shall know how to deal with them.' (This is word for word.) At this meeting I was quite astonished to notice that Beethoven, usually so careless about his dress, appeared in a most unusually elegant attire: blue tail-coat with yellow buttons, immaculate white trousers, a matching waistcoat, and a new beaver hat worn as usual towards the back of his head. I left him at the entrance of the shop, which was crowded with people, and he thanked me for my company and went with Herr Steiner to his office. I could not avoid reporting to my teacher *191* Mayseder, who lived nearby, the remarkable metamorphosis of Beethoven's elegance, an occurrence which surprised him less than myself, for he told me with a smile, 'That's not the first time his friends have stolen his old clothes during the night and replaced them with new ones; he won't have even noticed it and will have quite happily put on the new clothes which were lying handy.' This is the only remarkable anecdote that I have to tell about him. Nor did I pursue the matter further to find out if this was the way it really happened, but I must repeat that I never noticed Beethoven to be unobservant.

Hallelujah, 4th year, 1885, No. 20/21.   Kerst II, 14 f.

Beethoven's improvisation aroused considerable attention in the first years after his arrival in Vienna, even including the admiration of Mozart. It assumed various forms, depending on whether he improvised on themes of his own or on themes given to him [by others].

First: In the form of a first movement of a sonata or of a rondo finale: the first part would come to a regular close and he would use a related key for the middle melody. In the second part he would give free rein to his improvisation, making, however, every possible use of the main theme. He further enlivened the tempo allegro with *bravura* passages which were generally even more difficult than those found in his [written] compositions.

Second: A free variation form, more or less on the lines of his Choral Fantasia, Op. 80, or the choral finale of the Ninth Symphony, both of which provide an excellent example of the style of his improvisations.

Third: A mixed genre in which one idea would follow another, in the manner of a *pot-pourri*, as in his Fantasia, Op. 77.

A few insignificant notes often sufficed as material for the construction of a whole improvised work, similar to the finale of the Sonata in D Major, Op. 10 No. 3.

When he had finished such improvisations, Beethoven would break out into hearty and satisfied laughter. No one could equal him in the dexterity of his playing of scales, his double trills or his leaps: not even Hummel. His deportment while playing was exemplary: quiet, noble and beautiful. Nor did he indulge in any form of grimace. As his deafness increased, he tended to stoop. His fingers were very strong, not long, and the finger-tips were broadly shaped from much playing. He often told me that in his youth he practised an enormous amount, sometimes until long after midnight. When he taught he also insisted on a proper position of the fingers, according to the school of Emanuel Bach, which he used in teaching me. His own span was barely a tenth. He made considerable use of the pedal, far more than is indicated in his [published] works. His interpretations of the scores of Handel and Gluck and of the Fugues of Johann Sebastian Bach were unique: in the first he knew how to endow them with a full-voiced amplitude and a spirit which gave a new form to these works. He was the greatest sight-reader of his day, even of orchestral scores. As if by divination he could grasp an unfamiliar composition simply by leafing through it at speed. His judgments were always correct yet, especially in his younger years, sharp, biting and inconsiderate. Many works which the world admired, and still admires, he viewed from the high point of view of his genius in quite a different light.

Extraordinary as his improvisation was, his interpretation of those of his own compositions which had already appeared in print was less successful. He would not take enough trouble or time to practise again [something already familiar to him]. The success therefore depended on chance, or on his mood. Since both his playing and his compositions were in advance of his time, so also were the pianofortes of the time (up to 1810) often unequal to carrying his gigantic interpretations, being, as they were, still weak and imperfect. Because of this it came about that Hummel's pearly playing, with its brilliance calculated to a nicety, was far more comprehensible and attractive to the general public.

Nevertheless, Beethoven's interpretation of adagios and his lyric legato style exercised an almost magic spell on everyone who heard him and, to the best of my knowledge, has never been surpassed by anyone.

Czerny 21, 22.

194, 195

Letter from Beethoven to Sigmund Anton Steiner (1816):

We ask you not to forget our request today, since we cannot go out and need the money by tomorrow morning – as far as the Adjutant is concerned, he is to be put *in carcere** immediately and to be informed that he is to prepare himself for tomorrow's court session at 3.30 p.m. He will be accused there of great crimes against the state. Among other things he has not observed the rule of silence imposed on him regarding important affairs of state.

Given, without giving anything, etc. etc.

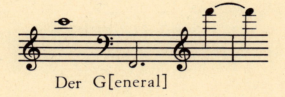

Der G[eneral]

[Address on the reverse side of the sheet:] To the/l-t g-l [Lieutenant General]/ Office/ (to be delivered personally).

TDR III, 626 f. Anderson 706.

Anton Schindler about Beethoven's financial difficulties:

As early as 1816, that is, in the days when his long-lasting embarrassments and calamities of all sorts began, the Leipzig publisher Hoffmeister proposed to our composer a plan for the publication of his complete pianoforte compositions, a plan which contained conditions that in the main did not differ too much from his [Beethoven's] own demands. In this matter he consulted Anton Diabelli, who had not yet become a publisher 225

The negotiations with Hoffmeister were not conducted with diplomatic secrecy and came to the ears of the friends of the great master in the Paternostergässchen in Vienna, who were equally constant in their affection for him and in their self-sacrifice in his interests.

Speculators like Messrs. Steiner and Comp. [i.e. Steiner and Haslinger] could hardly be unaware of the fact that if the Leipzig plan were to be consummated, they would find themselves at a disadvantage with their own Beethoven publications and that in the future they would receive no new works whatever from him. They

*Latin in original.

therefore approached him with a similar plan, requesting that the master grant them two or three years' time in order to begin the project. With arithmetical calculations they proved to him the great advantages, both specifically in reference to the fees and generally, if all his works, corrections, and so forth were to be accomplished under his own supervision. These chimerical propositions sufficed to scuttle the Hoffmeister plan at once.

Sometime later, this Vienna publishing house submitted to the master a price list for all the various forms of music beginning with the symphony and oratorio down to a song, in which the fee for every form was specified. This list, in Tobias Haslinger's handwriting, still exists. A symphony, for example, is priced at 60–80 ducats, a 'major' oratorio at 300 ducats, a smaller one at 200, a requiem at 120, an *opera seria* at 300, a sonata for the pianoforte alone at 30, a grand sonata for the pianoforte alone at 40 ducats. The whole thing was a much more seductive plan than had ever been made before to the master. That it found a willing ear goes without saying . . . .

It was a plan drawn up with the most refined cleverness, and it stipulated the condition that Beethoven was to bind himself to give everything he might compose in the future exclusively to this Viennese publisher. It was a condition he was willing to accept; yet this plan, too, suffered the same fate as the Hoffmeister plan: it was betrayed. Immediately the other Viennese publishers raised a hue and cry. In just such a manner might the ears of the Sultan of Turkey have been assaulted by the Pashas over some planned government reforms as were those of our master by the Artarias, Mollos and Cappis over Herr Steiner's proposed monopoly. And the musical Sultan of Vienna let himself be persuaded of the infallibility of the objections raised by the gentlemen of the competition: that the Steiner plan would work to his disadvantage. As before with the Leipzig proposal, this too was set aside, so that the little ship and its helmsman, though he continued to watch for every wind, remained grounded, high and dry, despite his own admonition, noted in his diary for 1816. But freedom and independence, the latter of a very dubious sort, were preserved. It was

49, 50   Domenico Artaria who reaped the first tangible fruits of this freedom: the great Sonata in B-Flat Major, Op. 106.

Schindler II, 38 ff.

Friedrich Johann Rochlitz describes walking in the country with Beethoven:

Our third meeting was the merriest of all. He came to Baden, and this time he was neat and well groomed, indeed elegant. This, however, did not prevent him from

197   taking off his fine black tail-coat during a walk in the Helenental (it was a hot day) – that is, on a road frequented by everyone, including the Emperor and his household, where people mostly walk along narrow paths and have to brush past one another – he carried his coat on his cane across his shoulder and walked around with his arms bare. He stayed from about ten o'clock in the morning to six o'clock in the afternoon. One of his friends and Gebauer were with him. He was in very high spirits all the time and occasionally very droll. He gave voice to everything that came into his mind. ('Today for once I am unbuttoned,' he called it, appropriately enough.) All he said and

292

all he did represented uniquely personal characteristics and sometimes curious ones, but through it all there shone a truly childlike good nature, a freedom from care, a trusting attitude towards all who approached him. Even his little acid tirades – such as the one against the Viennese of today, which I mentioned above – are merely outbursts of his imagination and expressions of a temporary excitement. He blurts them out without arrogance, bitterness or hatred – in a light spirit, amiable disposition and in a giddy and humorous mood; then it is all over.

Rochlitz, *op. cit.*, IV, 258 f.   Kerst I, 287.

Johann Sporschil's obituary of Beethoven in the Dresdener Abendzeitung (*July 1827*):

No longer will the citizens of friendly Vienna have the privilege of observing a man of compact build, carelessly dressed, a hat of indeterminate shape on his head, the head itself lifted up, the face with its grey shadows wearing an expression of deep abstraction. No longer will they see him hurrying through the street with his short yet firm steps barely touching the ground, until, fast as lightning, he vanishes around the corner. No longer will they be able to whisper with benevolent and indulgent pride to one another: 'Did you see? Beethoven!' Nor will the stranger, wandering through the romantically beautiful countryside of Baden or Mödling in the remotest part of the *197, 198* shady mountain woods, again see the same man leaning against a tree trunk or sitting on a rock, a notebook in one hand, a pencil in the other, now fixing his gaze through the green and leafy cover to the blue sky, now hastily filling the page with strange hieroglyphs. No longer will the stranger be able to observe this curious but fascinating apparition without himself being observed. Nor will the stranger, once his presence has been noticed and the apparition has vanished towards yet more remote depths, continue on his way and, when he has returned to the company of his happy fellow men, describe what he has just seen and ask: 'Was not that, perhaps – ?' receive the answer – 'Yes, it was Beethoven!'

Kerst II, 71 f. (Johann Sporschil, a poet and historian, lived in Vienna until 1827. He offered Beethoven an opera libretto, which Beethoven intended to use with his music to *The Ruins of Athens*.)

A page from Beethoven's notebook:

My decree is to remain in the country; how easy it is to do that in whatever corner. My unfortunate hearing does not plague me there./ It is as if/every tree spoke to me/in the country, holy! holy!/ Ecstasy in the woods! Who/can describe it?/ If all comes to nought/the country itself remains/, Gaden, Untere Brühl etc./in the winter/it would be easy/to rent a lodging from a peasant;/ around this time it is/surely not expensive./ Sweet stillness of the woods! The wind which blows already on the second nice day cannot retain me in Vienna, because it is my enemy.

Theodor Frimmel, *Beethoven Handbuch*, Hildesheim-Wiesbaden 1968, I, p. 423. (Facsimile in *Ein Wiener Beethovenbuch*, compiled by Alfred Orel, Vienna 1921, p. 231. This autograph was formerly in the possession of Guido Adler, Vienna.)

On 29 November 1814, Beethoven gave a brilliant concert in the Redoutensaal in which the Seventh Symphony was performed and was such a success that the slow movement had to be repeated.

Louis Spohr recalls the concert on 29 November 1814:

His friends grasped this favourable occasion [the success of the revival of *Fidelio*] to organize a concert in the Grand *Redoutensaal*, in which the newest compositions by Beethoven were to be performed. Anybody who could play a string or wind instrument, or sing, was invited to take part, and not one of the leading artists of Vienna was missing. I and my orchestra naturally consented to take part, and for the first time I saw Beethoven conduct. Although much had been told to me about his way of conducting, it nevertheless astounded me in the utmost degree. Beethoven was in the habit of giving dynamic indications to the orchestra by means of all sorts of peculiar movements of his body. When he wanted a *sforzando* he would vehemently throw out both his arms, which previously he had held crossed across his breast. For a *piano* he would crouch down, going down deeper as he wanted the sound to be softer. Then, at the beginning of a *crescendo* he would rise gradually and when the *forte* was reached he would leap up into the air. Occasionally he would shout with the music in order to make the *forte* stronger, without being conscious of it . . . .

The concert organized by his friends enjoyed a most brilliant success. The new compositions by Beethoven were exceptionally well received, particularly the Symphony in A Major (the Seventh); the wonderful second movement had to be repeated; it made a deep and lasting impression on me.

The execution was quite masterly despite Beethoven's uncertain and sometimes ludicrous conducting. It was evident that the poor deaf master was no longer able to hear the *pianos* in his music. This was particularly evident in a passage in the second part of the first *Allegro* of the symphony, where two *fermate* follow one another, of which the second is *pianissimo*. Beethoven probably had overlooked the second one, because he started off beating time again before the orchestra had even begun the second *fermata*. Therefore, without knowing it, he was ahead of the orchestra by as much as ten or twelve bars when it began to play the *pianissimo*. Beethoven, indicating the passage in his own way, had crouched down under the music stand; at the *crescendo*, which followed, he became visible once more, made himself taller, and then leapt high up in the air at the moment when, according to his calculation, the *forte* should have begun. When this did not happen, he looked about him in terror, stared in astonishment at the orchestra, which was still playing the *pianissimo*, and found his place only when the so-long-awaited *forte* began and became audible to him.

Fortunately this comic scene during the performance was not noticed by the audience; otherwise they would have laughed.

Since the hall was completely filled and the applause enthusiastic, Beethoven's friends organized a repetition of the concert, which brought in almost equal profits. By this means Beethoven was spared financial embarrassments for a while; yet these recurred once or twice before his death, due to the same reasons . . . .

Louis Spohr, *op. cit.*, 200, 201 f.   Kerst I, 173 ff.

Beethoven's apostles and followers spread his name throughout Europe. One of the finest women pianists of the period was Marie Leopoldine Pachler, née Koschak, a Beethoven enthusiast in Graz.

Anselm Hüttenbrenner about Leopoldine Koschak-Pachler:

The daughter of the lawyer Koschak was the most beautiful girl, and later, for some years, the most beautiful woman in Graz. She was called 'the daughter of heaven'. She had a passion for Jean Paul, Göthe [sic] and Schiller; for Beethoven, Mozart and Schubert.

202

TDR IV, 60.

Letter from Beethoven to Leopoldine Koschak-Pachler:

[Vienna, Summer 1817]

I am so happy that you will remain yet another day. We will make a lot of music – the Sonatas in F Major and C Minor – you will play them for me, won't you?

I have never found anybody who plays my compositions as well as you do – the greatest *pianonists* [sic] not excepted, they possess only mechanics or affectation. You are the true nurse of the children of my spirit.

TDR IV, 60.   Anderson 815.

Cipriani Potter tells Alexander Wheelock Thayer about his experiences with Beethoven:

Once Potter asked him his opinion about one of the foremost pianists who were then in Vienna: it was Moscheles. 'Don't ever speak about players of scales!' was the answer. Another time Beethoven told him that John Cramer gave him more satisfaction than anybody else.

74

Once Potter entered his anteroom in Mödling and heard him improvising in the next room. Naturally he waited, astonished and delighted at the same time by the wonderful playing, now expressed in incredible harmonies (or perhaps disharmonies, due to his deafness), now softening into delicate and swift passages. A little while later he opened the door and looked out. When he first noticed Potter he was taken aback and said, 'I do not like anyone to listen to me.'

Politics, too, played a rôle in their conversations. The very first time they were together, Beethoven started right in and berated the Austrian government with all sorts of names. He was filled with the thought of coming to England. He wanted so much to see the House of Commons. 'You people in England have heads on your shoulders.'

Potter imparted the interesting information that Beethoven spoke Italian fluently, French less easily. He must have received the impetus to perfect his knowledge of the Italian language through his intercourse with Salieri and the other Italian artists, and of course he often composed to Italian texts. Their conversations were for the most part held in that language. Potter could make himself understood when he spoke directly into Beethoven's ear through his cupped hand; sometimes it was obvious that Beethoven had not heard, yet it was sufficient if he could understand the essentials.

Potter often saw the copyist Schlemmer. When he could not decipher a certain passage, Schlemmer said: 'I am supposed to read everything!'

TDR IV, 57 f.

201   *August von Kloeber discusses Beethoven:*

A brother-in-law of mine, Baron von Skrbensky, who owned an estate in Austrian Silesia and died many years ago, asked me to do a portrait of Beethoven for him as part of a collection of famous Viennese artists and composers of the time.

Making Beethoven's acquaintance was a difficult task, and it was still more difficult to get him to sit for me. By a fortunate chance I had come to know a friend of Beethoven's, the cellist Dont, a member of the Imperial Court Opera Theatre; this proved to be helpful, the more so as Dont himself was most interested in the plan. Dont advised me to wait until the summer, since Beethoven usually spent the summer in Mödling and was then at his most easy-going and accessible. In a letter, our mutual friend told Beethoven that I would be arriving in Mödling, and also that I wished to draw him. Beethoven agreed, on condition that he would not have to sit for too long at a time.

Early in the morning I went to call on him. His old housekeeper told me he was still at breakfast but would soon be coming; in the meantime there were books by Goethe and Herder with which I could occupy myself. Beethoven finally came in and said, 'You want to paint me, but I am very impatient.' He was already quite deaf, and if I wanted to say something I had to write it, or else he used his ear-trumpet 247   when his *famulus* (a young relation of about twelve [nephew Carl]) was not present to shout the words into his ear.

Beethoven then sat down, and the boy had to begin practising the [Broadwood] piano, a gift from England and equipped with a large metal dome. The instrument stood roughly four to five paces behind him, and Beethoven, despite his deafness, corrected every mistake the boy made, had him repeat single passages, etc.

Beethoven always looked very serious, his extremely lively eyes usually wandered, looking upwards somewhat darkly and low-spiritedly, which I have attempted to capture in the portrait. His lips were shut, but the expression about the mouth was not unfriendly. – One of his favourite topics was the overweening vanity and perverted taste of the Viennese aristocracy, about whom he never had a good word to say, for he considered himself neglected by them, or not sufficiently understood.

After roughly 3/4 of an hour he became restless; remembering Dont's advice, I now knew it was time to stop, and asked him only if I could come again the next day, since I was staying in Mödling. Beethoven was quite agreeable and said, 'Then we can meet more often, for I cannot sit still too long at one time; you must also have a good look at Mödling, for it is quite lovely here, and as an artist you must certainly be a nature-lover.' I encountered Beethoven several times on my walks in Mödling, and it was most interesting to see him, a sheet of music paper and a stump of a pencil in his hand, stop often as though listening, look up and down and then write a few notes on the paper. Dont had told me that when I saw him thus, I should never speak to him or take any notice of him, because that would make him embarrassed or even unpleasant. Once, when setting out on a walk through the woods, I saw him climbing up the hill opposite, from the defile which separated us, his broad-brimmed, grey felt hat pressed under his arm; once at the top, he lay down full length under a pine-tree and looked at the sky for a long while. Every morning he sat a little less than an hour for me. When Beethoven saw my portrait, he mentioned that he liked the way the hair was done; other painters had always done it too elegantly dressed, as though he were appearing before a court official, and he was not like that at all. – I must mention that the oil painting done for my brother-in-law is larger than the lithograph, and that Beethoven is holding a sheet of music in his hand; the background is a Mödling landscape.

Beethoven's dwelling in Mödling was quite simple, as indeed was everything about him; his clothing consisted of a light blue frock-coat with yellow buttons, white waistcoat and necktie, as was then the fashion, but all in a quite neglected state. His complexion was healthy and robust, the skin somewhat pockmarked; his hair was the colour of blued steel, having already begun to change from black to grey. His eyes were blue-grey and quite lively. When his hair was tossed about by the wind, he had something absolutely Ossian-like and demoniacal about him. In friendly conversation, however, he took on a genial and mild expression, particularly when he was pleasantly affected by the subject. Every mood of his spirit was immediately and violently expressed in his countenance.

Allgemeine Musikalische Zeitung, No. 18, 4 May 1864.

One of the Viennese suburbs which Beethoven frequented was Nussdorf on the Danube. The composer was there in the summer of 1817.

From Beethoven's conversation books:

[April 1826]

Christoph Kuffner: Do you still remember the 'Fischerhaus' near Nussdorf where we sat on the terrace in the light of the full moon until close on to midnight, with the wind in the meadows and the swollen Danube before us? I was your guest there too. – – –

Kerst II, 296.

Letter from Beethoven to Nanette Streicher:

Nussdorf, 7 July [1817]

My dear friend!
I received your letter here, confirming your bad fall. I hope it will improve soon; warm, tepid baths heal all hurts. – The bad weather the day before yesterday kept me from coming to see you when I was in town. Yesterday morning I hurried back here,

199

but did not find my servant at home; he had even taken the keys to my lodgings with him. It was quite chilly and I had come out from town with nothing but a very thin pair of breeches and was forced to loaf about for three hours. This was injurious for me and put me in a foul humour for the whole day. – There you see what happens to households that depend on servants! . . .

Beethovens Briefe (Leitzmann), *op. cit.*, p. 133. Anderson 785. (Nanette Streicher was the daughter of the piano manufacturer Johann Andreas Stein. She carried on her father's firm.)

Louis Schlösser writes about Beethoven's method of composition (1822/23):

'I carry my ideas about with me for a long time, and often for a very long time, before I write them down,' he [Beethoven] answered. 'In doing so, my memory is so trustworthy that I am sure I will not forget, even after a period of years, a theme I have once committed to memory. I change a great deal, eliminate much and begin again, until I am satisfied with the result; then the working-out, in extension, in diminution, in height and in depth begins in my head, and, since I know what I want, the basic idea never leaves me, it mounts and grows, I hear and see the work in my mind in its full proportions, as though already accomplished, and all that remains is the labour of writing it out; this proceeds quickly, depending on the time I have available, since I often have several pieces in the works at once; I am certain, however, not to confuse one with the other. You will ask me where I get my ideas. That I cannot say with certainty. They come unbidden, indirectly, directly. I could grasp them with my hands; in the midst of nature, in the woods, on walks, in the silence of the night, in the early morning, inspired by moods that translate themselves into words for the poet and into tones for me, that sound, surge, roar, until at last they stand before me as notes.'

Kerst II, 15 f. *Hallelujah* 4th year, No. 20, 1885.

203   *Anton Schindler on Schimon's painting of Beethoven:*

. . . It is worth taking the space to report on the conditions under which this painting was done. At my intercession the artist, who was still quite young, received permission to set up his easel next to the master's workroom, and to work as he saw fit. Beethoven steadfastly refused to grant a sitting, for he was completely engrossed in work on the *Missa Solemnis* and declared that he could not spare a single hour. Schimon, however, had already secretly followed Beethoven's every footstep and had several studies for the painting in his portfolio, and was thus quite satisfied with the permission as granted. When the picture had been completed except for one significant detail, the expression of the eyes, the critical situation arose as to how to achieve this most difficult end; for the play of the eyes in Beethoven's head was of a singular nature, revealing a gamut of expressions, ranging from the wildest and most defiant to the gentlest and most affectionate, equal to the gamut of his emotions. For a painter this was, then, the most difficult obstacle. The master himself helped to overcome it. The uncouth, blunt nature of the young painter, his unceremonious behaviour as though he were in his own studio, his habit of arriving without saying 'Good morning' and leaving without saying 'Goodbye', had attracted Beethoven's attention even more than what stood on the easel; in short, the young man began to interest him. He invited him to coffee. Schimon used the impromptu sitting at the coffee table to work out the eyes. Further invitations to a cup of coffee, at 60 beans per cup, gave the painter the opportunity to finish his work, with which Beethoven was utterly satisfied.

Schindler II, 288 f.

Anton Schindler on Beethoven's eyes:

... Rochlitz reports how Beethoven received his suggestion concerning music to *Faust*, in the following words: 'He [Beethoven] read. Ha! he cried, and threw up his hands. That would be a piece of work! Something could come of that! He went on a while in this manner, proceeding forthwith to lay plans in his mind, and not at all badly, all the while staring at the ceiling, his head bent back.'

The latter observation belongs to the afore-mentioned play of the eyes in Beethoven's head. His eyes, which usually appeared to be small, frequently became large and prominent, and their gaze, directed upwards, would remain fixed for some time on the ceiling or on the sky, either in meditation or when something in the conversation had affected him strongly. Only Schimon caught that characteristic *203* completely; Stieler merely hinted at it. The illness Beethoven suffered at the beginning of 1825 had destroyed the brightness of his eyes, so that, as many inward and outward metamorphoses began at that time, nothing more of the curious play of the eyes could be perceived from then onwards. Stieler's painting agrees excellently with *207* that outward change.

Schindler II, 292 f.

Anton Schindler reports on Beethoven's clothing:

In choosing the articles of apparel to appear in the portrait of an historical figure, due consideration has to be given to a number of points; among them is the distinction that has to be made between everyday and festive clothing, and even between good and bad seasons of the year. Still more particular attention will have to be paid to a Beethoven, who knew how to dress decently for the street as well as for the drawing-room. In this regard it must be said of the master that, until the last days of his life, conditions permitting, he was fond of dressing painstakingly and that there was always harmony in his apparel. A frock-coat of fine blue cloth with metal buttons (blue was his favourite colour at that time) suited him excellently. Such a frock-coat, with another of dark green cloth, was never missing from his wardrobe. During the summer one always saw him in fair weather in white trousers, shoes and white stockings (then the fashion). His waistcoat and necktie were white at every season and were conspicuous for their exemplary cleanliness even on weekdays. Apart from this attire one must imagine a light step and an erect carriage, light movements in general, which were always characteristic of Beethoven, and one will have Beethoven's personality before one.

Schindler II, 294 f.

There is an illuminating report on Beethoven's creative powers during this period by his friend and later biographer, Anton Schindler. In many respects, Schindler was a small-minded and waspish pedant, but his personal recollections of Beethoven are of the utmost value and more than make up for his deficiencies. Both these opposing qualities can be seen in his report about the last great Sonatas, particularly the final one, in C Minor, Op. 111.

Anton Schindler on Beethoven's creative powers:

When the *Allgemeine Musikalische Zeitung* brought out the following item, which was reprinted in the Viennese newspapers – 'Beethoven is now engaged, like Father Haydn before him, in arranging Scottish folksongs; he appears to be utterly indifferent about larger works.' (XXIII, 539) – this gave still more weight to the comment already in circulation, that Beethoven had written himself out.

The master himself appeared to be amused at such definite statements concerning his intellectual exhaustion; however, they did in fact provide an unmistakable impulse towards a new, fresh spiritual effort. He was not lacking in pronouncements on the order of, 'Just wait, you'll soon be taught better.' On his return in late autumn from his summer sojourn in Mödling where he had, in customary fashion, collected ideas like a bee, he sat down at his desk and wrote the three Pianoforte Sonatas Op. 109, 110 and 111 'at one stretch', as he called it in a letter sent to Count Brunsvik to calm that friend about his mental state. Those who know these works will be able to consider what the words 'at one stretch' were meant to denote. The first of the Sonatas – there were indications during the previous winter that work on it was under way – was published by Schlesinger in 1822; but the other two at the beginning of the following year. The delay was caused at first by the difficulty of establishing the date of simultaneous publication in Berlin, Paris and Vienna, and then by Beethoven's own proof-reading. The Paris edition had to make the journey to Vienna twice; due to the extremely large number of errors remaining in the second proofs, the author demanded that Op. 111 be returned yet again, which the publishers would not agree to. At that, the heavens seemed about to fall on our composer.

I was charged with writing out the fair copy of the passages containing printer's errors, which Beethoven had excerpted for returning to the publisher. Occupied with this rather ungratifying job on the Sonata Op. 111, I allowed myself, in my innocence, to put a question to the master, who was seated opposite me; why, I asked, had he not written a third movement comparable in character to the first. Beethoven answered calmly that he had had no time for a third movement; that was why the second movement had had to be extended to such large proportions. Since I had not, until that time, heard more than fragments of the work while it was being composed, his

204

answer sufficed. Later on, when I had come to know the Sonata, I began to think about the reason given for the lack of a third movement, and I openly confess that I still truly regret it at this moment. I was unable to understand (and still cannot) how the two movements, so drastically opposed to one another in character, can be said to form a self-contained, coherent whole; on one hand the expression of almost violent passion, with only short interruptions by pleasant-sounding melodies; on the other hand a tonal painting which is sombre virtually throughout, a piece without an equal in Beethoven's works up to that time. It appeared (and still does) that the composer had surpassed himself in this movement with regard to multiplicity of form and the employment of an excess of scientific methods on such simple material as the 'Arietta' (the theme of the variations, etc.); this is something we encounter often in subsequent works. The critique from Leipzig contained, among other comments, the following remark on this movement: 'It has pleased the composer, in working out his fine material, to make use for the most part of such artificial means as we consider not quite worthy of his genius. He resembles, in this tonal painting, an artist who fills out his space in monochrome, using a miniature brush.' (XXXIV, 213)

In the introduction to the critique, which goes into great detail about the nature of the last three Sonatas, the author makes use of a telling comparison in relation to Beethoven's music in general; we include it verbatim here, particularly since it will serve us well in judging certain subsequent works. It reads:

'One may possibly compare an artistic life of such richness to a magnificent landscape park with excellently laid and often wonderfully meandering paths which wind their way through copses, meadows, valleys and rock-walled gorges. In a park of that kind there are points, for the most part unexpected, from which spread delightful prospects, to be enjoyed completely, it is true, by the armed eye only; likewise there are, in such a magnificent musical park as the one Beethoven has created for us, certain delightful parts that stand out marvellously. In the one as in the other there are times when the path turns abruptly – often at the most captivating resting-points – in the opposite way, so that one may think at first that one is walking back or that one has been diverted from the direction in which many an enjoyment was to be awaited, the lack of which now fills one with concern. However, in the one as in the other, one should let oneself, willingly and devotedly, be led by the creator (who could be a better guide than he?), and one will find to one's gratification that not every turning-point is a point of culmination.'

Schindler II, 2 ff.

Dr. W. Chr. Müller on the Viennese passion for music:

[26 October 1820]
It is incredible to what extent the Viennese are fond of music, especially of proficiency in Fortepiano playing. There is a good instrument in every house. At the banker Gaymüller's we found five by different manufacturers. Particularly the women play a great deal. Hummel told me that in Vienna there are a hundred women who play

more than he does. With regard to finger dexterity that may be true; but where is his strength and his extraordinary identification with the work? – We heard several ladies, for example Frau von Mosel, etc. Baroness Ertmann, who studied with Beethoven, appeared to excel all others in execution. The others rattle off the most difficult masses of notes with magical velocity; but the spirit of the composition, and even its character, remain alien to them; they act neither on the feelings nor on the imagination.

Dr. W. Chr. Müller, *Briefe an deutsche Freunde, von einer Reise durch Italien über Sachsen, Böhmen und Österreich, 1820 und 1821 geschrieben und als Skizzen zum Gemälde unserer Zeit herausgegeben*, Altona 1824, p. 130. (Müller and his daughter, a good pianist, visited Beethoven in Vienna on a journey to Italy in 1820.)

Anton Schindler writes about the painter Stieler:

In the autumn of 1821, the painter Stieler from Munich presented himself to Beethoven with good references and a good reputation as an artist. His personal character was especially praised. Stieler was able, to a rare degree, to make the moody master agreeable to his purpose. Sitting after sitting was granted, without one complaint about wasted time. As a work of art the portrait by Stieler is significant, although it is executed in the then modern convention which, despite a certain outward brilliance, admits of little virtuosity; the painting appears to be in a rather straightforward style. As to the expression of character, this is well caught and met with approval. On the other hand, the conception of the Titan favoured by the artist encountered opposition, in particular the inclination of the head; for the master was never known by his contemporaries to do other than carry his head proudly erect, even in moments of physical pain. A painter acquainted with his nature would never have given him that attitude.

Schindler II, 289 f.

This was the period of the tremendous *Missa Solemnis*, Op. 123, for Archduke Rudolph. It was Beethoven's faithful copyist, Schlemmer, who prepared the beautiful score given to the Archduke himself, which is now in the Gesellschaft der Musikfreunde.

From Beethoven's conversation books:

[1–14 April 1820]
Stieler: In what key is your Mass? I just want to write on the page Mass in ....
Beethoven: D Missa solemnis in D.
Stieler: a quarter-hour after the exhibition I will send it to Brentano.

A thousand thousand thanks for so much patience

Jos. Czerny: We were just talking about your portrait. – Oliva thinks – that it is a very good likeness –

[26 April 1820]

Oliva: Has Aulic Councillor Birkenstock's house been sold? She will be very glad about the portrait. Stieler has caught the spirit of your countenance.

Konv. Sch. 37, 42, 69.

Carl Friedrich Hirsch describes Beethoven's appearance, as taken down by Theodor von Frimmel:

Hirsch confirmed what was said about the musical Titan's powerful build and the healthy ruddy colouring of his face; Hirsch, too, drew my attention to the fact that Beethoven's eyebrows were quite bushy and his forehead low (a statement confirmed by the skull and the existing masks, but contradicted by less credible assertions about a high forehead which have come from various scattered quarters). The nose, Hirsch says, was large and broad, particularly the nostrils (which were always soundly 'worked over'). Beethoven's hair was quite thick, bushy and dark – though mixed with grey – and stood up from his forehead. Now and then, when reading music, the master used eyeglasses, but he did not wear them constantly. – On this occasion I showed Herr Hirsch my collection of Beethoven portraits, to ask him which were good likenesses and which were not. He found that a small medallion in my possession, showing the head turned to the right, was the most similar; it was done from life by a renowned old Viennese artist at the beginning of the 1820s. The artist in question is Josef Daniel Böhm (1794–1865). Of the other Beethoven portraits I showed him, Hirsch described the one made after the Schimon portrait as good. *203* In most of the others he found the forehead too high. Of the later ones, he approved of those which retained the Schimon or Waldmüller type, among them the medallion *224* by Brehmer, on which, however, the forehead was also much too high. The wrinkles in the forehead falling to the bridge of the nose, as shown in the Stieler portrait, he *207* considered especially true to life.

Beethoven's lack of order at home was also confirmed. Beethoven worked in a flowered cloth dressing-gown; when not at home he was to be seen in a dark green or brown coat and grey or black trousers. – In his room the greatest disorder reigned; music, manuscripts, books lay around, some on the writing desk, some on the floor. The revered head was covered by a sort of low top hat or, during the warmer seasons, a brown or dirty yellow straw hat. His service was seen to by a hotel.

Neue Zeitschrift für Musik, No. 35, 1880. (As a child, Hirsch had had piano lessons from Beethoven.)

Anton Schindler on the Missa Solemnis: *205, 206*

Towards the end of August [1819] I arrived at the house in Mödling where Beethoven was staying; with me was Johann Horzalka, a musician who is still living in Vienna. It was four in the afternoon. We had no sooner walked in when we were told that Beethoven's two maidservants had taken themselves off that same morning, and that all the occupants of the house had been disturbed by a scene which took place after midnight, because both servants had fallen asleep after waiting so long and the food they had prepared had turned inedible. In one of the living-rooms, behind closed doors, we heard the master singing, howling and stamping his foot over the *Credo* fugue. We had listened for some time to the awful scene and were about to leave, when the door opened and Beethoven stood facing us with features so distorted as to fill one with alarm. He looked as though he had just survived a life-and-death battle with the whole host of contrapuntalists, his perpetual opponents. His first remarks were confused, as though he were unpleasantly surprised at our eavesdropping. But he presently came to speak of the issues of the day and remarked with perceptible composure, 'A fine business. Everyone has run off and I have had nothing to eat since yesterday noon.' I sought to mollify him and helped him to dress. My companion hurried on ahead to the dining-room at the baths to have something prepared for our famished master. There he complained to us about the bad conditions of his household. For various reasons there was no remedying them. Surely no work of art of such magnitude has ever been created in more unpleasant living conditions than was the *Missa Solemnis*!

Schindler I, 270 f.

Franz Lachner on Beethoven and Nanette Streicher:

59   I had the privilege of making Beethoven's acquaintance at the Streichers'. Their home was the meeting place of all the leading figures in music; and so it happened that I found access, although I was merely an organist and a practising performer on the piano. One day I was there alone, and sat at the piano next to Nanette Streicher who was studying the Trio in B-Flat Major, Op. 97, by Beethoven. Suddenly Beethoven, on whose household affairs Frau Streicher had considerable influence, entered the room, just as we had reached the beginning of the last movement. He listened for a few moments, using the ear-trumpet he always carried with him, but soon showed that he was not in agreement with the too gentle execution of the principal motive of the Finale. He leaned over Nanette and played it for her, after which he left straight-away. I was so excited and thrilled by the loftiness of his aspect, his forceful action and the immediate proximity of his imposing personality, that it took some time until I was again in a tranquil state.

FRBS II, 265 f.

190. Ludwig van Beethoven. Engraving by Blasius Höfel, from a pencil drawing by Louis Letronne, 1814. Gesellschaft der Musikfreunde, Vienna. (*See Plate 188.*)

Höfel found Letronne's drawing not accurate enough and received permission to make a new sketch of Beethoven; the result was, according to contemporary opinion, one of the best portraits of the composer ever made.

191. Sigmund Anton Steiner (1773–1838). Lithograph by Joseph Teltscher, 1826. Historisches Museum of the City of Vienna.

In 1804, Steiner bought the printing firm of Senefelder together with Rochus Krasnitzky. Ten years later, Tobias Haslinger became a partner, the firm was turned into a music publishing house, and immediate contact with Beethoven was made. The firm in fact became one of Beethoven's principal publishers and the composer used amusing military titles when dealing with the various partners: Steiner was 'Lieutenant General', Haslinger was 'Adjutant', and the composer 'Generalissimus'. When the composer Anton Diabelli joined the firm, he became known as 'Diabolus'. In 1826 Haslinger became the sole proprietor.

192. Tobias Haslinger (1787–1842). Watercolour by Joseph Kriehuber, 1832. Historisches Museum of the City of Vienna.

193. Ludwig van Beethoven. Portrait in oils by Joseph Willibrord Mähler, signed 'J. Mähler pinx'. Wolfgang von Karajan, Salzburg.

This second Beethoven portrait by Mähler – the first one had been painted *c.* 1804 – seems to date about August 1815, for the *Allgemeine Musikalische Zeitung* wrote in that month: "The composers' portraits by Herr Mähler deserve special appreciation and public announcement. This clever young man studied for three years in Dresden with the famous Graff and then continued his apprenticeship at the Vienna Academy. As an admirer of the related art [of music] he completed in his spare time a series of portraits of local composers, which all distinguish themselves by the strength of their brush strokes, their great likeness, their subjects and their unmistakable expression. Up to now the following portraits have been completed: Beethoven, Eibler, Gelinek, Gyrowetz, Hummel, Seyfried, Weigl.' It is not clear if this portrait is the original or one of the copies that we know Mähler made.

197. The Helenental near Baden. Coloured steel plate engraving by Charles Westwood from a drawing by Lieut. Col. Robert Batty, London 1822. Antiquarian Ingo Nebehay, Vienna.

199. Danube landscape, seen from Nussdorf. Anonymous watercolour, end of the 18th century. Historisches Museum of the City of Vienna.

The year 1817 was a troubled one for Beethoven: the fight to gain adoption of his nephew Carl, financial worries, and sickness; all of these things made the composer troubled and ill-humoured. In June he moved to the nearby village of Nussdorf, but also kept his flat in town. During a walk into town, he caught cold and since his servant—'the ass'—had gone away with the keys to the flat, Beethoven, already soaked through, had to wait on the street in the rain.

◀ 198. The Hinterbrühl near Mödling. Coloured engraving by Laurenz Janscha from a drawing by Johann Ziegler, c. 1800. Historisches Museum of the City of Vienna.

Beethoven often spent the summer months in Baden or Mödling when he was not taking the cure at one of the Bohemian spas. These summer lodgings were inexpensive and the trip to and from Vienna easily accomplished; Beethoven always had financial worries and his inexpensive life during the summers was undoubtedly beneficial to his budget as well as his health.

200. Ludwig van Beethoven. Undated pencil drawing by Gustav Adolph Hippius. Collection Dr H. C. Bodmer, Beethovenhaus Bonn.

The portrait was made between the years 1814 and 1816, when Hippius was in Vienna. Beethoven is said to have sat for it.

201. Ludwig van Beethoven. Pencil drawing by Carl Friedrich August ▶ von Kloeber. Collection Dr H. C. Bodmer, Beethovenhaus Bonn.

This drawing would appear to have been a study for the large, now lost, painting which showed Beethoven and his nephew Carl while at Mödling. The painting was ordered by Kloeber's brother-in-law, Baron Skrbenski. The drawing, which was probably made at Mödling about 1818, shows considerable differences when placed beside the Klein mask. Apart from this study, Kloeber made at least two other drawings: one of Beethoven's head (C.F. Peters [Walter Hinrichsen], disappeared 1945 in Leipzig), and a study of the composer's hands, now in the Beethovenhaus in Bonn.

313

202. Marie Leopoldine Pachler, née Koschak (1794–1855). Anonymous miniature on ivory (10 × 9 cm). Beethovenhaus Bonn.

The young lady from Graz made a trip to Vienna, shortly after her marriage in 1816, and at that time made Beethoven's acquaintance; he held the gifted pianist in high regard. During a second trip to Vienna in the year 1823 Beethoven gave her a 'musical farewell' consisting of two bars (WoO 202).

314

203. Ludwig van Beethoven. Portrait in oils by Ferdinand Schimon. Beethoven-haus Bonn.

Beethoven, who was hard at work on the *Missa Solemnis*, did not at first wish to grant any sessions to the young painter Schimon. Several references to Schimon in Beethoven's conversation books enable us to date the work 1818 or 1819. The picture was owned by Beethoven's friend Anton Schindler and from him passed first to the Staatsbibliothek in Berlin and later to the Beethovenhaus in Bonn.

204. Piano Sonata in C minor, Op. 111. Autograph. First page of the first movement. Beethovenhaus Bonn.

At the top left corner Beethoven's pencilled note: 'am 13. Jänner 1822'. The handwriting at the bottom is that of Artaria, who owned the manuscript. The right-hand margin is also in Beethoven's hand. The Sonata was dedicated to the Archduke Rudolph. Beethoven worked at the three Piano Sonatas Opp. 109, 110 and 111 while composing the *Missa Solemnis*.

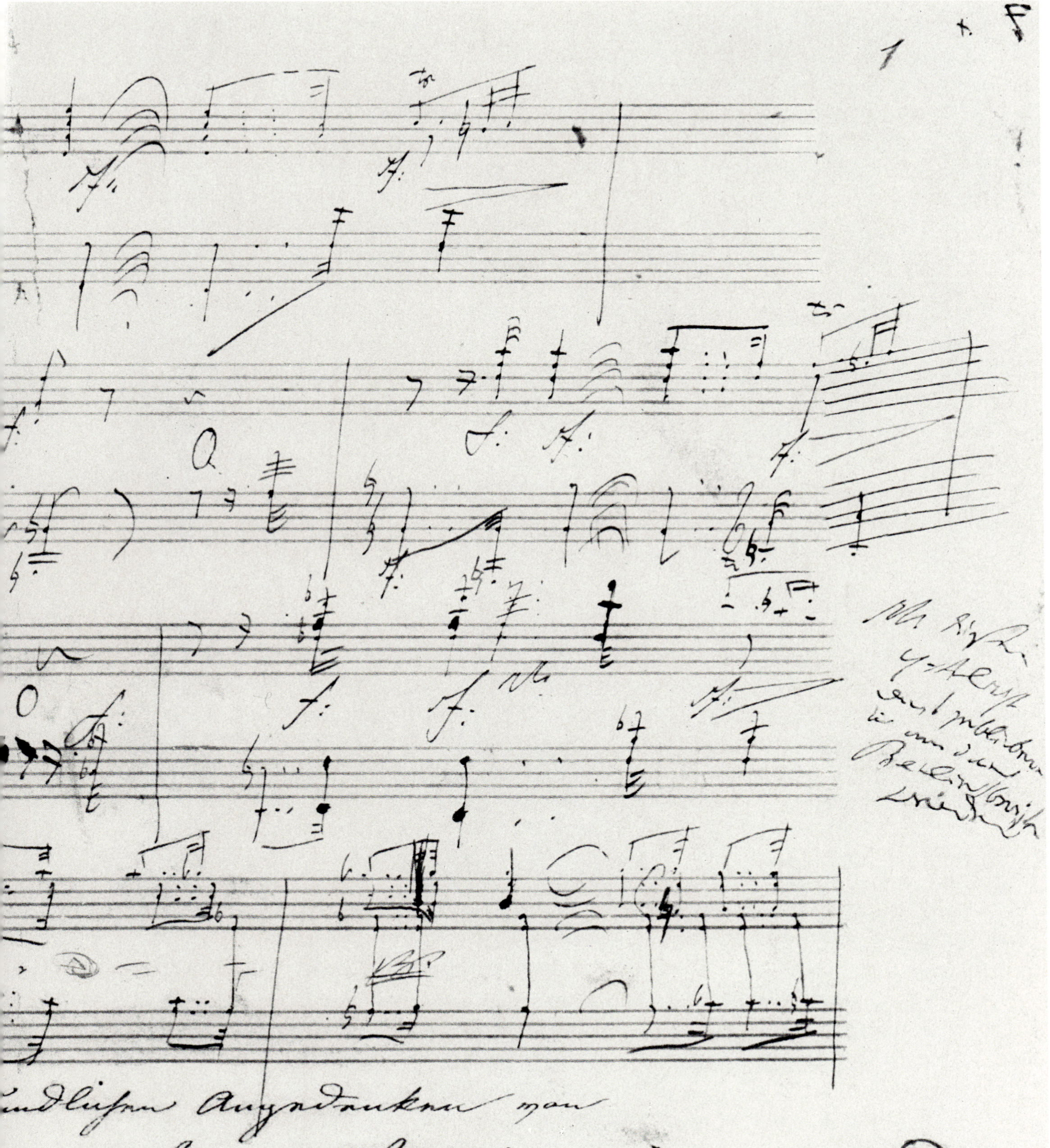
August Artaria

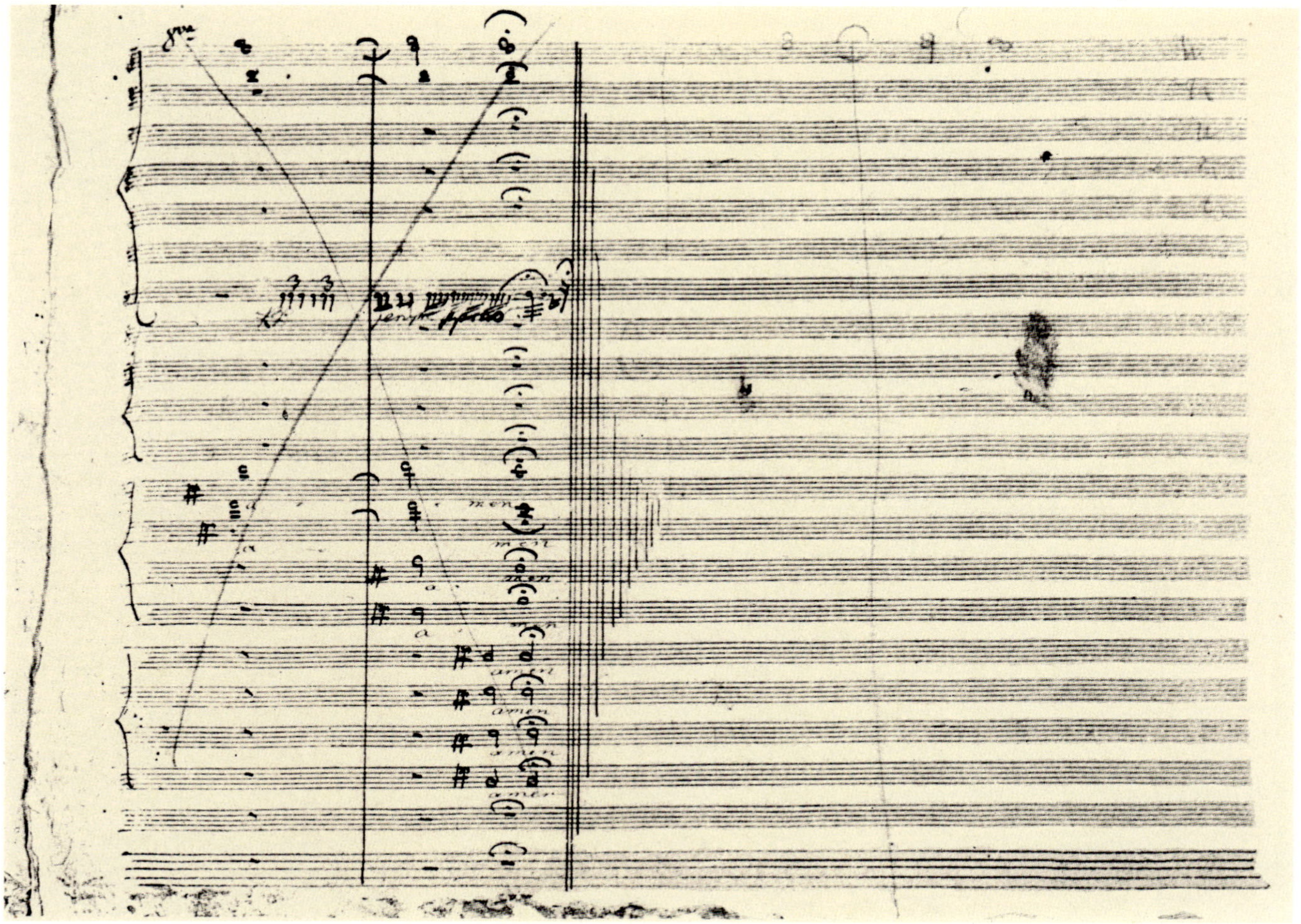
men
amen

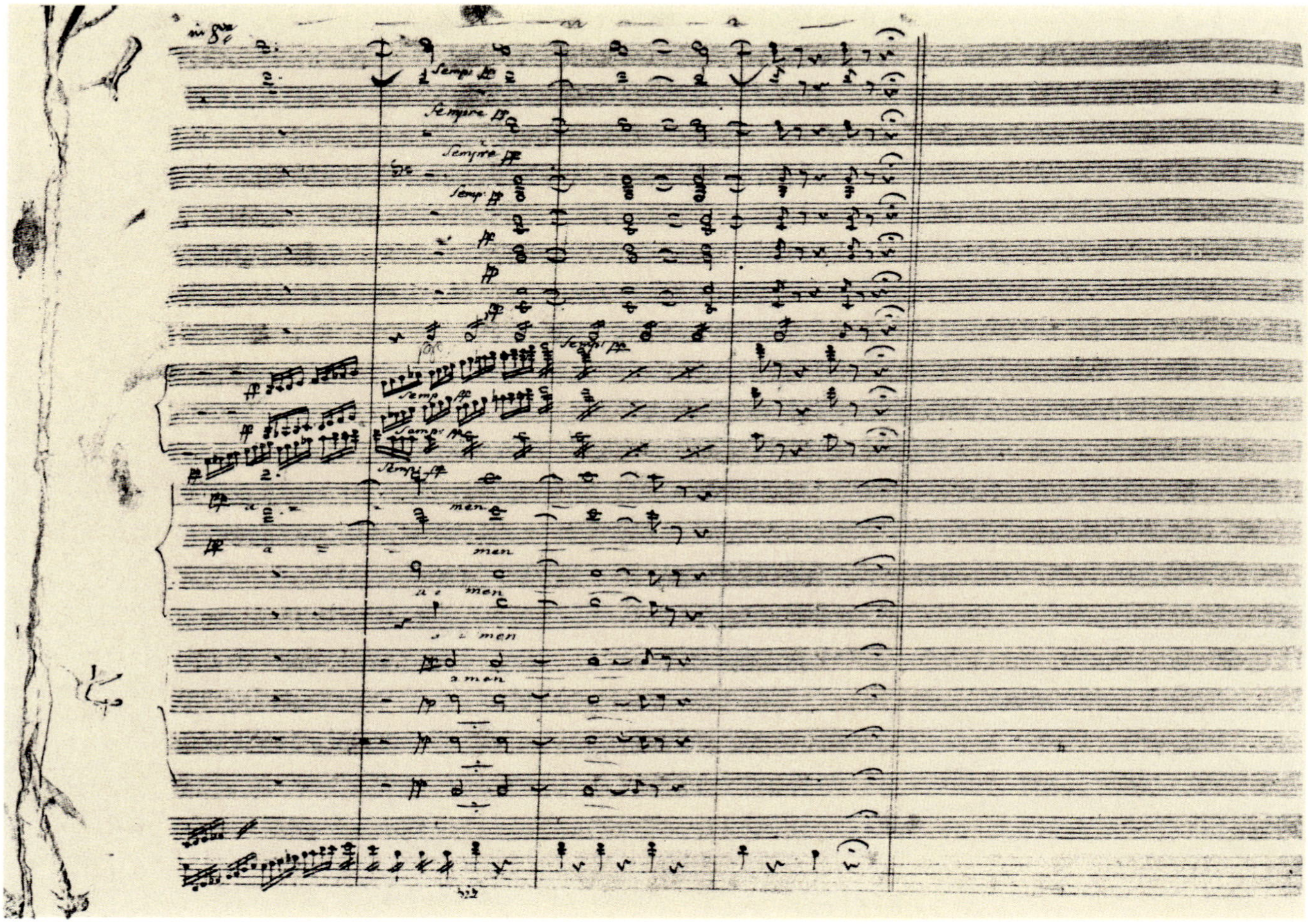
Sempre pp
men
amen

207. Ludwig van Beethoven. Portrait in oils by Joseph
Carl Stieler. Walter Hinrichsen, New York.

The celebrated painter Stieler, who made portraits of many of the Habsburgs, was granted
three sessions by Beethoven. According to the inscription on the back of the picture
('Ludwig v. Beethoven, Tonsetzer, nach der Natur gemalt von J. Stieler 1819') the painting dates from 1819, but in fact the strongly idealized portrait was not entirely completed
until about April 1820. Stieler had to finish the hands from memory.

◄ 205, 206. *Missa Solemnis*, Op. 123. Credo from the manuscript score, made by the copyist Schlemmer for
Archduke Rudolph, then Bishop of Olmütz; and the final version of the end of the Credo in *Missa Solemnis*.

The first page here reproduced shows the end of the Credo cancelled; the second page
shows the final version. Beethoven began writing down the Mass in 1819: it was intended
for the installation of the Archduke as Archbishop of Olmütz in 1820, but Beethoven was
not ready in time and did not deliver the completed Mass to his patron until 1823.

208. Ludwig van Beethoven. Drawing by Johann Peter Theodor Lyser. Beethovenhaus Bonn.

This drawing appeared in 1833 in the periodical *Cäcilia* in Hamburg with the following note: 'Drawn truthfully on the spot as, in the last years of his life, he jumped and ran rather than walked through the streets of Vienna'. Lyser appears not to have known Beethoven personally, for his daughter asserted that he did not arrive in Vienna before 1845. How it came that Lyser sketched Beethoven so often cannot satisfactorily be explained. (*See also Plates 214, 226, and 229.*)

Friedrich Johann Rochlitz describes Beethoven to his wife (1822):

Imagine a man of about fifty, of less than medium height, but of quite powerful, stocky build; thick-set, and in particular of strong bone structure – somewhat like Fichte, but more fleshy, especially the face, which is fuller and rounder; a red, healthy colour; restless, bright eyes, almost piercing when they gaze steadily; no movements, or else quick ones; in the expression of the countenance, particularly of the intelligent and lively eyes, a mixture or at times an instantaneous alternation of the most cordial good nature and shyness; in his whole attitude the tension, the uneasy, anxious listening of a deaf man who is highly sensitive; now a word thrown out happily and freely, followed by an immediate plunge into gloomy silence; added to all that, the feelings of the observer which unceasingly make themselves heard: this is the man who brings pure joy to millions – pure spiritual joy! – He said some friendly and cordial things to me in broken sentences; I raised my voice when I could, spoke slowly, accentuated carefully, and in the fulness of my heart thanked him for his works, what they mean to me and will mean to me all my life; drew special attention to some of my favourites and elaborated on them; I told him how masterly were the executions of his symphonies in Leipzig and how the public loudly expressed its approval, etc. He stood close to me, sometimes looking intently at my face and sometimes lowering his head; then he smiled, nodded in a friendly way, but said nothing. Had he understood me? Or not? Finally I had to stop; then he shook my hand vigorously and said, rather curtly, to ✳✳✳ [Carl, the nephew?]: 'I have some things to do.' And to me, as he left, 'We shall see each other again.' ✳✳✳ accompanied him out of the house. I was deeply moved and disturbed. Then ✳✳✳ came back. 'Did he understand me?' I asked. ✳✳✳ shrugged his shoulders: 'Not a word.' We were silent a long while, and I cannot express how moved I was. Finally I asked: 'Why didn't you repeat at least some of it, since he seems to understand you?' 'I didn't want to interrupt you and he's very touchy. But I'd hoped, really, that he would have understood some of it: however, the noises from the street, your speech (which he isn't used to), and perhaps even his haste to try to understand everything – because he probably saw that you were saying nice things to him – He was so sad.'

I cannot describe the mood in which I left. The same man, who delights all the world with the beauty of his tones, can hear none, not even the tones of him who wants to express his gratefulness; even more, it becomes a torment for him! . . . Roughly a fortnight later I was just on my way to lunch when I met the young composer Franz Schubert, an ardent admirer of Beethoven. He had spoken to him about me. 'If you want to see him merry and less self-conscious,' Schubert said, 'then you should lunch now at the inn where he has just gone.' – He took me there. Most of the tables were occupied. Beethoven sat surrounded by several of his acquaintances, who were strangers to me. He actually did seem merry. He returned my salutation; but I deliberately did not join him. I found a place at a table where I could see him and could make out most of what he said, for he spoke loudly enough. What he carried on was not actually a conversation; he spoke alone, and for the most part rather steadily, as though at random and into the blue. His listeners added little, only laughing or nodding in approbation. He – philosophized, and talked politics in his own way. He spoke of England and the English, he conceived of them

247

222

as being incomparably excellent – which to some extent sounded quite curious. Then he told stories about the French from the two times they occupied Vienna. He could not stand them at all. He said everything with the greatest carelessness and without the least restraint, but spiced with highly original, naive judgments or droll fancies.

Kerst I, 282 f. Rochlitz, *op. cit.*, 351 ff.

From Sir George Smart's diary for Sunday, 11 September 1825:

[original English]
... From hence I went alone to Schlesinger's, at the 'Wildemann', where was a larger party than the previous one. Among them was l'Abbé Stadler, a fine old man and a good composer of the old school, to whom I was introduced. There was also present a pupil of Moscheles, a Mademoiselle Eskeles and a Mademoiselle Cimia, whom I understood to be a professional player. When I entered Messrs. C. Czerny, Schuppanzigh and Lincke had just begun the trio, op. 70 of Beethoven, after this the same performers played Beethoven's trio, op. 97 – both printed singly by Steiner. Then followed Beethoven's quartette, the same that I heard on September the 9th, and it was played by the same performers. Beethoven was seated near the pianoforte beating time during the performance of these pieces. This ended, most of the company departed, but Schlesinger invited me to stop and dine with the following party of ten. Beethoven, his nephew, Holz, Weiss, C. Czerny, who sat at the bottom of the table, Lincke, Jean Sedlatzek – a flute player who is coming to England next year, and has letters to the Duke of Devonshire, Count St. Antonio, etc. – he has been to Italy – Schlesinger, Schuppanzigh, who sat at the top, and myself. Beethoven calls Schuppanzigh Sir John Falstaff, not a bad name considering the figure of this excellent violin player.

65, 66

We had a most pleasant dinner, healths were given in the English style. Beethoven was delightfully gay but hurt that, in the letter Moscheles gave me, his name should be mixed up with the other professors.... After dinner he was coaxed to play extempore, observing in French to me, 'Upon what subject shall I play?' Meanwhile he was touching the instrument thus

to which I answered, 'Upon that.' On which theme he played for about twenty minutes in a most extraordinary manner, sometimes very fortissimo, but full of genius. When he rose at the conclusion of his playing he appeared greatly agitated. No one could be more agreeable than he was – plenty of jokes. He was in the highest of spirits. We all wrote to him by turns, but he can hear a little if you halloo quite close to his left ear.

Leaves from the Journals of Sir George Smart, edited by H. Bertram Cox and C. L. E. Cox, London 1907, p. 113 ff. (Sir George Smart, musician and organist, came to Vienna in 1825, in the course of a European tour, and met Beethoven there.)

By this time, Beethoven was a well-known figure in Vienna. People were used to his rather wild appearance and also proud of his presence in the Royal and Imperial city. Beethoven was often seen walking in the popular Paradeplatz, and there is a detailed description of him at this period by Dr Gerhard von Breuning, son of Stephan, Beethoven's old friend.

Dr Gerhard von Breuning describes Beethoven's appearance:

Beethoven's outward appearance, due to his quite peculiar nonchalance in the matter of dress, had something uncommonly conspicuous about it in the street. Usually lost in thought and humming to himself, he often gesticulated with his arms when walking by himself. When in company, he would speak quite animatedly and loudly, and, since his companion then had to write his rejoinder in the conversation book, an abrupt halt would have to be made; this was conspicuous in itself, and was still more so when the rejoinder was communicated in mime.

208–215

And so it happened that most of the passers-by would turn around to stare at him; the street urchins also made their gibes and shouted after him. For that reason his nephew Carl refused to go out with him and once told him straight out that he was ashamed to accompany him in the street because of his 'comical appearance'; at this, so he told us, he was greatly insulted and hurt. For my part, I was proud to be able to show myself with a man of his importance.

247

The crown of the felt hat he wore at that time had lost its shape and bulged towards the top where it had been stretched; this was the result of Beethoven's habit, on coming in, of clapping his hat over the topmost point of the hall-stand; should the hat be dripping with rain, he would simply shake it lightly first, which he also did at our house without a thought for the furniture. The hat was rarely if ever brushed, either before or after rain, and, becoming increasingly dusty, it took on a permanently matted appearance. He wore it, when feasible, at the back of his head to have his forehead free, while his grey, unkempt hair (in Rellstab's apt words, 'not frizzly, not straight, but a mixture of everything') flew out on both sides. By wearing the hat far out of the face and tilting it towards the back while keeping his head erect, the rear part of the brim collided with the collar of the coat, which at that time was worn quite high; this gave the brim a turned-up shape, while the collar, due to constant contact with the hat-brim, appeared to have been rubbed threadbare. The lapels of the coat (especially those of the blue frock-coat with brass buttons) were not fastened, and flapped back against his arms, particularly when he walked into the wind; the two long points of the neckcloth, which was knotted about the wide shirt-collar, likewise flew outwards. The double lorgnette, which he wore for his nearsightedness, hung loose. The coat-tails were rather heavily laden: apart from a pocket handkerchief, which often showed, they contained a quite thick, folded, quarto music notebook and an octavo conversation book with a thick carpenter's pencil,* for communicating with friends and acquaintances he might happen to meet; and at an earlier period, so long as it was of any use, an ear-trumpet. The weight of the music notebook lengthened the one coat-tail considerably, and the pocket was often turned inside out when the notebook and conversation book were extracted from it . . . . I often saw him thus

---

*In the same way that Beethoven was peculiarly awkward when it came to cutting quill pens for himself, his rather clumsy fingers also proved to be ill suited to sharpening pencils without quickly breaking them. This may have been the reason he preferred to procure thick-gauge pencils for himself, similar to those used by carpenters.

from our windows, when I was not with him myself, coming at about two o'clock –
his dinner hour – from the Schottentor across the part of the Glacis where the
Votivkirche now stands, sailing towards his lodgings in his customary posture, his
body leant forward (but not bowed), his head erect.

Breuning 96 ff. (Footnote in the original text.)

Ferdinand Ries on Beethoven's irritability:

Beethoven was sometimes extremely violent. One day we were dining at the Swan;
the waiter brought him the wrong dish. Beethoven had scarcely said a few choice
words about it, which the waiter had answered perhaps not quite so politely as he
should have, when Beethoven laid hold of the dish (it was a so-called 'Lungenbratel'
[a kind of roast-beef] with lots of sauce) and flung it at the waiter's head. The poor
fellow still had on his arm a large number of plates containing various dishes (a
dexterity which Viennese waiters possess to a high degree) and could do nothing
to help himself; the sauce ran down his face. He and Beethoven shouted and cursed
at each other, while all the other guests laughed out loud. Finally Beethoven began
laughing at the sight of the waiter, who lapped up with his tongue the sauce that was
running down his face, tried to go on hurling insults, but had to go on lapping
instead, pulling the most ludicrous faces the while, a picture worthy of Hogarth . . . .

Beethoven hardly knew what money was, which often gave rise to unpleasant
scenes because, mistrustful in general, he often believed he had been cheated when in
fact he had not. Quickly aroused, he bluntly called people cheats, which in the case
of waiters had to be made good by a tip. Ultimately his peculiarities and his absent-
mindedness became so well known at the inns he most frequented, that everything was
tolerated, even when he left without paying.

Kerst I, 98.

Carl Czerny writes about Beethoven's reputation in Vienna:

It has sometimes been said abroad that Beethoven was neglected and oppressed in
Vienna. The truth is that he enjoyed, even as a young man, all possible support and
an encouragement and respect on the part of our high nobility which has rarely been
the portion of a young composer.

Later too, when he had alienated many of his well-wishers by his hypochondria,
no difficulties were ever put in the way of his often conspicuous idiosyncrasies;
this accounts for his preference for Vienna. And it is doubtful whether he would have
remained so unchallenged in any other country. It is true that, as an artist, he had to
contend with intrigues, but the public had no part in them. He was always esteemed
and stared at in wonder as an exceptional being, and his greatness was also sensed by
his opponents, who did not understand him. He could have been well off, but he was
not made for domestic order.

Czerny 14.

Anton Schindler on Beethoven's daily schedule:

As regards our composer's daily schedule, he customarily arose at dawn at every season of the year and went at once to his writing-desk. He worked until 2 or 3 o'clock, at which hour he ate his dinner. During his working hours he would usually go out of doors once or twice, where he (in Saphir's words) worked while walking. Such excursions seldom lasted more than an hour and resembled the flights of bees to gather honey; they took place whatever the season, and neither heat nor cold were heeded. The afternoons were kept for regular walks; later he would stop in at a favourite tavern to peruse the daily newspapers, if this need had not already been satisfied at a coffee-house. When the English parliament was in session, however, the *Allgemeine Zeitung* was regularly read at home for its reports of the debates. It will be easily understood that our amateur politician was on the side of the opposition; this would have been so even if he had not been partial to Lord Brougham, Hume and other opposition orators. Beethoven always stayed home on winter's evenings, which were devoted to serious reading. Only rarely did one see him engaged in writing music in the evening, because this was too tiring to his eyes. This might not have been the case when he was younger. It is certain, however, that at no time did he use the evening hours for composition. He went to bed at 10 o'clock at the latest.

Schindler II, 192.

From Beethoven's conversation books:

[January 1820]
Böhm: manager in a wholesale house.   *211, 213*
Young Carl Beethoven must show me your portrait very soon.   *247*

I have been here quite some time; I am glad to see you, because my medallion is nearing completion. I want to do the hair this way in the middle, somewhat less and shorter than it is now; I will let you see it before I finish it – goodbye

Konv. N. 274.

Dr. W. Chr. Müller describes Beethoven's appearance in 1820:

Everything about his appearance is powerful, much of it coarse, like the raw-boned   *216*
structure of his face, with a high, broad forehead, a short, angular nose, with hair standing stubbornly up and divided into thick locks. – But he is blessed with a delicate mouth and with beautiful, eloquent eyes which reflect at every moment his quickly changing ideas and feelings – charming, affectionate, fierce, wrathful, dreadful .... How little he knew of the world, and how little care he paid to conventional forms and earthly things, is shown by his outward appearance during the period when he was composing most prolifically. He did not know, for example, of the fashion of wearing frilled shirts. So that he would look more presentable when

giving lessons to his female pupils, a woman friend of his had shirts made for him, with frills added as an embellishment. 'What is this for?' he asked her when he saw them. 'Ah, yes, to keep me warm,' he said, answering his own question, and stuffed the frills under his waistcoat.

FRBS I, 101.

Nanette Streicher tells Mary and Vincent Novello about Beethoven:

[original English]

...Madame Streicher called to take leave – told us that Beethoven's life might probably have been prolonged for some time had he continued to employ the King's Physician whom he had consulted at the commencement of his illness – but he was fearful that his means would be inadequate to meet the fees that might be thus incurred and he had too high a spirit to accept any attendance as a favour conferred upon him.

Mme. Streicher's opinion arises from the great skill this eminent medical Gentleman possesses, especially in the complaint (dropsy) under which Beethoven was suffering.

Hummel was much with him during his last illness – about four days before he died Hummel told Madame Streicher that Beethoven made an effort to overcome the langour that was creeping over him – he arose from the bed and dressed himself – saying to Hummel that it was necessary to make some exertion to stand up against illness and that he would endeavour to overcome his painful and languid sensation – this was said with great energy and he appeared for the moment to be much better – but unfortunately this flash of his former spirit did not last, his feebleness rapidly returned, and he gradually grew weaker until he sank at last into death.

On one occasion, when he began to get infirm and his legs failed him, on arriving near his own house his foot slipped and he fell to the Earth where some mud had been left by a Shower of Rain. A Lady who happened to be standing at a window in the neighbourhood, and who knew Beethoven, saw the accident and immediately sent her servant to assist him, but some unfeeling Brutes who had gathered round him, instead of helping, began to laugh at the accident that had befallen him which so enraged Beethoven that although he was scarcely able to move from the united effects of weakness and pain, he indignantly refused all aid whatever, turning fiercely away from the proffered assistance of the servant sent by the Lady, who could not refrain from tears at the miserable situation in which this great man was placed – deaf, covered with mud, scarcely able to walk from intense pain, and subjected to the jeering insults of a ruffian-like mob.

In excuse for his complaints of poverty to the Philharmonic Society Mme. Streicher accounted for that circumstance by declaring that she believed he was so harassed by different vexations and the infirmity of his irritable temper, that he really scarcely knew what was in his possession or what was not.

That he was more anxious for his nephew than for himself. That almost all his thoughts and cares were dedicated towards making some provision for this Person, who after all did not act in such a manner as to give satisfaction either to Beethoven himself or to any of his friends.

Beethoven rather fond of 'les plaisirs de la table', his favourite dish was a Cold Turkey in Jelly – and the Pâtés de Périgord – Strasburg Pâté de foie gras.

A Mozart Pilgrimage, Being the Travel Diaries of Vincent & Mary Novello in the year 1829, transcribed and compiled by Nerina Medici di Marignano, edited by Rosemary Hughes, London 1955, p. 203 ff. (The Novello family had a large musical circle in London. Vincent Novello was an organist, his daughters were singers.)

Louis Schlösser tells about Beethoven's visit:

Spring had come virtually overnight, the 3rd of March [1822] was a bright morning and I sat, carefully attired, at the piano waiting for the appointed hour and making some small corrections in the cantata, when the servant opened the door and – to my not inconsiderable astonishment – there stood Beethoven himself on the threshold. I scarcely believed my eyes; the celebrated composer had not disdained to climb four flights of stairs to return the call of a 22-year-old neophyte. I do not know what I said in my initial confusion, he, however, surely aware of my embarrassment, quickly interrupted. He had come, he said, to fetch me for a short walk before dinner, since the weather was so fine, and at the same time to see my rooms, instruments, musical effects and the pictures of my parents, about which I had told him. And he actually began to leaf through my booklets of counterpoint exercises, to look through my reference library – in which he found his favourites, Homer and Goethe – and I even had to show him drawings of mine; he looked attentively at everything and was full of praise. I need not assure you that I was exultant at strolling through the crowded streets towards the Volksgarten at the side of a man I so revered, or to what extent his spirited comments and universal knowledge made me recognize the high flight of his genius in every direction. At such moments when he spoke, utterly consumed by the subject at hand, the wealth of the ideas that poured from him appeared truly miraculous.

In his absence the housekeeper had made the necessary preparations. The table was nicely laid, and the dinner was served with the greatest care, so that everything went like clockwork. Beethoven was the paragon of a fatherly Amphitryon in word and deed; he begged me repeatedly to excuse the shortcomings of his bachelor household (which that day at least left nothing to be desired), saw to it that conversation never lagged, and talked of the time when as a young man of 22, after the death of his father Johann (18 December 1792), he had come for the second time to Vienna, which city he had not left since. He prepared the coffee himself, using a machine of new invention, and even explained its construction to me in all details; we had coffee in the next room, which I had never entered, although the door was always open. There I saw the magnificent piano by Broadwood and on it the de luxe edition of Handel's works; both had been gifts from London, and a volume of Handel lay open on the music-rest.

Kerst II, 10 f.

For the opening of the Josephstadt Theatre in October 1822, Beethoven composed an overture in the Handel style called *Die Weihe des Hauses* (*The Consecration of the House*), Op. 124.

Anton Schindler on The Consecration of the House:

197 While walking one day with Beethoven and his nephew in the lovely Helenental near Baden, Beethoven told us to go on ahead a little and wait for him at a certain spot. He soon caught us up, remarking that he now had two motives for an overture committed to paper. He immediately began talking about the plan of composition: one was to be treated in a free style, the other in a strict style, Handelian, to be precise. He sang the motives as well as he could and then asked which one we liked better. This may serve to illustrate the momentary rosy mood in which he found himself as a result of discovering two precious stones for which he had, perhaps, long searched. His nephew chose both, while I uttered the wish to have the fugal motive used for the above purpose. On no account, however, did Beethoven compose *The Consecration of the House* simply because I so desired it, but rather because he had long planned to write an overture in a strict, exclusively Handelian style . . . .

218, 219   The newly-formed orchestra of the Josephstädter Theater saw the overture for the first time on the afternoon of the day the theatre was to be opened; there were countless errors in every part. What effort could be spent learning it — it was late and the stalls were already almost filled — hardly sufficed to correct the most glaring errors of the copyist.

At Beethoven's request, the musical direction was left to him. Accordingly, he sat at the piano so that he was facing most of the orchestra, with his left ear — which still functioned to a certain extent — turned towards the stage. Kapellmeister Franz Gläser (at present Court Kapellmeister in Copenhagen) stood at his right where he could supervise everything, and I led the orchestra at the head of the first violins; shortly before, I had left the law office and with it the circle of dilettantes, a change of situation in which our composer had a large share. As for the musical success of the celebration, it could not, on the whole, be called favourable, despite the enthusiastic cooperation of all concerned, roused still more by encouraging words from the master. Repeated hitches on the stage and in the orchestra, caused by strained listening and a lack of movement on the part of the conductor-in-chief (who was now and then utterly at odds with his two sub-conductors), resulted in general alarm. Beethoven did not sense that he was principally at fault. His admonitions about 'too much hurry' could not have any effect on the course of the performance, simply because such was not the case. Nevertheless, the performance was brought safely to an end without obvious mishap, and the sublime master was called again and again to the stage by a highly excited audience. He came out hand in hand with the estimable director, Hensler.

During the dress rehearsal for the celebration something had happened which was a pleasant surprise for all those present. In a duet for soprano and tenor, the young soprano conducted herself irresolutely and dragged noticeably. Beethoven also noticed it and called her towards him, drawing her attention to the places in which she should pick up the tempo; he then cheered her up and recommended that she follow the more experienced tenor. Then he had the number repeated, expressing his satisfaction at the end with the words, 'That time it was good, Fräulein Heckermann!' The tenor in the duet was the present director of the Stadt-Theater in Aachen, Herr Michael Greiner, whom our composer knew from the theatre in Baden.

Schindler II, 7 ff.

Wilhelmine Schröder-Devrient recalls the rehearsals for Fidelio: 220

I was scarcely out of my teens and had already begun to make my first timid efforts as an inexperienced singer; it was probably the lack of another, more suitable, interpreter and not the conviction that I was already equal to the rôle of Leonore, that caused that difficult part to be entrusted to me. With youthful naïveté and without the least idea of the magnitude of my task, I began to study a rôle which I later had especially to thank for the fact that my name, among those of German artists, was mentioned abroad with particular distinction. Under the guidance of my intelligent mother, many traits in Leonore's character had become clear to me; however, I was still too young, too little developed inwardly, to have a complete understanding of everything that went on in the soul of a Leonore, for whose emotions Beethoven had invented his immortal harmonies. At the rehearsals, which were conducted by the then Kapellmeister Umlauf, the inadequacy of my underdeveloped child's voice was soon realized, and many changes were made in my part so that the effect would not suffer too greatly. The last rehearsals were scheduled when I learned, before the dress rehearsal, that Beethoven had requested the honour of conducting his opera himself, in observance of the occasion. At this news an unspeakable anxiety befell me, and the memory of my boundless clumsiness at the last rehearsal, which had driven my poor mother and my colleagues to distraction, was still fresh. But Beethoven sat before the orchestra, all participants depending on his baton, and I had never laid eyes on the man before! – At that time the master's physical ear was already closed to all sounds. Waving his baton to and fro with violent movements, a puzzled expression on his face and celestial inspiration in his eyes, he stood among the playing musicians and did not hear a note! When, in his opinion, a passage was to be played *piano*, he would creep almost under the music-stand, when he wanted *forte* he would leap upwards with the most curious gestures and utter the strangest sounds. With every number our anxiety grew, and it seemed to me that I was watching one of Hoffmann's weird figures emerge before me. It was inevitable that the deaf composer caused the most complete confusion among the singers and orchestra and got everyone quite out of time, so that no one knew any longer where they were. But Beethoven observed nothing of all that, and so we somehow managed to finish the rehearsal, with which he seemed to be quite satisfied, for he laid aside the baton with a cheerful smile. It was unthinkable, however, that he should be entrusted with the performance, and Kapellmeister Umlauf had to take on the heart-breaking task of telling him that the opera could not be put on with him conducting.

Kerst II, 39 ff.

and others. Again and again he cried out enthusiastically, 'Truly, there is a divine spark in Schubert!' – 'If I had had this poem I would have set it to music too!' he said of most of the poems, the subject and content of which, together with Schubert's original setting, he could not praise enough . . . . In short, Beethoven gained such great respect for Schubert's talent that he now wanted to see his operas and piano pieces too; but his illness had advanced to the point where he could no longer satisfy that desire. But he spoke often of Schubert, prophesying that 'he will cause a stir in the world,' and regretting that he had not come to know him earlier.

Kerst I, 274f.

251   *Letter from Anselm Hüttenbrenner to Professor Luib:*

I know for certain that Professor Schindler, Schubert and I paid a visit to Beethoven's bedside roughly a week before he died. Schindler announced us both and asked Beethoven which one of us he wished to see first. Beethoven answered, 'Let Schubert come in first.'

Kerst I, 276. TDR V, 480.

Anton Schindler on Beethoven and the painter Waldmüller:

. . . In early 1823 the publishers Breitkopf & Härtel wanted a portrait of our com-
224   poser, and Waldmüller, a professor at the Academy, was chosen to do it. There were unfavourable portents to this plan: urgent work to be finished and persistent eye trouble, and ill-humour in consequence. After a long delay, the first sitting was at last arranged. Waldmüller conducted himself deferentially and much too timidly, a demeanour which, with Beethoven, usually led to no success whatever. We have only just heard in what utterly different ways the two painters mentioned previously
203, 207   [Stieler and Schimon] achieved their purpose. Even though Waldmüller made great haste in sketching the head and in roughing, the master, who was deep in thought, found he was taking too long; he left his seat now and again, pacing sulkily up and down the room or going to his writing-desk in the next room. The roughing was not yet finished when Beethoven made it plain that he could bear it no longer. When the painter had left, Beethoven's anger erupted and Waldmüller was called the most miserable of daubers – because he had made him sit facing the window. He stub-bornly refused to admit any argument in defence. There were no more sittings. The painter finished the portrait from his imagination, because, as he replied to my remonstrances, he could not do without the contracted fee of 20 ducats . . . .

Schindler II, 290 f. (Waldmüller received only 12 ducats.)

John Russell about Beethoven:

[original English]
Beethoven is the most celebrated of the living composers in Vienna, and, in certain departments, the foremost of his day. Though not an old man, he is lost to society in consequence of his extreme deafness, which has rendered him almost unsocial. The neglect of his person which he exhibits gives him a somewhat wild appearance. His features are strong and prominent; his eye is full of rude energy; his hair, which neither comb nor scissors seem to have visited for years, overshadows his broad brow in a quantity and confusion to which only the snakes round a Gorgon's head offer a parallel. His general behaviour does not ill accord with the unpromising exterior. Except when he is among his chosen friends, kindliness or affability are not his characteristics. The total loss of hearing has deprived him of all the pleasure which society can give, and perhaps soured his temper. He used to frequent a particular cellar, where he spent the evening in a corner, beyond the reach of all the chattering and disputation of a public room, drinking wine and beer, eating cheese and red herrings, and studying the newspapers. One evening a person took a seat near him whose countenance did not please him. He looked hard at the stranger, and spat on the floor as if he had seen a toad, then glanced at the newspaper, then again at the intruder, and spat again, his hair bristling gradually into more shaggy ferocity, till he closed the alternation of spitting and staring, by fairly exclaiming, 'What a scoundrelly phiz!' and rushing out of the room. Even among his oldest friends he must be humoured like a wayward child. He has always a small paperbook with him, and what conversation takes place is carried on in writing. In this, too, although it is not lined, he instantly jots down any musical idea which strikes him. These notes would be utterly unintelligible even to another musician, for they have thus no comparative value; he alone has in his own mind the thread by which he brings out of this labyrinth of dots and circles the richest and most astounding harmonies. The moment he is seated at the piano, he is evidently unconscious that there is any thing in existence but himself and his instrument; and, considering how very deaf he is, it seems impossible that he should hear all he plays. Accordingly, when playing very *piano*, he often does not bring out a single note. He hears it himself in the 'mind's ear'. While his eye, and the almost imperceptible motion of his fingers, show that he is following out the strain in his own soul through all its dying gradations, the instrument is actually as dumb as the musician is deaf.

I have heard him play, but to bring him so far required some management, so great is his horror of being any thing like exhibited. Had he been plainly asked to do the company that favour, he would have flatly refused; he had to be cheated into it. Every person left the room, except Beethoven and the master of the house, one of his most intimate acquaintances. These two carried on a conversation in the paperbook about bank stock. The gentleman, as if by chance, struck the keys of the open piano, beside which they were sitting, gradually began to run over one of Beethoven's own compositions, made a thousand errors, and speedily blundered one passage so thoroughly, that the composer condescended to stretch out his hand and put him right. It was enough; the hand was on the piano; his companion immediately left him, on some pretext, and joined the rest of the company, who, in the next room, from which they could see and hear every thing, were patiently waiting the issue of this tiresome conjuration. Beethoven, left alone, seated himself at the piano. At first he only struck now and then a few hurried and interrupted notes, as if afraid of being detected in a crime; but gradually he forgot every thing else, and ran on during half an hour in a phantasy, in a style extremely varied, and marked, above all, by the most abrupt transitions. The amateurs were enraptured; to the uninitiated it was more interesting, to observe how the music of the man's soul passed over his countenance. He seems to feel the bold, the commanding, and the impetuous, more than what is soothing or gentle. The muscles of his face swell, and its veins start out; the wild eye rolls doubly wild; the mouth quivers, and Beethoven looks like a wizard, overpowered by the demons whom he himself has called up.

John Russell, *A Tour in Germany and some of the Southern Provinces of the Austrian Empire, in the Years 1820, 1821, 1822,* 2 Vols., 3rd edition, Edinburgh 1825; Vol. II, pp. 273 ff.

We have to thank Nikolai Borissovich, Prince Galitzin, for the late Quartets that are among the very greatest creations in all music. It is generally asserted that they were not understood when they were first performed at Vienna, but as the documents show this is again one of the half-truths that seem to bedevil Beethoven biographies. This is also the period of the 'Diabelli Variations', Op. 120, which carried to new heights the art of piano variations which Beethoven had so assiduously cultivated throughout his life.

Dr Gerhard von Breuning visits Beethoven:

Once, as often happened, I found him sleeping when I came. I sat down quietly next to his bed so as not to wake him from what I hoped would be an invigorating sleep, and in the meantime leafed through the conversation books lying ready for use on the bedside table, to find out who had been there since my last visit and what had been discussed. I found, among other things, the note: 'Your quartet that Schuppanzigh played yesterday was not well received.' After a short time he awoke, and I showed him that comment, asking him what he had to say about it. 'They will like it, one of these days' was the laconic reply, and he deliberately added curt remarks to the effect that he writes what he considers good and does not allow himself to be influenced by the judgment of the day. 'I know, I am a musician.' –

Breuning 142 f.

Carl Holz tells Ludwig Nohl about Beethoven composing the late Quartets:

221 While composing the three quartets requested by Prince Galitzin, such a wealth of new quartet ideas flowed from Beethoven's inexhaustible imagination that he virtually had to write the Quartets in C-Sharp Minor and F Major involuntarily. 'My dear fellow, I've just had another idea,' he would say jocularly and with glistening eyes when we were out walking, and would write down a few notes in his sketchbook. – –

Kerst II, 187 f.

During the winter of 1822–23 [actually 1820], the publishers Diabelli & Co. presented to a large number of composers a plan to publish a collective set of variations for the pianoforte. The theme, waltz-like in character, was of Diabelli's own invention. Each composer was to contribute a single variation only. Beethoven was also invited to participate. The invitation immediately put him in mind of the collective vocal work on the words 'In questa tomba oscura, etc.' in 1808. . . . At the same time, the master's wrath at the persiflage that had befallen that work was reawakened. He declared that he had resolved never to participate in a collective work again; if people had dared then to banter about a poem so elevated and serious, the present theme offered every opportunity to hold all participants up to ridicule; he did not care for the theme with its *Schusterfleck* ['cobbler's patch'] (Rosalie)*, and so on. The invitation was therewith disposed of. Not long after this categorical statement he called upon me to ask Diabelli at my leisure whether he would agree to Beethoven's writing a set of variations by himself, and what fee he would offer. The publisher, pleasantly surprised, immediately said 80 ducats and sent a few lines on the spot to notify the master of his decision, asking for 6 or 7 variations only. Beethoven, in his turn not less pleasantly surprised at the uncommonly high fee for a set of variations, accepted quickly in writing, saying to me, 'Well, he'll have a variation or two on his cobbler's patch!'

*[Footnote by Schindler:] For readers who are not musically educated it will be necessary to explain that in the theory of composition the term 'Rosalie' is understood to mean a little pattern of a few bars which is repeated stepwise, the intervals usually remaining the same, like the beads of a rosary. For example:

Among musicians, little patterns of this sort are commonly known as 'cobbler's patches'; patch after patch.

Schindler II, 34 f.

Letter from Beethoven to Ferdinand Ries:

Baden, 5 September [1823]

My dear friend!

You say I should have a look round for someone to attend to my things; well, that has been the case with the variations, namely that my friends and Schindler attended to them for me. The variations were to appear here only after being published in London, but everything went wrong; the dedication to Brentano was to have been for Germany only, for I am much obliged to her and had nothing else to publish at the moment; by the way, only the local publisher Diabelli received them from me; but everything was handled by Schindler – I have never yet met a more wretched creature on God's earth, an arch scoundrel whom I have sent packing. – I can dedicate another work to your wife in its place . . . .

TDR IV, 432. Anderson 1237.

221 *Letter from Prince Nikolai Galitzin to Beethoven:*

[St. Petersburg, 30 December 1823]

[original French]

227   I do not yet have the music you advised me has been sent. – But I found, at the music vendor's here, your Opus 120, the 33 Variations etc. The piece is a masterpiece, as is everything you write; one cannot but admire the felicitous fecundity to which the science of harmony has inspired you in this piece. – . . .

TDR V, 558.

Advertisement in the Wiener Zeitung, *No. 136, 16 June 1823:*

Cappi & Diabelli, am Graben No. 1133;
Thirty-three Variations/ on a Waltz/ for Pianoforte,/ composed/ by/ L. van Beethoven./ Opus 120. . . .

    With this work we do not offer the world Variations of the usual kind, but rather a great and important masterpiece, . . . as only Beethoven, the greatest living representative of true art, can produce. The most original forms and ideas, the most audacious turns of phrase and harmonies are exhausted in it, all pianistic effects based on a well-grounded manner of playing are employed; and the work is made still more interesting by the fact that it was produced on a theme which surely no one else would have considered capable of such treatment . . . .

209. Ludwig van Beethoven. Water-coloured pencil drawing by Joseph
Weidner. Collection Dr H. C. Bodmer, Beethovenhaus Bonn.

The sketch shows Beethoven from behind,
lost in thought and waving a stick.

210. Ludwig van Beethoven. Lithograph by Martin Tejček, 1841. Gesellschaft der Musikfreunde, Vienna.

The artist is supposed to have seen Beethoven while walking on the Glacis and the city walls.

211. Ludwig van Beethoven. Drawing by Joseph Daniel Böhm. Beethovenhaus Bonn.

The engraver Joseph Daniel Böhm was with Beethoven in the years 1819 and 1820, and made this drawing as a study for an engraved silver plate.

212. The *Paradeplatz* (parade square) in front of the Burgtor in Vienna. Coloured engraving by Leopold Beyer, 1805. Antiquarian Gilhofer und Ranschburg, Vienna.

The *Paradeplatz* was a popular walking spot for the Viennese, Beethoven included.

213. Ludwig van Beethoven from behind. Drawing by Joseph Daniel Böhm. Beethovenhaus Bonn.

This drawing is the second that the engraver Böhm made as a study for an engraved silver plate. (*See Plate 211.*)

214. Ludwig van Beethoven. Pencil drawing by Johann Peter Theodor Lyser. Gesellschaft der Musikfreunde, Vienna.

This drawing, which according to contemporary opinion showed Beethoven's figure realistically, is not a good likeness of Beethoven's facial features.

215. Beethoven in the rain. Water-coloured pen-and-ink drawing by Johann Nepomuk Hoechle. The original has disappeared. Photograph H. C. Robbins Landon, Buggiano Castello, Italy.

216. Ludwig van Beethoven. Plaster bust by Anton Dietrich
(detail). Historisches Museum of the City of Vienna.

On the right-hand side of the pedestal there is the inscription
'Ant. Dietrich, nach dem Leben modellirt 1821' ('Ant. Dietrich,
modelled from life, 1821'). Dietrich made portraits of Beethoven:
there is a drawing of 1826 and several other versions of the bust,
the first of which was exhibited in 1820.

Sonntag den 3. N

Im k. k. Hoftheater nächst dem Kärnthnerthore.

Fidelio.

Oper in zwey Aufzügen, nach dem Französischen.

Musik von L. v. Beethoven.

Neu in die Scene gesetzt.

Personen.

Don Fernando, Minister	— —	Hr. Nestroy.
Don Pizarro, Gouverneur eines Staatsgefängnisses		Hr. Forti.
Florestan, ein Gefangener	— —	Hr. Haizinger.
Leonore, seine Gemahlinn, unter dem Nahmen Fidelio		Dlle. Schröder.
Rokko, Kerkermeister	— —	Hr. Zeltner.
Marzelline, seine Tochter	— —	Dlle. Demmer.
Jaquino, Pförtner	— —	Hr. Rauscher.
Staatsgefangene. Offiziere. Wachen. Volk.		

Vor Anfang der Oper wird das Volkslied: „Gott erhalte Franz den Kaiser" angestimmt.

Meds. Rozier, Courtin und Dlle. Vio sind unpäßlich.

Freibillete sind heute ungültig.

Der Anfang ist um halb 7 Uhr.

217. Hand-bill of the revival of *Fidelio* on 3 November 1822 at the Kärntnerthortheater, Vienna. Österreichische Nationalbibliothek, Vienna.

To celebrate the name day of the Empress Caroline, *Fidelio* was put back into the repertoire after an interval of three years. The title rôle was sung by Wilhelmine Schroder (*see Plate 220*), then seventeen years of age, for whose benefit the performance was organized. Beethoven was at the beginning rather unhappy to see 'such a young girl' sing the part.

218. The Josephstadt Theatre after its reconstruction in 1822. Watercolour by Schestauber after an old engraving. Historisches Museum of the City of Vienna.

On 3 October 1822, the theatre in the Viennese suburb of Josephstadt was ceremoniously opened with the première of Beethoven's Overture *Die Weihe des Hauses* ('The Consecration of the House'), Op. 124. *Die Weihe des Hauses*, re-written by the poet Carl Meisl from August von Kotzebue's *Ruinen von Athen* ('Ruins of Athens'), contained music by Beethoven, partly newly composed. The other festive piece, *Das Bild des Fürsten* ('The Picture of the Prince'), was also written by C. Meisl, but had music by Joseph Drechsler. The director of the theatre, Carl Friederich Hensler, was a friend of Beethoven's.

219. Interior of the Josephstadt Theatre. Anonymous coloured engraving, *c.* 1825.

220. Wilhelmine Schröder-Devrient (1804–60). Steel plate engraving by Karl
Mauer from a painting by J. K., *c.* 1825. Gesellschaft der Musikfreunde, Vienna.

Wilhelmine Schröder, who later married the actor Devrient, studied
the rôle of Fidelio with her mother Sophie Schröder, a celebrated
actress. In later years Schröder's interpretation of the part became
world-famous.

221. Nikolai Borissovich, Prince Galitzin (1794–1860). Lithograph by Georg Christian Hahn and Franz Seraph Hanfstaengl. Gesellschaft der Musikfreunde, Vienna.

Prince Galitzin, a gifted amateur cellist, had a considerable influence on the musical taste of St Petersburg. He was responsible for the first complete performance of the *Missa Solemnis*, which took place at St Petersburg in April 1824. He had Beethoven's piano compositions, which he could not play himself, arranged for string quartet, and finally, in 1822, he wrote a letter to Beethoven, asking the master to write some quartets, and set his own price. Beethoven asked fifty ducats apiece.

222. Franz Schubert (1797–1828). Anonymous portrait in oils, attributed to Leopold Kupelwieser. Gesellschaft der Musikfreunde, Vienna.

Schubert, long an admirer of Beethoven's, made his personal acquaintance in 1822; the young composer dedicated to Beethoven 'Variationen über ein französisches Lied', Op. 10.

223. Anton Haizinger (1796–1869). Anonymous portrait in oils. Historisches Museum of the City of Vienna.

Haizinger sang Florestan and was later to sing in the first performance of the Ninth Symphony.

224. Ludwig van Beethoven. Portrait in oils ▶ by Ferdinand Georg Waldmüller, 1823. Original destroyed at Breitkopf and Härtel's. Photograph H. C. Robbins Landon, Buggiano Castello, Italy.

Waldmüller was commissioned to paint this famous portrait by Breitkopf and Härtel, the Leipzig publishers. Schindler, Beethoven's secretary and faithful companion during the master's last years, describes Waldmüller's as the most unsuccessful of all Beethoven portraits—certainly an exaggeration. A repetition of the Waldmüller picture, made by the artist himself, was sold by the antiquarian Schneider in Tutzing über München in 1968.

225. Anton Diabelli (1781–1858). Lithograph by Joseph Kriehuber. Historisches Museum of the City of Vienna.

226. Ludwig van Beethoven. Drawing by Johann Peter Theodor Lyser. André Meyer, Paris.

A lithograph was later made from this drawing.

227. '33 Variations on a Waltz, for Piano-Forte', Op. 120. First edition, first page of music. Gesellschaft der Musikfreunde, Vienna.

Diabelli came to Vienna in 1803 and entered Steiner's publishing house. In 1818 he founded his own house together with Cappi, and from 1824 ran his own firm. In 1819 he asked a large group of well-known musicians to write variations on a waltz which he had composed. Among the composers was also Beethoven, who, instead of one, wrote thirty-three variations and dedicated the gigantic opus to his friend Antonie von Brentano, née Birkenstock.

228. The Kärntnerthortheater in Vienna. Anonymous coloured engraving, *c.* 1825. Historisches Museum of the City of Vienna.

The large concert at the Kärntnerthortheater on 7 May 1824 included the following works by Beethoven: Overture in C ('Die Weihe des Hauses'), Op. 124; Kyrie, Credo and Agnus Dei from the *Missa Solemnis*, Op. 123; and to conclude, the Ninth Symphony.

229. Ludwig van Beethoven. Pen-and-ink drawing by Johann Peter Theodor Lyser, 1833. André Meyer, Paris.

From a sheet with four persons (Paganini, [E.T.A?] Hoffmann, Lyser himself and Beethoven).

230. Friedrich Wilhelm III, King of Prussia (1770–1840). Detail from a painting by Nicolas Louis François Gosse. Arenenberg Castle, Switzerland.

231. Symphony No. 9 in D minor, Op. 125. Manuscript copy of the score with Beethoven's autograph dedication to the King of Prussia. Beethovenhaus Bonn.

At the end of 1826, the King of Prussia received this copy of the score with Beethoven's dedication. The score was written by the copyist Peter Gläser, but he took so long over it that the first printed copies had already been delivered to subscribers before the King received his dedication manuscript.

232, 233. Caroline Unger or Ungher (1803–1877). Silver medal by Nicolo Segnani, 1837. Kunsthistorisches Museum, Vienna; Numismatic Collection.

The medal has the inscription: 'Karolina Ungher. Musicis Summa Gestu Maior' and 'Regii Lepidi Mundinarius Ludis Scenicis Amphificatis. Anno MDCCCXXXVII'. Caroline Unger, later Madame Sabatier, sang the alto part in the Ninth Symphony.

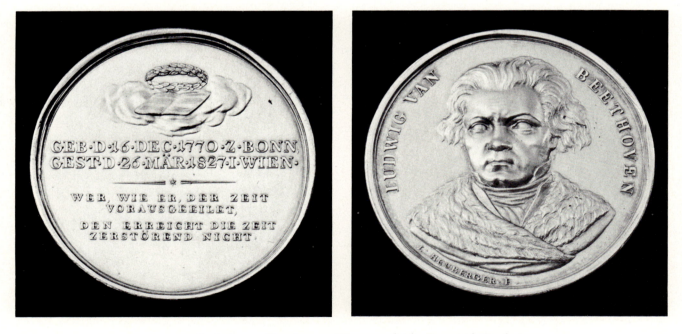

234, 235. Ludwig van Beethoven. Silver medal by Leopold Heuberger. Kunsthistorisches Museum, Vienna; Numismatic Collection.

This medal was struck shortly after Beethoven's death in 1827. Apart from his dates, it has the following inscription: 'Wer wie er der Zeit vorauseilet/Den erreicht die Zeit zerstörend nicht' ('He, who hastens before his time, will not be destroyed by time itself').

Apart from the unbelievably rich list of late Quartets, the *Missa Solemnis*, the last Piano Sonatas and the Diabelli Variations, Beethoven was also working on the Ninth Symphony, which he dedicated to the King of Prussia. The documents show how Vienna came to have the world première of the Ninth Symphony and parts of the *Missa Solemnis*. There was a plan afoot to lure Beethoven to Berlin and to have these works performed for the first time in the Prussian capital. As had happened in 1809 when Jerome Bonaparte threatened to take Beethoven away from Vienna, the composer's Viennese friends, appalled at the idea that these great works should be first performed elsewhere, gathered together and submitted a petition to the composer, asking him to give Vienna the honour of these new masterpieces. The concert of 7 May 1824, which was repeated, was a financial disaster for Beethoven, although the Ninth Symphony was an enormous success. We know from the conversation books and from other sources that the Viennese broke into applause at the timpani solo in the Scherzo. Among the solo singers were Henriette Sontag and Caroline Unger, attractive young girls who often visited Beethoven during the preparation of the Ninth Symphony.

Letter from Beethoven to the publisher Schott:

Vienna, 26 July 1826.

 I see from the postscript of your letter of the 8th that you want to send two printed copies of the symphony to the King of Prussia. I beg you to postpone that for the time being, since I intend to send, from here, a manuscript copy of the work to the King by courier, which can be done in this way without risk. I ask you only to delay publication until I can report that the King has received the copy; you will understand that with the publication of a work, a copy ceases to have any value. For the King's printed copies, I beg you to procure fine, choice paper . . . .

230

TDR V, 316. Anderson 1492. (The Bernhard Schott publishing house was founded in Mainz in 1773 and published several of Beethoven's best works, among them Op. 123, 125 and 131.)

Beethoven's letter to the King of Prussia accompanying the copy of the Ninth Symphony:

[Vienna, about 27 September 1826]

Your Majesty:

 Receiving Your Majesty's most gracious permission to dedicate to Your Majesty the present work, has brought great happiness to my life.

 Your Majesty is not only the father of Your Majesty's subjects, but also the protector of the arts and sciences; and how much more am I gladdened at your most gracious permission, since I myself enjoy the good fortune, as a citizen of Bonn, of counting myself Your Majesty's subject.

 I beg Your Majesty to accept most graciously this work as a small token of the great respect I pay to Your Majesty's virtues.

Your Majesty's
most humble and obedient
Ludwig van Beethoven.

TDR V, 368 f.

The Prussian Royal Librarian, Dr Spicker, describes his visit to Beethoven:

[about 25 September 1826]

230, 231 As we know, Beethoven, after obtaining the permission of His Majesty the King of Prussia, dedicated to his Majesty his last symphony with choruses, and desired to send, quickly and safely, the fair copy of the original score with all holograph corrections and interpolations to his Majesty. In this regard, certain points had to be agreed upon, and this was the reason for proposing a visit to Beethoven, which he accepted .... B. spoke with great enthusiasm of our King, to whose love of the arts, in particular of music, he did full justice; he also showed his great joy at the permission granted him (of which he had been notified by the now deceased Prince Hatzfeldt) to dedicate his last symphony to the monarch ....

TDR V, 370 f. (Spicker published his account in the *Berliner Nachrichten* in April 1827.)

Letter from King Friedrich Wilhelm III of Prussia to Beethoven:

In view of the acknowledged excellence of your compositions, I have had great pleasure in receiving the new work you have presented to me. I thank you for sending it, and send you the enclosed diamond ring as a token of my sincere esteem.

Berlin 25 November 1826
Friedrich Wilhelm.

To the composer Ludwig van Beethoven.

TDR V, 369.

From Beethoven's conversation books:

[End of April 1824]
Schindler: Both of them must come to rehearsal again tomorrow morning at 9. Both ladies lack the vocal training necessary to sing such sustained lines. Sontag admits it, and has asked me to go through Durante's, Leo's and Porpora's methods with her, which I have promised to do. We will begin just after the concert. That Italian warbling has made them stray from the right path. –

Sontag says she has never sung anything so difficult. –

233 You know in any case that Unger is a silly goose, full of fun and banter even when and where it is out of place.

Kerst II, 278.

The violinist Joseph Böhm on the first performance of the Ninth:

The work was studied with the diligence and conscientiousness that such a huge and

354

difficult piece of music demanded. It came to the performance. An illustrious, extremely large audience listened with rapt attention and did not stint with enthusiastic, thundering applause. Beethoven himself conducted, that is, he stood in front of a conductor's stand and threw himself back and forth like a madman. At one moment he stretched to his full height, at the next he crouched down to the floor, he flailed about with his hands and feet as though he wanted to play all the instruments and sing all the chorus parts. – The actual direction was in Duport's hands; we musicians followed his baton only. – Beethoven was so excited that he saw nothing that was going on about him, he paid no heed whatever to the bursts of applause, which his deafness prevented him from hearing in any case. – He had always to be told when it was time to acknowledge the applause, which he did in the most ungracious manner imaginable.

Kerst II, 73. TDR V, 93.

From the Diary of Joseph Carl Rosenbaum:

Friday, 7 [May 1824]. Warm . . . At the K. Th. van Bethowen's concert, with Sontag, Unger, Heitzinger and Seipelt singing, Umlauf conducting. He sympathizes with it. Overture and three Hymns with Kyrie and Ode to Joy; lovely but tedious – not very full – . . . to the K. Th. Many boxes empty, no one from the Court. For all the large forces, little effect. B.'s disciples clamoured, most of the audience stayed quiet, many did not wait for the end. –   *228, 236*

Autograph, Österreichische Nationalbibliothek, Handschriftensammlung.

Leopold Sonnleithner reports on the performance of the Ninth Symphony *in the* Allgemeine Musikalische Zeitung, *No. 14, 6 April 1864:*

You ask me to inform you, on the basis of my personal recollection, about the tempo Beethoven took in the double-bass recitatives in the last movement of his Ninth Symphony. I do not hesitate to comply with that request, and state first of all that in the spring of 1824 I attended all (or most) of the orchestral rehearsals of the Ninth Symphony, which was performed for the first time on 7 May 1824. Beethoven himself   *237* stood at the head of the forces, but the actual conducting of the orchestra was looked after by Umlauf, who beat time, and Schuppanzigh as first violin. – I can confirm from my own experience that Beethoven had the recitatives played quickly, that is, not exactly *presto* but not *andante* either. The whole symphony, especially the last movement, caused great difficulty for the orchestra, which did not understand it at first, although leading musicians (such as Mayseder, Böhm, Jansa, Linke) were playing in it. The double-bass players had not the faintest idea what they were supposed to do with the recitatives. One heard nothing but a gruff rumbling in the basses, almost as though the composer had intended to offer practical evidence that instrumental music is absolutely incapable of speech. The more often this gigantic work was performed subsequently, the better the musicians and the audience came to terms with it. – . . .

On this occasion I cannot refrain from mentioning something my deceased friend Carl Czerny (a favourite pupil of Beethoven's) repeatedly related to me and which he confirmed as being reliably true. Some time after the first performance of the Ninth Symphony, Beethoven is supposed to have announced to a small group of his closest friends, among them Czerny, that he realized he had committed a blunder with the last movement of the symphony; he wanted, therefore, to eliminate it and write an instrumental movement without voices in its place; he already had an idea in mind for it.

Although the less favourable reception of the final movement with chorus was probably not entirely without influence on this statement of Beethoven's, he was certainly not the man to waver in his views as a result of criticisms of the day or less than customary applause. Therefore, it seems in fact that he did not feel quite comfortable on the new path he had taken. In any event it is greatly to be regretted that his announced intention was never carried out.

Kerst II, 78 f.

Joseph Hüttenbrenner tells how Beethoven, who had expected a large profit from the concert on 7 May 1824, took the news that only 420 Gulden had been realized:

I handed him the ticket-office figures. He collapsed at the sight of them. We picked him up and laid him on the sofa. We stayed at his side until late at night; he did not ask for food or anything else, and did not speak. Finally, on perceiving that Morpheus had gently closed his eyes, we went away. His servants found him the next morning as we had left him, asleep and still in the clothes in which he had conducted.

Kerst II, 79.

Anton Schindler describes Beethoven's mistrustfulness:

241   Beethoven believed that he owed Umlauf, Schuppanzigh and me some thanks for our efforts. A few days after the second academy, therefore, he ordered a meal at the *Wilder Mann* in the Prater. He arrived in the company of his nephew, his brow hung round with dark clouds, acted coldly, using a biting, carping tone in everything he said. An explosion was to be expected. We had only just sat down at the table when he brought the conversation round to the subject of the pecuniary result of the first performance in the theatre, blurting out point-blank that he had been defrauded by the administrator Duport and me together. Umlauf and Schuppanzigh made every effort to prove the impossibility of a fraud of any sort, pointing out that every piece of money had passed through the hands of the two theatre cashiers, that the figures tallied precisely, and that furthermore his nephew, on the instructions of his apothecary brother, had superintended the cashiers in defiance of all custom. Beethoven, however, persisted in his accusation, adding that he had been informed of the fraud from a reliable quarter. Now it was time to give satisfaction for this affront. I went off

quickly with Umlauf, and Schuppanzigh, after having to endure several volleys at his voluminous person, soon followed. We gathered at the *Goldenes Lamm* in the Leopoldstadt to continue our interrupted meal undisturbed. The furious composer, however, was left to vent his anger at the waiters and the trees, and as punishment had to eat the opulent meal alone with his nephew.

Schindler II, 88.

Felix von Weingartner writes in his book Akkorde:

Frau Grebner told me and several other devout listeners that she had taken part in the first performance as a soprano in the chorus. Beethoven sat among the performers from the first rehearsal onwards, to be able to hear as much as his condition would permit. He had a stand in front of him, on which his manuscript lay. The young girl, who now sat before me as a venerable old lady, stood just a few steps away from that stand and thus had Beethoven constantly in view. Her description of him is the same as the one that has been handed down to us: a thick-set, very robust, somewhat corpulent man, with a ruddy, pock-marked face and dark, piercing eyes. His grey hair often fell in thick strands over his forehead. His voice, she said, was a sonorous bass; he spoke little, however, for the most part reading pensively in his score. One had the tragic impression that he was incapable of following the music. Although he appeared to be reading along, he would continue to turn pages when the movement in question had already come to an end. At the performance a man went up to him at the end of each movement, tapped him on the shoulder and pointed to the audience. The motions of the clapping hands and the waving handkerchiefs caused him to bow, which always gave rise to great jubilation. Altogether, the effect made by the work at its first performance was quite prodigious. At times there was a burst of applause during a movement. One such moment, Frau Grebner recalled, was the unexpected entrance of the timpani in the Scherzo.

This had the effect of a bolt of lightning and produced a spontaneous show of enthusiasm. Anyone who knows the Viennese public will not be surprised.

Kerst II, 80 f.   F. von Weingartner, *Akkorde*, Leipzig 1912, p. 1 f.

From Beethoven's conversation books about the second concert, 23 May:

[May 1824]
[Carl:] It was not full, because many people are already in the country. — Some stayed away because they were disgusted about the Rossini aria, as was I.

I was in the auditorium to hear the comments too. Everyone was infuriated at the aria. Stadler had a small group about him who poked fun at it. It cannot harm you, only insofar as people may dwell on the thought that your compositions are desecrated by being, as it were, put into the same category as Rossini's strummings.

Kerst I, 293. (At the second concert an aria by Rossini was put on the programme between Beethoven's Mass and the Ninth Symphony.)

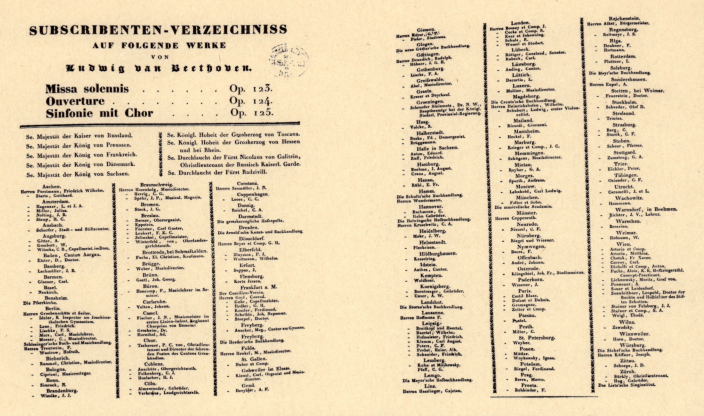

List of subscribers for the orchestral scores of Beethoven's *Missa Solemnis* (Op. 123), Overture *Die Weihe des Hauses* (The Consecration of the House, Op. 124) and Ninth Symphony (Op. 125), published in 1825 by Schott & Co., Mainz. Gesellschaft der Musikfreunde, Vienna.

If we compare this impressive and international list of subscribers with that to the Trios Op. 1 (*see pp. 64 – 5*), we can see that Beethoven's reputation, in the thirty years that separate the two subscription lists, has increased from brilliant local patronage to European recognition. The Schott list is a concrete measure of the immense respect in which Beethoven's music was held throughout Europe in 1825.

Anton Schindler discusses Beethoven's relations with the Viennese musical élite:

The year 1823 witnessed the reawakening of a frenzy for Italian opera which degenerated into a veritable Italian *fanatismo* . . . two years later this state of affairs had reached such a pitch of depravity that the *Allgemeine Musikalische Zeitung* published the following item from Vienna: 'For years now hardly a single significant interesting piece of music has been published in Vienna; nothing but pianoforte arrangements of Rossini's operas. All is barren. Whither next?'

The depressing character of this period must form the predicate for the events we are about to discuss if we are to achieve a correct understanding of them. It is not difficult to imagine how hard-hit our sublime master was by these conditions. The *Missa Solemnis* had been completed two years earlier, and the Ninth Symphony was finished except for the last touches. How was a performance of the two works to be brought about, with prospects of artistic as well as financial success (the latter taking into account the costs of mounting the performance), in the presence of such general depravity? Therefore, Beethoven had taken advantage of his correspondence with Count Brühl to ask whether a performance of the two works in Berlin could be arranged under his auspices. Count Brühl encouraged the master to proceed on that assumption and promised a successful outcome. When this became known in Vienna, a small group of musicians and music-lovers, who still retained a genuine and sober-minded interest in their art, was moved to band together for the purpose of averting the disgrace threatening the imperial city. An address to the master was drafted and a deputation of the élite presented it to him. It follows verbatim:

To Herr Ludwig van Beethoven.

'A small group of disciples and lovers of the arts steps forward today from the large circle of respectful admirers surrounding your genius in its second native city, to express desires long cherished, to give modest voice to requests long restrained.

'The spokesmen are few in number when compared to the company of those who recognize your worth with rejoicing and who are conscious of what you have come to mean to times present and future; and those desires and requests are by no means limited to the spokesmen representing so many like-minded persons. We may affirm in the name of all those to whom art and the realization of their ideals are more than means and objects of amusement, that our desires are the desires of countless people, that our requests are repeated, aloud and silently, by everyone whose breast is stirred by the awareness of the divine in music.

'We express in particular the desires of the music-lovers of our own nation, for although Beethoven's name and works belong to the age and to every land in which sensitive minds are receptive to art, Austria may still claim him for its own at present. Its inhabitants have not yet lost their appreciation of the great and immortal works created for all time by Mozart and Haydn in the bosom of their homeland, and they are conscious, with joyful pride, that the sacred trinity in which those names and yours shine as the symbol of the sublime in the realm of harmony, has sprung from native soil.

'Thus it is all the more painful for us to be forced to watch an alien influence invade the citadel of that musical nobility; to see figures that can claim no relationship to the princely spirits of that dynasty lead a dance of victory over the burial mounds of the deceased and about the abode of the one man of that trinity who is left to us; to see inanity abuse the name and insignia of art; to watch the understanding for the pure and the eternally beautiful darken and vanish in unseemly dalliance with a sacred art.

'We therefore feel more strongly than ever that one thing is needed precisely at this moment: a revival led by a strong hand, a reappearance of the monarch of his realm. This need brings us to you today, and the following are the requests we address to you for all those by whom these desires are cherished, and in the name of the art of their homeland.

'Withhold no longer from the public, deny no longer to the suffering sense of greatness and consummateness, the performance of the latest masterpieces from your hand. We know that a large sacred composition has followed that first such work in which you immortalized the feelings of a soul pervaded and transfigured by the power of faith and celestial light. We know that in the garden of your glorious and unexcelled symphonies a new blossom glows. For years, since the thunder of the Battle of Vittoria died away, we have waited and hoped to witness the bestowal, within the circle of your own disciples, of new gifts from the abundance of your riches. Disappoint our expectations no longer! Deepen the impression of your newest works by allowing us the pleasure of making their acquaintance through yourself! Do not permit your most recent children to be introduced to their birthplace perhaps as foreigners, by people to whom you and your spirit are alien! Appear soon among your friends, your admirers and venerators! – This is our first and foremost request.

'But other demands upon your genius have become audible too. The desires and offers addressed to you more than one year ago by the directors of the Court Opera and somewhat thereafter by the Society of Austrian Friends of Music, were too long the silent desires of all venerators of music and your name, and raised too many hopes and expectations, not to have found the swiftest dissemination near and far, not to have awakened the most universal interest. – Poetry has done its part to give support to such great hopes and desires. A worthy subject, from the hand of an esteemed poet, waits for your imagination to call it to life. Do not let that fervent summons to so noble a goal remain unheard! Delay no longer in reconveying to us those vanished days when Polyhymnia's song moved and delighted the initiates of art and the heart of the masses in equal measure!

'Should we tell you with what deep regret your seclusion has long been felt? Must we assure you that, as all eyes were turned hopefully towards you, we were aggrieved to see the man we regard as the first among the living in his realm watch silently as foreign art encamps on German soil and sits in the place of honour of the German muse; as German works degenerate into mere echoes of foreign tunes, and a dotage of taste threatens to follow the golden age of art.

'Only you can secure victory for the efforts of the best of us. The musical societies of the fatherland and the German opera await a new efflorescence, a regeneration and a new reign of the true and the beautiful over the foreign power to which the fashion of the day seeks to subjugate the eternal precepts of art. Give us the hope that the desires of all those people who have been reached by the sounds of your harmonies may soon be fulfilled. This is our second most earnest request. – May the year now beginning not come to a close without gratifying us with the fruits of our requests; may the coming spring bring one of the desired gifts with it, and so become a twofold time of efflorescence for us and for the whole world of art.'

Vienna, February 1824.

Signed:

Prince C. Lichnowsky.	Ferd. Count Palfy	M. Count Dietrichstein.
Artaria und Comp.	Ed. Frh. v. Schweiger.	Ig. Edler von Mosel,
v. Hauschka.	Count Czernin, Chamberlain.	I. & R. Hofrat.
M. J. Leidesdorf.	Moritz Count Fries.	Karl Czerny.
J. E. von Wayna.	I. F. Castelli.	M. Count Lichnowsky.
Andreas Streicher.	Prof. Deinhardtstein.	v. Zmeskall.
Anton Halm.	Ch. Kuffner.	Hofrat Kiesewetter.
Abbé Stadler.	F. R. Nehammer, perm.	L. Sonnleithner, Dr.
von Felsburg, Court Sec'y.	Sec'y.	Steiner und Comp.
Ferd. Count Stockhammer.	Steiner von Felsburg,	Lederer.
Anton Diabelli.	Banker.	J. N. Bihler.

It had been expected that Beethoven would read the address in the presence of Court Secretary von Felsburg and J. N. Bihler, the two signatories delegated to hand it to him; this would give them a chance to discuss various other points and to obtain a definite promise from him. The hour after dinner was chosen for the presentation of the paper, for at that time the master was usually accessible for an extended conversation. The deputies erred, however. Beethoven wanted to read the document later, when he would be alone. It may be taken for granted that he was not a little surprised at receiving it, especially since his trust in everyone's attitude towards him was already quite shaken and his trust in the corps of musicians was completely non-existent; he had spoken his mind about that to Court Councillor Rochlitz in 1822 in no uncertain terms, . . . It may be guessed to what extent I, for my part, was interested in the impression the address would make. I could not refrain from calling on the master immediately after it was presented. I found him with the paper in his hand. After he had told me what had just happened, he handed me the page with a composure that showed only too clearly how moved he was by its contents. While I read what I already knew, he went to the window and looked at the clouds floating past. I put the paper aside without speaking, waiting for him to begin. He remained in the position I have described. Finally he turned to me and spoke in a curiously high-pitched tone: 'It is really very nice! – I am happy about it!' This was the cue for me to express my happiness too – unfortunately in writing. He read it and said quickly, 'Let us go out!' Out of doors he remained monosyllabic in contrast to his customary behaviour, again an unmistakable sign of what was going on in his soul.

Schindler II, 59 ff.

Letter from Georg August Griesinger to Court Councillor Böttiger in Dresden:

Vienna, 21 May 1825 . . . I was pleased that Sontag found an engagement here; her moral character was always highly praised here, and her chastity is the more praiseworthy since her mother sets a bad example *236*

Autograph, Sächsische Landesbibliothek, Dresden.

From Beethoven's conversation books:

[Autumn 1823]
Schindler: You can also put Sontag to good use, for the girl has a rare diligence and a rare culture. She wants to take the liberty of visiting you, but she does not quite dare. –

Sontag is remarkable, a paragon of rare morality.
God grant it. –

[November 1823]
Lichnowsky: I hear that Fidelio is being prepared again, with Sontag. –

Sontag is the better singer, but Schröder has more power and acting ability. *220*

Sontag has a tolerable upper register and very true intonation. –

Unger: Fräulein Sontag is as happy as I at your kindness in inviting us. We have come straight from the rehearsal, so please forgive us for coming so early. I have not come to have a good meal, but to make your esteemed acquaintance, which I have long looked forward to doing.

Schindler has told us that you have finally decided, to everyone's delight, to give a concert; we would be grateful if you should consider us worthy of singing in it. – May we go into the other room to sing something? Do you have *Fidelio* close to hand?

[March 1824]
Schindler: Now some unpleasant news about Sontag, which will surely distress you. The few drops of wine from ... Ausbruch have caused an explosion in her, so that the *Taucher* had to be cancelled yesterday. –

She vomited fifteen times the night before last. Last night she was better. With Unger the effect was in the opposite direction. What a pair of heroines! They are not used to drinking wine; it is a bad wine, too, it appears. –

Sontag was supposed to go to the rehearsal of the Court concert yesterday morning. When she heard that she stood to lose the 24 ducats, she sent word that she had recovered from her illness and would come. Both beauties send you their regards and ask for a better and more wholesome wine in future; with good reason, for otherwise your dinners could prove too costly for them. –

Kerst II, 264, 271 ff.

Letters from Georg August Griesinger to Court Councillor Böttiger in Dresden:

233   Vienna, 15 March 1826 .... She [Caroline Unger] is a well-bred, rather pretty person of unimpeachable behaviour. As for her singing, she really has made every effort, and has had the good sense to attach herself to the Italians and to profit from their method. But the one thing her voice lacks ... is timbre! Therefore she can never make a sensation as prima donna; as seconda, however, she will fill her post well ....

Vienna, 23 June 1827 .... You asked me recently how Mlle Unger was trained as a singer in Naples. During her short stay in Vienna she appeared just once in a concert, and was a success. Her voice is not a fully professional voice [?], and she never sang leading rôles with the Italians; she is more suitable for German opera, in which less is demanded. In Naples she was not engaged at San Carlo, but at the Teatro dal Fondo.

Autograph, Sächsische Landesbibliothek, Dresden.

From Beethoven's conversation books:

[October 1823]
Caroline Unger: Do not be angry with me for disturbing you; I could not resist any longer the desire to see you and to ask whether you still remember me. I thank you for

362

your sweet, friendly letter; I will treasure it like a sacred object; it is only a pity I do not deserve the title.

Schindler: Unger was indisposed for several days, otherwise she would have paid a call. She takes too little care of herself concerning what she eats and drinks. –

Sontag is more cautious. –
Unger is too spirited.

[before May 1824]
Schindler: Unger greatly regrets that she must rehearse both mornings and afternoons, and cannot come to call on you. Singing in the concert is the greatest honour imaginable, no matter what tasks you have set for her. She sings from F to A and B. – She recommends Preisinger for the bass part rather than Forti, for Preisinger is better than Forti in such compositions.

Kerst II, 262, 263, 267

Letter from Caroline Unger to Ludwig Nohl in 1873:

I have read your article, which charmed me back to the happiest period of my youth and made that dinner with Beethoven even more vivid in my mind's eye. You do me too much honour in believing that Beethoven had a weakness for me. His great goodness to me was the legacy of his friendship for my father. As far back as I can remember, I see the greatest master of all time meeting us in Dornbach or elsewhere on solitary walks, generously encouraging me to continue with my progress in music, until the moment when I was so fortunate as to be permitted to participate in that great work, which was not so completely recognized then as it is now.

I still see that simple room in the Landstrasse [district], where a rope served as bell-pull, and in the middle a large table on which the excellent roast and that capital sweet wine were served. I see the room next door, piled to the ceiling with orchestral parts. In the middle of it stood the piano that Field (if I am not mistaken)* had sent to Beethoven from London.

Jette Sontag and I entered that room as though entering a church, and we attempted (alas in vain) to sing for our beloved master.

I remember my insolent remark that he did not know how to write for the voice, because one note in my part in the symphony lay too high. He answered, 'Just learn it! The note will come.' His words spurred me on to work from that day on.

L. Nohl, *Mosaik*, 1881, p. 282. Kerst II, 77 f.

The journalist Anton Wilhelm von Zuccamaglio visits Beethoven in Baden in 1824:

I recognized him immediately from the pictures I had seen of him, of which the portrait by Kreuzhuber [Kriehuber] seemed to me then to be the best likeness; but

*The piano by Broadwood.

236

241

I was forced to admit that they all expressed only a part of his character, that none had captured the whole man, when compared to the original. In particular, none of the artists seemed to me to have done full justice to the idea-laden forehead, or to have caught in the least the fire of the eyes, which seemed to look straight through me. The master's locks had already turned quite white and floated about his head in a not unattractive confusion. Despite the white hair, however, despite the high forehead and the flashing eyes, Beethoven did not give the impression of loneliness, seclusion and gloomy retirement I had imagined he would; on the contrary, an air of extraordinary good nature hovered over his whole countenance, and kindliness was expressed in all his words and gestures. As to his physique, he seemed to me of somewhat less than medium height; his frame was squat and thick-set, but still proclaimed its power and soundness despite its advanced years. As for his clothing, I recall only that he wore a long, grey frock-coat which, as clean as it was unpretentious, could have been his house-coat, for he had just got up from his work to receive me; further, that he had on a plainly-bound neckcloth; in short, nothing in his attire was either dirty or neglected, as one usually expects the clothing of a great artist to be; neither was it so foppish and affected as that of many people I know, who try to pass for boundlessly gifted artists in the salon. His attire proclaimed the honest German burgher.

When I spoke to him, however, I saw only too clearly that he did not understand my words, that he had become deaf, that the man who has spoken to the world for all time through his tones can hear no tone in reply, and stands lonely and isolated in the midst of the happy sphere of language. This feeling pervaded me so violently, so disconcerted me, that I could conceal my tears no longer and broke out in loud sobs and weeping in the master's presence. Beethoven comprehended my grief immediately; the strength of his nature placed him above it, and while I dissolved in sorrow, his features were not darkened by any cloud of affliction. On the contrary, he seemed much more cheerful, and he attempted to console and calm me. Like a father fondling his child, he patted my cheek and embraced me. 'I am not so completely cut off from the world nor from those who are fond of me,' he began again. 'Here is my book and here are my writing utensils, so you can answer every question for me in writing.'

Kerst II, 84 f. (Anton Wilhelm von Zuccamaglio wrote under various *noms-de-plume. Neue Zeitschrift für Musik*, Leipzig, No. 4 of 12 January 1838.)

The new Quartets were now being played in Vienna. We have various and interesting eye-witness reports, among others from Carl Holz, who was at this time Beethoven's amanuensis, taking the place of Schindler. Schinlder loathed Holz and has given us a very warped view of him and his relations with Beethoven. Holz left memoirs about Beethoven which are, how-ever, extremely interesting; and his account of the great Cavatina from the Quartet Op. 130 has the indubitable ring of truth. In the autumn of 1826 Beethoven went to Gneixendorf near Krems to visit his brother Nikolaus Johann, and there he wrote his last completed work, the *Ersatz* Finale of the String Quartet Op. 135. He was now living in the Schwarz-spanierhaus and returned from Gneixendorf to his flat a very ill man.

From the diary of Sir George Smart:

[original English]
Friday 9 September 1825:

. . . At twelve I took Ries to the Hotel Wildemann, the lodgings of Mr. Schlesinger, the music seller of Paris, as I understood from Mr. Holz that Beethoven would be there and there I found him. He received me in the most flattering manner. There was a numerous assembly of professors to hear Beethoven's second new manuscript quartette, bought by Mr. Schlesinger. This quartette is three-quarters of an hour long. They played it twice. The four performers were Schuppanzigh, Holz, Weiss, and Lincke. It is most chromatic and there is a slow movement entitled 'Praise for the recovery of an invalid.' Beethoven intended to allude to himself I suppose for he was very ill during the early part of this year. He directed the performers, and took off his coat the room being warm and crowded. A staccato passage not being expressed to the satisfaction of his eye, for alas, he could not hear, he seized Holz's violin and played the passage a quarter of a tone too flat. I looked over the score during the performance. All paid him the greatest attention. About fourteen were present, those I knew were Boehm (violin), Marx ('cello), Carl Czerny, also Beethoven's nephew, who is like Count St. Antonio, so is Boehm, the violin player. The partner of Steiner, the music-seller, was also there. I fixed to go to Beethoven at Baden on Sunday and left at twenty-five minutes past two.

Leaves from the Journals of Sir George Smart, edited by H. Bertram Cox and C. L. E. Cox, London 1907, p. 108 f.

Carl Holz recalls how, in the spring of 1825, Beethoven talked about his favourite among his works:

For him the crowning achievement of his quartet writing, and his favourite piece, was the E-Flat Cavatina in 3/4 time from the Quartet in B-Flat Major. He actually composed it in tears of melancholy (in the summer of 1825) and confessed to me that his own music had never had such an effect on him before, and that even thinking back to that piece cost him fresh tears.

Kerst II, 187.   L. Nohl, *Beethoven*, III, 1867.

240

Dr Gerhard von Breuning on Beethoven's brother Johann:

242

For several years after the death of the great 'brainowner', his brother, the 'land-owner', played a quite singularly naïve rôle. During Ludwig's lifetime, Johann was interested in his brother's works only for the profit that might be realized from them; now, however, he strove to feign the appreciative admirer of those same works. Splendidly bedizened (blue frock-coat, white waistcoat), he would be seated in the front row of the concert hall at performances of his late brother's works; following each one he would shout 'Bravo', his broad mouth wide open, while applauding mightily with his bony hands, clumsily gloved in white.

Breuning 182.

Dr Gerhard von Breuning describes Johann van Beethoven to Alexander Wheelock Thayer:

His hair was blackish brown and combed down smoothly; his hat was well brushed, his clothing clean like that of a man who wants to dress elegantly for Sunday, but more pedantic and awkward, due to his bone structure, which was angular and un-attractive. His waist was rather narrow, not a bit of embonpoint; his shoulders were broad; if I recall correctly, he held one shoulder a little lower than the other, or else it was his angular build which made his figure seem somewhat odd. He usually wore a blue frock-coat with brass buttons, a white cravat, white waistcoat, light-coloured breeches, buff-coloured I believe, and cotton gloves, the fingers of which were too long, so that the tips turned over or flopped limply. His hands were broad and bony. His frame was not actually large, but was much larger than Ludwig's. His nose was large and rather long; his eyes were not evenly set, so that one got the impression he had a cast in one eye. His mouth was crooked, one corner was drawn somewhat crookedly upwards, which made him look as though he were smiling mockingly. In his clothing he played the well-to-do dandy, but that did not suit his bony, angular figure. He bore no resemblance whatever to his brother Ludwig.

TDR IV, 264.

From Beethoven's conversation books (about Johann van Beethoven):

[Winter 1822/23]
76 Count Moritz Lichnowsky: Everyone makes a fool of him; we call him simply 'the Chevalier'. — Everybody says his only merit is that he bears your name.

TDR IV, 264 f.

Ludwig Cramolini, tenor and later producer at the Vienna Court Opera, tells about his last visit to Beethoven:

I saw Beethoven just one more time, at the urging of my mother. It was the 15th or 16th of December 1826. I had already been singing for two years as a tenor at the Imperial and Royal Court Opera and was engaged to be married to Nanette Schechner, an excellent singer. After a performance of *Fidelio*, which Nanny sang and acted beautifully, my mother said, 'I would never have believed the old crosspatch could write such heavenly music, music which quite squeezed the tears out of me.' My mother had never had an opportunity to hear any of Beethoven's music until then. 'You should go call on him; perhaps Beethoven will remember us both. It would be ungrateful of him not to, but I can hardly believe he would be; for someone who feels so deeply, as his composition of *Fidelio* proves he does, must have a kind heart, and I have never doubted that he has.' Nanny also urged me to go, and expressed the desire to make his acquaintance herself on the occasion. I finally agreed, and spoke to Schindler who was then the musical director of the Theater in der Josefstadt, begging

366

him to remind Beethoven of Frau Cramolini's son Louis, who had so often tormented him, but who was now mature enough to recognize and admire his immortal works. A few days later Schindler told me that Beethoven was prepared to receive us, Nanny and me, but we would have to excuse his receiving us lying in bed. We should also bring some music with us, for he wanted to hear or at least to see us sing. Thus we drove out to see him on the afternoon of that December day.

When we entered the room the poor man was lying on his sick-bed seriously ill with dropsy. He looked at me, his eyes wide and glowing, then held out his left hand and said, 'So this is young Louis, and already engaged.' Then he nodded to Nanny and said, 'A handsome couple and, so I hear, a couple of able artists too. And how is your dear mother?' He handed us paper and a pencil, and we carried on the ensuing conversation in writing, while he sometimes spoke rather incomprehensibly. Then he asked us to sing for him. Schindler sat down at one of the two pianos that stood side by side in the middle of the room, and we stood facing Beethoven. I wrote that I would sing his 'Adelaide', with which I actually made my initial reputation as a singer. Beethoven nodded affably. But when I tried to begin, my palate and throat had become so dry from anxiety that I could not sing. I asked Schindler to wait a few moments until I could collect myself. Beethoven asked what had happened and why I was not singing, and laughed out loud when Schindler wrote down the reason. Then he said, 'Just sing, dear Louis. Unfortunately I can hear nothing; I only want to see you sing.' Finally I took courage and sang, with true fervour, the song of songs, Beethoven's divine 'Adelaide'. When I finished, Beethoven motioned me over to him, pressed my hand cordially and said, 'From your breathing I can see that you sing correctly, and in your eyes I have read that you feel what you sing. It has been a great pleasure for me.' I was overjoyed at the great man's judgment and had to dry away a tear. When I tried to kiss his hand he withdrew it quickly, saying, 'Kiss the hand of your good mother and remember me often to her, and tell her what a joy it was for me that she still recalls me and has sent her little Louis to see me.'

Then Nanny sang Leonore's aria from *Fidelio*, with such intensity that Beethoven repeatedly began beating time and absolutely devoured her with his wide-open eyes. After the aria, Beethoven held his hand over his eyes for a long while, and then said, 'You are a masterful singer, with a voice possibly somewhat like Milder's, but she did not have the depth of feeling at her command that you do, which showed clearly in your face. What a pity I cannot . . . .' He probably wanted to say 'hear you', but he stopped abruptly and then went on, 'Thank you, Fräulein, for a lovely hour, and may you both be very happy together.' Nanny was also deeply touched and pressed his hand to her heart. There was a short silence. Then Beethoven said, 'I feel quite exhausted after all.'

We made ready to go, but before leaving we wrote our thanks and begged his pardon for disturbing him, adding the wish that God might restore him to health soon. With a smile Beethoven said, 'Then I will write an opera for the two of you. My greetings to your father and your dear mother, and if I do regain my health I will ask Schindler to bring them to see me. Adieu my little Louis, and adieu my dear Fidelio.' He pressed our hands again, looked at us sadly but amiably, and finally turned his face to the wall. We went out quietly so as not to disturb him, and were driving back towards town when Nanny broke the silence and said, 'We have probably seen that godlike man for the last time.' The same thought had struck me. I gave Nanny my hand and we wept bitterly.

Kerst II, 217 f. *Frankfurter Zeitung*, No. 270, 29 Sept. 1907.

Ludwig Rellstab on Beethoven's deafness:

[Beethoven:] 'This is a beautiful piano! I got it as a gift from London. Look at the name!' He pointed with his finger to the strip of wood above the keyboard. In fact I saw several names written there which I had not hitherto noticed. There were Moscheles, Kalkbrenner, Cramer, Clementi, Broadwood himself. The circumstance was an impressive one. The wealthy, artistically minded manufacturer could not have found a worthier object on whom to bestow an instrument, which he seems to have found particularly successful, than on Beethoven. The aforementioned great artists had reverently signed their names, as it were, rather like godparents; and thus the peculiar remembrance-book travelled far across the seas and was laid at the feet of the highest and most famous as a token of honour from those famous men. 'It is a wonderful present,' said Beethoven looking at me, 'and it has a beautiful tone,' he continued, turning towards the piano without taking his eyes off me. He struck a chord softly. Never will another chord pierce me to the quick with such sadness and heartbreak. He had played C major in the right hand and B natural in the bass; he looked at me steadily and repeated the false chord several times to let the mild tone of the instrument sound, and the greatest musician on earth could not hear the dissonance!

Kerst II, 136 f.

236. Henriette Walpurgis Gertrude Sontag (1806–1854) as Donna Anna in Mozart's *Don Giovanni*. Reproduction after a portrait by P. Delaroche. Antiquarian Ingo Nebehay, Vienna.

Henriette Sontag came to Vienna in 1822. She sang the soprano part in the concert of 7 May 1824. Beethoven, who found the sixteen-year-old girl very attractive, wrote her a letter of praise after the concert.

237. Hand-bill for the concert on 7 May 1824 in the Kärntnerthortheater. Österreichische Nationalbibliothek, Vienna. (*See Plate 228.*)

Freytag den

K. K. Hoftheater nächst dem Kärnthnerthore.

Große musikalische Akademie

von

Herrn L. van Beethoven,

Ehrenmitglied der königl. Akademie der Künste und Wissenschaften zu Stockholm und Amsterdam, dann Ehrenbürger von Wien.

Die dabey vorkommenden Musikstücke sind die neuesten Werke des Herrn Ludwig van Beethoven.

Erstens. Große Ouverture.
Zweytens. Drey große Hymnen, mit Solo- und Chor-Stimmen.
Drittens. Große Symphonie, mit im Finale eintretenden Solo- und Chor-Stimmen, auf Schillers Lied, an die Freude.

Die Solo-Stimmen werden die Dlles. Sontag und Unger, und die Herren Haizinger und Seipelt vortragen. Herr Schuppanzigh hat die Direction des Orchesters, Herr Kapellmeister Umlauf die Leitung des Ganzen, und der Musik-Verein die Verstärkung des Chors und Orchesters aus Gefälligkeit übernommen.

Herr Ludwig van Beethoven selbst, wird an der Leitung des Ganzen Antheil nehmen.

(Die Eintrittspreise sind wie gewöhnlich.)

Freybillets sind heute ungültig.

Der Anfang ist um 7 Uhr.

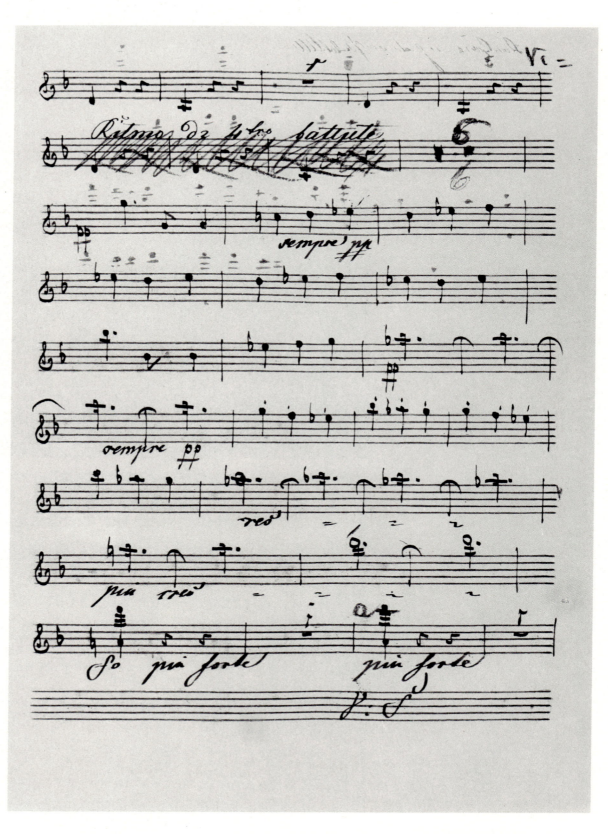

238. Symphony No. 9, Op. 125, Scherzo 'ritmo di 3 battute'. Original performance
material, first violin part with changes in Beethoven's hand. Gesellschaft der
Musikfreunde, Vienna.

This page of the original performance material shows some bars cancelled by Beethoven: in the first edition the passage is changed.

239. Symphony No. 9, Op. 125, Scherzo, p. 56 of the first edition in score by Schott. Gesellschaft der Musikfreunde, Vienna.

This page shows the final version of the passage illustrated in Plate 238.

240. Cavatina, fifth movement from the String Quartet in B-flat, Op. 130. Autograph. Staatsbibliothek, Preußischer Kulturbesitz, Berlin.

This, the third of the works commissioned by Prince Galitzin, was written down in August 1825 at Gutenbrunn near Baden and, with the *Grosse Fuge* (Op. 133) as finale, completed in November. At the suggestion of the publisher Mathias Artaria, Beethoven wrote a new finale to take the place of the technically difficult *Fuge*; this second finale movement was sketched in September 1826, and completed in October and the beginning of November in Gneixendorf. Beethoven sent it to Vienna on 11 November 1826; it was the master's last completed work.

241. Ludwig van Beethoven. Chalk drawing by Stephan Decker, May ▶ 1824. Historisches Museum of the City of Vienna.

When Decker drew Beethoven, the master was rather thin and the round cheeks of earlier times somewhat sunken; he was perhaps liverish. Decker's portrait soon became the prototype of similar Beethoven portraits which were circulated after the master's death. According to a report in the *Wiener Allgemeine Musikalische Zeitung* of 5 June 1824 by Siegfried August Kanne, Decker's drawing was made a few days after the performance of the 'big concert', in other words shortly after 7 or 23 May 1824.

373

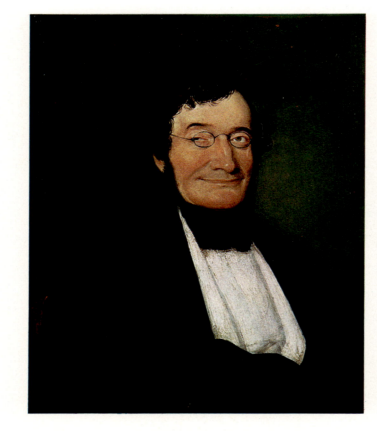

242. Nikolaus Johann van Beethoven (1776–1848). Portrait in oils by Leopold Gross, 1841. Historisches Museum of the City of Vienna.

The apothecary Johann van Beethoven, the composer's youngest brother, was the only one of the three brothers who managed to be a success in business. In 1819, he was already able to retire to his estate 'Wasserhof' at Gneixendorf near Krems, and to lead the life of a country squire. When he once signed a New Year's card to his brother Ludwig with the word 'Gutsbesitzer' ('landowner'), Beethoven promptly answered with his signature as 'Hirnbesitzer' ('brain owner'). The composer visited Johann and his wife in Gneixendorf at the end of September 1826, and completed there the String Quartet in F, Op. 135. On the return journey to Vienna in an open carriage, he caught pneumonia. (*See also Plates 180, 181.*)

243. Carl Holz (1798–1858). Miniature on ivory by Barbara Fröhlich-Bogner (7 × 5.5 cm). Signed 'B. F. pinx. 22. Febr. 1824.' Historisches Museum of the City of Vienna.

Carl Holz was a clerk, but a good enough violinist to play second violin in Schuppanzigh's quartet. Thus he soon made Beethoven's acquaintance and the two became intimate friends. It was because of Holz that Schindler left his beloved master and did not return to him until December 1826, when Beethoven was very ill.

244. Beethoven's study in the Schwarzspanierhaus. Coloured lithograph from a sepia drawing by Johann Nepomuk Hoechle, about the beginning of April 1827 (?). Advance study for an engraving by Leybold. Historisches Museum of the City of Vienna.

In 1825, Beethoven took rooms in the former monastery buildings of the Schwarzspanier in the Alser Vorstadt. 'Schwarzspanier' was the name of the Spanish monks, thus called because of their black ('schwarz') cassocks. The monastery moved into the city in 1779, and the old building in the outskirts of Vienna was turned into an apartment house.

247. Carl van Beethoven (1806–1858) in cadet's uniform. Unsigned miniature (6.3 × 5.2 cm). Original disappeared. Historisches Museum of the City of Vienna.

Beethoven's younger brother Carl Anton Caspar died of tuberculosis and made his wife Johanna and his brother Ludwig the guardians of his son Carl. This joint guardianship caused Beethoven a great deal of worry and care. Since he strongly disapproved of his sister-in-law, he attempted with every means at his disposal to secure the sole guardianship over his nephew. As a result of this extended legal battle, not only the child suffered, but also Beethoven, whose possessive love of his nephew was repulsed.

245, 246. Beethoven in a coma. Both drawings by Joseph Eduard Teltscher. Mrs Eva Alberman, London.

Beethoven returned from Gneixendorf, where he had visited his brother Johann in the late autumn of 1826, a sick man. Teltscher visited Beethoven on the latter's deathbed and made three sketches, two with the master and one with only the deathbed. Beethoven's body, swollen with dropsy, can be clearly seen underneath the bedclothes.

248. Beethoven's last will of 23 March 1827. Archiv der Stadt Wien.

Three days before his death, Beethoven was able to write his last will, aided by Schindler, who held the pen in Beethoven's hand and propped him up in a sitting position; Beethoven made his nephew Carl sole beneficiary.

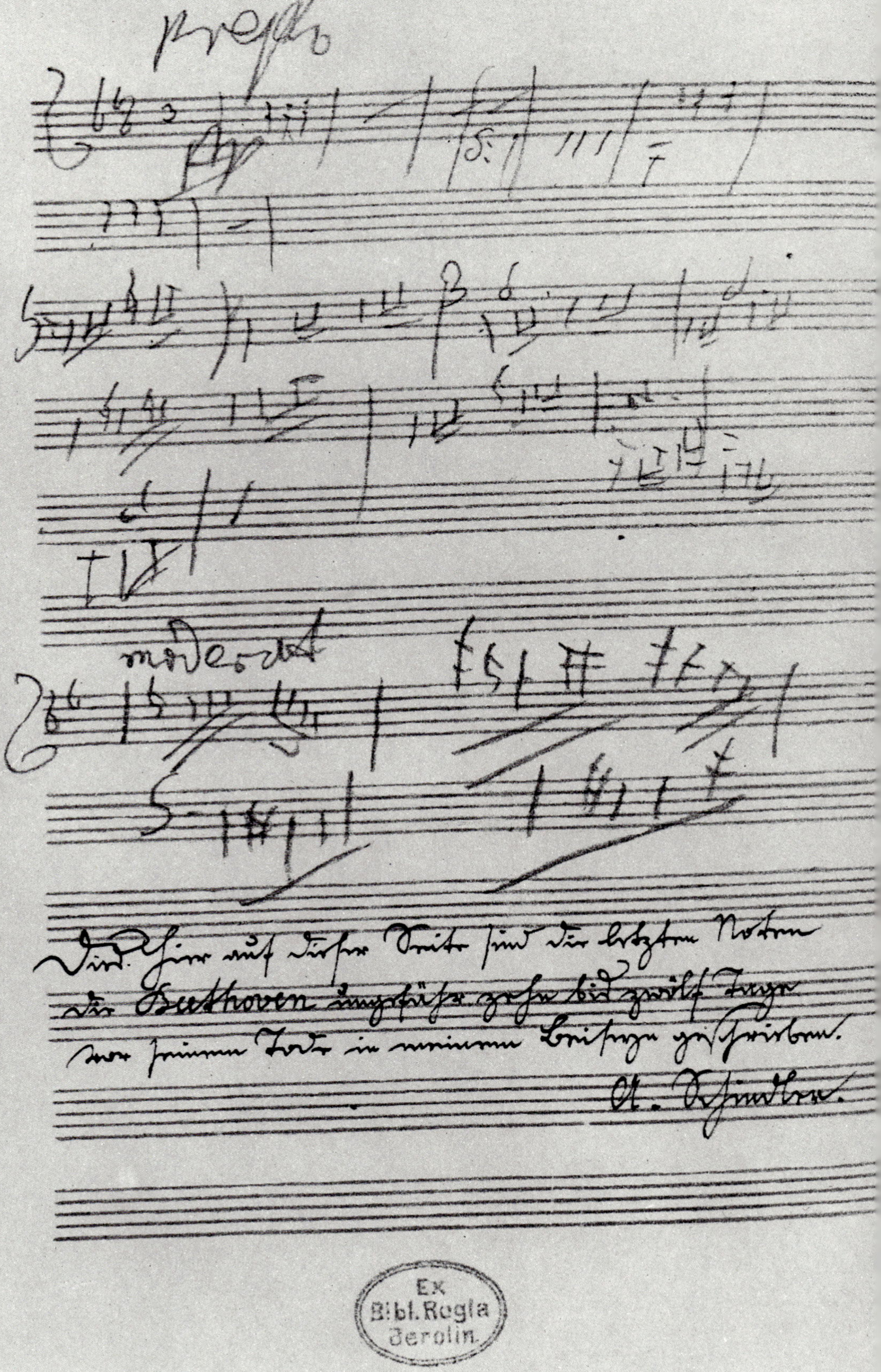
Presto
moderato
Dies hier auf dieser Seite sind die letzten Noten
die Beethoven ungefähr zehn bis zwölf Tage
vor seinem Tode in meinem Beiseyn geschrieben.
A. Schindler.
Ex Bibl. Regia Berolin.

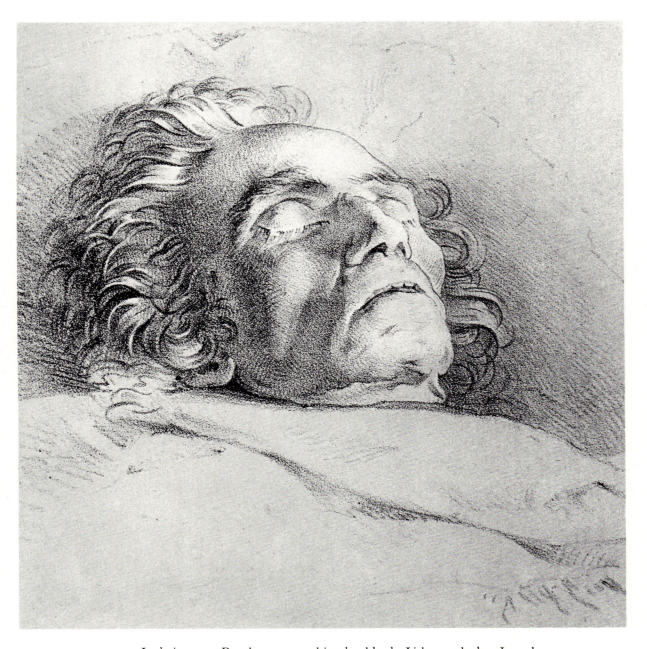

250. Ludwig van Beethoven on his deathbed. Lithograph by Joseph Danhauser from his own drawing. Gesellschaft der Musikfreunde, Vienna.

Danhauser, who had been commissioned to do Beethoven's death mask, also made a drawing of the dead composer. Whether this sketch was made after the autopsy (during which the middle and inner ears were removed to discover the reason for Beethoven's deafness), or before, is not known.

◄ 249. The last music that Beethoven wrote. Autograph. Staatsbibliothek, Preussischer Kulturbesitz, Berlin.

Sketches for the Tenth Symphony. Schindler wrote underneath the following note: 'The music on this page is the last that Beethoven wrote in my presence about ten or twelve days before his death. A. Schindler.'

251. Anselm Hüttenbrenner (1794 – 1868). Chalk drawing by Joseph Teltscher, from his sketchbook. Historisches Museum of the City of Vienna.

Anselm Hüttenbrenner came to Vienna in 1815 to study with Salieri, and became an intimate friend of Schubert's. Hüttenbrenner, a young man in comfortable circumstances, met Beethoven in 1816, when he and another friend paid a visit to the master. Beethoven at that time had looked through Hüttenbrenner's compositions and had said complimentary things about them. He was fated to be present at the very moment that Beethoven died.

380

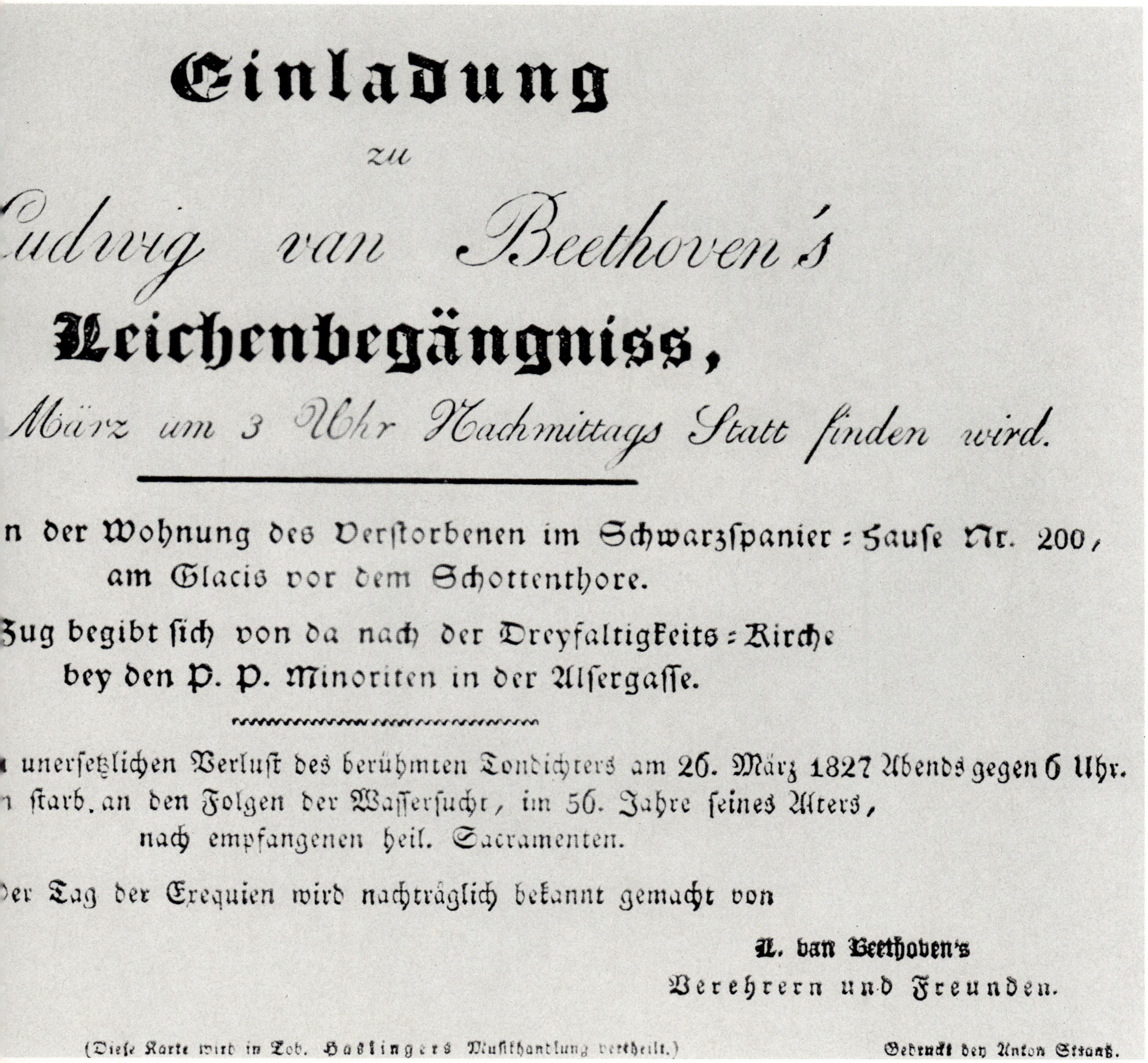

Einladung

zu

Ludwig van Beethoven's

Leichenbegängniss,

März um 3 Uhr Nachmittags Statt finden wird.

_____

n der Wohnung des Verstorbenen im Schwarzspanier = Hause Nr. 200,
am Glacis vor dem Schottenthore.

Zug begibt sich von da nach der Dreyfaltigkeits = Kirche
bey den P. P. Minoriten in der Alsergasse.

_____

unersetzlichen Verlust des berühmten Tondichters am 26. März 1827 Abends gegen 6 Uhr.
starb, an den Folgen der Wassersucht, im 56. Jahre seines Alters,
nach empfangenen heil. Sacramenten.

er Tag der Exequien wird nachträglich bekannt gemacht von

L. van Beethoven's
Verehrern und Freunden.

(Diese Karte wird in Tob. Haslingers Musikhandlung vertheilt.)   Gedruckt bey Anton Strauß.

252. Invitation to Beethoven's funeral procession.
H. C. Robbins Landon, Buggiano Castello, Italy.

Beethoven's life-long friend Stephan von Breuning formulated the wording of this invitation.

253. Beethoven's death mask, by Joseph Danhauser; in profile.
Historisches Museum of the City of Vienna.

Both the Beethovenhaus in Bonn and the Historisches Museum of the
City of Vienna own casts of Danhauser's death mask. The copy in the
Beethovenhaus came into the possession of the museum in 1890, while
the Vienna mask was acquired by Franz Liszt in 1840, and later belonged
to his friend, the Princess Marie von Hohenlohe; it was from her that
the Historisches Museum acquired the mask; the Vienna mask is far
preferable, for it is a more faithful copy.

254. Beethoven's funeral procession. Watercolour by Franz Stöber. Beethovenhaus Bonn.

It is reported that some 20,000 persons took part in this solemn ceremony.

255. Franz Grillparzer (1791–1872). Watercolour by Michael Moritz Daffinger, 1827. Historisches Museum of the City of Vienna.

The great Austrian poet, who had known Beethoven personally since 1805, wrote the funeral oration; it was spoken by the actor Heinrich Anschütz at the entrance of the cemetery in Währing, because it was not permitted to hold speeches within the actual confines of a cemetery.

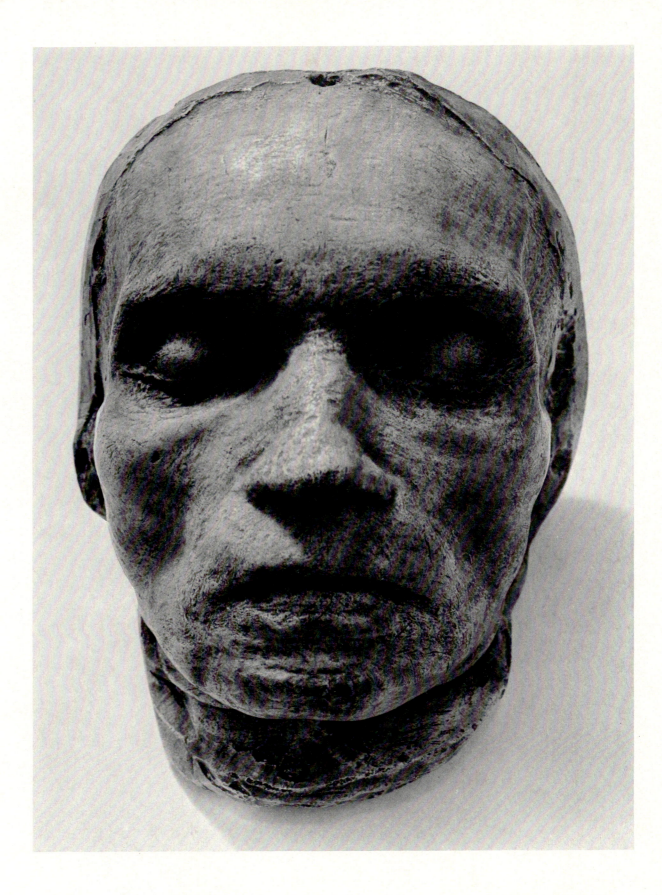

256. Beethoven's death mask by Joseph Danhauser. View from the front. Historisches Museum of the City of Vienna.

Carl Holz was a respectable man who had studied the classics and who had a good knowledge of music, the latter borne out by his place in the quartet association that has gone down in musical history. But Carl Holz was every inch a Viennese 'Phaeacian' and of the first water, too, towards which class our Beethoven had always revealed a deeply-rooted antipathy; nor was it in his nature for him to overlook it. The young man was, however, quite an excellent mathematician, and it was this quality alone which made Beethoven overlook both the Phaeacian and the musician. For with his dual personality Beethoven needed such a specialist in the same way that Wallenstein needed the astrologer Seni. . . .

Noticeable were not only the buffooneries which Carl Holz had written in his own hand, not the frequent attacks on very highly placed persons and others, but rather the high degree of inner irritability in which the master was henceforth kept, and in which state he was obviously pleased with himself. The divergence from old, deeply-rooted principles even revealed itself in Beethoven's accompanying his young friend to gatherings of utter strangers in public places, taverns and wine-shops, and to the shops of music-dealers favoured by him. This did not fail to cause a stir. C. Holz seemed intent on proving that he could do anything with the otherwise retiring composer and subject him to his will. And truly he was able to achieve the unbelievable. Does one need stronger evidence of this than the fact that Beethoven, in the midst of all the frenzy of speculation in which he found himself at the time, stood godfather to his new friend's first-born son? This revealed that our master's mind was in a state of metamorphosis that dumbfounded those who thought that they knew him. It is unfortunately true that under such guidance sacrifices were sometimes made to Bacchus – before the eyes of strangers; precisely this increased the regret of all true friends and disciples. Dr. Wawruch's accusing words, 'sedebat et bibebat,' refer to this association only. The period of these excesses extended, thank heaven, only from the autumn of 1825 until the summer of 1826.

Schindler II, 108 ff.

Fanny Linzbauer on Carl Holz's last visit to Beethoven:

'Haslinger, Castelli and I went to see him. All three of us knelt at his bedside.' – Holz's voice failed him, he covered his face and wept. – 'He blessed us,' he said with great effort, 'and we kissed his hand and never saw him again!'

Kerst II, 216 f.

From Beethoven's conversation books:

[End of February 1827]
Young Breuning: No one can stand Holz; all who know him say he is deceitful. He acts as though he likes you, God knows how much. –

He is very able at shamming. –

He can lie like a book. –

You are the best of all, the others are all scoundrels. –

If you were not so good-natured you could ask him to pay for his board, and with good reason. –

He likes your wine best of all. –

Schindler: I gave Herr Holz a good piece of my mind yesterday. –

The result was that he was quite courteous when he left. –

I heard that he let it be known somewhere that he does not like my coming to see you. –

I called him to account for that, but he insisted he had not said anything whatever about jealousy of that kind. He said he must divide his time between his office, his lessons and his bride, and cannot come to see you for that reason. –

[*A later holograph note by Schindler:* It must be stated here that it was Herr Holz and no one else who openly said everywhere that Beethoven had contracted dropsy purely as a result of too much wine-drinking. This is how the belief spread that he was a drinker. The truth is that Herr Holz, who was a heavy drinker himself, often induced our Beethoven to drink more than usual. But thank heaven that this period, during which he let himself be led about by Herr Holz and drank a great deal, lasted approximately 18 months only, from the early summer of 1825 until the end of September 1826.]

Kerst II, 307 f.

247 *Dr Gerhard von Breuning on Carl van Beethoven:*

The time for examinations at the Technical Institute came, and there were again debts to be settled. Time was pressing, and Carl, prepared neither in knowledge nor in pocket, and fearing his uncle's reproaches more and more (he was 'tired of them long since' and found them 'absurd'), decided to make a change; not for the better, as his uncle longed for him to do, but for the worse, by killing himself. He bought two pistols, drove to Baden and climbed the tower of the ruins of Rauhenstein Castle. Once at the top, he put both pistols to his temples and fired. He wounded himself only superficially – the periosteum was injured – but he still had to be taken to the *Allgemeines Krankenhaus* [General Hospital] in Vienna.

Beethoven was badly shaken by the news. His grief at this event was indescribable; he was as despondent as a father who has lost his adored son. My mother met him on the Glacis looking quite stricken. 'Do you know what has happened to me? My Carl has shot himself!' – 'And is he dead?' 'No, he only grazed himself. He is still alive, and there are hopes of saving him. But the disgrace he has brought on me – and I loved him so much . . . . – '

The surgeon Ignaz Seng, who died as recently as 16 September 1879, told me the following account of his meeting Beethoven: 'I was *Secundarius* at the *Allgemeines Krankenhaus* in Vienna, working in the surgical clinic headed by *Primarius* Gassner, a part of which was the so-called 3-Gulden floor; I lived to the left of the large courtyard facing the middle house, on the ground floor of which the administrative offices were located. In the late summer of 1826, on a day when I had inspection duty, a man dressed in a grey coat came up to me. I thought at first he was just an ordinary burgher. He asked coolly, 'Are you *Herr Secundarius* Seng? They told me at the reception office that I should see you. Is my nephew one of your patients, that wretch, that scoundrel, etc.?' After asking the patient's name, I said he was, and added that he was in a room on the 3-Gulden floor, had been treated for a gunshot wound, and did he want to see him?, at which he answered, 'I am Beethoven.' And while I led him to his nephew, he went on speaking: 'I actually did not want to visit him because he does not deserve it. He has caused me too much annoyance, but . . .' And he went on talking about the catastrophe and about his nephew's behaviour, and how he spoiled him too much, and so on. I was quite astonished to have, beneath that outward appearance, the great Beethoven before me, and promised him I would do everything to look after his nephew.'

Breuning 119 ff.

From Beethoven's conversation books:

[Summer 1826]
Carl: Dearest father, you can be certain that the sorrow I have brought you causes me more grief than you. Fear has restored my reason, and I now see what I have done. If I thought that you believe I did it deliberately, I would be inconsolable. It happened in a state of drunkenness. If you can forgive me, I promise you I will never touch another drop of wine, so that I do not lapse into that condition again. But it causes me great pain to know that you can think such things about me. What sort of person would I be if I had even the remotest intention of causing you grief? Forgive me just this once more! I will certainly not drink wine any more; that was the cause of everything; I could not restrain myself and did not know where I was. I beg you once more, forgive me!

Kerst II, 304.

Ferdinand Hiller visits the ailing Beethoven with Hummel and his wife:

[8 March 1827]
We drove out to the suburb. We walked through a large anteroom in which stood high cupboards holding thick bundles of music tied with string, and then entered

Beethoven's sitting room and were not a little amazed to find the master sitting, apparently quite comfortably, at the window. He wore a long, grey dressing-gown, which at that moment was completely open, and high boots up to the knee. Emaciated from his serious illness, he seemed tall when he stood up; he was unshaven, and his hair fell in disorderly fashion about his temples. The expression on his face became friendly and bright when he saw Hummel, and he seemed as exceptionally pleased at seeing Hummel as Hummel was to see him. The two men embraced warmly. Hummel introduced me; Beethoven was quite gracious towards me, and I was made to sit opposite him by the window. It is known that conversation with Beethoven had in part to be written; he spoke, but those with whom he spoke had to write down their questions and answers. For this purpose thick booklets of normal quarto writing paper and pencils were always close at hand . . . . Beethoven followed the writer's hand with eager eyes, and took in the written words at a glance rather than reading them. The liveliness of the conversation of course suffered greatly by the visitor's having constantly to write . . . . At the start the conversation, as was customary, concerned household affairs, the journey and our stay, my connection with Hummel and such things. Beethoven asked after Goethe's health with unusual concern, and we were able to report that all was well. As to his own health, Beethoven complained greatly. 'I have lain about for four months already,' he exclaimed, 'and one's patience finally wears out!' – In addition to that, there was much about Vienna that was not to his liking, and he spoke bitingly about the 'present taste in art' and the 'dilettantism that is ruining everything here.' Nor was the government spared, even its highest representatives. 'Write a bookful of penitential songs and dedicate it to the Empress,' he said to Hummel with an ill-humoured laugh; but Hummel made no use of that well-intentioned advice.

[13 March 1827]
We found his condition appreciably worsened. He lay in bed, seemed to be in pain and groaned at times, but spoke much and animatedly despite it. He seemed now to regret that he had not married, and at our first visit he had joked with Hummel about it . . . . 'You', he said this time, 'are a lucky fellow; you have a wife who looks after you, who loves you – but poor me!' And he gave a deep sigh. He also begged Hummel to bring his wife again; she had not come, for she could not bring herself to see, in such a state, a man she had known at the height of his powers. A short time before, he had been given a picture of the house in which Haydn was born; he had it near the bed and showed it to us. 'I was happy as a child to receive it,' he said, 'the cradle of a great man!' He also asked a favour of Hummel with regard to Schindler, whose name has been mentioned so often subsequently. 'He is a good fellow,' he said, 'and has done quite a lot for me. He is to give a concert soon, and I promised I would take part in it. But nothing will come of that now. I would like you to do me the favour of playing. One has to help poor artists to get on.' Hummel of course said he would.

Visit of 20 March: 'I will probably be up above soon,' he whispered after greeting us. He made other similar exclamations. He spoke of his plans and prospects and announced his intention of making a journey to London as soon as he was better, to show his gratitude to the English for their gift. 'I will compose a big overture and a symphony for them,' he said. And then he wanted to visit Frau Hummel and stay for a time in various places. His eyes, still quite full of life at Hummel's last visit, dimmed today, and he had difficulty from time to time in sitting up.

March 23, just three days before Beethoven's death: He lay there feeble and forlorn, *245, 246* occasionally sighing softly. Not another word passed his lips; the sweat stood out on his forehead. He could not find his handkerchief immediately, so Hummel's wife took her fine cambric hankderchief and wiped his face again and again. I shall never forget the grateful look in his dulled eyes . . .

March 26: While I was in convivial company at the home of the musical amateur Herr von Liebenberg [a former pupil of Hummel's], guests arrived with the news that Ludwig van Beethoven was no longer alive; he had died at about 5:45.

On Thursday, 29 March, the funeral was held. We gathered at the lodgings of *254* the deceased . . . . From there the cortège began moving towards the *Dreifaltigkeits-kirche* [Church of the Trinity] at about 3 o'clock. Eight Kappelmeister, Eibler, Hummel, Seyfried, Kreutzer, Weigl, Gyrowetz, Wurfel and Gänsbacher were the pall-bearers . . . I could not get into the church, but I drove from there with Hummel to the Währing Cemetery, which was crowded with people . . . The coffin was lowered into the earth; deeply moved, Hummel threw some laurel wreaths after it; others followed . . . .

K. Benyovszky, *J. N. Hummel, Der Mensch und Künstler*, Bratislava 1934, p. 151 ff. (As a pianist, Hiller was a pupil of Johann Nepomuk Hummel.)

Letter from Johann Baptist Jenger, an official in Graz, to Leopoldine Koschak-Pachler: *202*

[29 December 1826]
– – – He asked for me because he had heard from my friend Schindler (who carries great weight with Beethoven) that I had letters for him from Graz. I was dismayed when I entered his room, for everything lay about in confusion, as in an old store-room. He himself lay seriously ill in bed, and since he had not shaved for three weeks at least, you can easily imagine how he looked. He greeted me quite cordially and I was made to sit at his bedside. I wrote what was necessary and handed him both your letters, which he read carefully; he was extremely happy to get them. He thanked me for the letters and asked me to express his warmest thanks to you, adding that he, so far as his condition will permit, will write to you himself. He then spoke with much pleasure of your outstanding musical talents, and ended by saying that it would have been more prudent of him to have gone to you in Graz rather than to his brother in Upper Austria. He still hopes, however, to see you in Graz, which may be possible next year; I often advise him to do that, and perhaps I will make the journey with him.

Kerst II, 202 f.

Letter from Anton Schindler to Ignaz Moscheles:

Vienna, 24 March 1827
. . . My dear Moscheles, when you read these lines our friend will no longer be among

the living. His death is approaching rapidly, and all of us wish only to see him released from his terrible suffering. There is nothing else left to hope for. For a week he has lain as though almost dead, but has pulled his remaining strength together now and again to put a question or to ask for something. His condition is terrible and exactly like that of the Duke of York, about which we read recently. He is in a permanent state of dull brooding; his head hangs forward onto his breast and he stares fixedly at one spot for hours; he seldom recognizes his closest acquaintances unless he is told who they are. In short, it is dreadful to see. This condition can last just a few days more, for all bodily functions have ceased since yesterday. So if God will, he is soon released, and we with him. People have begun to come in droves to have a last look, although no one is admitted except for those who are so impudent as to badger a dying man in his final hours.

Apart from a few words at the beginning, he dictated the letter to you word for word; it is probably the last of his life, although he whispered the words 'Smart – Stumpff – write' disjointedly to me today. If he can still write so much as his name, I will see that it is done. – He knows the end is coming, for he said to Herr von Breuning and me yesterday, 'Plaudite, amici, comoedia finita est!' Yesterday we were also able to put his testament in order, although there is nothing but a few old pieces of furniture and manuscripts. He was at work on a string quintet and his tenth symphony, which he mentions in his letter to you. Two movements of the quintet are finished. It was intended for Diabelli. –

Kerst II, 222 f.

248   *The last testament:*

prs. 29 March 1827.

My nephew Karl shall be my sole heir; the capital of my estate, however, shall go to his natural or testamentary heirs. –

Vienna, 23 March 1827.
Ludwig van Beethoven mp.

TDR V, 485.

Dr Gerhard von Breuning on Beethoven's final hours:

... My father, Schindler and Johann gave Beethoven to understand – he was already lying in a twilight sleep – that he would have to sign something; they raised him up as much as possible and put pillows behind him. One after the other, the papers were placed before him, my father dipping the pen each time afresh and placing it in his hand. The dying man, whose writing had been so energetic, even lapidary, now wrote with trembling hand and great effort his testament, the curt lines of which had been drawn up by my father. –

Breuning, 157 f.

Professor Dr Wawruch's medical report on Beethoven's final illness:

... During January, February and March, emaciation increased rapidly and there was a considerable loss in vital power. In dejected moments following the fourth puncture, Beethoven prognosticated his approaching death, and he was not mistaken. No words had the power to console him any longer, and when I told him that the coming spring weather would alleviate his suffering he answered me with a smile, 'My day's work is done; if there were a physician who could still help, [the next words in English] his name shall be called wonderful!' – This distressing reference to Handel's *Messiah* affected me so greatly that I, deeply moved, was forced to confirm silently the truth of those words.

The fatal day drew nearer. My professional obligations as a physician, so gratifying and yet at times so grievous, demanded that I draw my suffering friend's attention to it, so that he could meet his civil and religious obligations. With the tenderest consideration, I wrote the words of admonition on a sheet of paper (for we had long been able to communicate only in this way). Beethoven read the writing with unparalleled composure, slowly and pensively, his face as though transfigured; he gave me his hand gravely and warmly, and said, 'Let the priest come.' Then he became quiet and thoughtful and nodded to me kindly, 'I will see you again soon.' Shortly thereafter, Beethoven performed his devotions with meek submission and turned to the friends standing about him with the words, 'Plaudite amici, finita est comoedia!'

A few hours later he lost consciousness, lapsed into a coma and the death rattle began in his throat. The next morning all symptoms of the approaching end were present. The 26th of March was stormy and dull; towards 6 in the afternoon a snowstorm began, accompanied by thunder and lightning. – Beethoven died. – What would a Roman augur have concluded about his apotheosis from the fortuitous unrest of the elements?

Kerst II, 214 f.

From the Diaries of Joseph Carl Rosenbaum:

Monday, 26 March 1827: freezing, snow flurries, north wind .... After 4 o'clock the sky grew darker; snowstorm and thunder and lightning. A revolution in nature; three violent thunderclaps followed. Bab. Beck's funeral at the same hour .... Death of Ludwig van Bethowen about 6 o'clock, of dropsy of the abdomen, aged 56. He is no more! His name lives in the light of glory.

Wednesday, 28 March 1827: Changeable, not so cold .... At Haslinger's I spoke with Steiner about Bethowen's will; he left 7 bank shares and 1,000 Florins from London in trust for his dissolute nephew the cadet. A string quartet was his swansong. – Haslinger published an invitation to the funeral.

252

Autograph. Österreichische Nationalbibliothek, Handschriftensammlung.

When I entered Beethoven's bedroom just before 3 o'clock on the afternoon of 26 March 1827, I found Breuning, his son and Frau van Beethoven, the wife of Johann van Beethoven, landowner and apothecary from Linz, and also my friend Joseph Teltscher, the portraitist. I believe Professor Schindler was also present. After a time the afore-mentioned gentlemen left the composer, who was in the throes of death, and harboured little hope of finding him still alive on their return.

245, 246

During Beethoven's last moments there was no one present in the death-chamber but Frau van Beethoven and myself. Beethoven lay in the final agony, unconscious and with the death-rattle in his throat, from 3 o'clock, when I arrived, until after 5 o'clock; then there was suddenly a loud clap of thunder accompanied by a bolt of lightning which illuminated the death-chamber with a harsh light (there was snow in front of Beethoven's house). After this unexpected natural phenomenon, which had shaken me greatly, Beethoven opened his eyes, raised his right hand and, his fist clenched, looked upwards for several seconds with a very grave, threatening countenance, as though to say, 'I defy you, powers of evil! Away! God is with me.' It also seemed as though he were calling like a valiant commander to his faint-hearted troops: 'Courage, men! Foward! Trust in me! The victory is ours!'

As he let his hand sink down onto the bed again, his eyes half closed. My right hand lay under his head, my left hand rested on his breast. There was no more breathing, no more heartbeat! The great composer's spirit fled from this world of deception into the kingdom of truth. I shut the half-open eyes of the deceased, kissed them, and then his forehead, mouth and hands. At my request Frau van Beethoven cut a lock of his hair and gave it to me as a sacred relic of Beethoven's last hour.

Kerst II, 232 f. (Hüttenbrenner published this report in the Graz *Tagespost* of 23 October 1868.)

From the diary of Franz von Hartmann:

28 March 1827.

244

I went out to the Schwarzspanier House where I looked at the body of the divine Beethoven, who died the day before yesterday at about 6 in the evening. As I entered his room, which is large and somewhat neglected, I was touched at its sad appearance. It is sparsely furnished, and only the piano, which the English gave him as a present, and a very grand coffin stood out by virtue of their quality. Music and some books lay about here and there. A bed had not yet been prepared for the lying in state and he still lay on the mattress of his bed. A blanket covered him, and a venerable old man, who looked to me more like his servant than an attendant, uncovered him for me. Thus I saw his magnificent face, which unfortunately I had never had the chance to see in life. There was such a celestial dignity about him, despite the disfiguration he is said to have suffered [at the post-mortem], that I could not look at him long enough. I went away deeply moved. Once below, I could have wept that I did not ask the old man to cut a few hairs for me. Ferdinand Sauter, whom I had planned to meet there but had missed, came at that moment and I returned to the room with him, telling him of my plan. The old man showed him to us again, uncovering the breast too, which was already completely blue, as was the badly swollen stomach. There was already a very strong cadaverous smell. We gave the old man a tip and begged him for a few of Beethoven's hairs. He shook his head and motioned to us to be silent. We were going slowly and sadly down the steps when the old man called softly from the balustrade above that we should wait at the gate until three fops had left, who had stood tapping their swagger-sticks on their pantaloons while looking at the dead man. Then we went up once more; the old man came out of the door, his finger on his lips, and handed us the hair in a bit of paper. We left with a feeling of mournful joy. We met Fritz, whom we told of our action, at which he did the same. – At the Kohlmarkt we looked at the most recent portrait of Beethoven, and found that his face in death still bore a great resemblance to it.

Kerst II, 248. (Franz von Hartmann was a friend of Franz Schubert's.)

Letters from Georg August Griesinger to Court Councillor Böttiger in Dresden:

Vienna, 28 March 1827 ... Ludwig van Beethoven died of dropsy the day before yesterday and will be buried tomorrow ...

Vienna, 7 April 1827 ... Beethoven's many admirers have had three Requiems held for him. The Mozart Requiem was done on the 3rd of this month at the Augustiner-kirche, Lablache singing the 'Tuba mirum'; Cherubini's Requiem was sung at the Karlskirche on the 5th, and Vogler's will be done at the Schottenkirche. The churches are always filled to bursting, and the funeral itself was most ceremonious. It is a great exaggeration to call Beethoven destitute: in his estate were 7 or 9 bank shares, he had a pension of 300 Thaler from the Archduke Rudolph, and publishers paid anything he asked for his compositions. He could have amassed much more, but he was utterly heedless of money, especially as a young man, so that his brothers had a sort of guardianship over him. Hummel knows how to derive more benefit from his talent. He gave a well-attended concert at Prince Schwarzenberg's at 4 Gulden per person. He played at the Theater am Kärntner Thor and is playing tonight at the Theater in der Josephstadt to benefit a poor family, as he had promised Beethoven he would.

Vienna, 25 April 1827 ... Beethoven always had a large group of adherents here. Short notices about him have appeared in several periodicals here, and I have heard of no one who wants to raise a full biographical monument of him. The outward events of his destiny were quite simple, and his actual life is in his works. A musical adept could find a great deal to say about them, but it would be of interest only to musicians and could ultimately be reduced to a few words: *His mighty genius drove him*! He owed virtually everything to that natural gift, not to the instruction he received from Haydn, about which he sometimes talked with a smile. Because of his utter deafness I did not see him at all during recent years ....

Autograph, Sächsische Landesbibliothek, Dresden.

He was an artist, but also a man, a man in every sense, in the highest sense. Because he shut himself off from the world, they called him hostile; and callous, because he shunned feelings. Oh, he who knows he is hardened does not flee! (It is the most delicate point that is most easily blunted, that bends or breaks.)

The excess of feeling avoids feelings. He fled the world because he did not find, in the whole compass of his loving nature, a weapon with which to resist it. He withdrew from his fellow-men after he had given them everything and had received nothing in return. He remained alone because he found no second self. But until his death he preserved a human heart for all men, a father's heart for his own people, the whole world.

Thus he was, thus he died, thus will he live for all time!

And you who have followed our escort to this place, hold your sorrow in sway. You have not lost him but have won him. No living man enters the halls of immortality. The body must die before the gates are opened. He whom you mourn is now among the greatest men of all time, unassailable for ever. Return to your homes, then, distressed but composed. And whenever, during your lives, the power of his works overwhelms you like a coming storm; when your rapture pours out in the midst of a generation yet unborn; then remember this hour and think: we were there when they buried him, and when he died we wept!

Kerst II, 250 f.

253, 256 *The provenance of Beethoven's death-mask:*

On 26 March [1827] early in the morning while we were still asleep, Ranftl* knocked on our door and brought in the news that Beethoven had died in the night.

Since we had a plasterer in our firm,** my brother Joseph, who in the course of his studies of heads had been prompted to try that sort of work, immediately struck on the idea of taking a death mask of the departed great man. We dressed quickly, had the horses harnessed and since the stucco worker Hofmann had arrived in the meanwhile, we took him along with us in the carriage.

It was still early in the morning as we arrived at the dead man's house, and we could find no one who could tell us anything. Finally, a woman let us go upstairs, and as we arrived at the landing we found an open entrance hall; the door leading to the next room was ajar, so we lifted the latch and went in. A bed stood against the main wall of this room, and in this bed lay Beethoven's body.

Since during the dead man's illness his beard had grown very thick, we sent the plasterer to fetch a barber, who shaved him clean. The barber's apprentice said that he could never use the razor again after he had shaved a dead man with it. I bought it from him.

In the meanwhile we had cut off two locks from the temple where it grew thickly, as a memento of the celebrated head, and then we went to work. My brother, who knew

*Ranftl later became a well-known animal painter.

**The father of the painter Joseph Danhauser founded at the beginning of the 19th century a large furniture factory in Vienna, which combined a large variety of activities, namely: Cabinet making, upholstery, locksmith-shop, metal working, plastering and many others.

less about this kind of work than the plasterer, was glad to have him help, and so we soon obtained a good cast which we brought home with great care; for my brother, a painter, had conceived the idea of trying his hand at modeling and at producing a bust of Beethoven. He went right away to work and actually succeeded in making a bust of the master which astounded the whole world and aroused admiration for the young artist. A number of casts were made. One of the first very successful copies which was sent to Moscheles in London, and on the success of which we had counted — we hoped that it would be executed there in marble — arrived in fragments.

The mask of Beethoven from life was made by Dietrich or Klein. The razor is still in my possession. The original death-mask (by my brother), the life mask and the locks of Beethoven's hair are now your property and in your possession. Since you, gracious Madam, wished however to have precise information about the origin of these objects, and in particular, how I came into possession of the locks of hair, I herewith send you this statement.

175

Carl Danhauser.

The text and signature are from the hand of the now eighty-year old Karl Danhauser. Collated with the unstamped original now before me, consisting of one sheet, this has been found to be a complete and true copy.

Währing, on the 19/nineteenth/May 1891/ninety one:/. —

Dr. Peter Gasser
Notary.

Authentication Fee 65 x.
St 50 x.
Total 1.15 x.

This copy has been shown to me for inspection supplied with a fifty kreutzer authentication seal as a true copy. Vienna, on Seventh December One thousand eight hundred and ninety-two.

Karl R.v. Olschbaur,
Notary.

Copying Fee   50
Authentication
seal   60
Stamp   50
Total   160

Franz Glück: *Prolegomena zu einer neuen Beethoven Iconographie*. Anniversary volume for Otto Erich Deutsch on the occasion of his 80th birthday on 5 September 1963. Published by Walter Gerstenberg, Jan La Rue and Wolfgang Rehm, Bärenreiter, Kassel, Basel, Paris, London, New York 1963, 211 f.

INDEX OF PEOPLE AND PLACES

(Numbers in italics refer to illustrations.)

INDEX OF COMPOSITIONS BY BEETHOVEN

(Within each category, works are arranged by Opus no.)